that we in the att[...]
being uniform[...]
[a]t night, sleep in baskets

footman

head
footman
Dusty

chauffer

catch and eat

mice and nuts

DISCARD

gardener
Stu

Who Will Make the Pancakes

MEGAN KELSO

FANTAGRAPHICS

FIVE STORIES

ALSO BY MEGAN KELSO

Queen of the Black Black
The Squirrel Mother
Artichoke Tales

Table of Contents

To my sister, Jenny

1

Watergate Sue

MEGAN KELSO

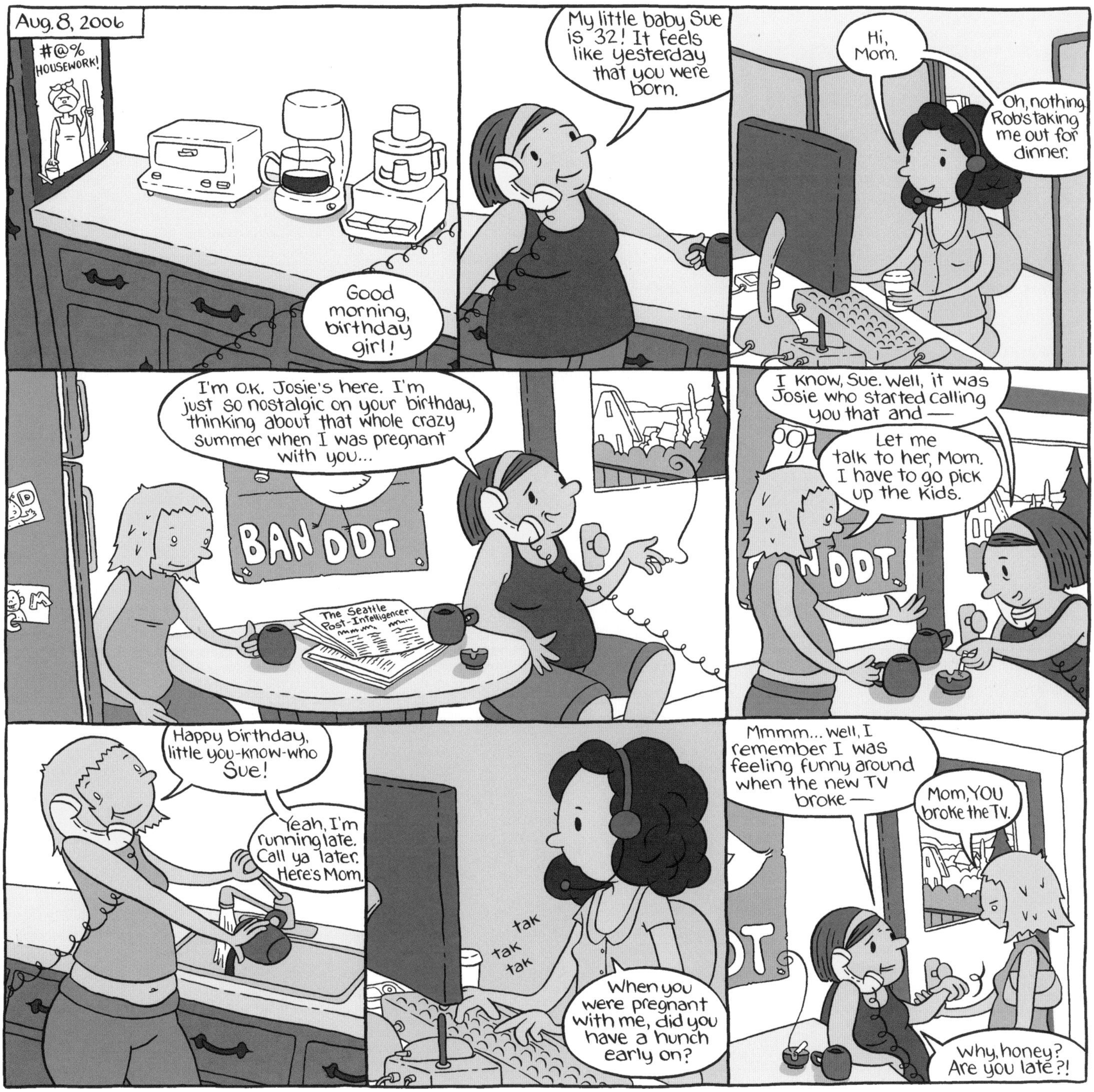
Aug. 8, 2006
#@% HOUSEWORK!
Good morning, birthday girl!
My little baby Sue is 32! It feels like yesterday that you were born.
Hi, Mom.
Oh, nothing. Rob's taking me out for dinner.
I'm O.K. Josie's here. I'm just so nostalgic on your birthday, thinking about that whole crazy summer when I was pregnant with you...
BAN DDT
The Seattle Post-Intelligencer
I know, Sue. Well, it was Josie who started calling you that and —
Let me talk to her, Mom. I have to go pick up the kids.
Happy birthday, little you-know-who Sue!
Yeah, I'm running late. Call ya later. Here's Mom.
tak tak tak
When you were pregnant with me, did you have a hunch early on?
Mmmm... well, I remember I was feeling funny around when the new TV broke —
Mom, YOU broke the TV.
Why, honey? Are you late?!

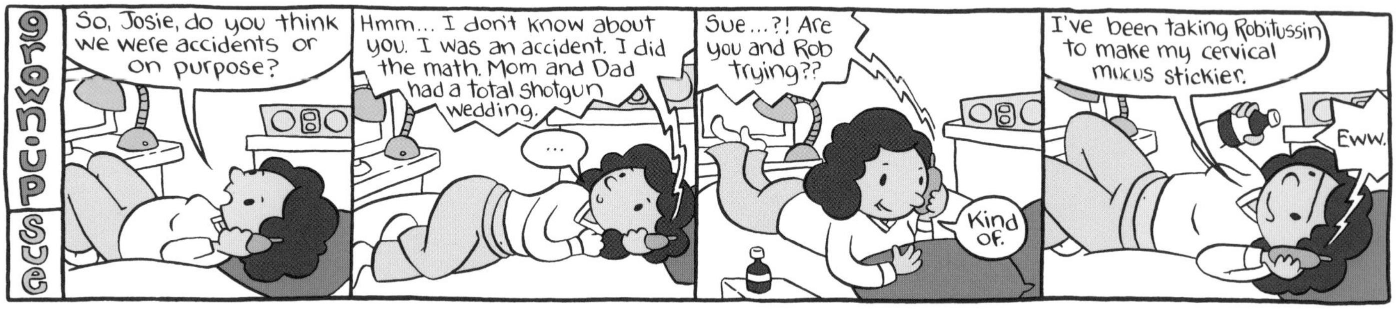
grown-up Sue
So, Josie, do you think we were accidents or on purpose?
Hmm... I don't know about you. I was an accident. I did the math. Mom and Dad had a total shotgun wedding.
...
Sue...?! Are you and Rob trying??
Kind of.
I've been taking Robitussin to make my cervical mucus stickier.
Eww.

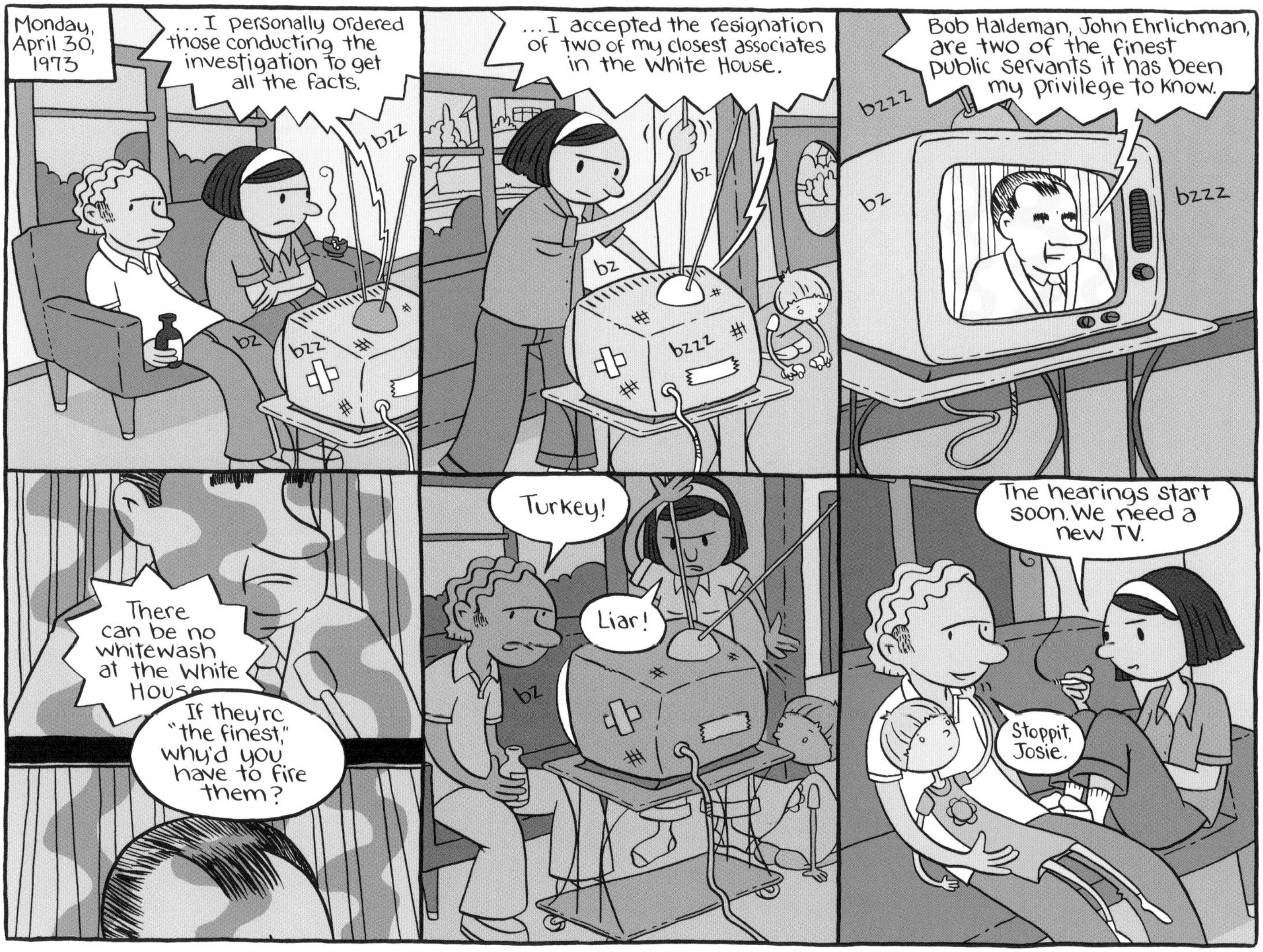
Monday, April 30, 1973
...I personally ordered those conducting the investigation to get all the facts.
bzz
bz
bzz
...I accepted the resignation of two of my closest associates in the White House.
bz
bz
bzzz
Bob Haldeman, John Ehrlichman, are two of the finest public servants it has been my privilege to know.
bzzz
bz
bzzz
There can be no whitewash at the White House
If they're "the finest," why'd you have to fire them?
Turkey!
Liar!
bz
The hearings start soon. We need a new TV.
Stoppit, Josie.

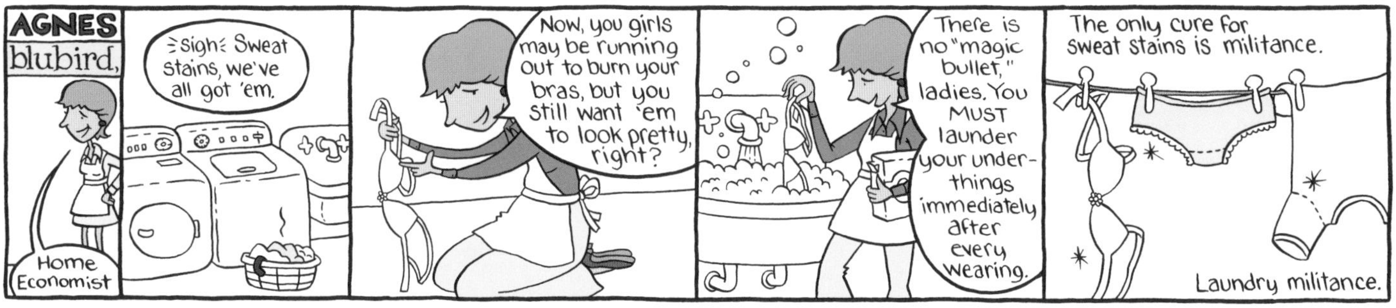
AGNES blubird, Home Economist
≶sigh≷ Sweat stains, we've all got 'em.
Now, you girls may be running out to burn your bras, but you still want 'em to look pretty, right?
There is no "magic bullet," ladies. You MUST launder your under-things immediately after every wearing.
The only cure for sweat stains is militance.
Laundry militance.

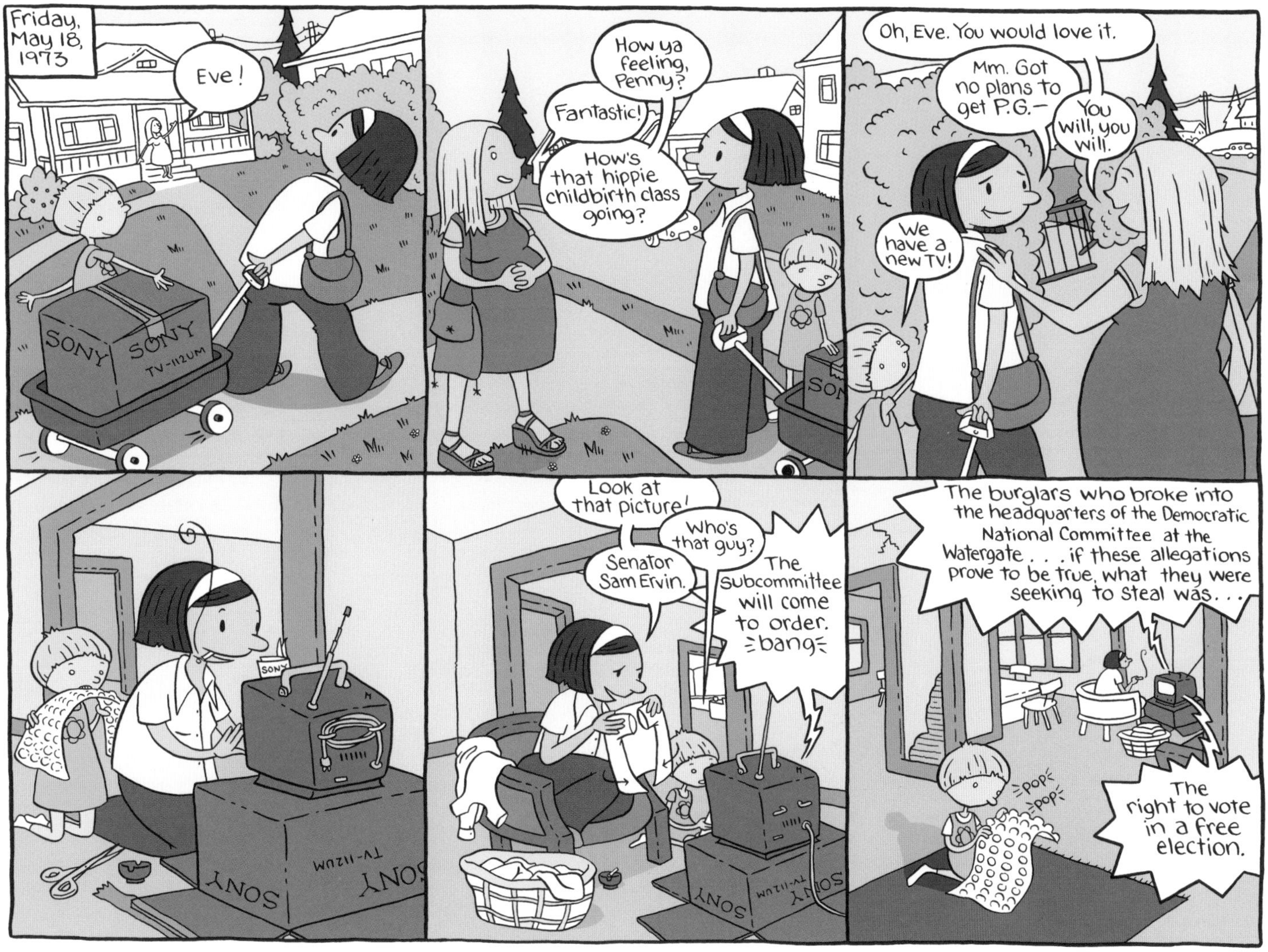
Friday, May 18, 1973
Eve!
SONY
SONY TV-112UM
How ya feeling, Penny?
Fantastic!
How's that hippie childbirth class going?
Oh, Eve. You would love it.
Mm. Got no plans to get P.G.—
You will, you will.
We have a new TV!
SONY
Look at that picture!
Who's that guy?
Senator Sam Ervin.
The subcommittee will come to order. ≶bang≷
The burglars who broke into the headquarters of the Democratic National Committee at the Watergate . . . if these allegations prove to be true, what they were seeking to steal was . . .
≶pop≷ ≶pop≷
The right to vote in a free election.

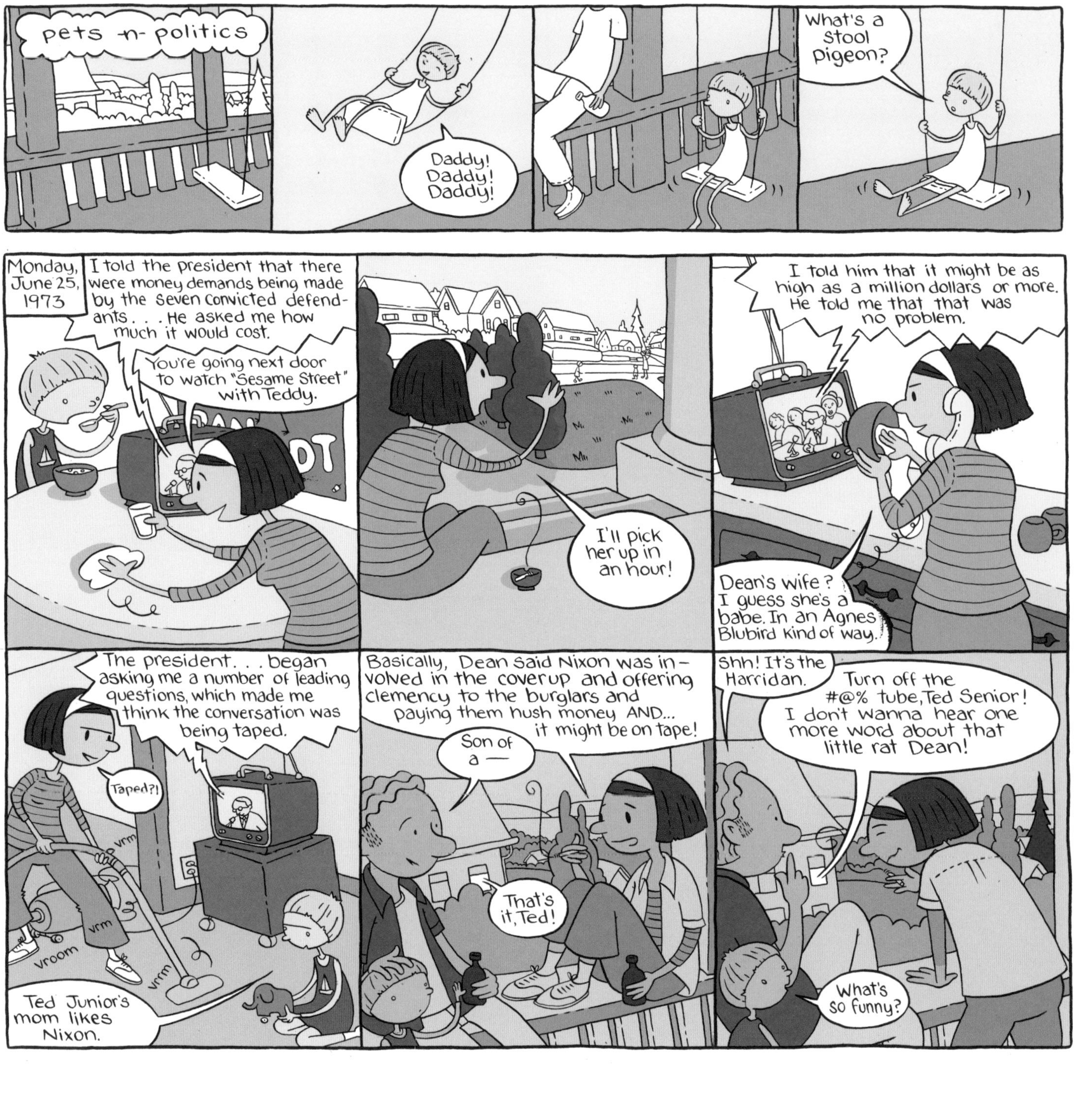
pets -n- politics
Daddy! Daddy! Daddy!
What's a stool pigeon?
Monday, June 25, 1973
I told the president that there were money demands being made by the seven convicted defendants. . . He asked me how much it would cost.
You're going next door to watch "Sesame Street" with Teddy.
I'll pick her up in an hour!
I told him that it might be as high as a million dollars or more. He told me that that was no problem.
Dean's wife? I guess she's a babe. In an Agnes Blubird kind of way.
The president. . . began asking me a number of leading questions, which made me think the conversation was being taped.
Taped?!
vrm
vrm
vroom
vrrm
Ted Junior's mom likes Nixon.
Basically, Dean said Nixon was involved in the coverup and offering clemency to the burglars and paying them hush money AND... it might be on tape!
Son of a —
That's it, Ted!
Shh! It's the Harridan.
Turn off the #@% tube, Ted Senior! I don't wanna hear one more word about that little rat Dean!
What's so funny?

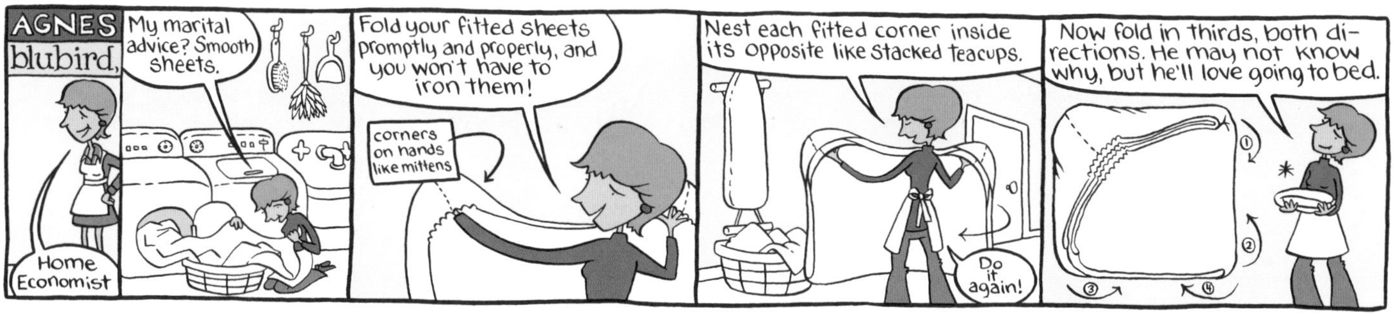
AGNES blubird, Home Economist
My marital advice? Smooth sheets.
Fold your fitted sheets promptly and properly, and you won't have to iron them!
corners on hands like mittens
Nest each fitted corner inside its opposite like stacked teacups.
Do it again!
Now fold in thirds, both directions. He may not know why, but he'll love going to bed.

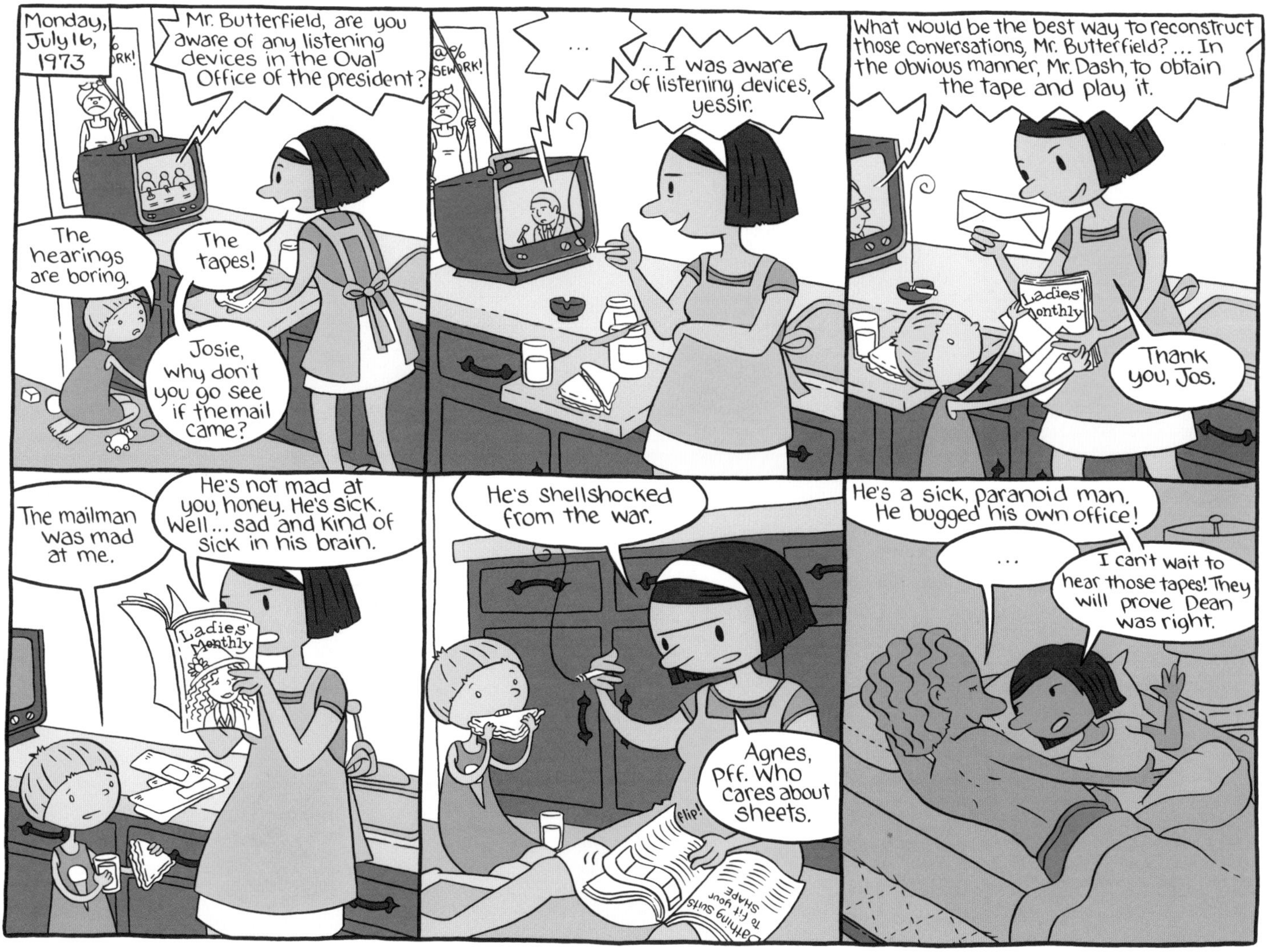
Monday, July 16, 1973
Mr. Butterfield, are you aware of any listening devices in the Oval Office of the president?
The hearings are boring.
The tapes!
Josie, why don't you go see if the mail came?
...
...I was aware of listening devices, yessir.
What would be the best way to reconstruct those conversations, Mr. Butterfield? ... In the obvious manner, Mr. Dash, to obtain the tape and play it.
Ladies' Monthly
Thank you, Jos.
The mailman was mad at me.
He's not mad at you, honey. He's sick. Well... sad and kind of sick in his brain.
Ladies' Monthly
He's shellshocked from the war.
Agnes, pff. Who cares about sheets.
flip!
He's a sick, paranoid man. He bugged his own office!
...
I can't wait to hear those tapes! They will prove Dean was right.

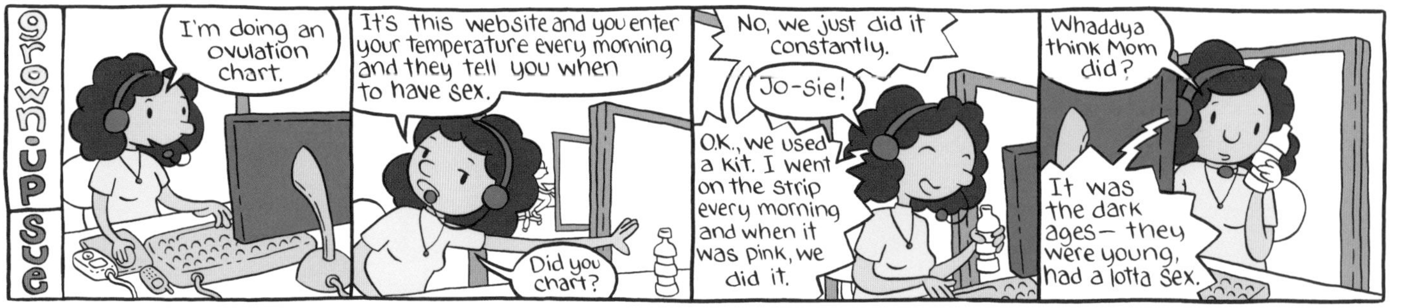
grown-up sue
I'm doing an ovulation chart.
It's this website and you enter your temperature every morning and they tell you when to have sex.
Did you chart?
No, we just did it constantly.
Jo-sie!
O.K., we used a kit. I went on the strip every morning and when it was pink, we did it.
Whaddya think Mom did?
It was the dark ages— they were young, had a lotta sex.

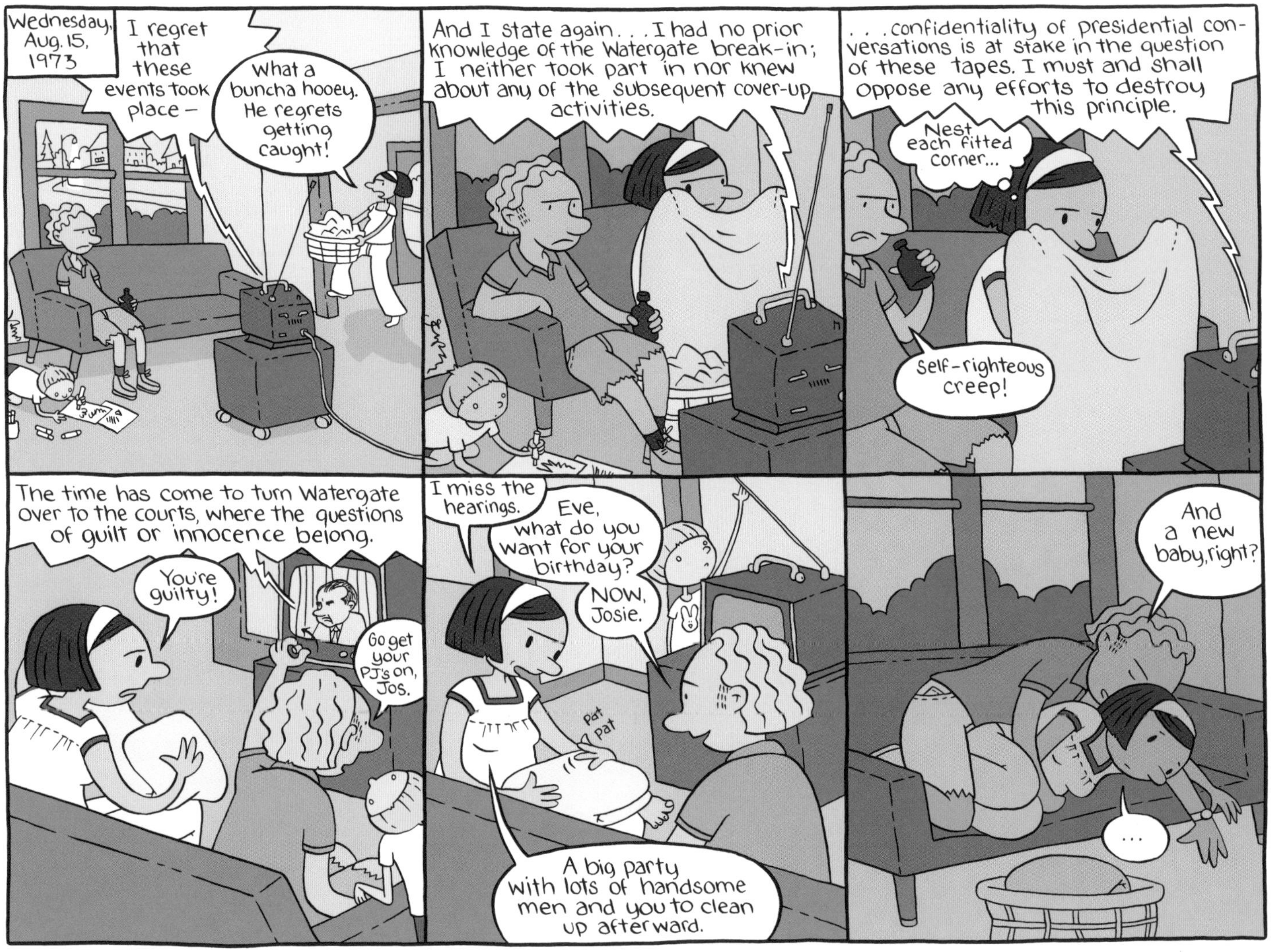
Wednesday, Aug. 15, 1973
I regret that these events took place—
What a buncha hooey. He regrets getting caught!
And I state again. . . I had no prior knowledge of the Watergate break-in; I neither took part in nor knew about any of the subsequent cover-up activities.
. . . confidentiality of presidential conversations is at stake in the question of these tapes. I must and shall oppose any efforts to destroy this principle.
Nest each fitted corner...
Self-righteous creep!
The time has come to turn Watergate over to the courts, where the questions of guilt or innocence belong.
You're guilty!
Go get your PJ's on, Jos.
I miss the hearings.
Eve, what do you want for your birthday?
NOW, Josie.
Pat pat
A big party with lots of handsome men and you to clean up afterward.
And a new baby, right?
. . .

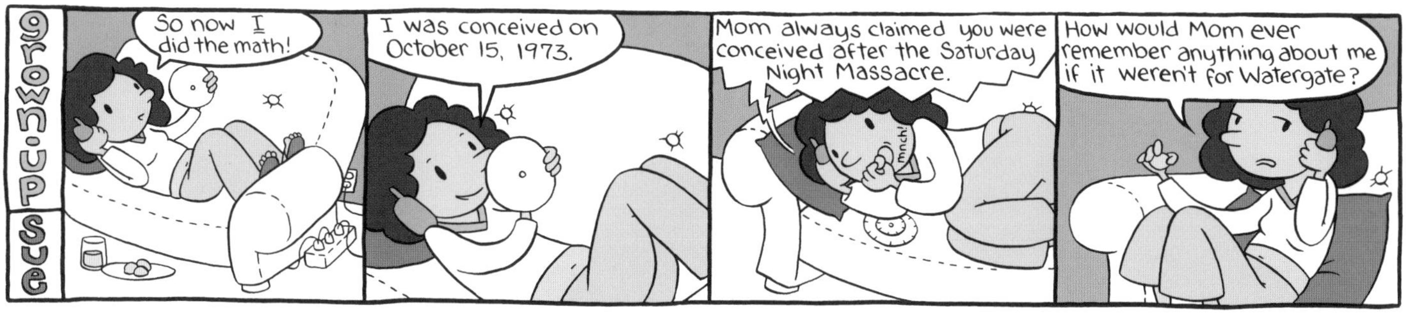
grown-up Sue
So now I did the math!
I was conceived on October 15, 1973.
Mom always claimed you were conceived after the Saturday Night Massacre.
mnch!
How would Mom ever remember anything about me if it weren't for Watergate?

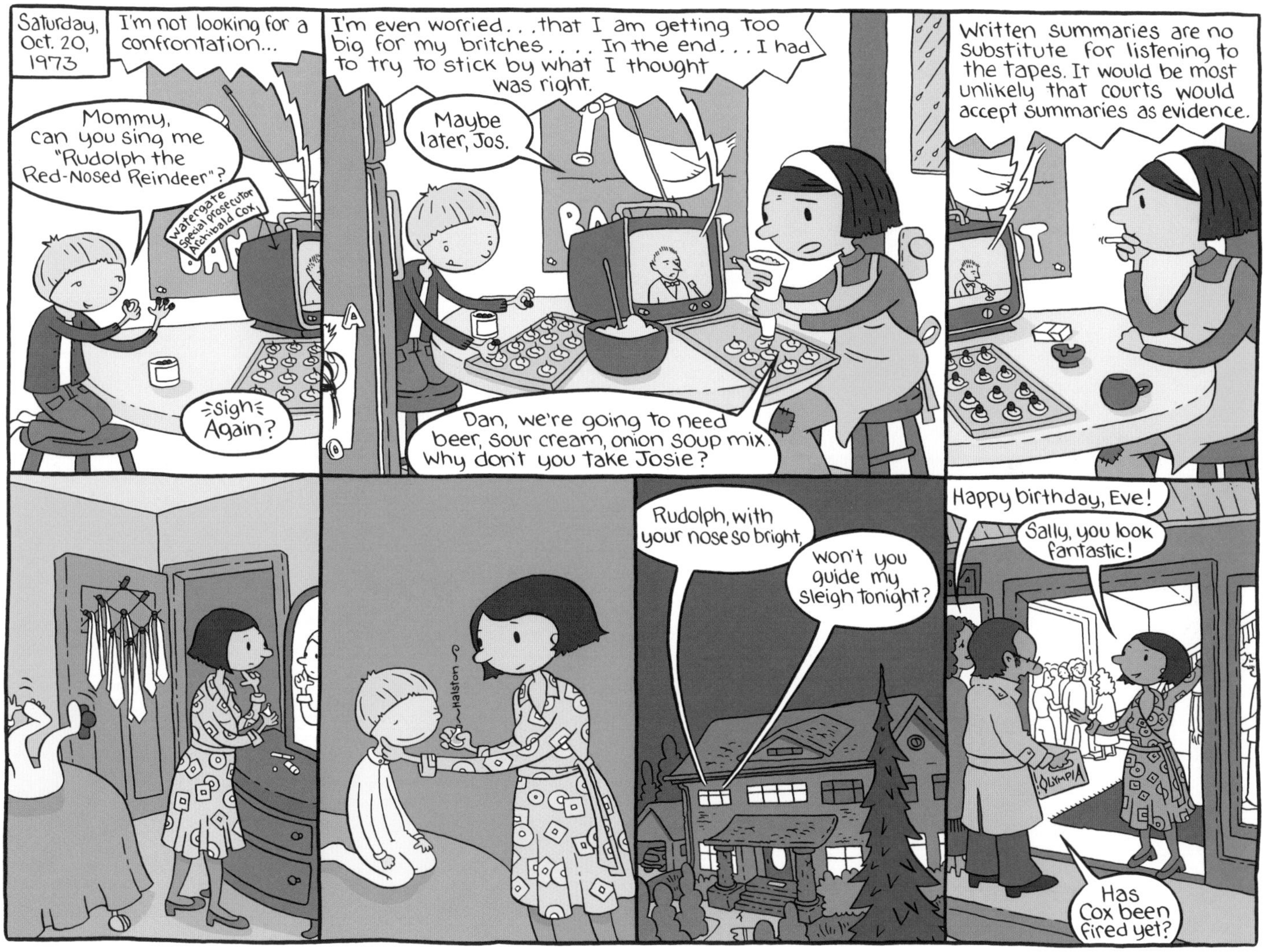
Saturday, Oct. 20, 1973
I'm not looking for a confrontation...
Mommy, can you sing me "Rudolph the Red-Nosed Reindeer"?
Watergate Special Prosecutor Archibald Cox
Sigh
Again?
I'm even worried. . .that I am getting too big for my britches. . . . In the end. . . I had to try to stick by what I thought was right.
Maybe later, Jos.
Dan, we're going to need beer, sour cream, onion soup mix. Why don't you take Josie?
Written summaries are no substitute for listening to the tapes. It would be most unlikely that courts would accept summaries as evidence.
Halston
Rudolph, with your nose so bright,
won't you guide my sleigh tonight?
Happy birthday, Eve!
Sally, you look fantastic!
OLYMPIA
Has Cox been fired yet?

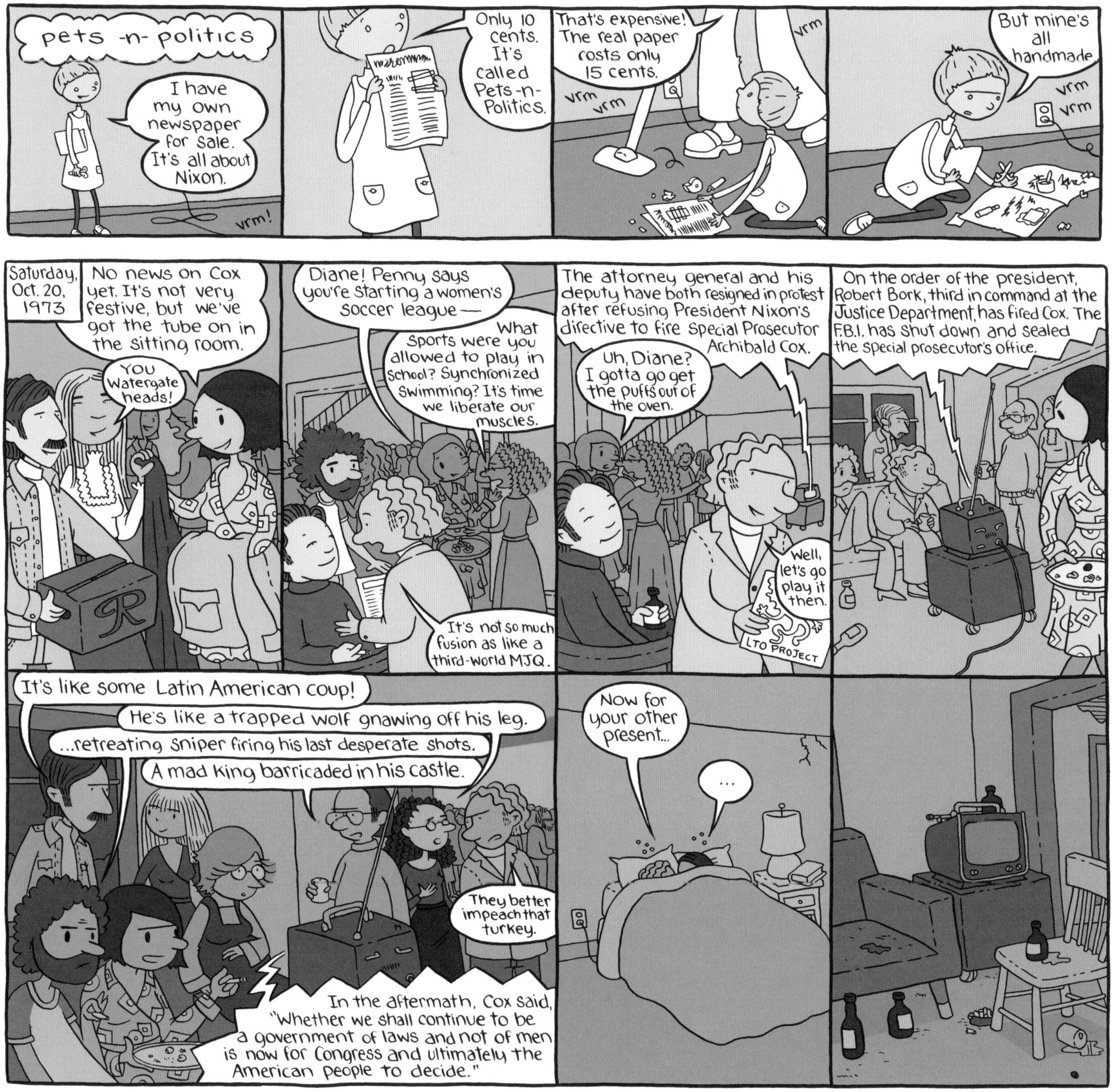
pets -n- politics
I have my own newspaper for sale. It's all about Nixon.
vrm!
Only 10 cents. It's called Pets-n-Politics.
That's expensive! The real paper costs only 15 cents.
vrm
vrm vrm
But mine's all handmade.
vrm vrm
Saturday, Oct. 20, 1973
No news on Cox yet. It's not very festive, but we've got the tube on in the sitting room.
YOU Watergate heads!
Diane! Penny says you're starting a women's soccer league—
What sports were you allowed to play in school? Synchronized swimming? It's time we liberate our muscles.
It's not so much fusion as like a third-world MJQ.
The attorney general and his deputy have both resigned in protest after refusing President Nixon's directive to fire Special Prosecutor Archibald Cox.
Uh, Diane? I gotta go get the puffs out of the oven.
Well, let's go play it then.
LTO PROJECT
On the order of the president, Robert Bork, third in command at the Justice Department, has fired Cox. The F.B.I. has shut down and sealed the special prosecutor's office.
It's like some Latin American coup!
He's like a trapped wolf gnawing off his leg.
...retreating sniper firing his last desperate shots.
A mad king barricaded in his castle.
They better impeach that turkey.
In the aftermath, Cox said, "Whether we shall continue to be a government of laws and not of men is now for Congress and ultimately the American people to decide."
Now for your other present...
...

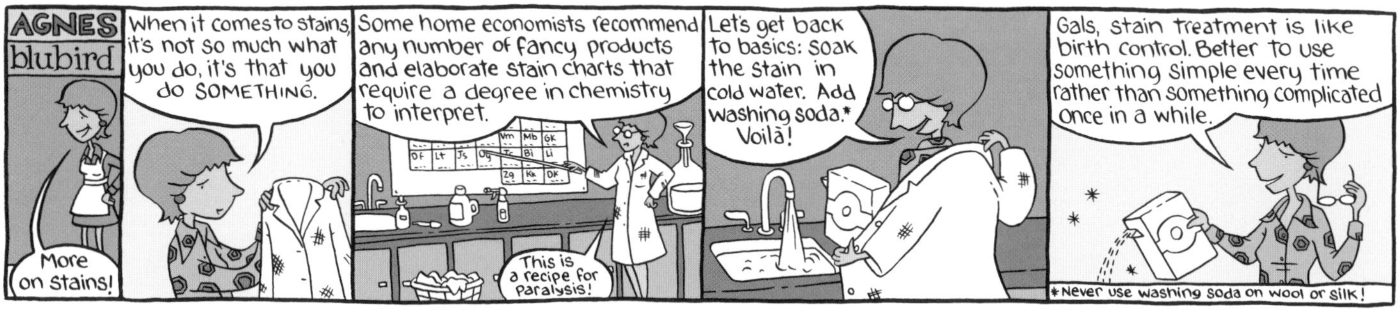
AGNES blubird
More on stains!
When it comes to stains, it's not so much what you do, it's that you do SOMETHING.
Some home economists recommend any number of fancy products and elaborate stain charts that require a degree in chemistry to interpret.
This is a recipe for paralysis!
Let's get back to basics: soak the stain in cold water. Add washing soda.* Voilà!
Gals, stain treatment is like birth control. Better to use something simple every time rather than something complicated once in a while.
* Never use washing soda on wool or silk!

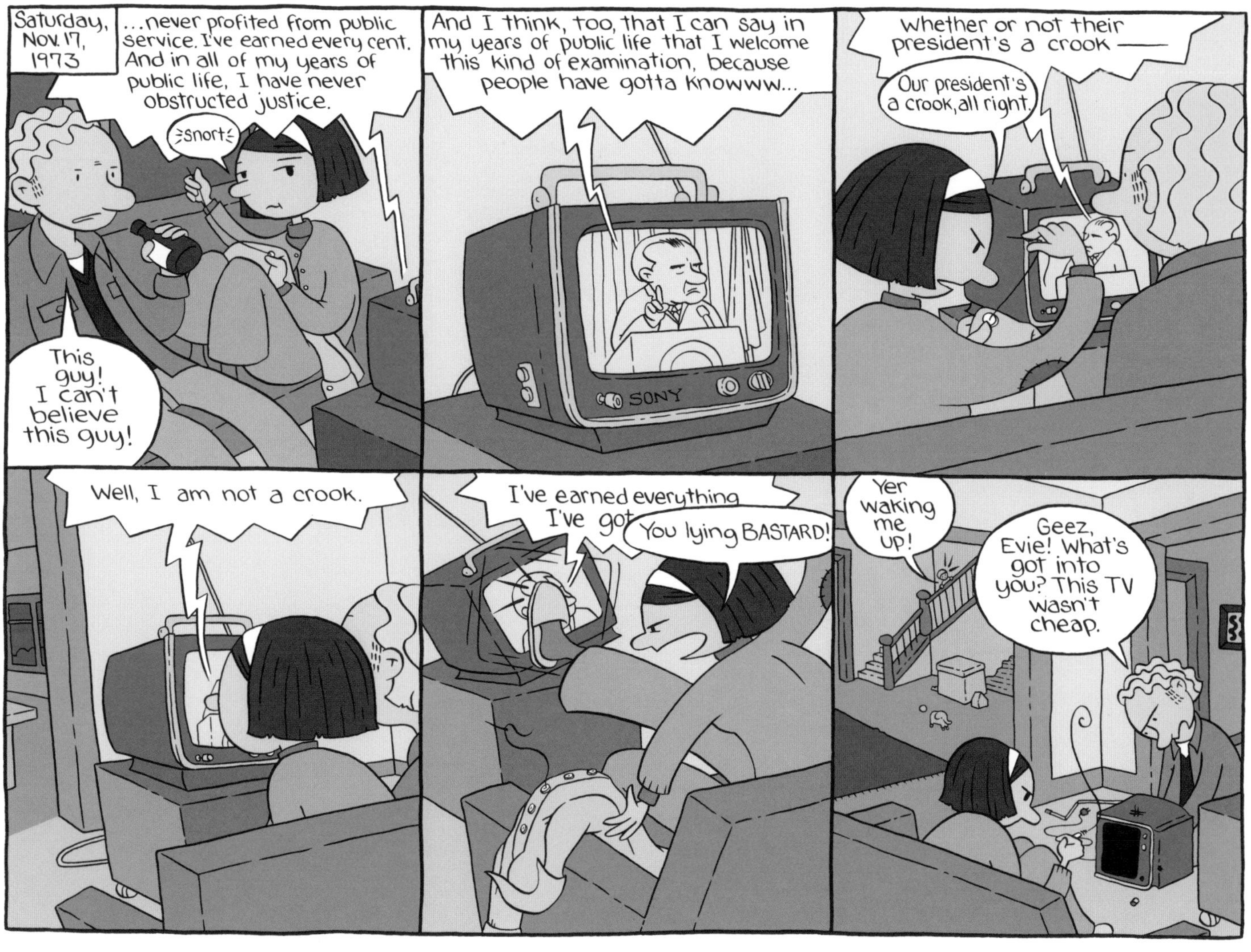
Saturday, Nov. 17, 1973
...never profited from public service. I've earned every cent. And in all of my years of public life, I have never obstructed justice.
snort
This guy! I can't believe this guy!
And I think, too, that I can say in my years of public life that I welcome this kind of examination, because people have gotta knowww...
SONY
Whether or not their president's a crook ——
Our president's a crook, all right.
Well, I am not a crook.
I've earned everything I've got
You lying BASTARD!
Yer waking me up!
Geez, Evie! What's got into you? This TV wasn't cheap.

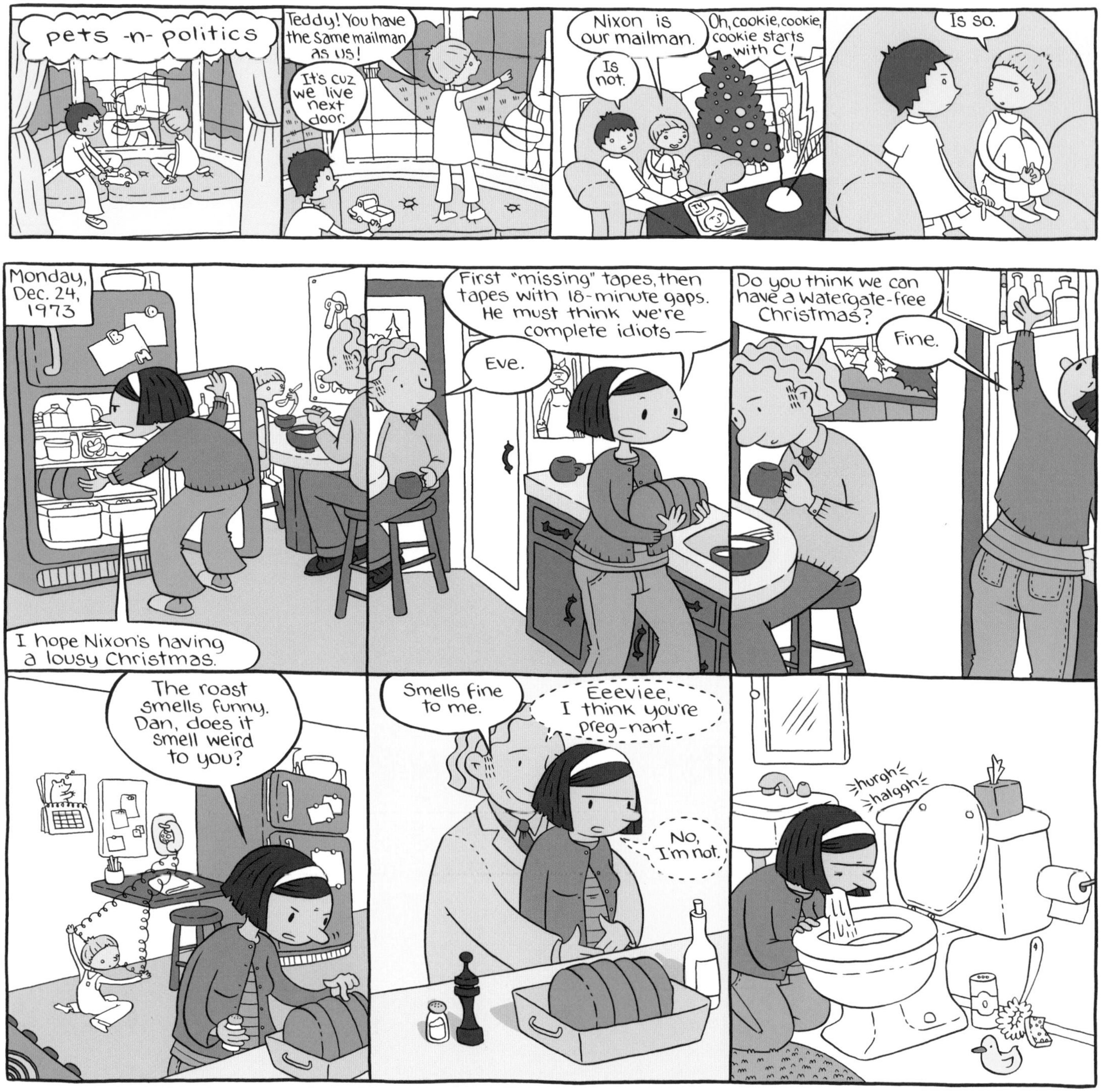
pets -n- politics
Teddy! You have the same mailman as us!
It's cuz we live next door.
Nixon is our mailman.
Is not.
Oh, cookie, cookie, cookie starts with C!
Is so.
Monday, Dec. 24, 1973
I hope Nixon's having a lousy Christmas.
Eve.
First "missing" tapes, then tapes with 18-minute gaps. He must think we're complete idiots—
Do you think we can have a Watergate-free Christmas?
Fine.
The roast smells funny. Dan, does it smell weird to you?
Smells fine to me.
Eeeviee, I think you're preg-nant.
No, I'm not.
hurgh
halggh

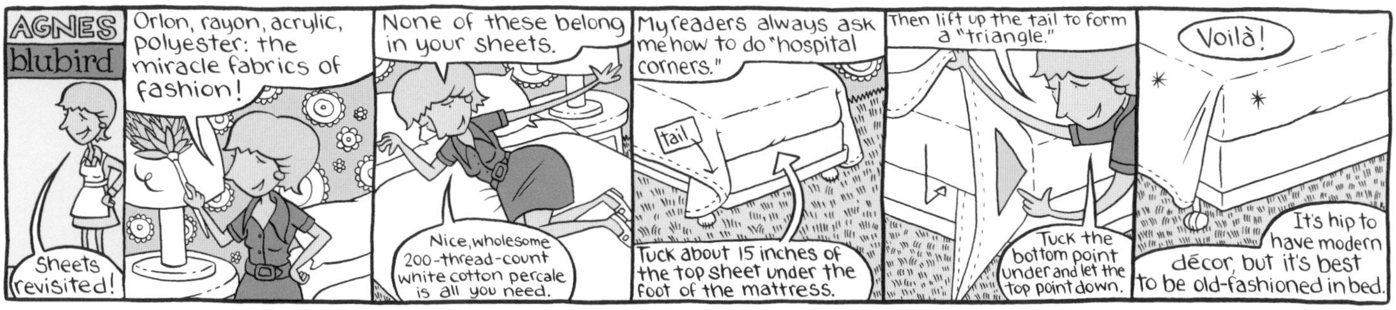
AGNES blubird
Sheets revisited!
Orlon, rayon, acrylic, polyester: the miracle fabrics of fashion!
None of these belong in your sheets.
Nice, wholesome 200-thread-count white cotton percale is all you need.
My readers always ask me how to do "hospital corners."
tail
Tuck about 15 inches of the top sheet under the foot of the mattress.
Then lift up the tail to form a "triangle."
Tuck the bottom point under and let the top point down.
Voilà!
It's hip to have modern décor, but it's best to be old-fashioned in bed.

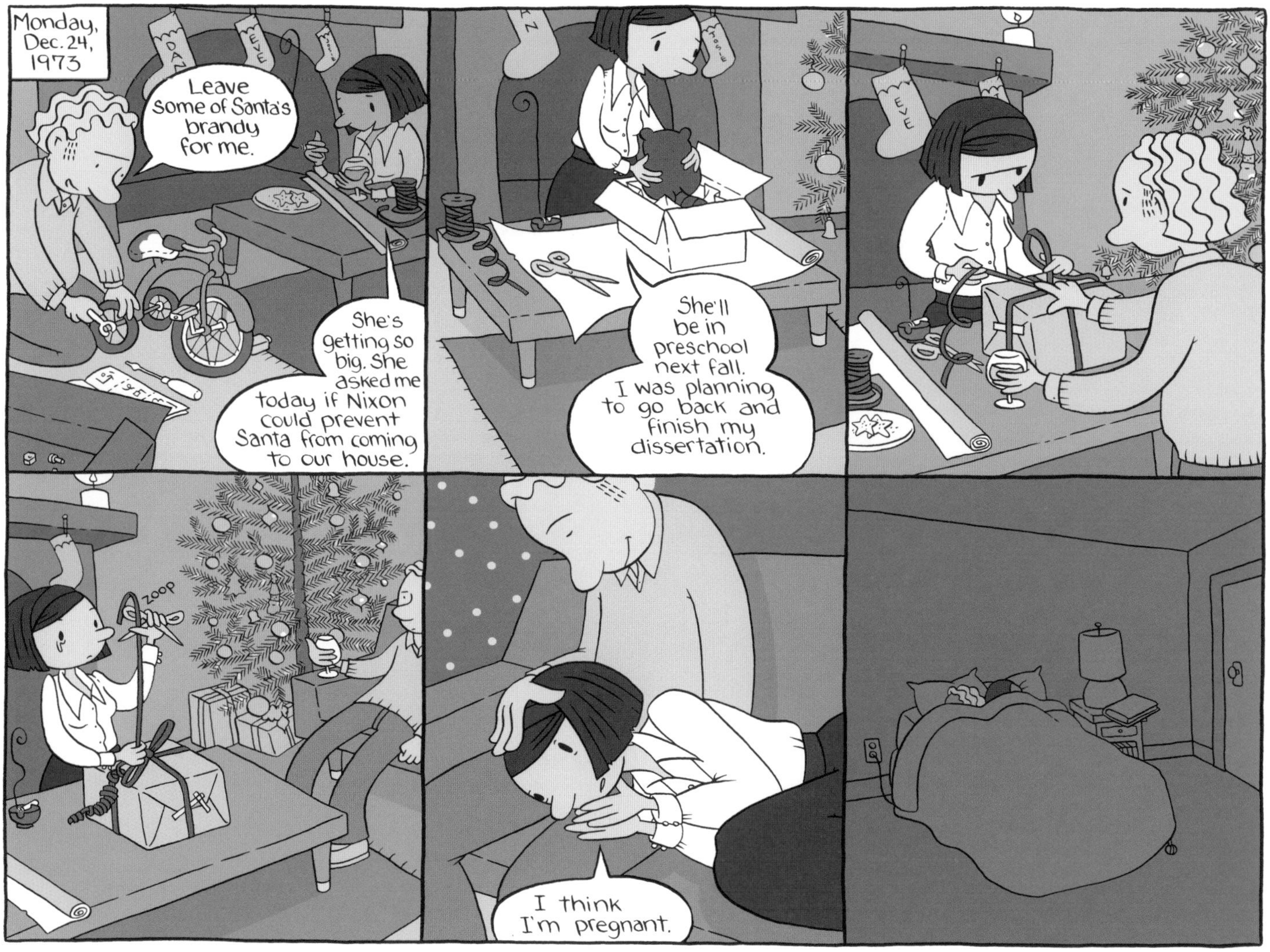
Monday, Dec. 24, 1973
Leave some of Santa's brandy for me.
She's getting so big. She asked me today if Nixon could prevent Santa from coming to our house.
She'll be in preschool next fall. I was planning to go back and finish my dissertation.
ZOOP
I think I'm pregnant.

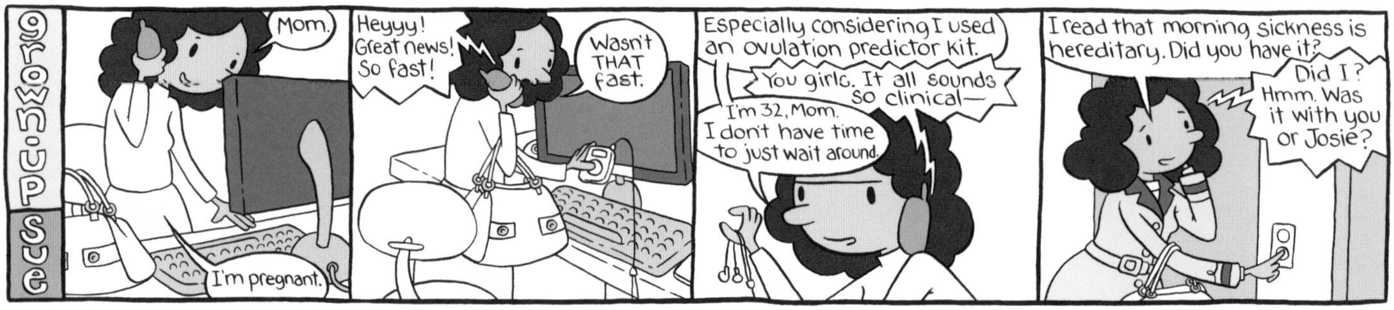
grown-up Sue
Mom.
I'm pregnant.
Heyyy! Great news! So fast!
Wasn't THAT fast.
Especially considering I used an ovulation predictor kit.
You girls. It all sounds so clinical—
I'm 32, Mom. I don't have time to just wait around.
I read that morning sickness is hereditary. Did you have it?
Did I? Hmm. Was it with you or Josie?

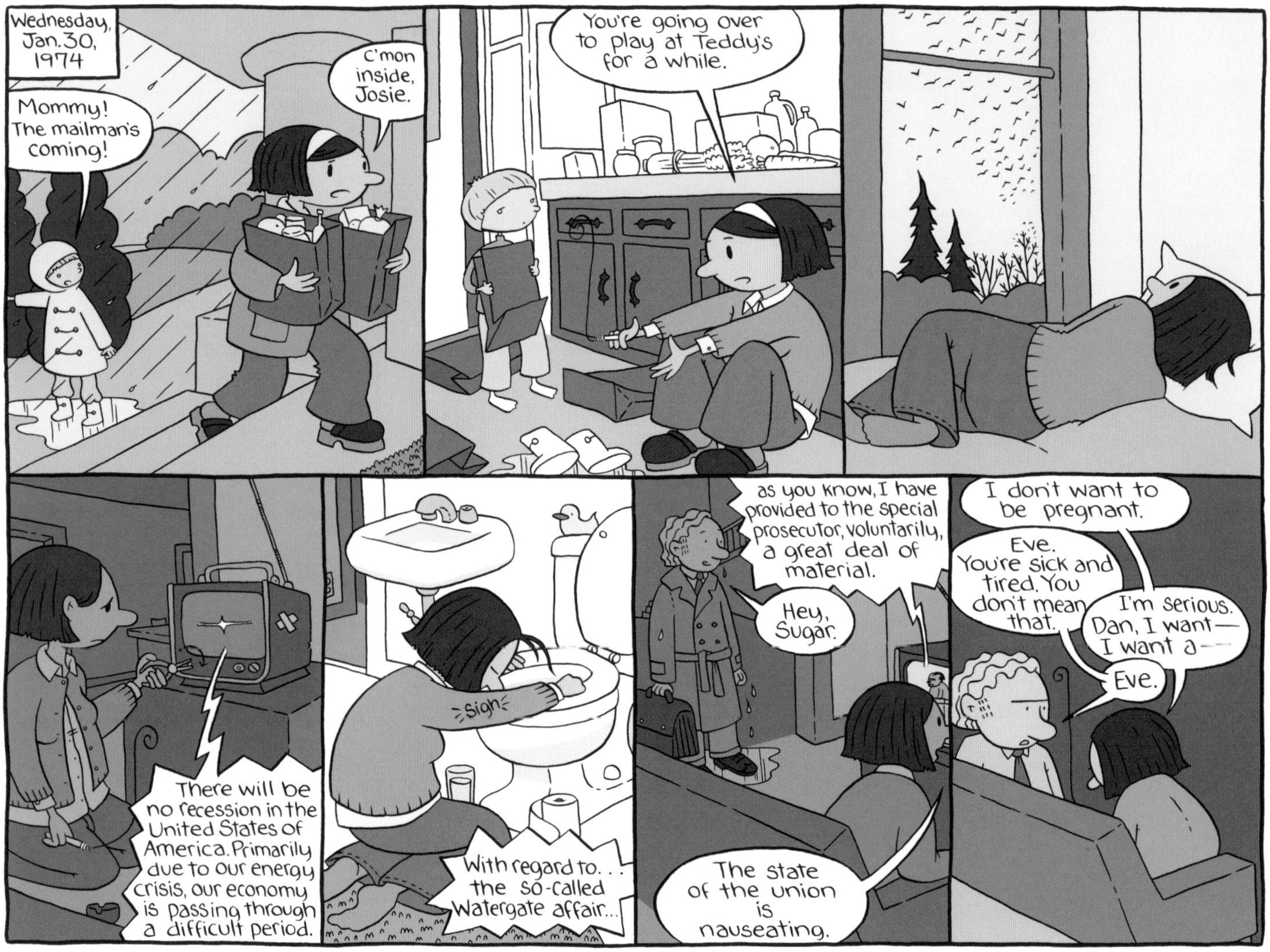
Wednesday, Jan. 30, 1974
Mommy! The mailman's coming!
C'mon inside, Josie.
You're going over to play at Teddy's for a while.
There will be no recession in the United States of America. Primarily due to our energy crisis, our economy is passing through a difficult period.
sigh
With regard to... the so-called Watergate affair...
as you know, I have provided to the special prosecutor, voluntarily, a great deal of material.
Hey, Sugar.
The state of the union is nauseating.
I don't want to be pregnant.
Eve. You're sick and tired. You don't mean that.
I'm serious. Dan, I want— I want a—
Eve.

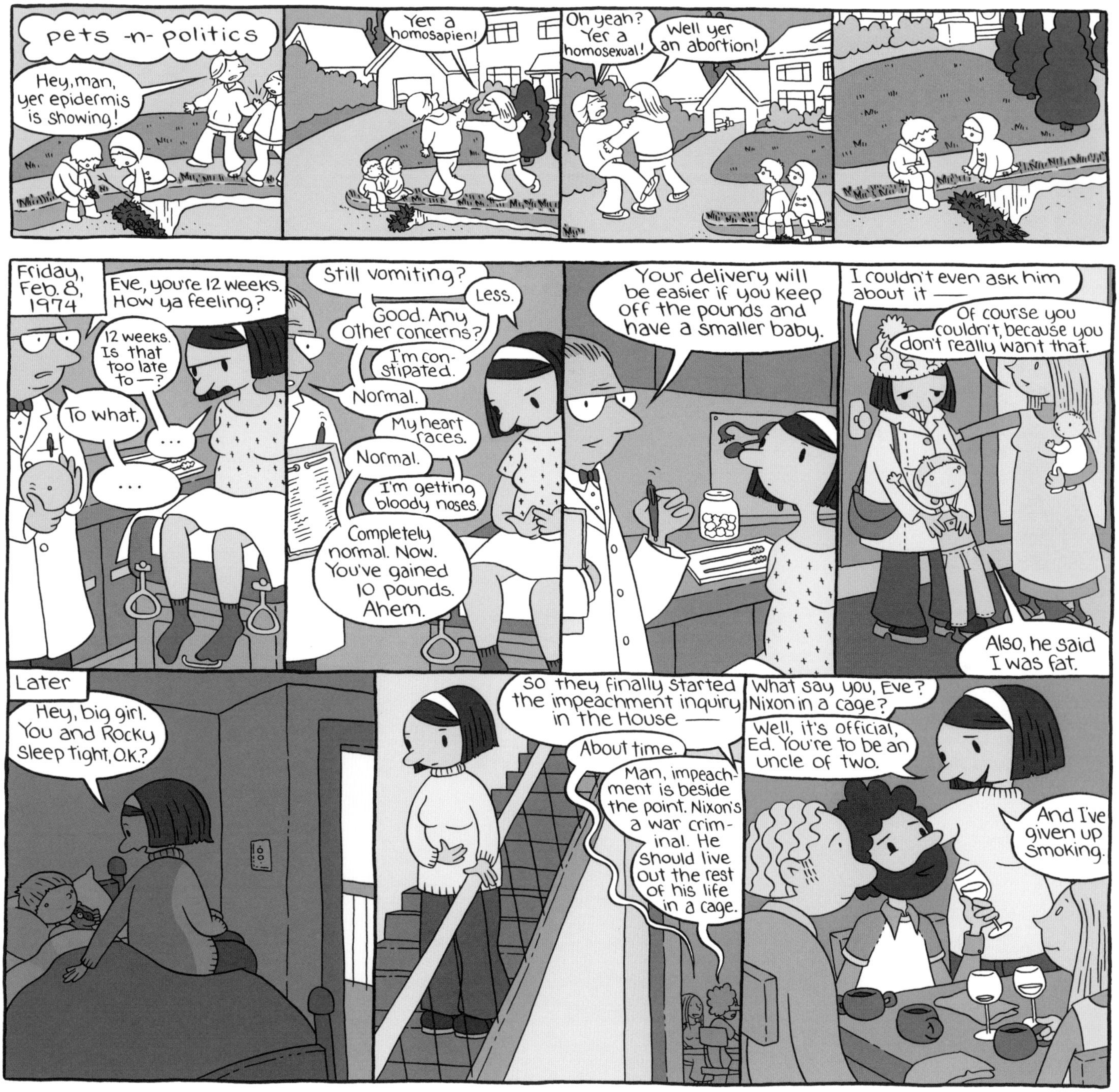
pets -n- politics
Hey, man, yer epidermis is showing!
Yer a homosapien!
Oh yeah? Yer a homosexual!
Well yer an abortion!
Friday, Feb. 8, 1974
Eve, you're 12 weeks. How ya feeling?
12 weeks. Is that too late to—?
To what.
...
...
Still vomiting?
Less.
Good. Any other concerns?
I'm constipated.
Normal.
My heart races.
Normal.
I'm getting bloody noses.
Completely normal. Now. You've gained 10 pounds. Ahem.
Your delivery will be easier if you keep off the pounds and have a smaller baby.
I couldn't even ask him about it —
Of course you couldn't, because you don't really want that.
Also, he said I was fat.
Later
Hey, big girl. You and Rocky sleep tight, O.K.?
So they finally started the impeachment inquiry in the House —
About time.
Man, impeachment is beside the point. Nixon's a war criminal. He should live out the rest of his life in a cage.
What say you, Eve? Nixon in a cage?
Well, it's official, Ed. You're to be an uncle of two.
And I've given up smoking.

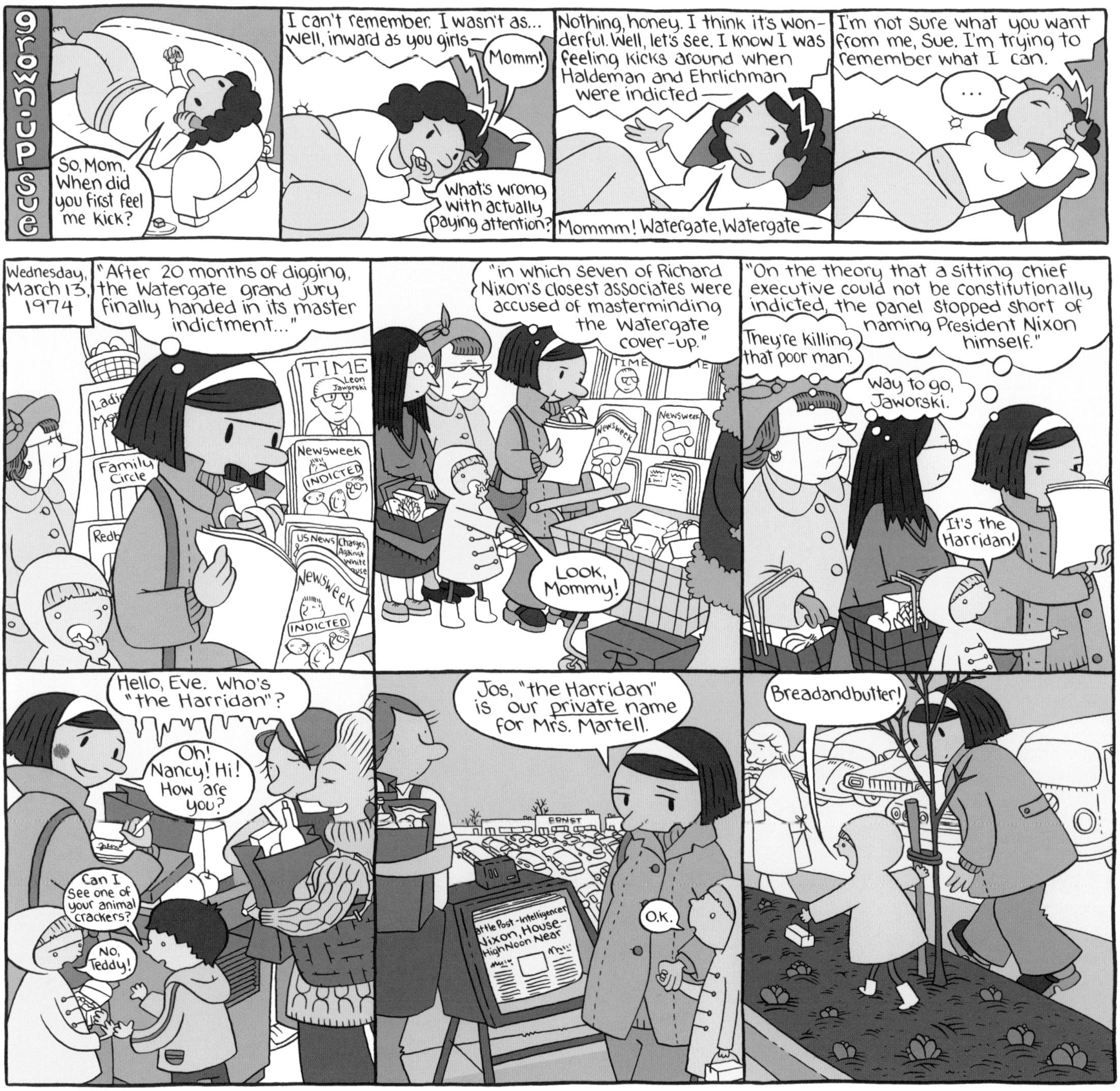
grown-up Sue
So, Mom. When did you first feel me kick?
I can't remember. I wasn't as... well, inward as you girls—
Momm!
What's wrong with actually paying attention?
Nothing, honey. I think it's wonderful. Well, let's see. I know I was feeling kicks around when Haldeman and Ehrlichman were indicted—
Mommm! Watergate, Watergate—
I'm not sure what you want from me, Sue. I'm trying to remember what I can.
...
Wednesday, March 13, 1974
"After 20 months of digging, the Watergate grand jury finally handed in its master indictment..."
TIME
Leon Jaworski
Family Circle
Newsweek
INDICTED
US News
Charges Against White House
"in which seven of Richard Nixon's closest associates were accused of masterminding the Watergate cover-up."
Look, Mommy!
"On the theory that a sitting chief executive could not be constitutionally indicted, the panel stopped short of naming President Nixon himself."
They're killing that poor man.
Way to go, Jaworski.
It's the Harridan!
Hello, Eve. Who's "the Harridan"?
Oh! Nancy! Hi! How are you?
Can I see one of your animal crackers?
No, Teddy!
Jos, "the Harridan" is our private name for Mrs. Martell.
ERNST
ttle Post-Intelligencer
Nixon, House-
High Noon Near
O.K.
Breadandbutter!

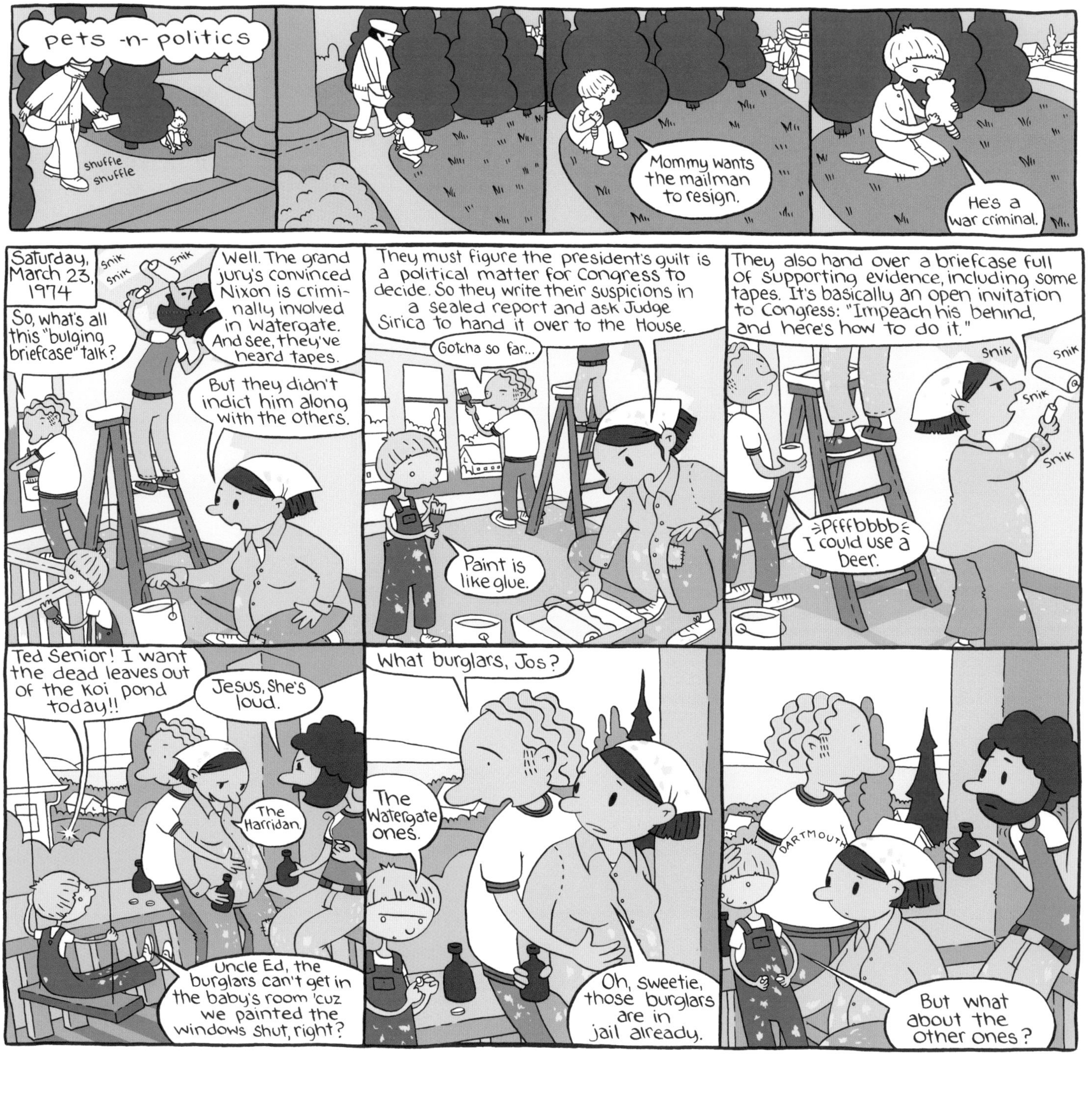
pets -n- politics
shuffle shuffle
Mommy wants the mailman to resign.
He's a war criminal.
Saturday, March 23, 1974
snik snik snik
So, what's all this "bulging briefcase" talk?
Well. The grand jury's convinced Nixon is criminally involved in Watergate. And see, they've heard tapes.
But they didn't indict him along with the others.
They must figure the president's guilt is a political matter for Congress to decide. So they write their suspicions in a sealed report and ask Judge Sirica to hand it over to the House.
Gotcha so far...
Paint is like glue.
They also hand over a briefcase full of supporting evidence, including some tapes. It's basically an open invitation to Congress: "Impeach his behind, and here's how to do it."
snik snik snik snik
Pfffbbbb I could use a beer.
Ted Senior! I want the dead leaves out of the Koi pond today!!
Jesus, she's loud.
The Harridan.
Uncle Ed, the burglars can't get in the baby's room 'cuz we painted the windows shut, right?
What burglars, Jos?
The Watergate ones.
Oh, sweetie, those burglars are in jail already.
DARTMOUTH
But what about the other ones?

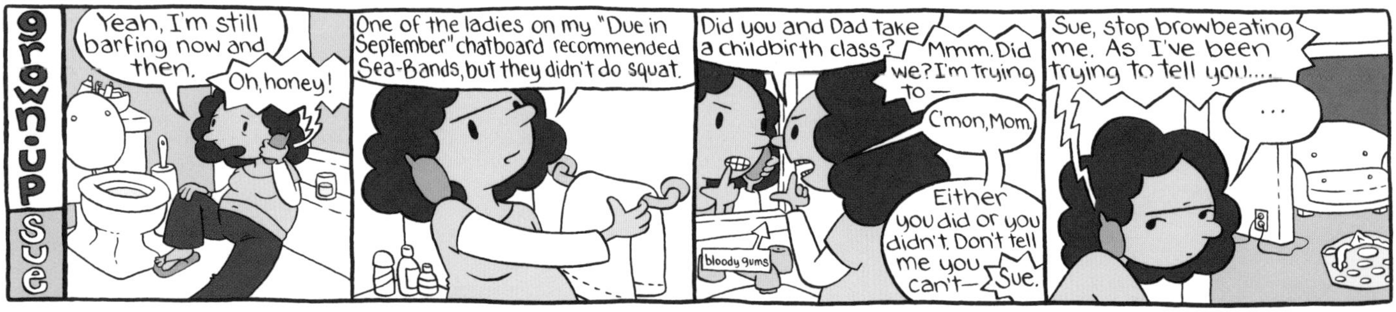
grown-up Sue
Yeah, I'm still barfing now and then.
Oh, honey!
One of the ladies on my "Due in September" chatboard recommended Sea-Bands, but they didn't do squat.
Did you and Dad take a childbirth class?
Mmm. Did we? I'm trying to—
C'mon, Mom.
Either you did or you didn't. Don't tell me you can't—
Sue.
bloody gums
Sue, stop browbeating me. As I've been trying to tell you....
...

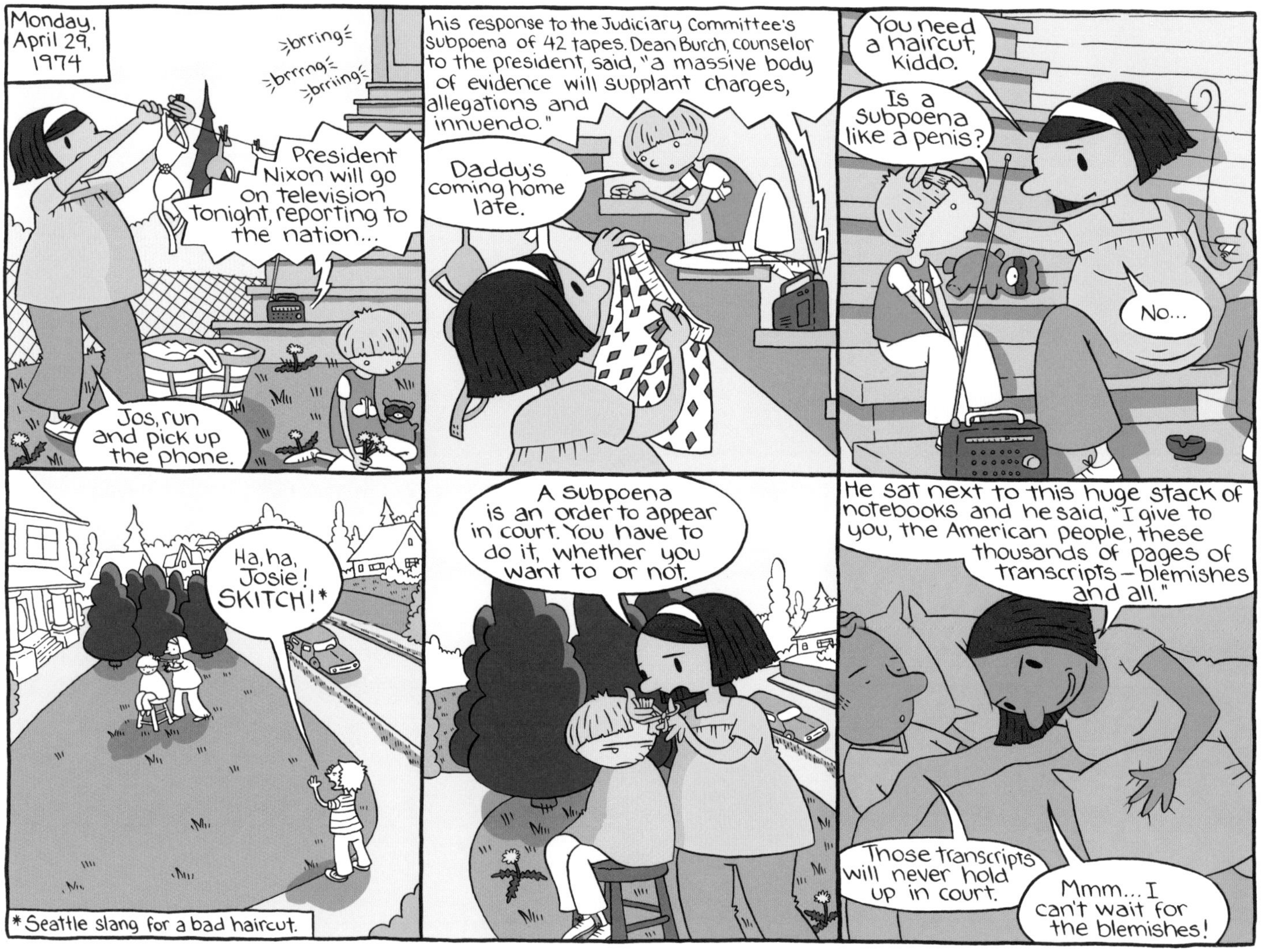
Monday, April 29, 1974
brring
brrrng
brriing
President Nixon will go on television tonight, reporting to the nation...
Jos, run and pick up the phone.
his response to the Judiciary Committee's subpoena of 42 tapes. Dean Burch, counselor to the president, said, "a massive body of evidence will supplant charges, allegations and innuendo."
Daddy's coming home late.
You need a haircut, Kiddo.
Is a subpoena like a penis?
No...
Ha, ha, Josie! SKITCH!*
*Seattle slang for a bad haircut.
A subpoena is an order to appear in court. You have to do it, whether you want to or not.
He sat next to this huge stack of notebooks and he said, "I give to you, the American people, these thousands of pages of transcripts—blemishes and all."
Those transcripts will never hold up in court.
Mmm... I can't wait for the blemishes!

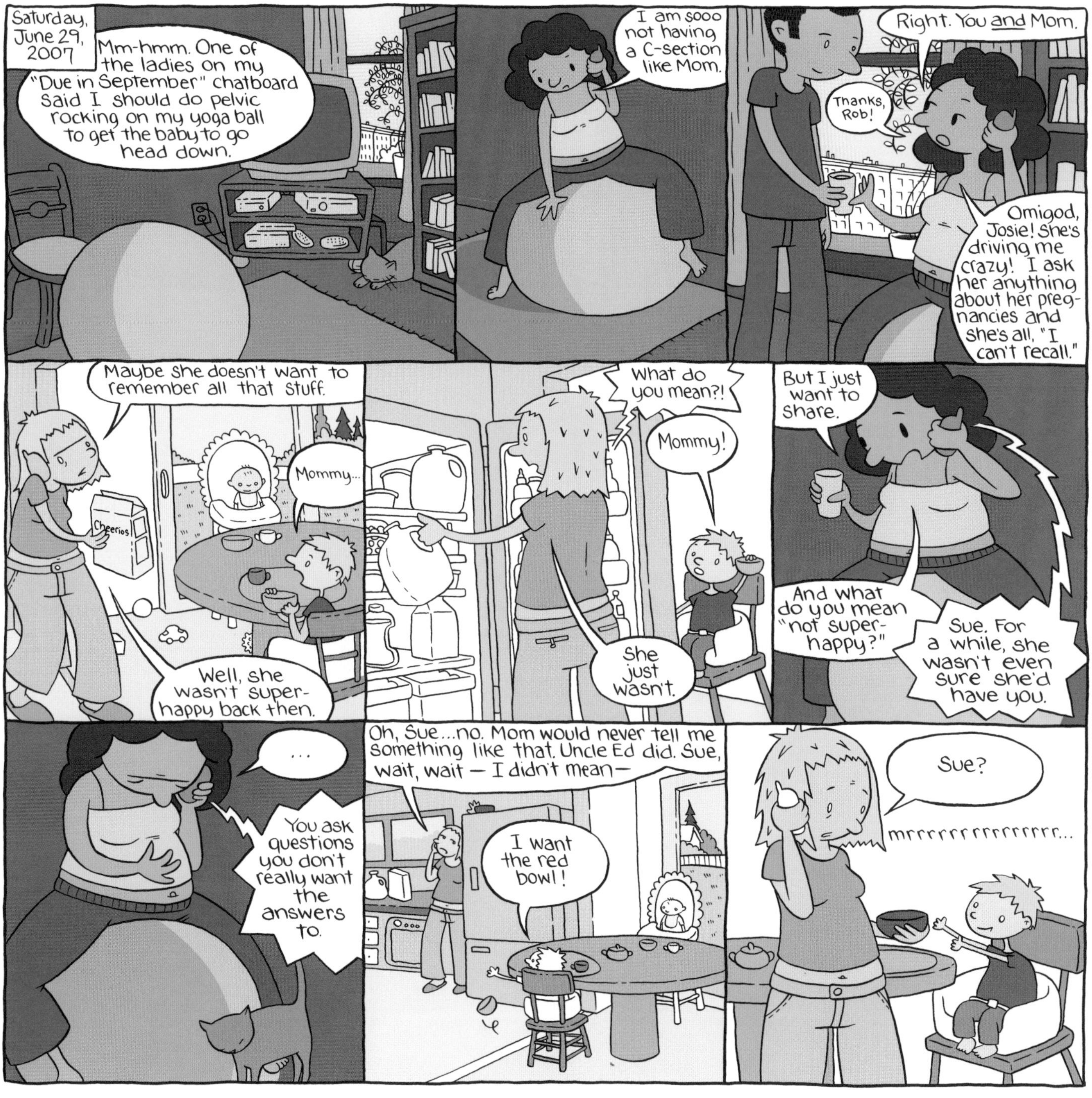
Saturday, June 29, 2007
Mm-hmm. One of the ladies on my "Due in September" chatboard said I should do pelvic rocking on my yoga ball to get the baby to go head down.
I am sooo not having a C-section like Mom.
Right. You and Mom.
Thanks, Rob!
Omigod, Josie! She's driving me crazy! I ask her anything about her pregnancies and she's all, "I can't recall."
Maybe she doesn't want to remember all that stuff.
Cheerios
Mommy...
Well, she wasn't super-happy back then.
What do you mean?!
Mommy!
She just wasn't.
But I just want to share.
And what do you mean "not super-happy?"
Sue. For a while, she wasn't even sure she'd have you.
...
You ask questions you don't really want the answers to.
Oh, Sue...no. Mom would never tell me something like that. Uncle Ed did. Sue, wait, wait — I didn't mean—
I want the red bowl!
Sue?
mrrrrrrrrrrrrrrr...

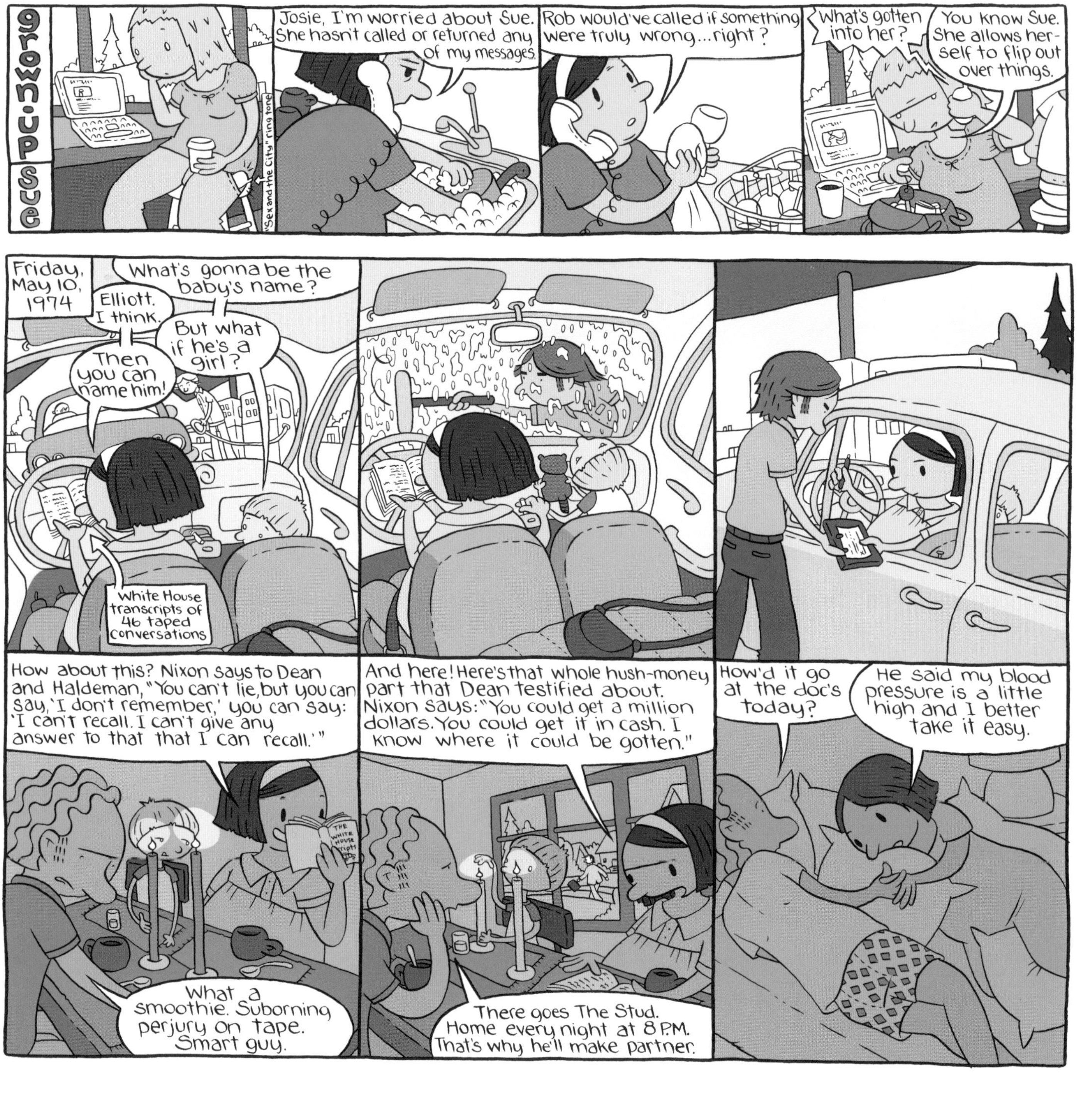
grown-up sue
"Sex and the City" ring tone
Josie, I'm worried about Sue. She hasn't called or returned any of my messages.
Rob would've called if something were truly wrong...right?
What's gotten into her?
You know Sue. She allows herself to flip out over things.
Friday, May 10, 1974
What's gonna be the baby's name?
Elliott. I think.
But what if he's a girl?
Then you can name him!
White House transcripts of 46 taped conversations
How about this? Nixon says to Dean and Haldeman, "You can't lie, but you can say, 'I don't remember,' you can say: 'I can't recall. I can't give any answer to that that I can recall.'"
THE WHITE HOUSE
What a smoothie. Suborning perjury on tape. Smart guy.
And here! Here's that whole hush-money part that Dean testified about. Nixon says: "You could get a million dollars. You could get it in cash. I know where it could be gotten."
There goes The Stud. Home every night at 8 P.M. That's why he'll make partner.
How'd it go at the doc's today?
He said my blood pressure is a little high and I better take it easy.

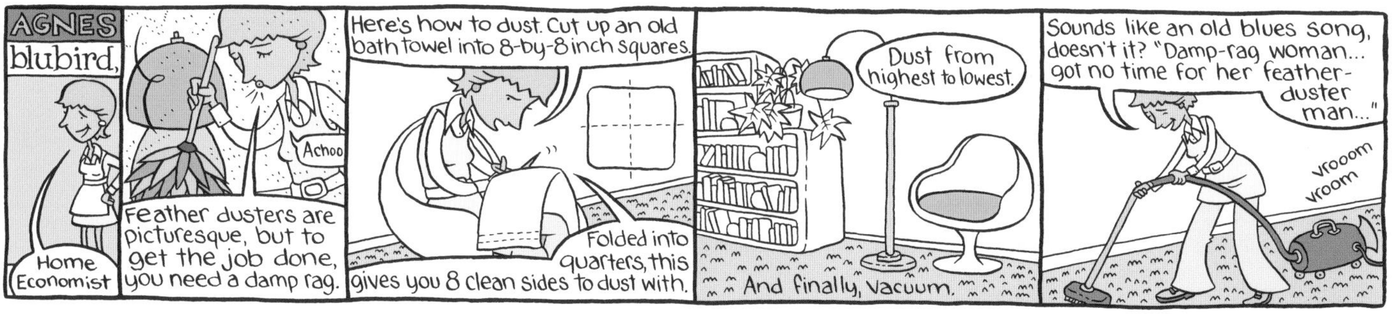
AGNES blubird,
Home Economist
Achoo
Feather dusters are picturesque, but to get the job done, you need a damp rag.
Here's how to dust. Cut up an old bath towel into 8-by-8 inch squares.
Folded into quarters, this gives you 8 clean sides to dust with.
Dust from highest to lowest.
And finally, vacuum.
Sounds like an old blues song, doesn't it? "Damp-rag woman... got no time for her feather-duster man..."
vrooom vroom

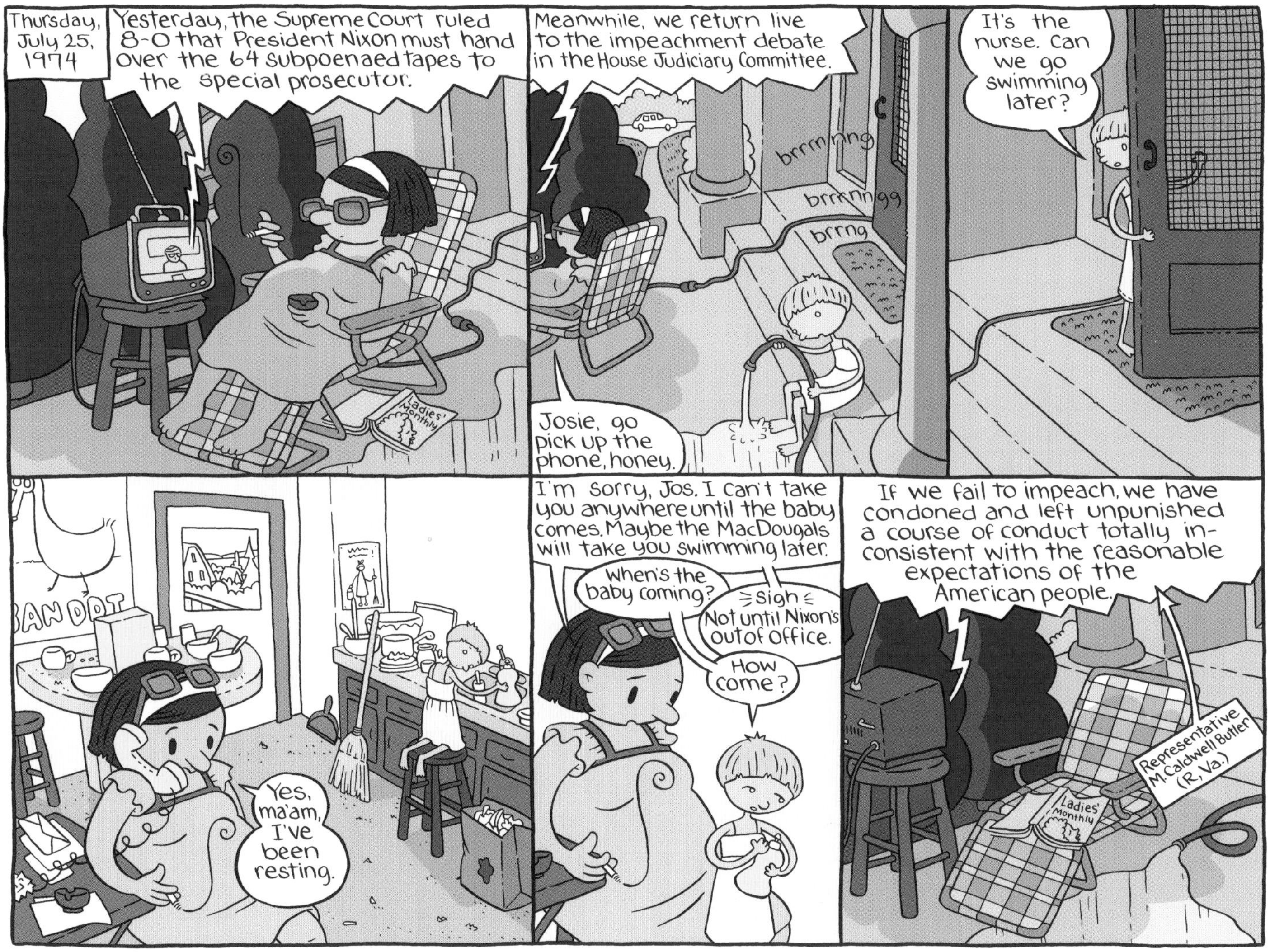
Thursday, July 25, 1974
Yesterday, the Supreme Court ruled 8-0 that President Nixon must hand over the 64 subpoenaed tapes to the special prosecutor.
Ladies' Monthly
Meanwhile, we return live to the impeachment debate in the House Judiciary Committee.
brrrnnng
brrrnnngg
brrng
Josie, go pick up the phone, honey.
It's the nurse. Can we go swimming later?
Yes, ma'am, I've been resting.
I'm sorry, Jos. I can't take you anywhere until the baby comes. Maybe the MacDougals will take you swimming later.
When's the baby coming?
Sigh
Not until Nixon's out of office.
How come?
If we fail to impeach, we have condoned and left unpunished a course of conduct totally inconsistent with the reasonable expectations of the American people.
Representative M. Caldwell Butler (R, Va.)
Ladies' Monthly

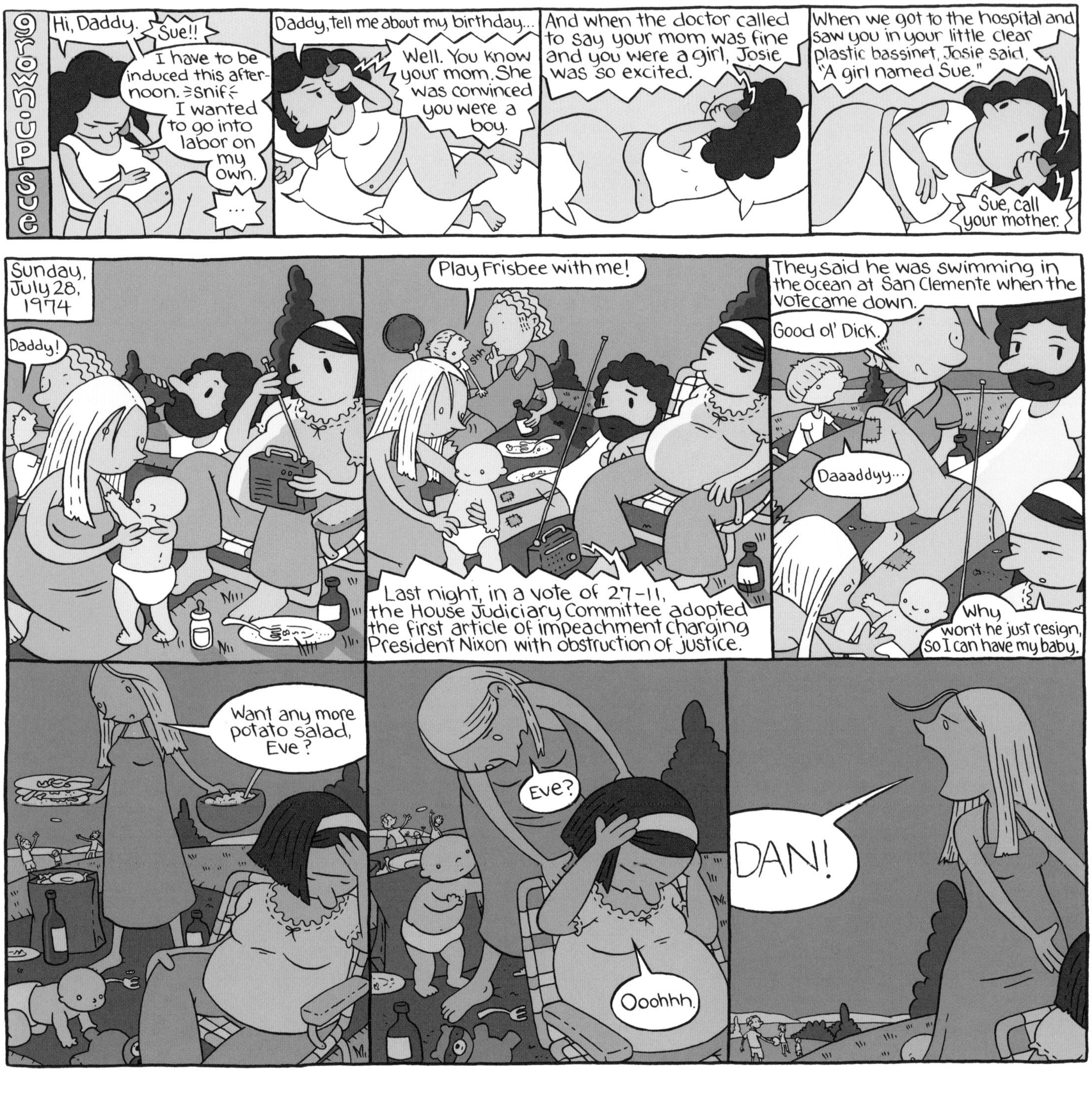
grown-up sue
Hi, Daddy.
Sue!!
I have to be induced this afternoon. ≥snif≤ I wanted to go into labor on my own.
...
Daddy, tell me about my birthday...
Well. You know your mom. She was convinced you were a boy.
And when the doctor called to say your mom was fine and you were a girl, Josie was so excited.
When we got to the hospital and saw you in your little clear plastic bassinet, Josie said, "A girl named Sue."
Sue, call your mother.
Sunday, July 28, 1974
Daddy!
Play Frisbee with me!
shh
Last night, in a vote of 27-11, the House Judiciary Committee adopted the first article of impeachment charging President Nixon with obstruction of justice.
They said he was swimming in the ocean at San Clemente when the vote came down.
Good ol' Dick.
Daaaddyy...
Why won't he just resign, so I can have my baby.
Want any more potato salad, Eve?
Eve?
Ooohhh.
DAN!

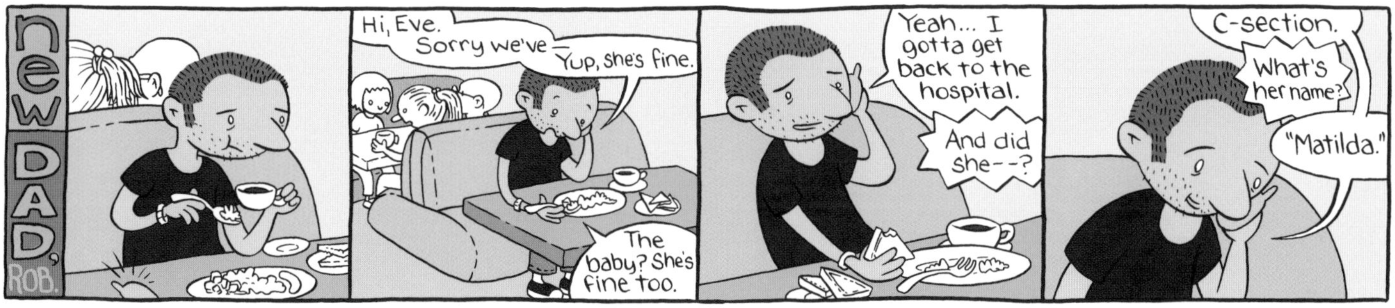
new DAD,
ROB.
Hi, Eve.
Sorry we've—
Yup, she's fine.
The baby? She's fine too.
Yeah... I gotta get back to the hospital.
And did she--?
C-section.
What's her name?
"Matilda."

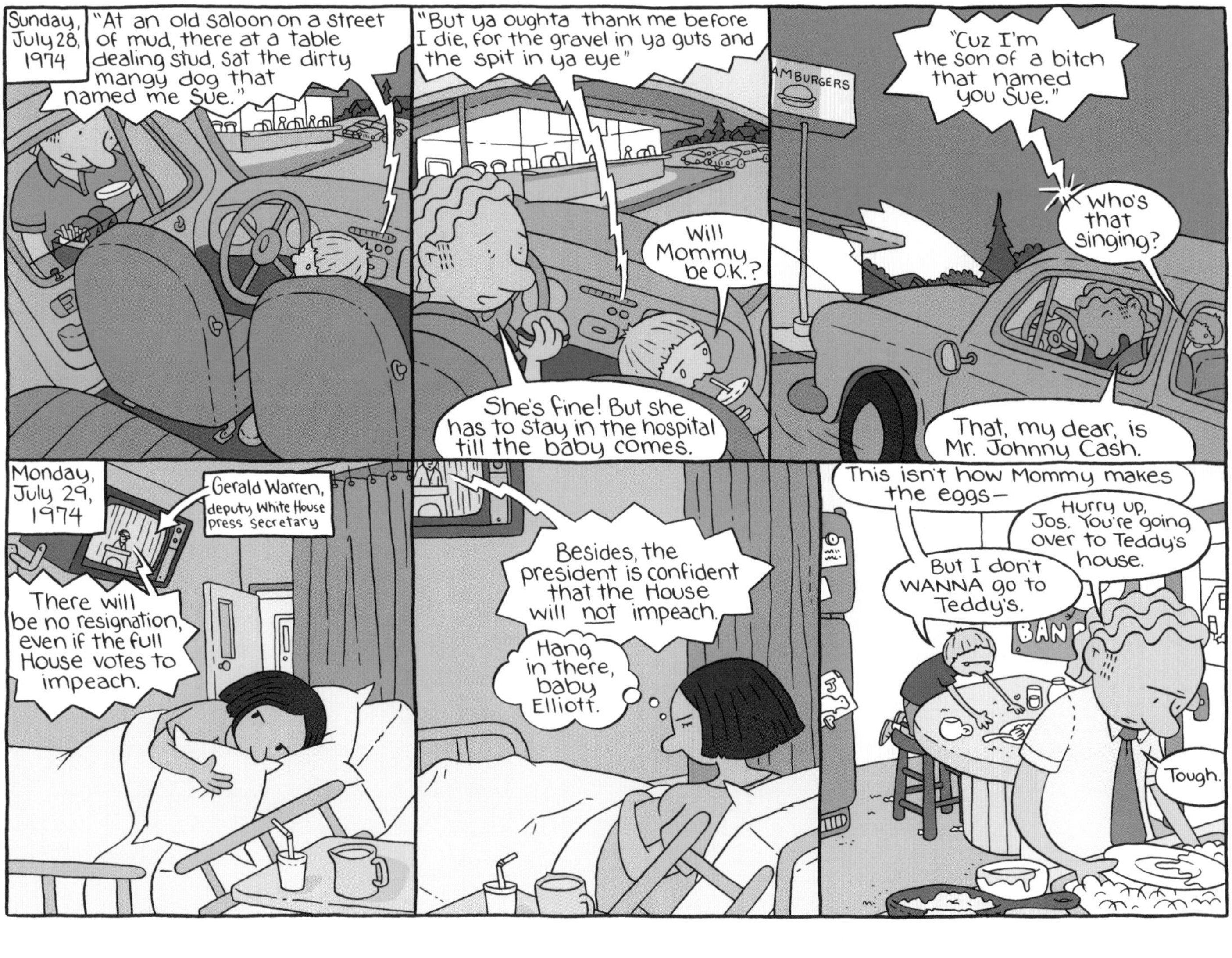
Sunday, July 28, 1974
"At an old saloon on a street of mud, there at a table dealing stud, sat the dirty mangy dog that named me Sue."
"But ya oughta thank me before I die, for the gravel in ya guts and the spit in ya eye"
Will Mommy be O.K.?
She's fine! But she has to stay in the hospital till the baby comes.
AMBURGERS
"Cuz I'm the son of a bitch that named you Sue."
Who's that singing?
That, my dear, is Mr. Johnny Cash.
Monday, July 29, 1974
Gerald Warren, deputy White House press secretary
There will be no resignation, even if the full House votes to impeach.
Besides, the president is confident that the House will not impeach.
Hang in there, baby Elliott.
This isn't how Mommy makes the eggs—
Hurry up, Jos. You're going over to Teddy's house.
But I don't WANNA go to Teddy's.
Tough.

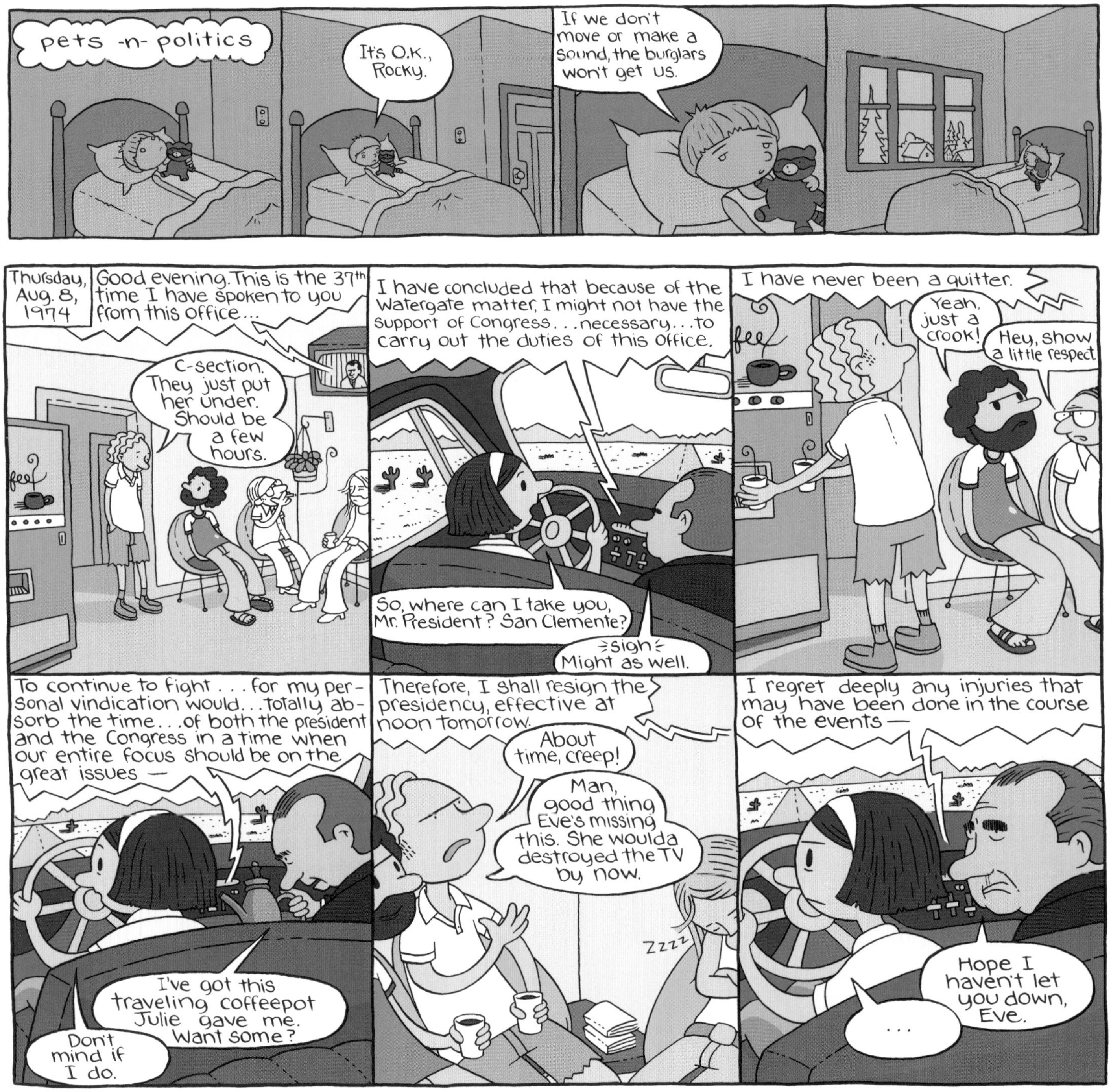
pets -n- politics
It's O.K., Rocky.
If we don't move or make a sound, the burglars won't get us.
Thursday, Aug. 8, 1974
Good evening. This is the 37th time I have spoken to you from this office...
C-section. They just put her under. Should be a few hours.
I have concluded that because of the Watergate matter, I might not have the support of Congress... necessary... to carry out the duties of this office.
So, where can I take you, Mr. President? San Clemente?
sigh
Might as well.
I have never been a quitter.
Yeah, just a crook!
Hey, show a little respect.
To continue to fight... for my personal vindication would... totally absorb the time... of both the president and the Congress in a time when our entire focus should be on the great issues —
I've got this traveling coffeepot Julie gave me. Want some?
Don't mind if I do.
Therefore, I shall resign the presidency, effective at noon tomorrow.
About time, creep!
Man, good thing Eve's missing this. She woulda destroyed the TV by now.
Zzzz
I regret deeply any injuries that may have been done in the course of the events —
Hope I haven't let you down, Eve.
...

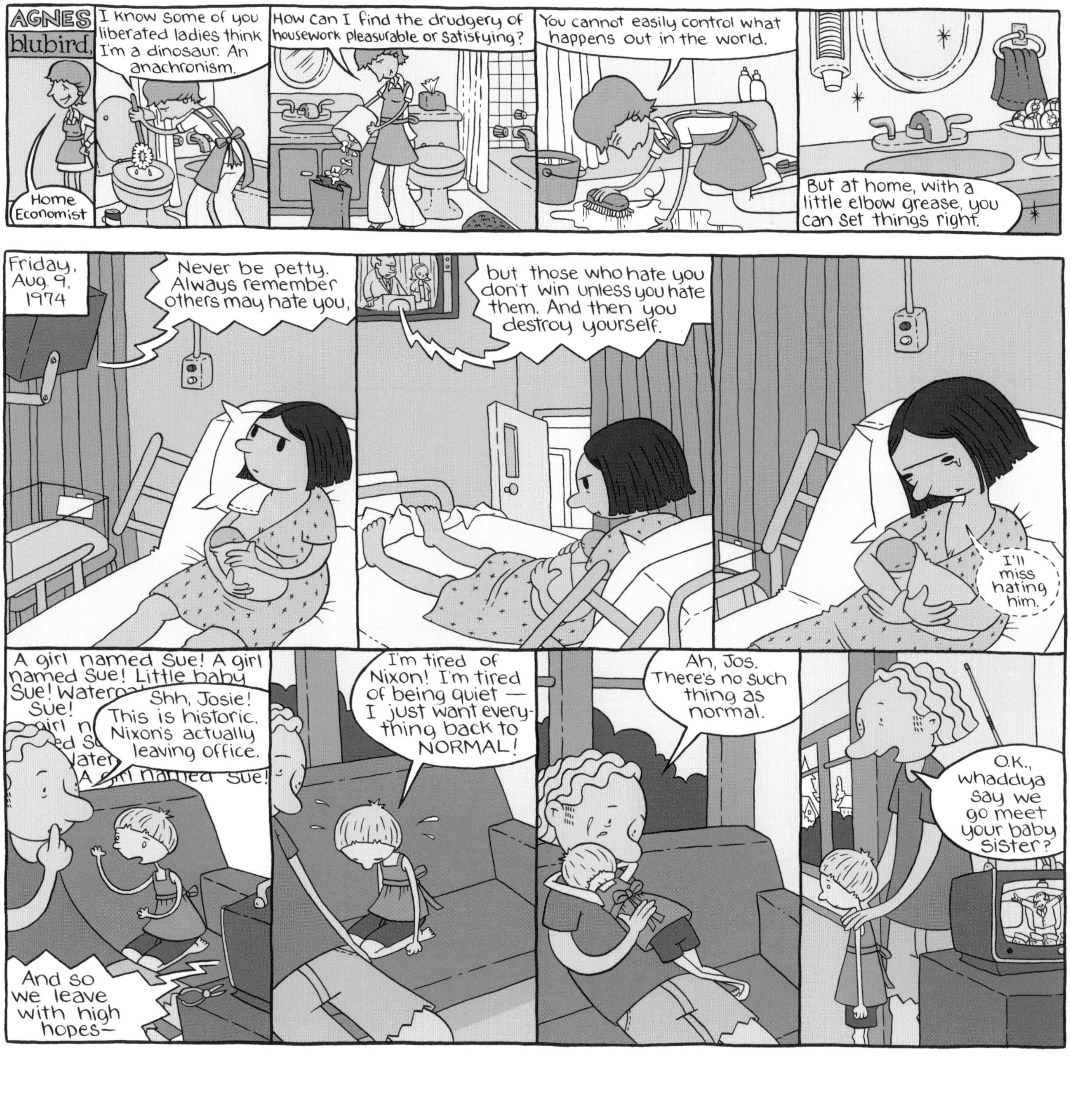

AGNES
blubird,
Home Economist
I know some of you liberated ladies think I'm a dinosaur. An anachronism.
How can I find the drudgery of housework pleasurable or satisfying?
You cannot easily control what happens out in the world.
But at home, with a little elbow grease, you can set things right.
Friday, Aug. 9, 1974
Never be petty. Always remember others may hate you,
but those who hate you don't win unless you hate them. And then you destroy yourself.
I'll miss hating him.
A girl named Sue! A girl named Sue! Little baby Sue!
Sue!
A girl named Sue!
Shh, Josie! This is historic. Nixon's actually leaving office.
And so we leave with high hopes—
I'm tired of Nixon! I'm tired of being quiet — I just want everything back to NORMAL!
Ah, Jos. There's no such thing as normal.
O.K., whaddya say we go meet your baby sister?

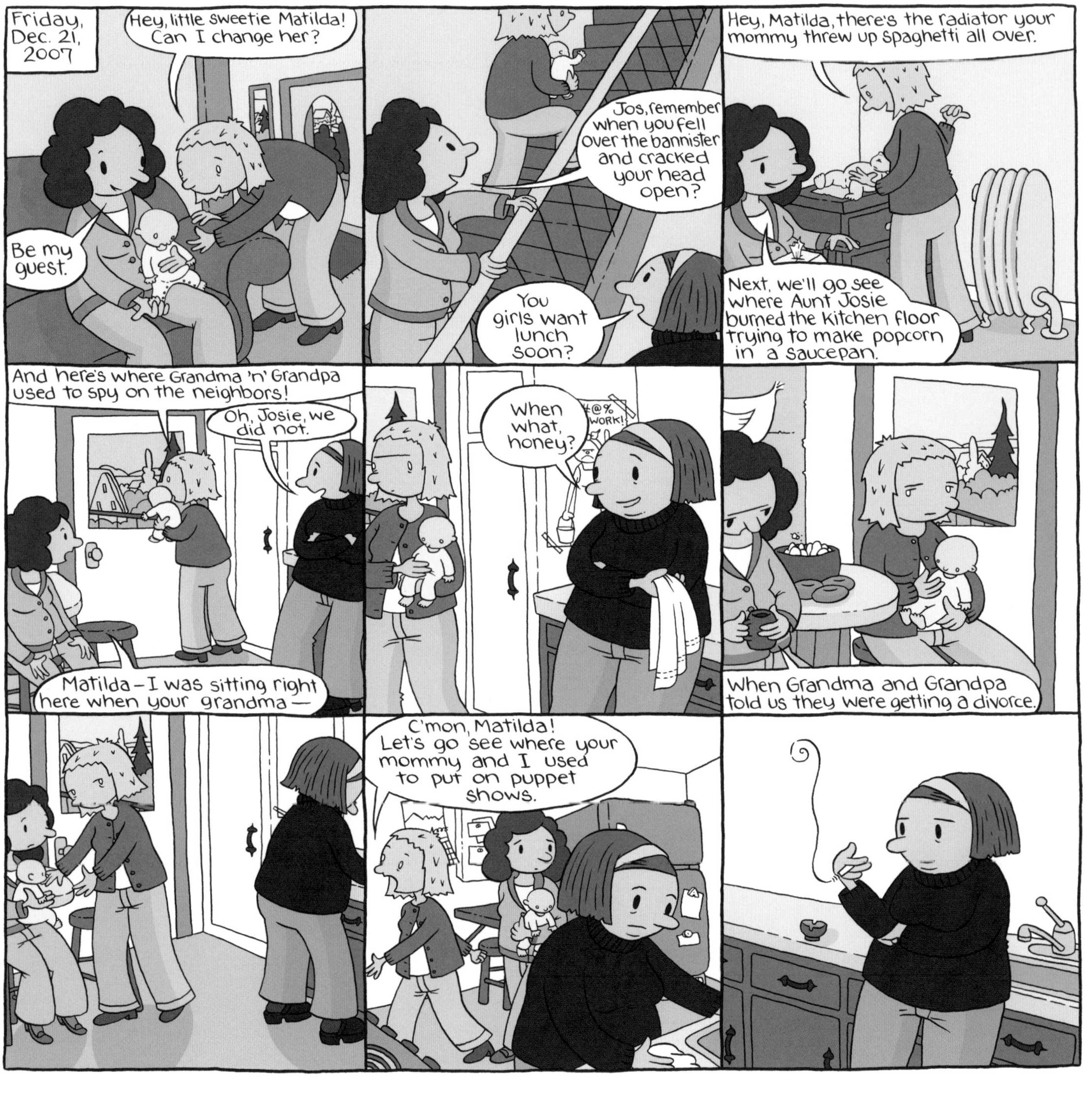

Friday, Dec. 21, 2007
Hey, little sweetie Matilda! Can I change her?
Be my guest.
Jos, remember when you fell over the bannister and cracked your head open?
You girls want lunch soon?
Hey, Matilda, there's the radiator your mommy threw up spaghetti all over.
Next, we'll go see where Aunt Josie burned the kitchen floor trying to make popcorn in a saucepan.
And here's where Grandma 'n' Grandpa used to spy on the neighbors!
Oh, Josie, we did not.
Matilda—I was sitting right here when your grandma—
When what, honey?
When Grandma and Grandpa told us they were getting a divorce.
C'mon, Matilda! Let's go see where your mommy and I used to put on puppet shows.

2

Cats in Service

MEGAN KELSO

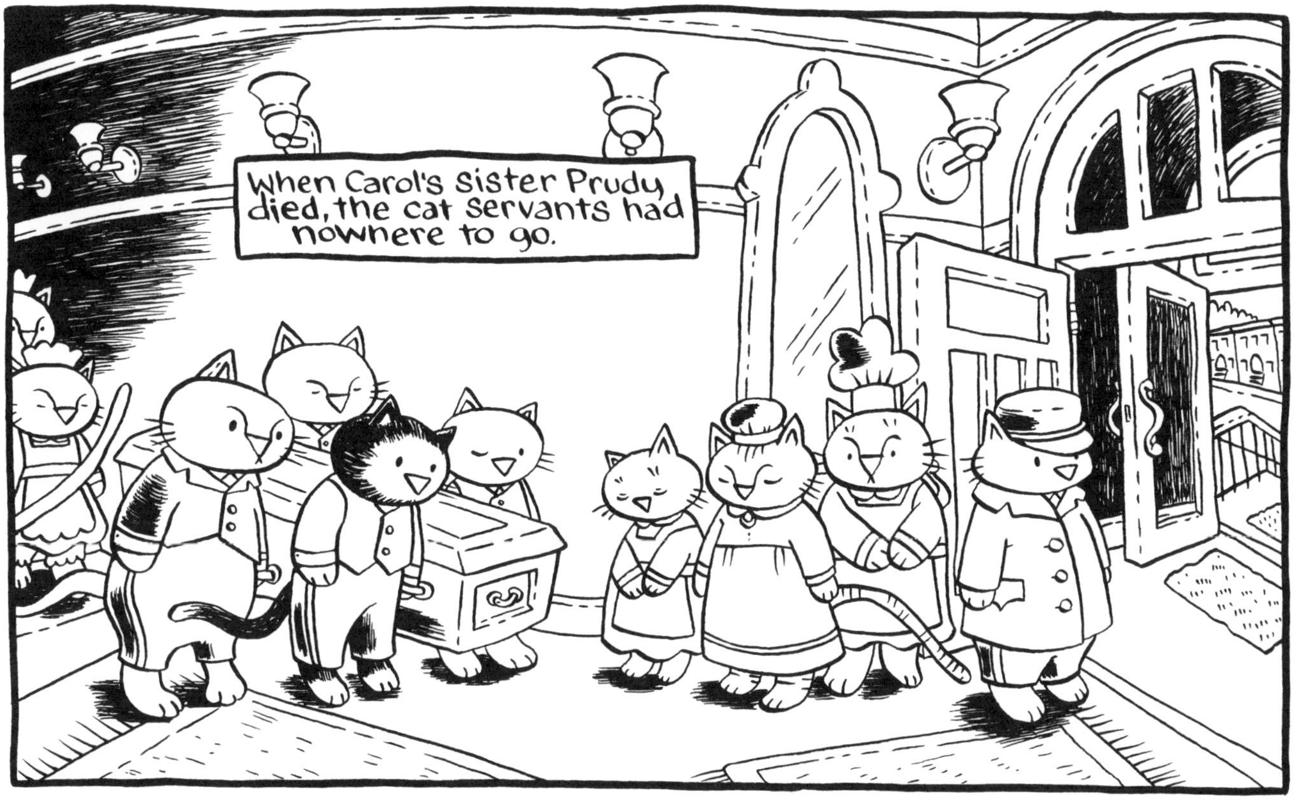
When Carol's sister Prudy died, the cat servants had nowhere to go.

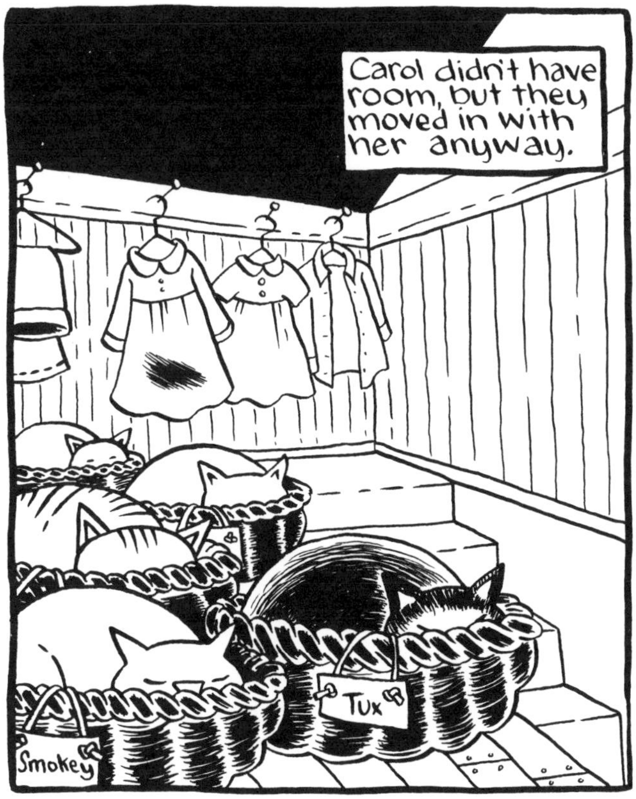
Carol didn't have room, but they moved in with her anyway.
Smokey
Tux

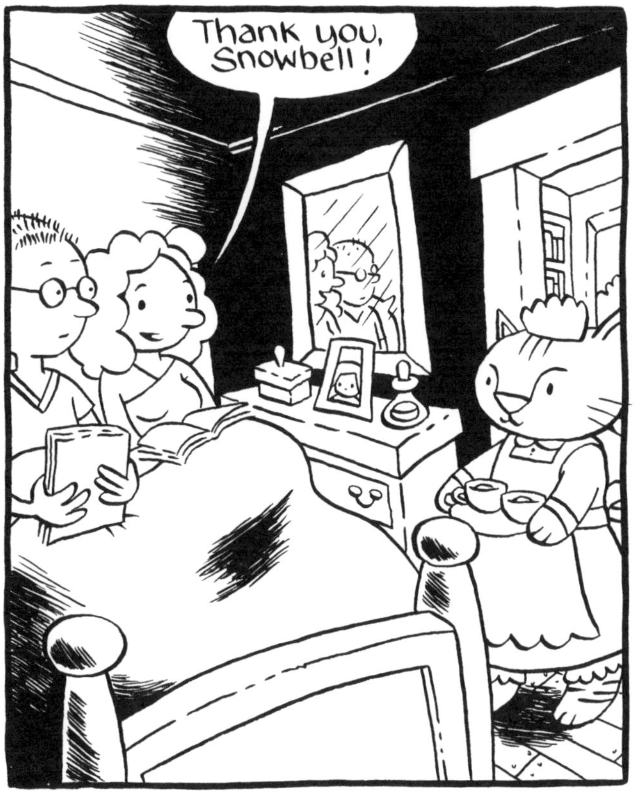
Thank you, Snowbell!

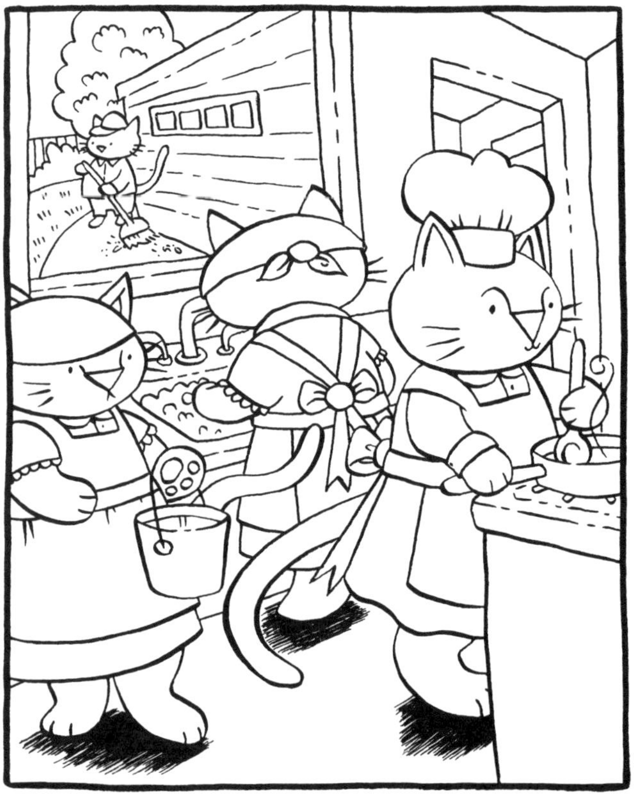

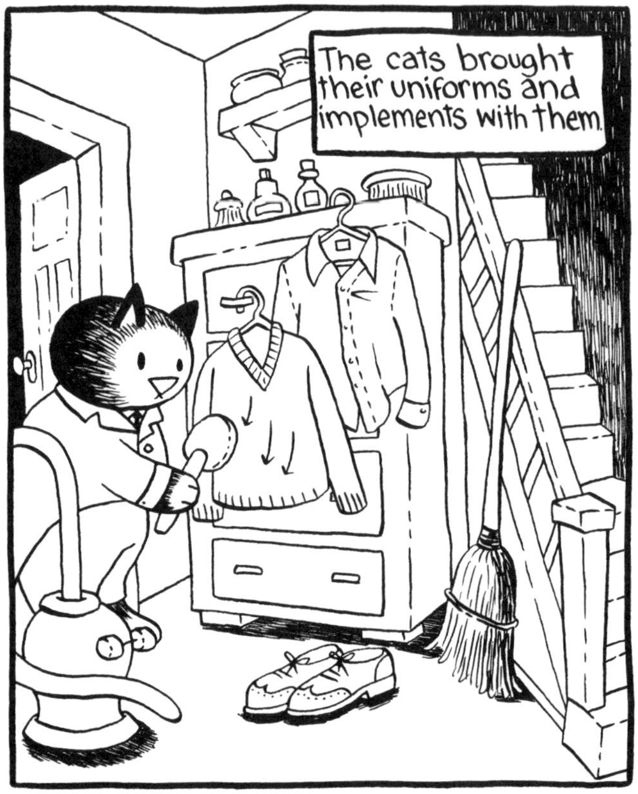
The cats brought their uniforms and implements with them.

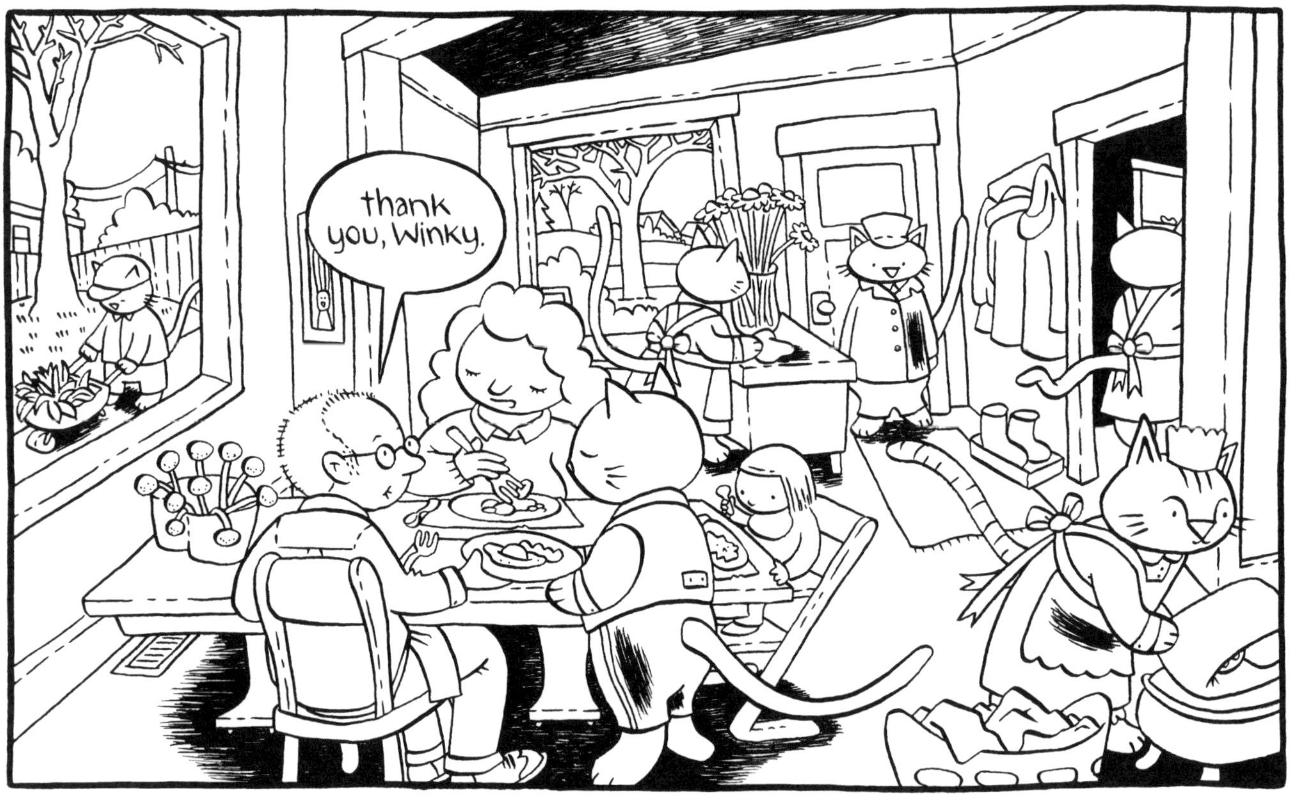
thank you, Winky.

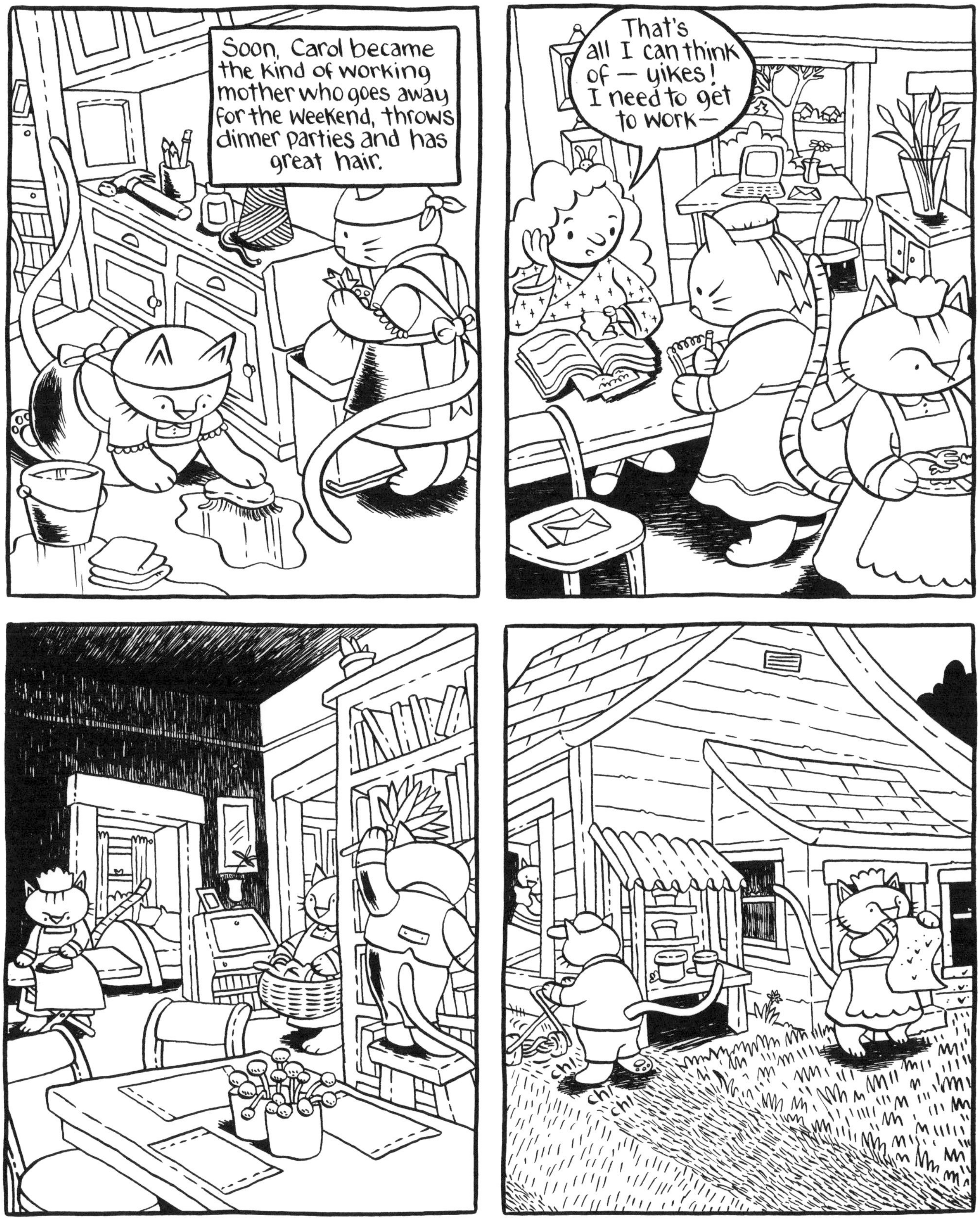
Soon, Carol became the kind of working mother who goes away for the weekend, throws dinner parties and has great hair.
That's all I can think of — yikes! I need to get to work—
chi
chi
chi

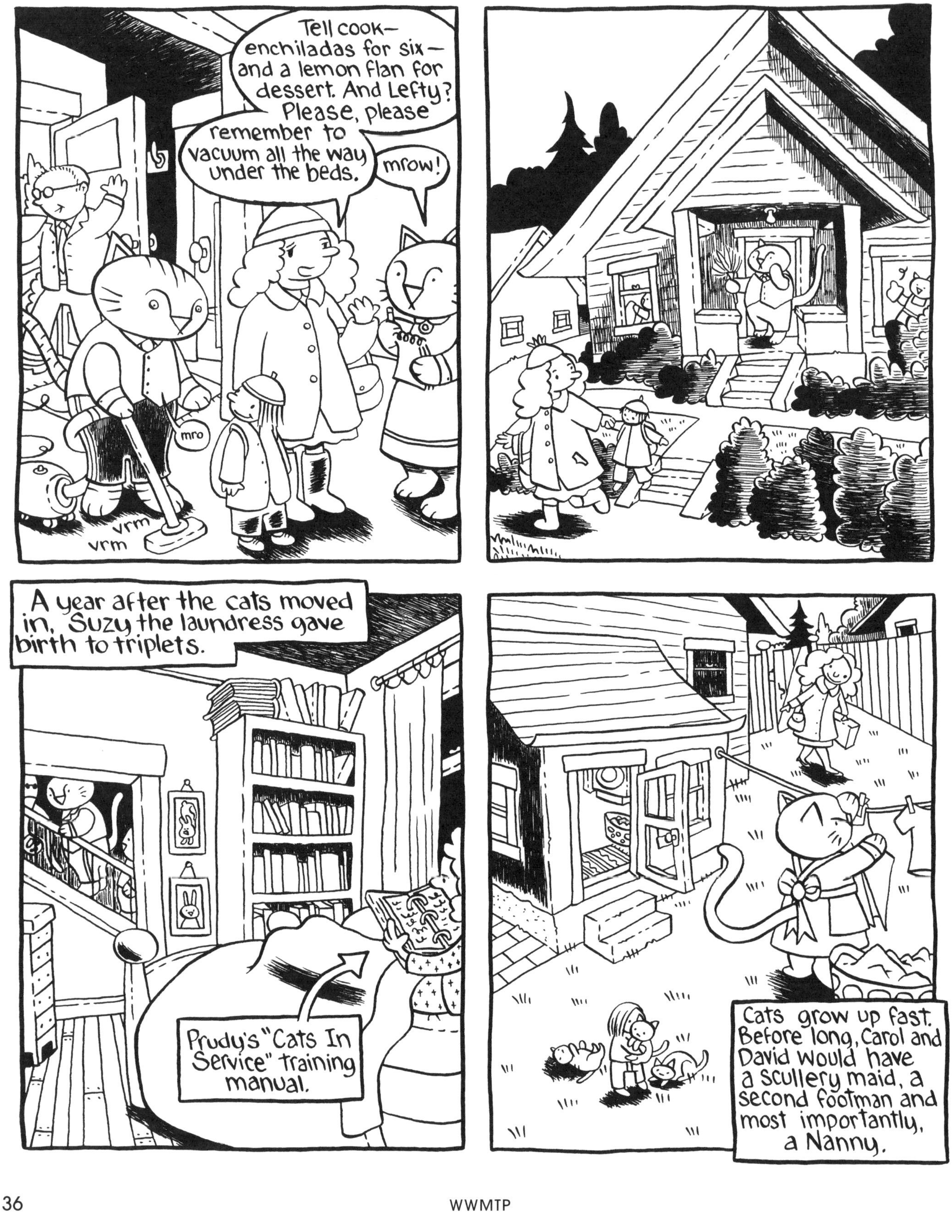
Tell cook—
enchiladas for six—
and a lemon flan for
dessert. And Lefty?
Please, please
remember to
vacuum all the way
under the beds.
mrow!
mro
vrm
vrm
A year after the cats moved in, Suzy the laundress gave birth to triplets.
Prudy's "Cats In Service" training manual.
Cats grow up fast. Before long, Carol and David would have a scullery maid, a second footman and most importantly, a Nanny.

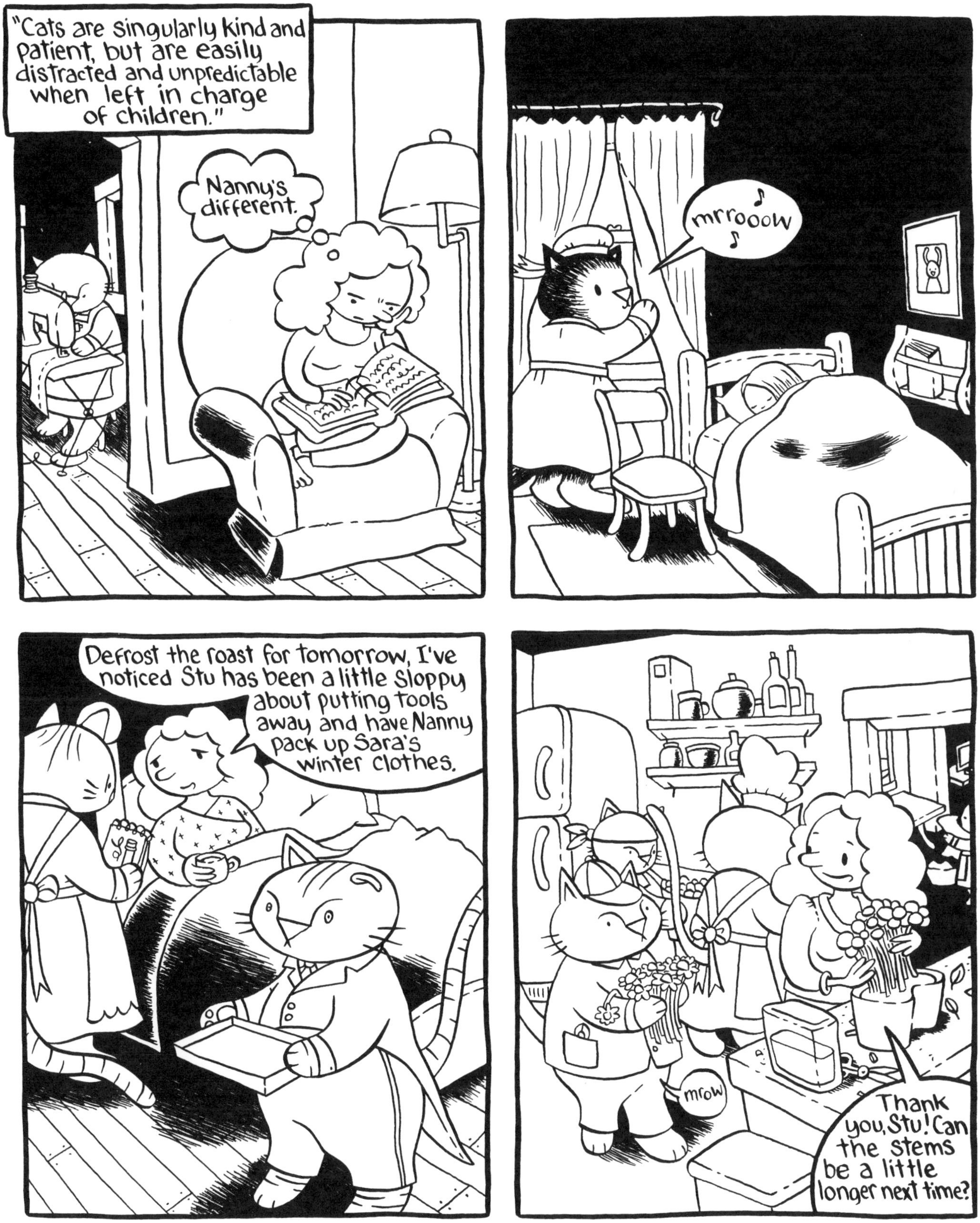
"Cats are singularly kind and patient, but are easily distracted and unpredictable when left in charge of children."
Nanny's different.
mrrooow
Defrost the roast for tomorrow, I've noticed Stu has been a little sloppy about putting tools away and have Nanny pack up Sara's winter clothes.
mrow
Thank you, Stu! Can the stems be a little longer next time?

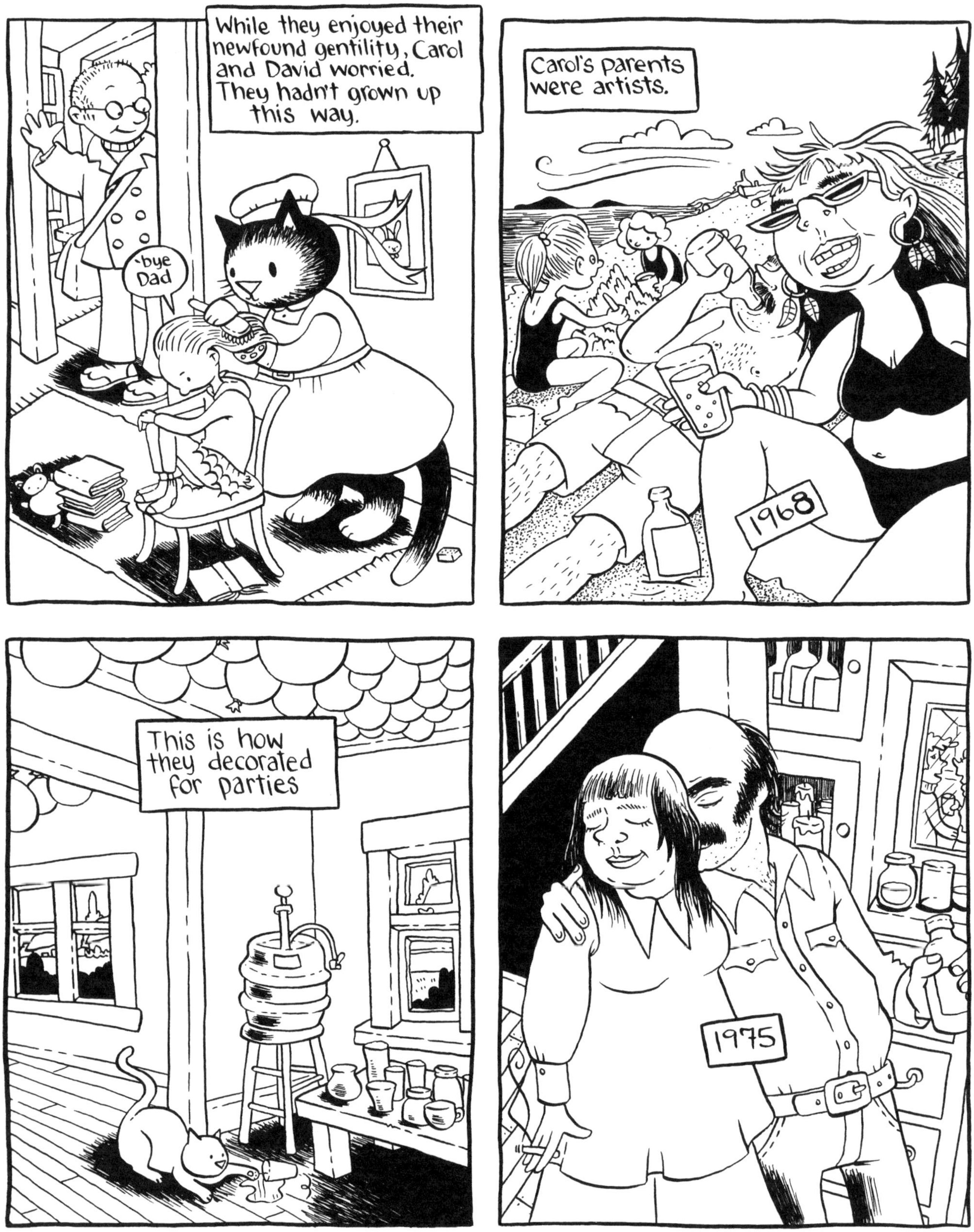
While they enjoyed their newfound gentility, Carol and David worried. They hadn't grown up this way.
`bye Dad
Carol's parents were artists.
1968
This is how they decorated for parties
1975

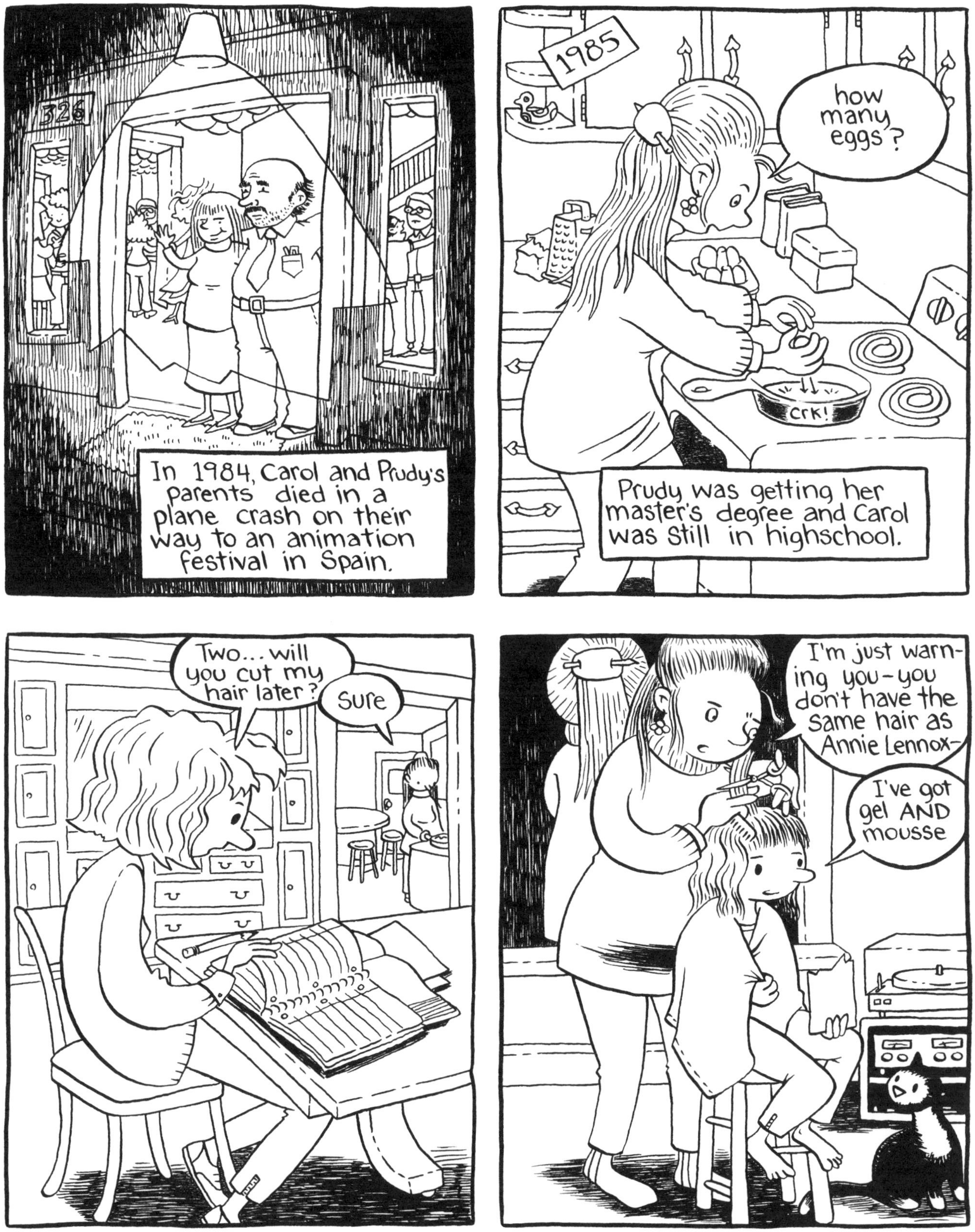
326
In 1984, Carol and Prudy's parents died in a plane crash on their way to an animation festival in Spain.
1985
how many eggs?
CRK!
Prudy was getting her master's degree and Carol was still in highschool.
Two... will you cut my hair later?
Sure
I'm just warning you-you don't have the same hair as Annie Lennox-
I've got gel AND mousse

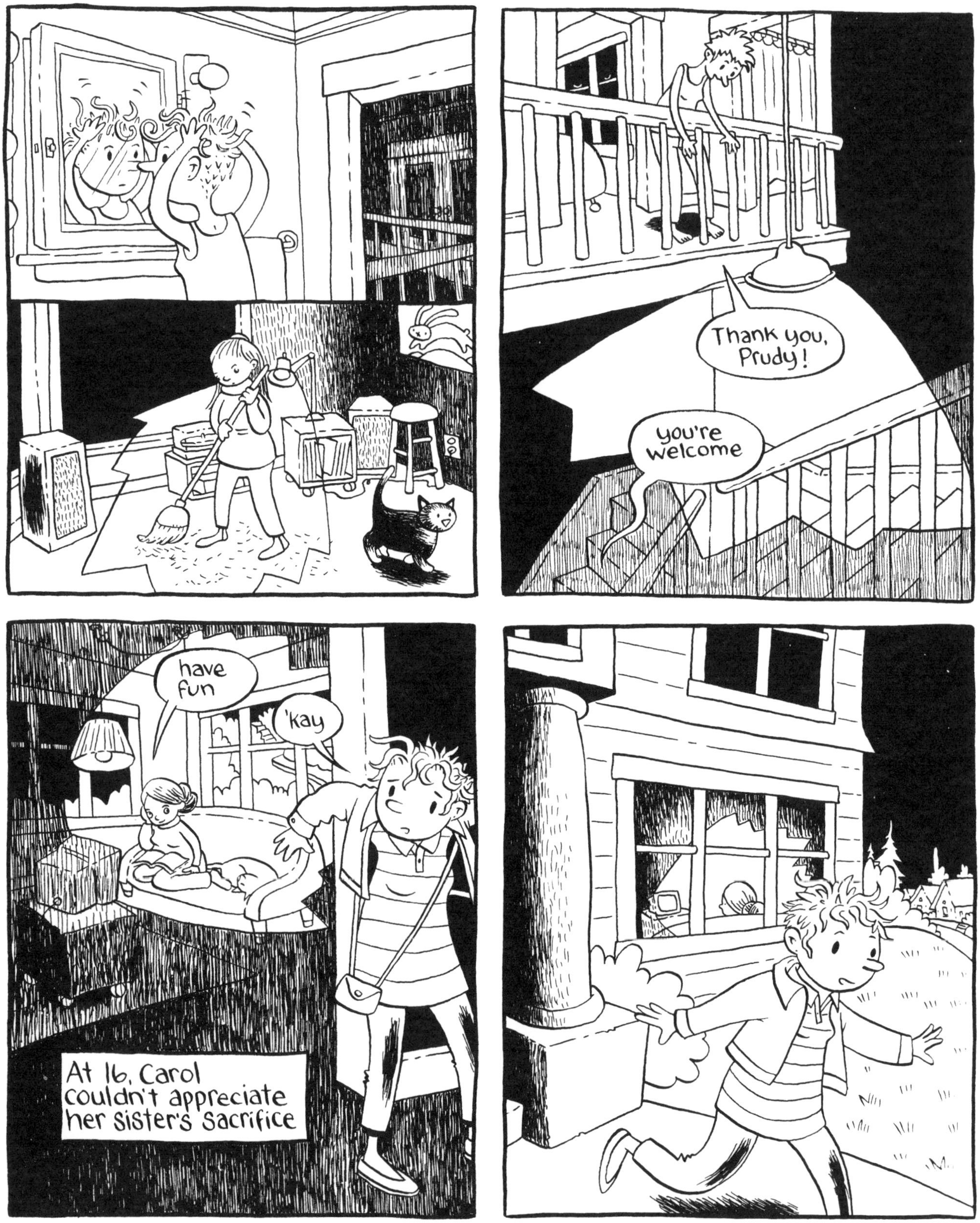
Thank you, Prudy!
you're welcome
have fun
'kay
At 16, Carol couldn't appreciate her sister's sacrifice

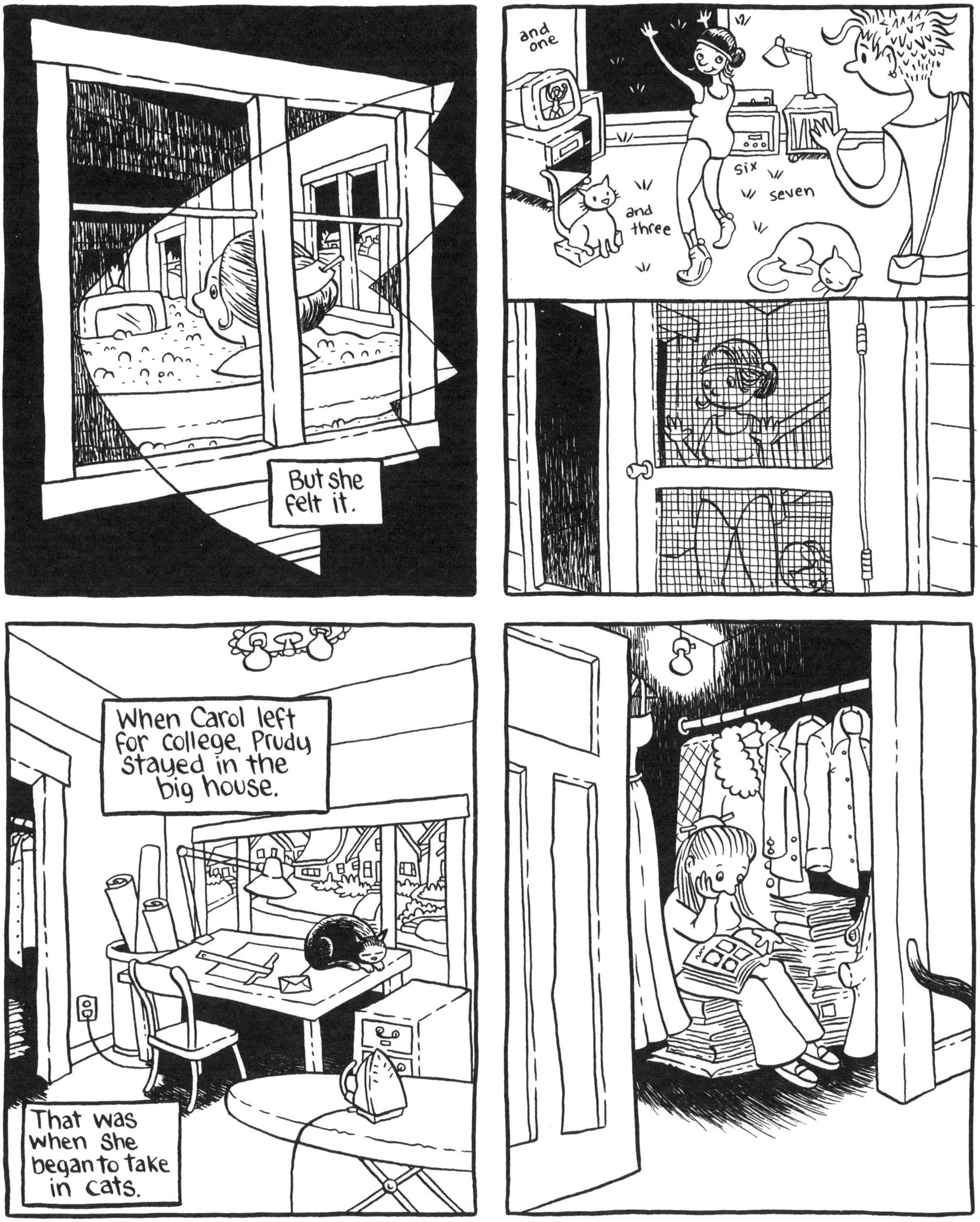
But she felt it.
and one
and three
six
seven
When Carol left for college, Prudy stayed in the big house.
That was when she began to take in cats.

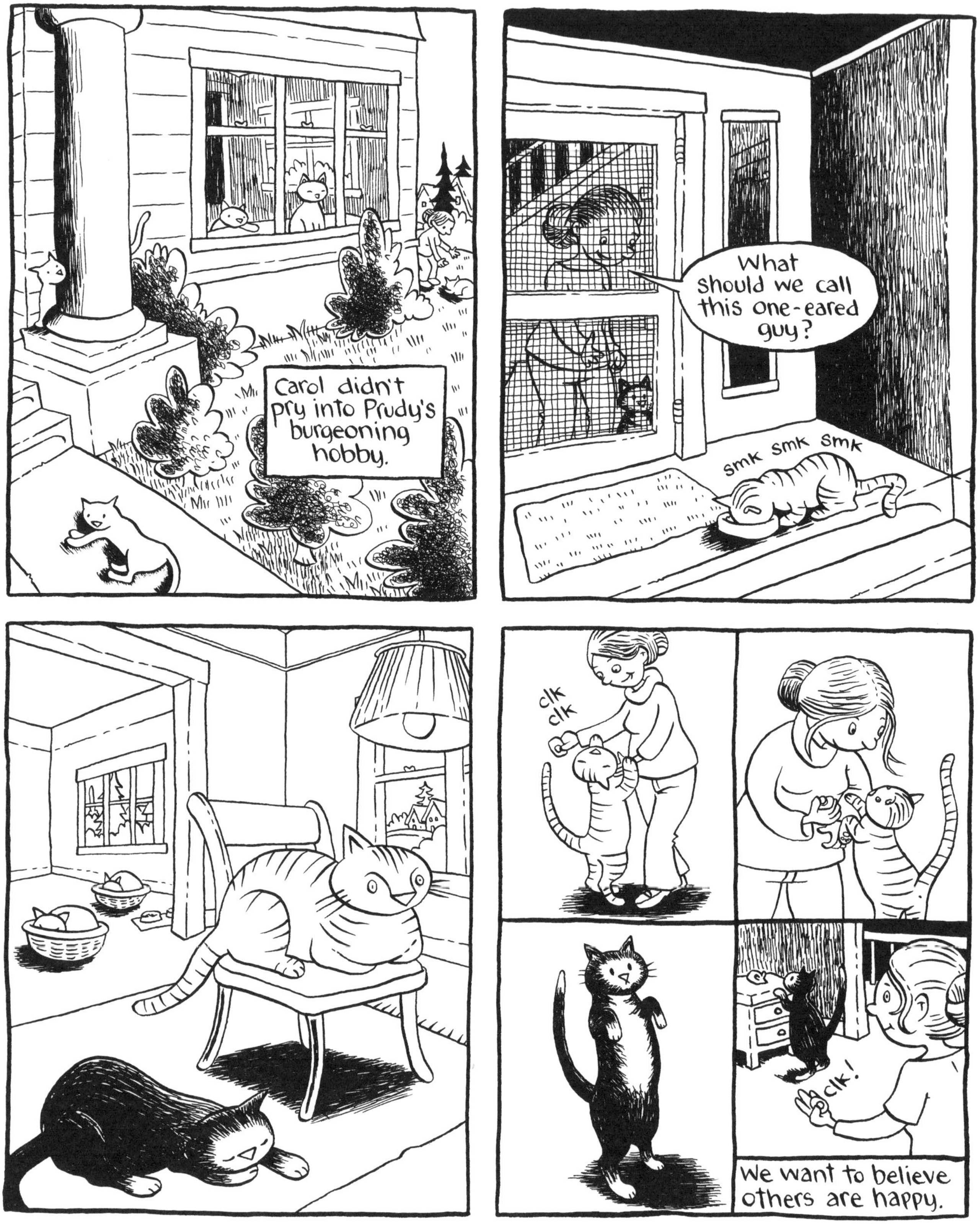

Carol didn't pry into Prudy's burgeoning hobby.
What should we call this one-eared guy?
smk smk smk
clk clk
clk!
We want to believe others are happy.

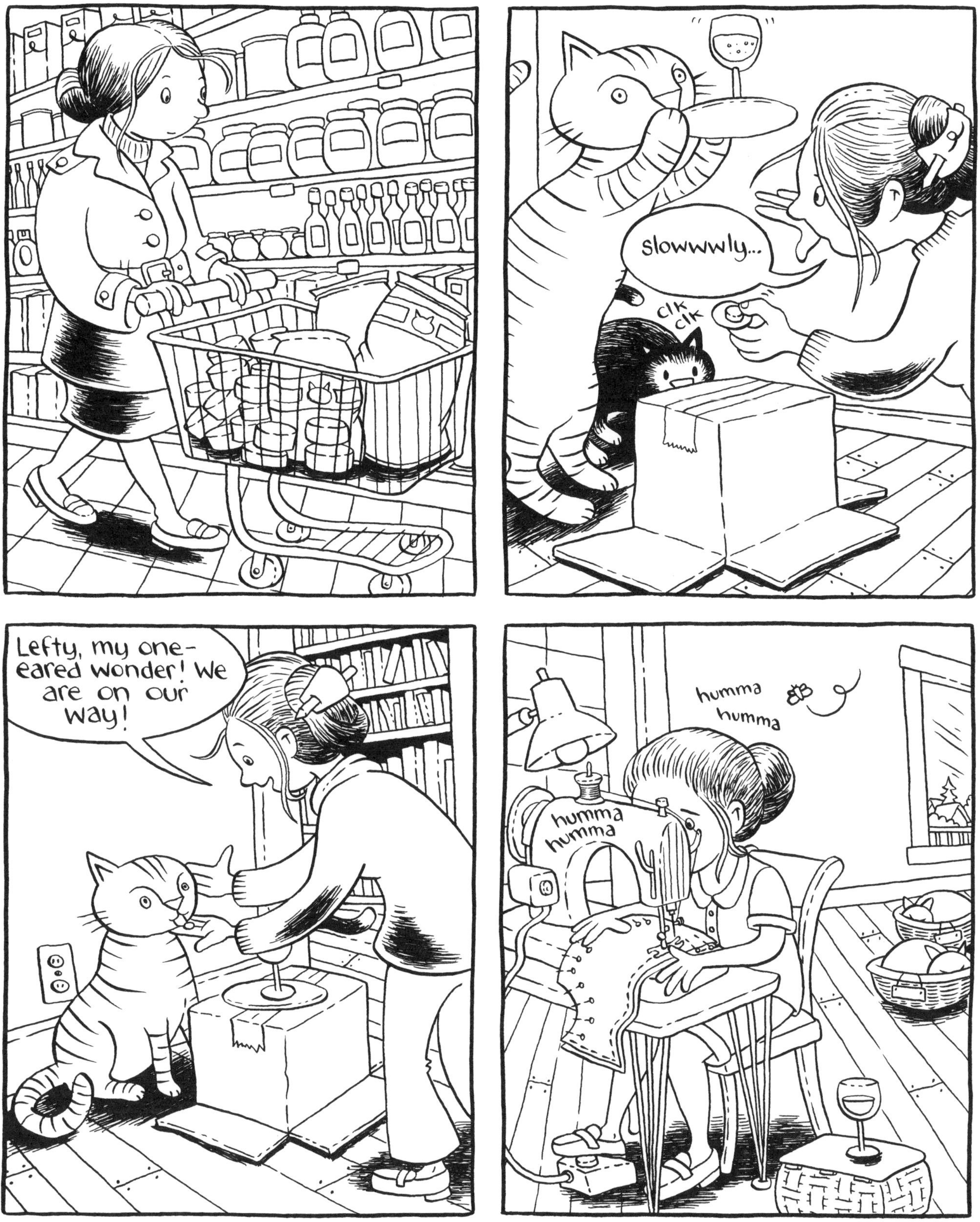
slowwwly...
clk
clk
Lefty, my one-eared wonder! We are on our way!
humma
humma
humma
humma

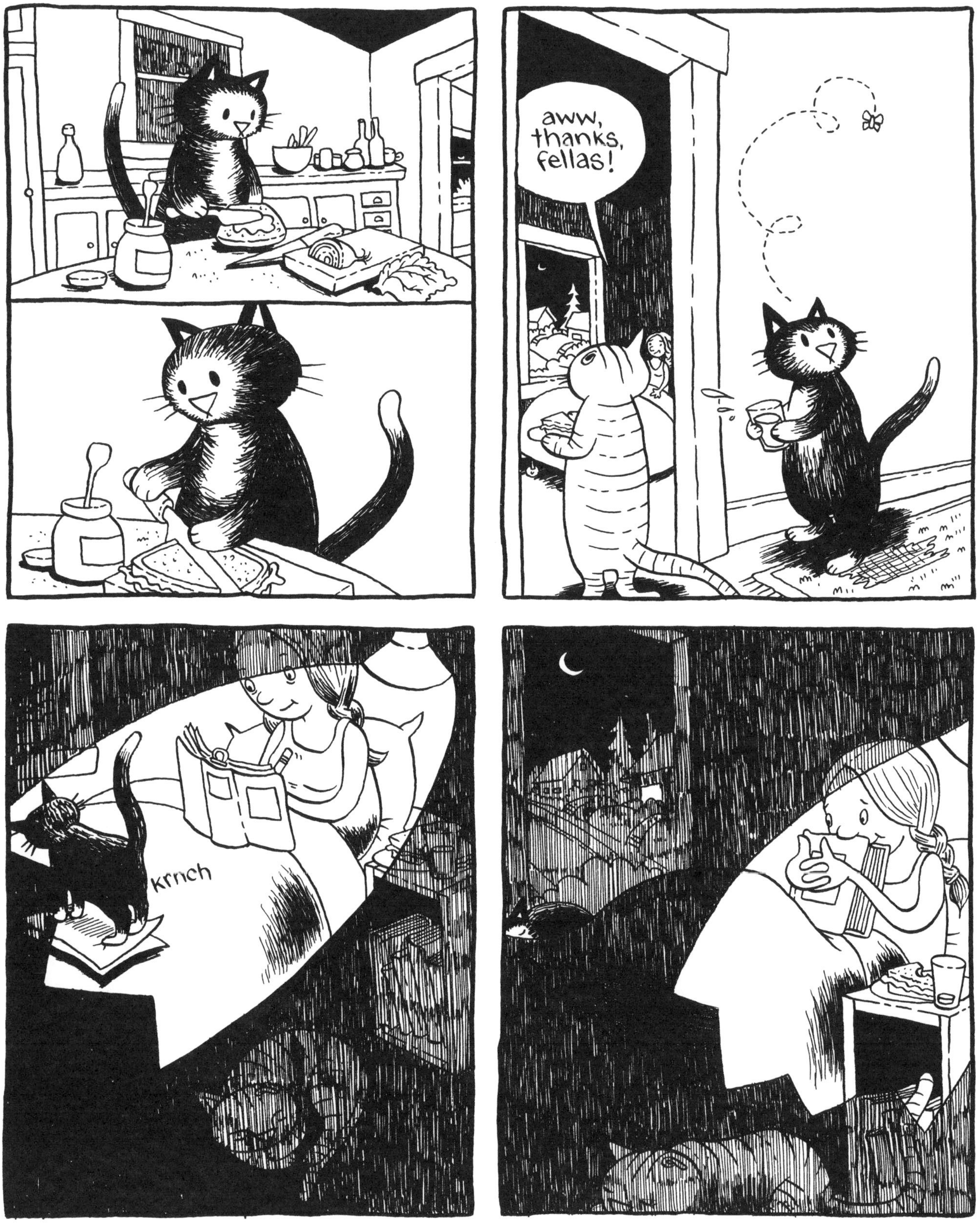
aww, thanks, fellas!
krnch

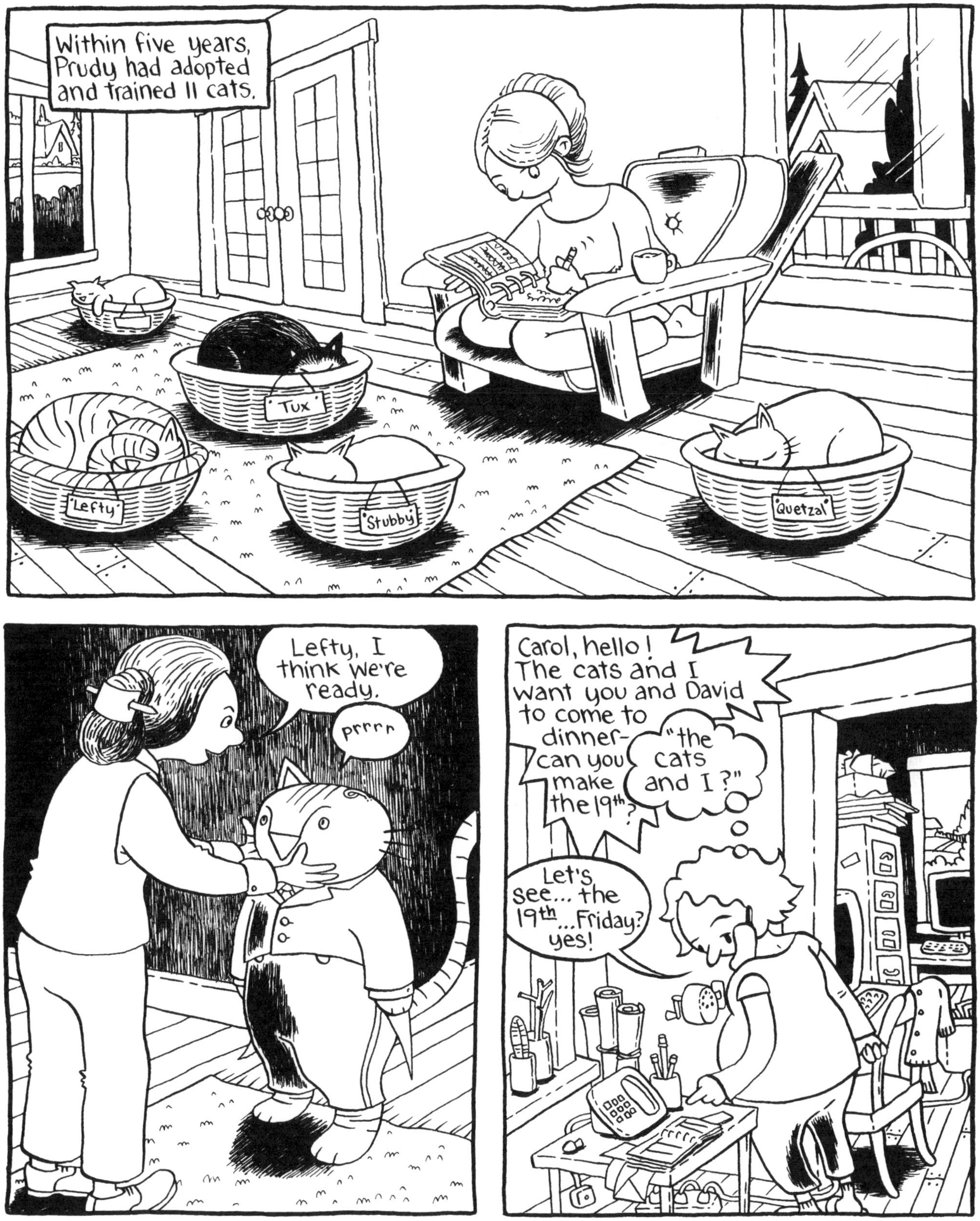
Within five years, Prudy had adopted and trained 11 cats.
Tux
Lefty
Stubby
Quetzal
Lefty, I think we're ready.
prrrr
Carol, hello! The cats and I want you and David to come to dinner- can you make the 19th?
"the cats and I?"
Let's see... the 19th... Friday? yes!

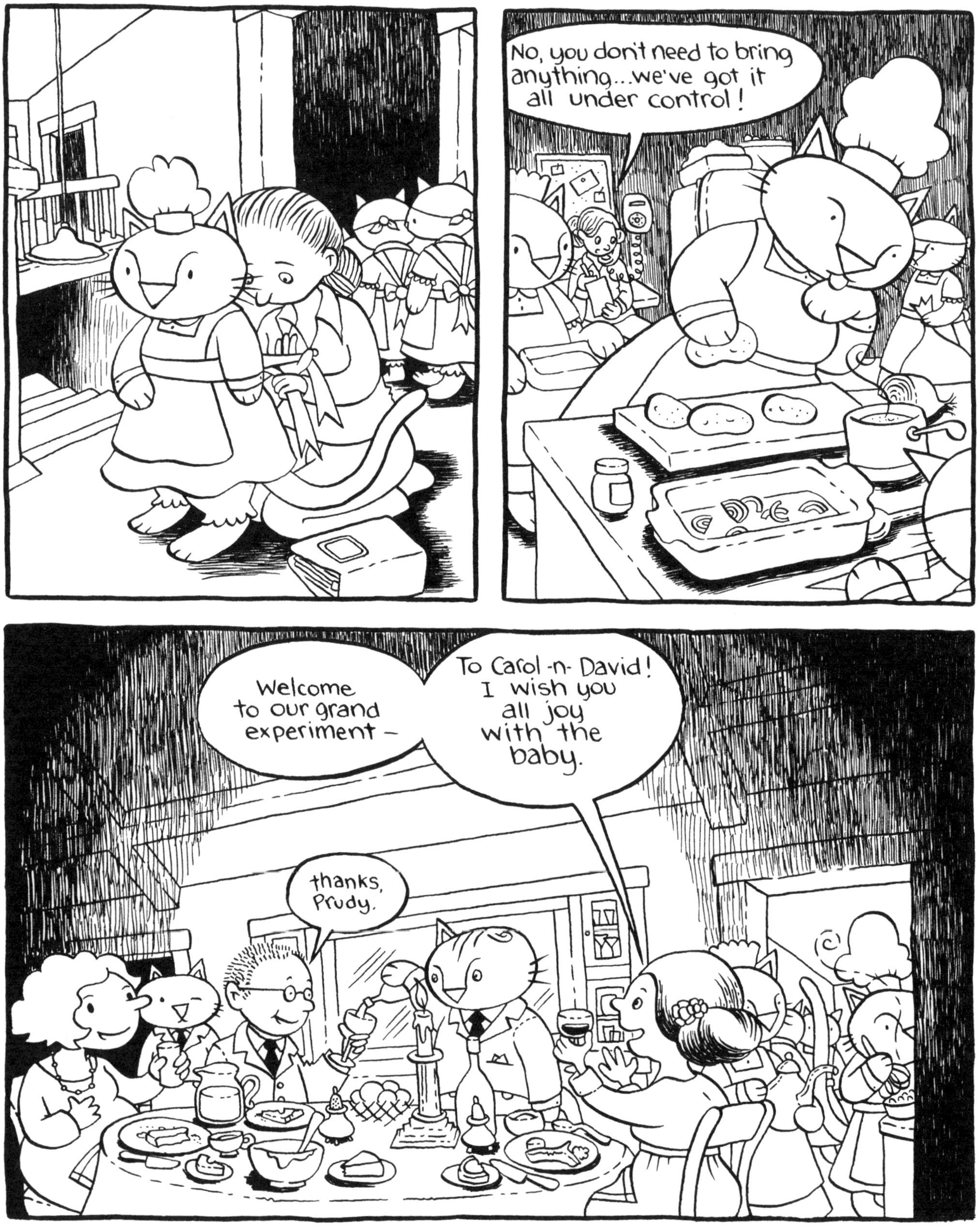
No, you don't need to bring anything...we've got it all under control!
Welcome to our grand experiment –
To Carol-n-David! I wish you all joy with the baby.
thanks, Prudy.

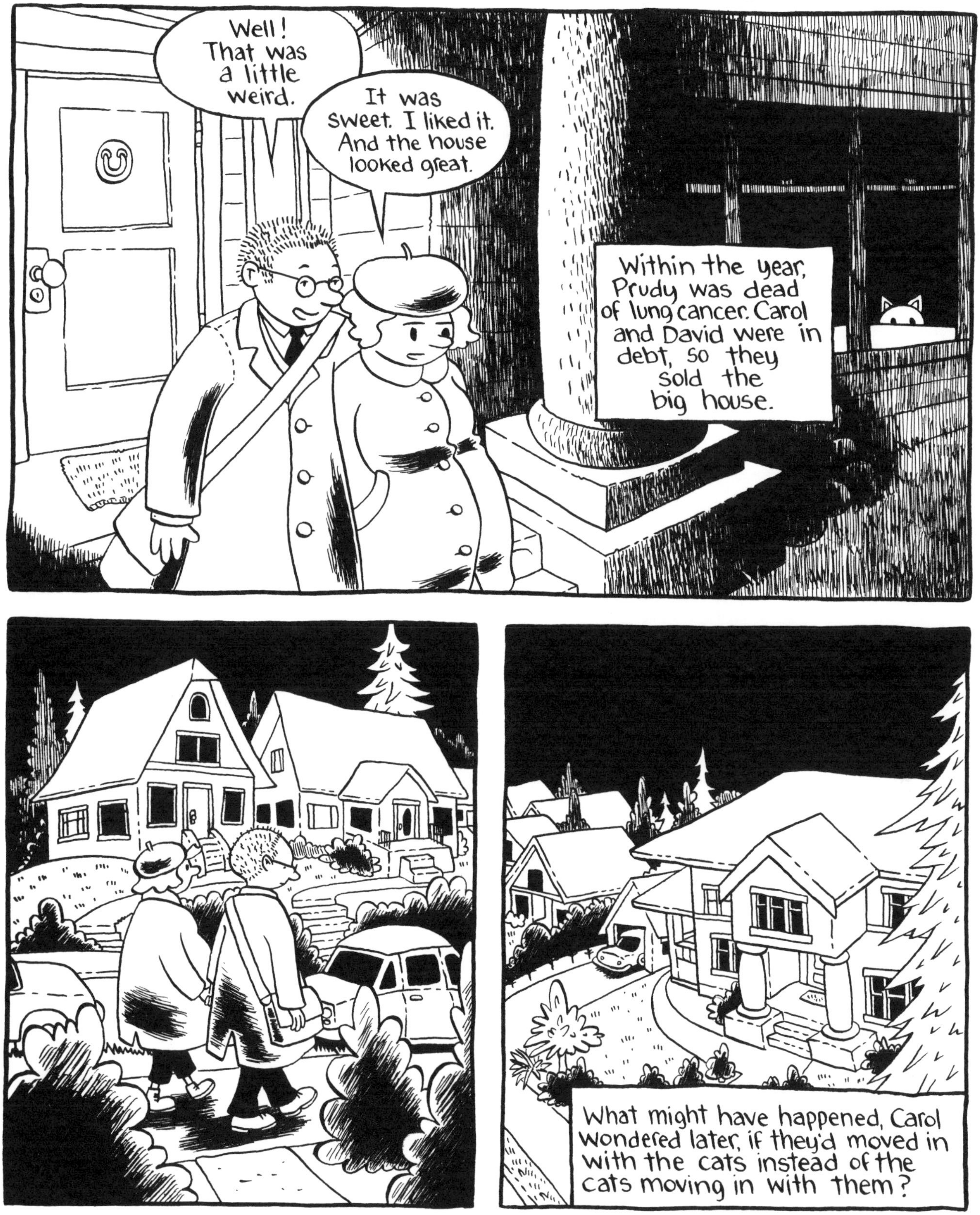
Well! That was a little weird.
It was sweet. I liked it. And the house looked great.
Within the year, Prudy was dead of lung cancer. Carol and David were in debt, so they sold the big house.
What might have happened, Carol wondered later, if they'd moved in with the cats instead of the cats moving in with them?

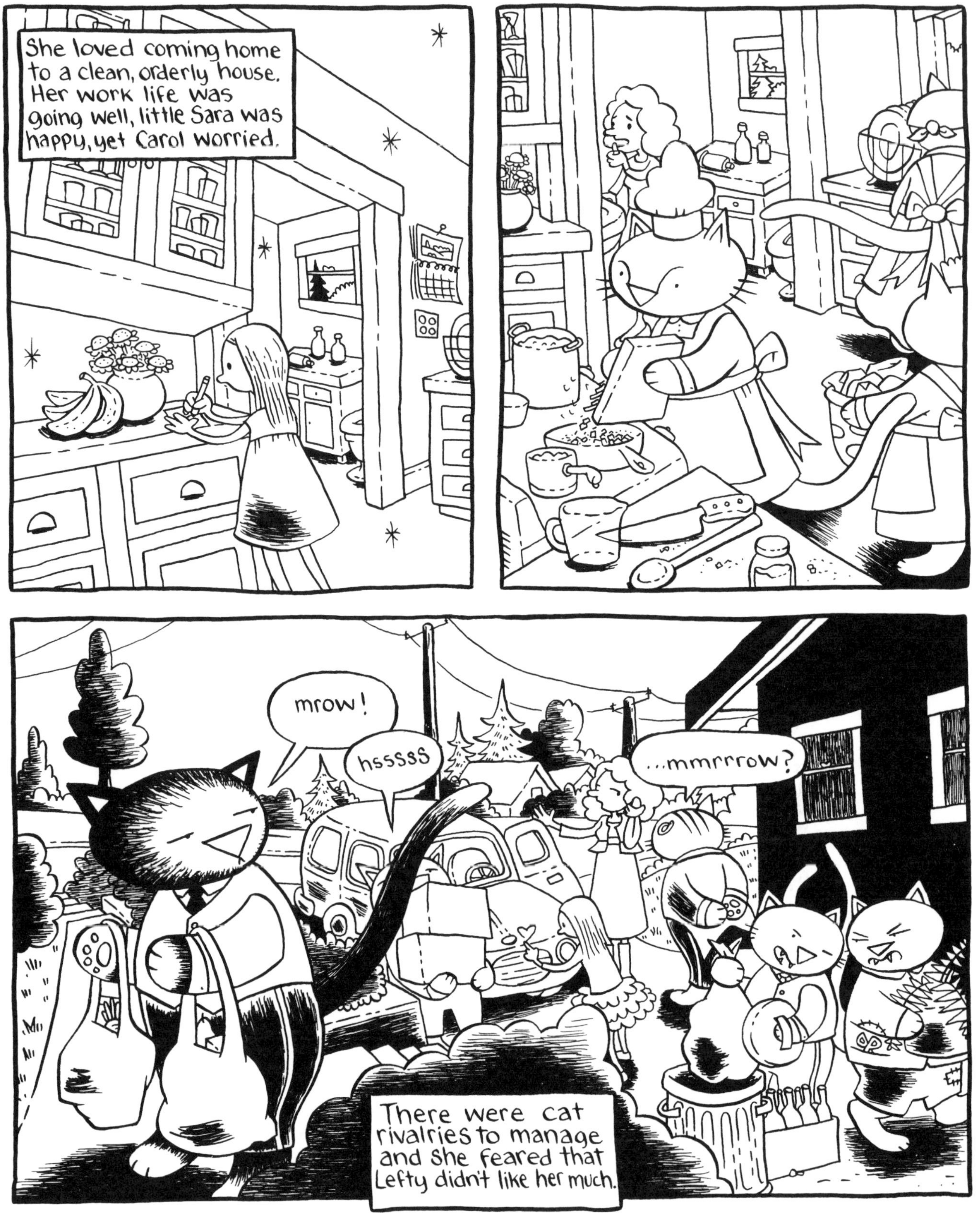
She loved coming home to a clean, orderly house. Her work life was going well, little Sara was happy, yet Carol worried.
mrow!
hsssss
...mmrrrow?
There were cat rivalries to manage and she feared that Lefty didn't like her much.

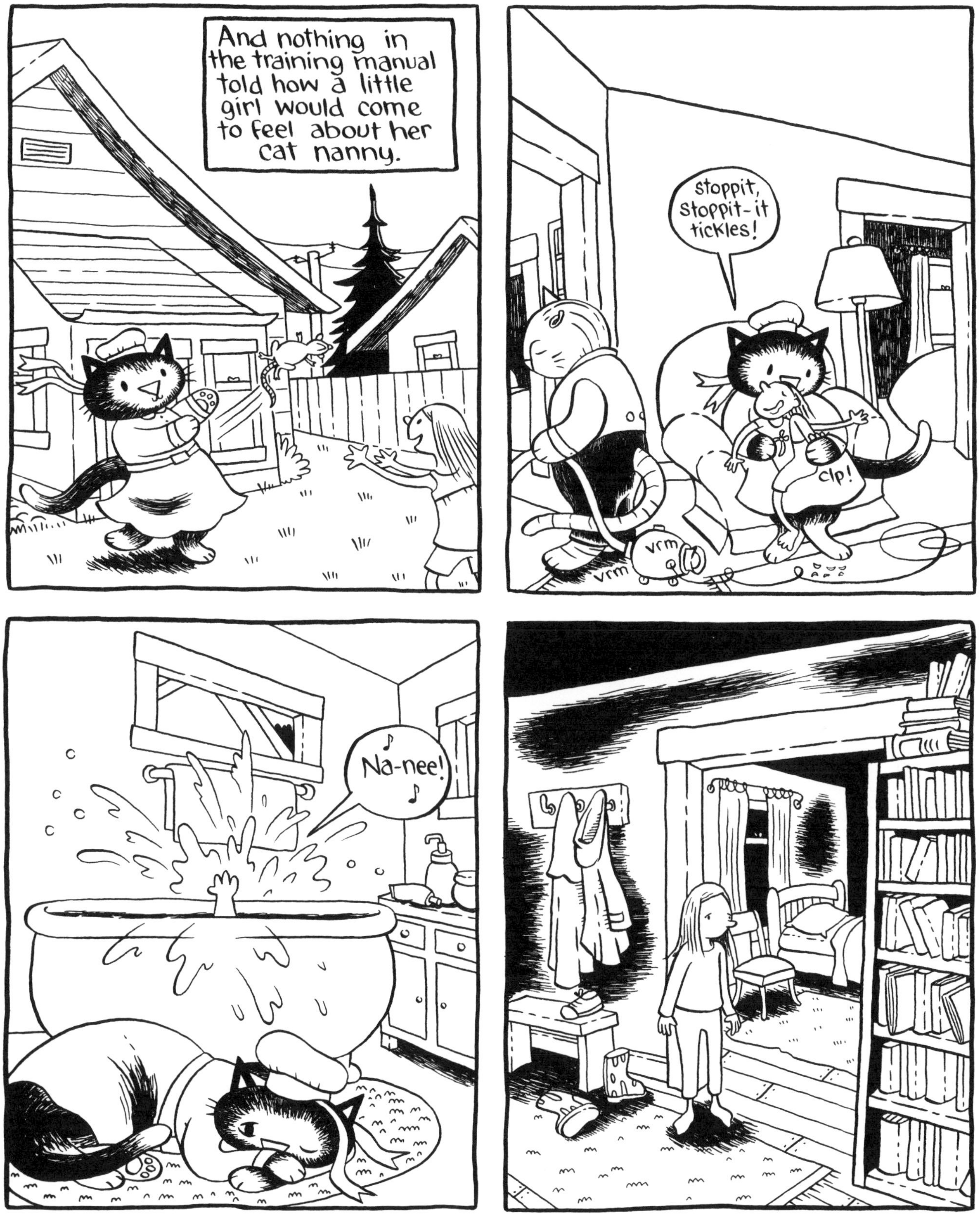
And nothing in the training manual told how a little girl would come to feel about her cat nanny.
Stoppit, Stoppit- it tickles!
clp!
vrm
vrm
Na-nee!

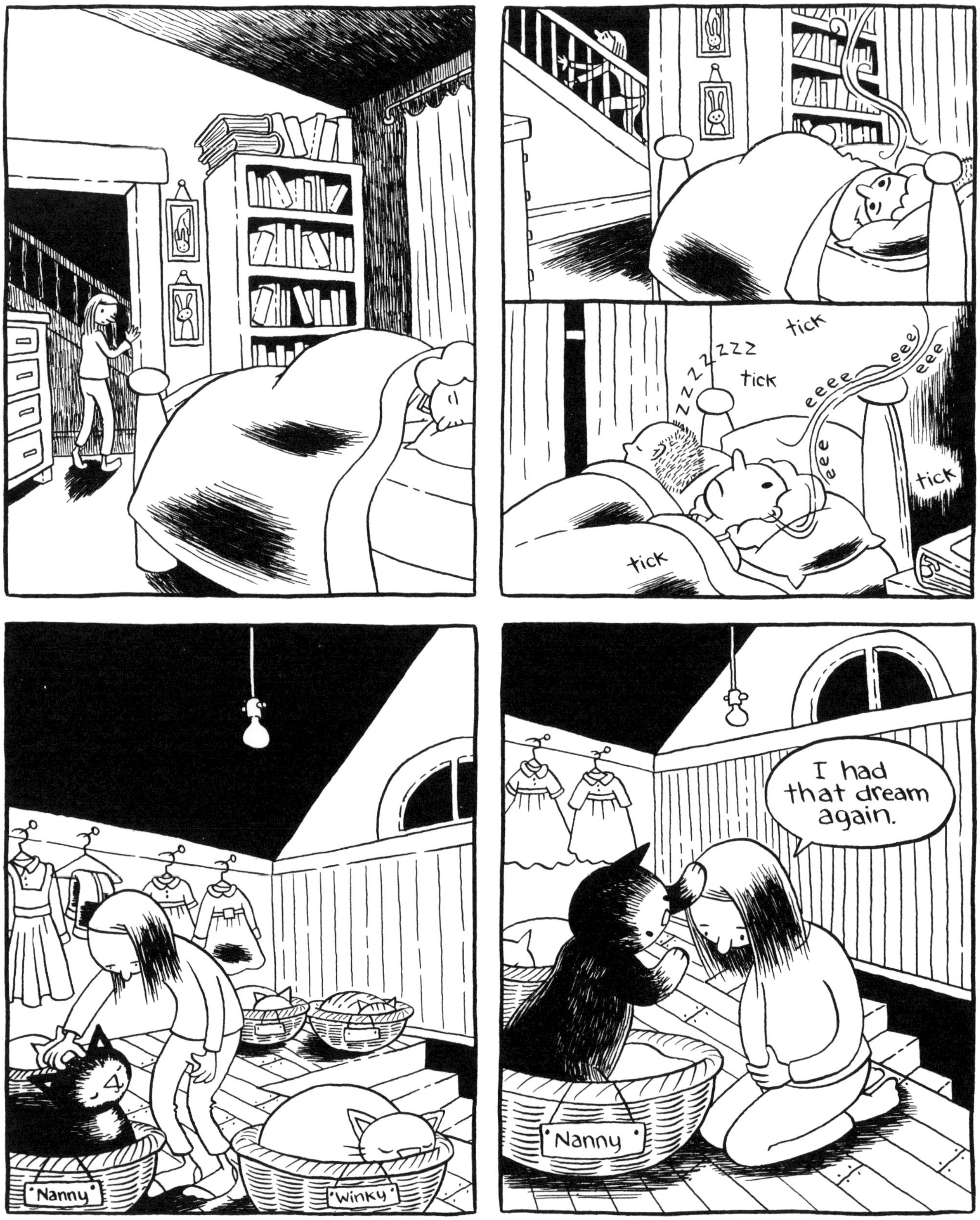

ZZZZZZZ
tick
tick
eeee
eeee
eee
eee
tick
tick
I had that dream again.
Nanny
Winky
Nanny

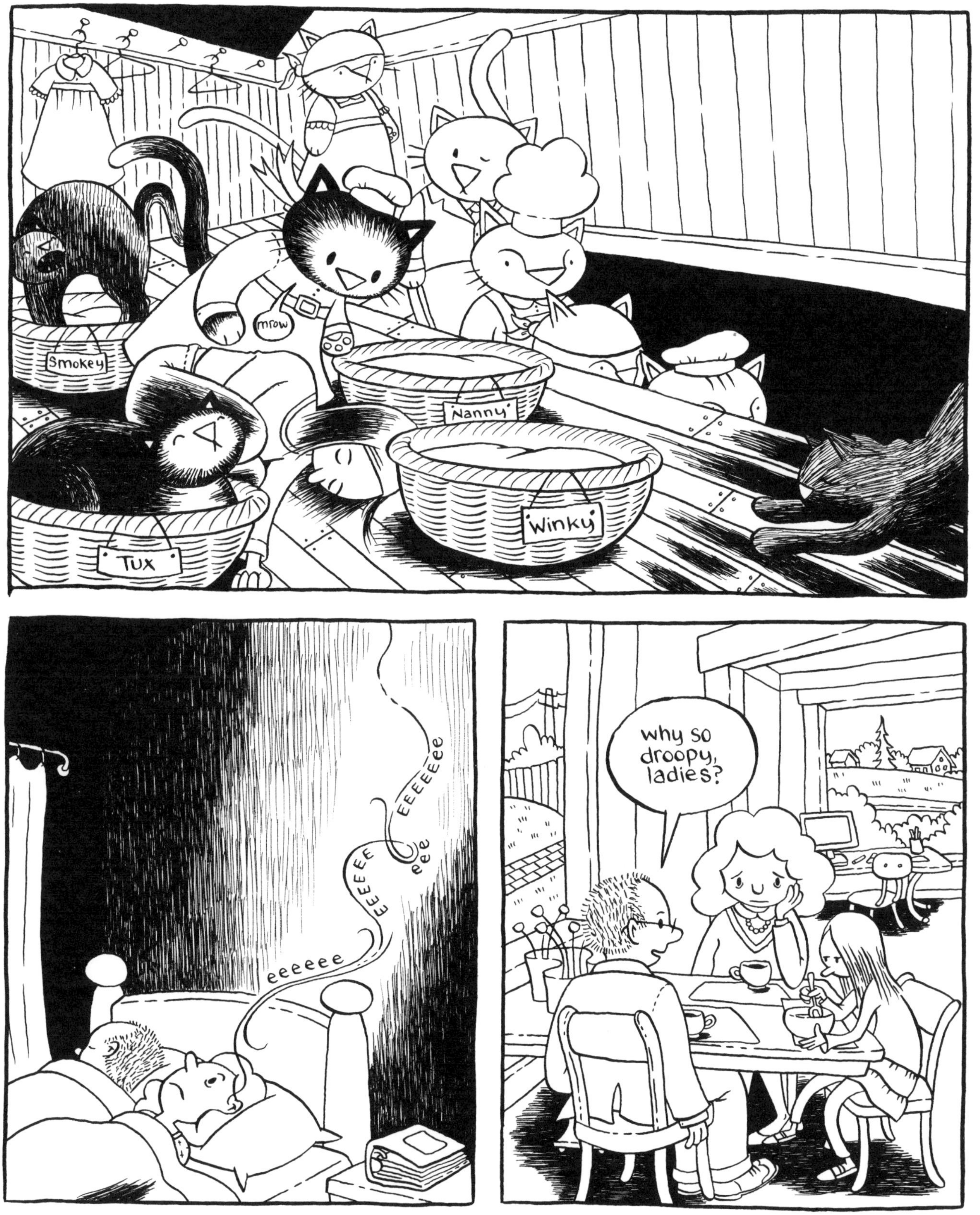
mrow
Smokey
Nanny
Tux
Winky
eeeeee
EEEEEE
eee
EEEEEEeee
why so droopy, ladies?

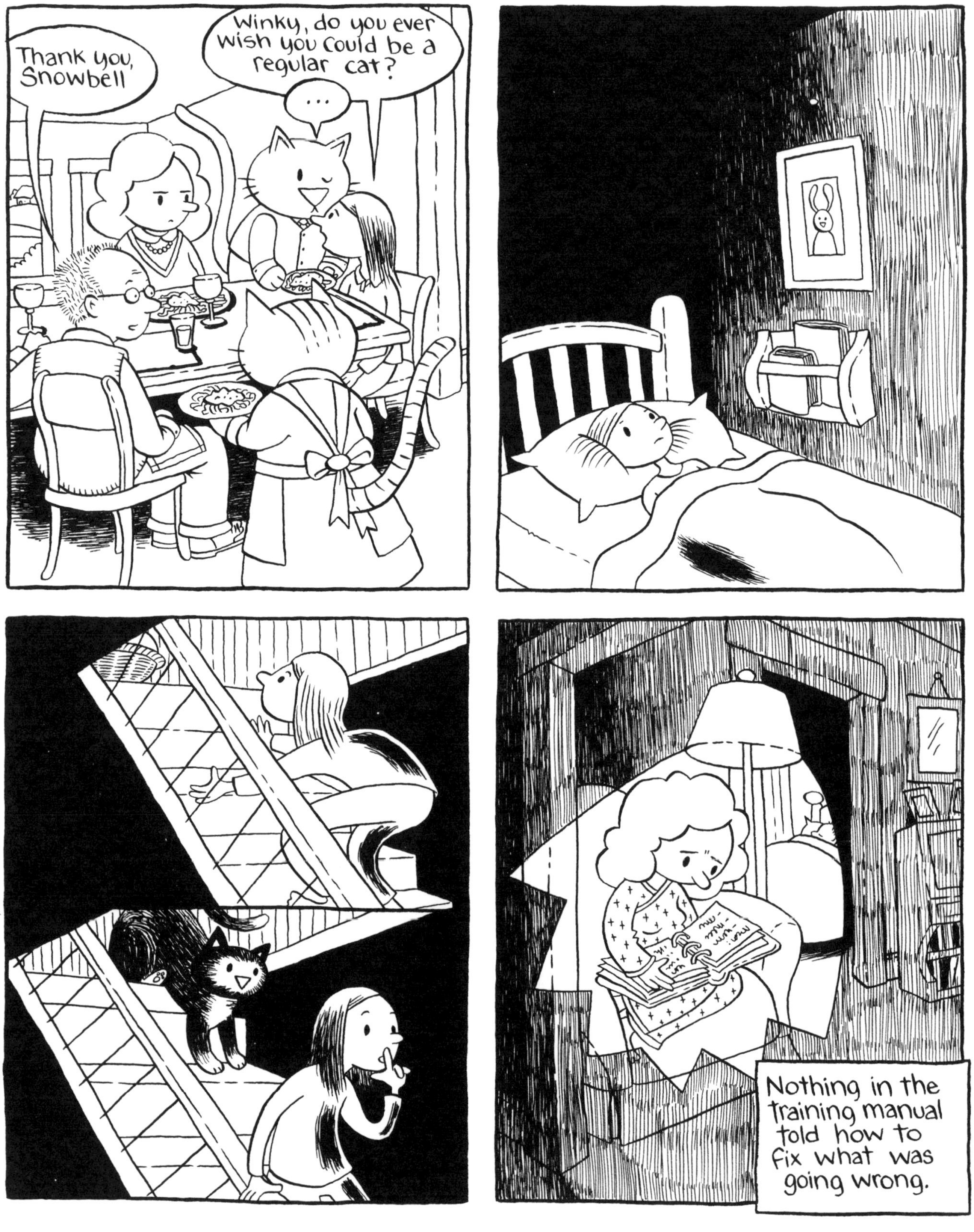
Thank you, Snowbell
Winky, do you ever wish you could be a regular cat?
...
Nothing in the training manual told how to fix what was going wrong.

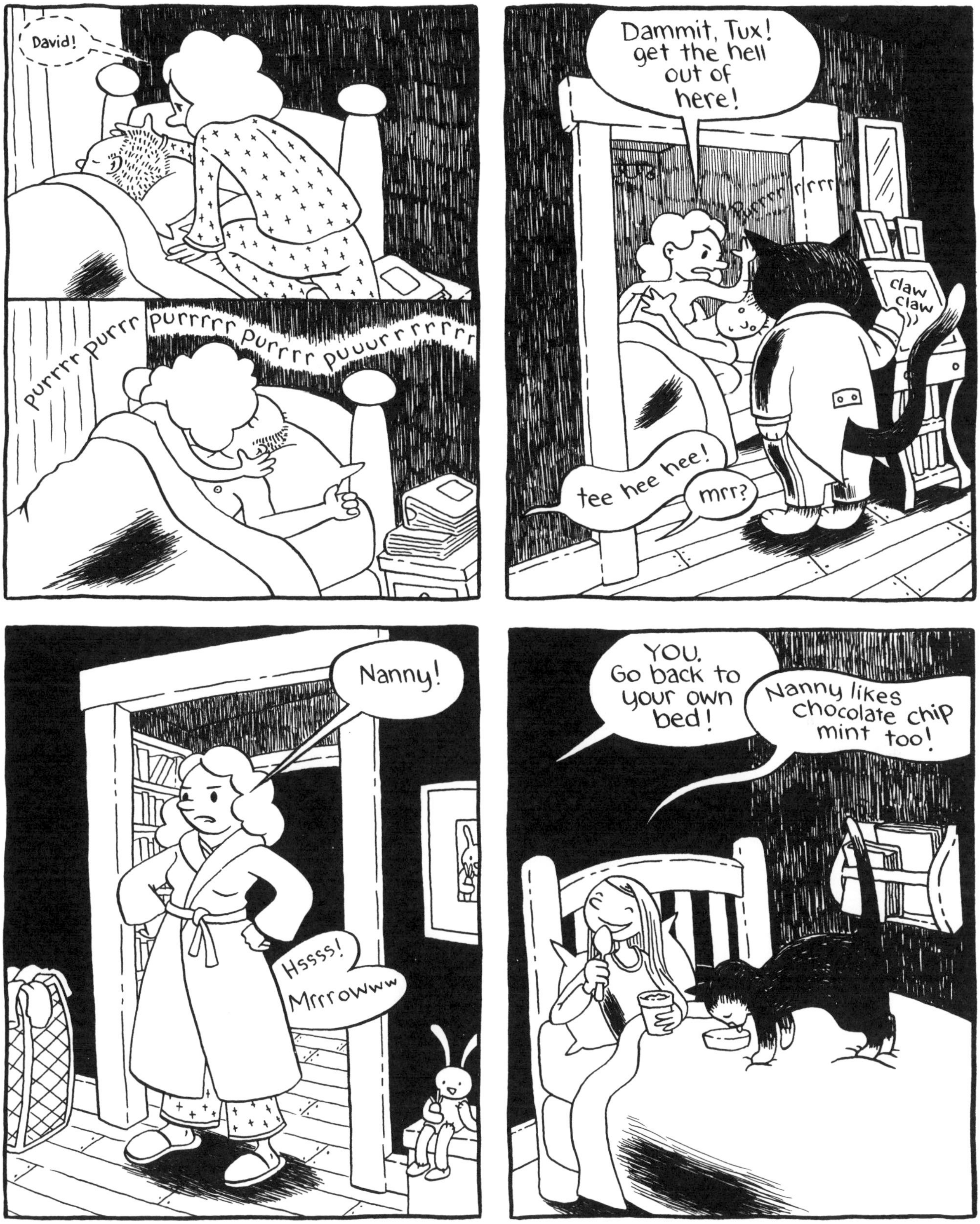
David!
purrrr purrr purrrrr purrrr puuurrrrrr
Dammit, Tux! get the hell out of here!
purrrr rrrr
claw claw
tee hee hee!
mrr?
Nanny!
Hssss! Mrrrowww
YOU. Go back to your own bed!
Nanny likes chocolate chip mint too!

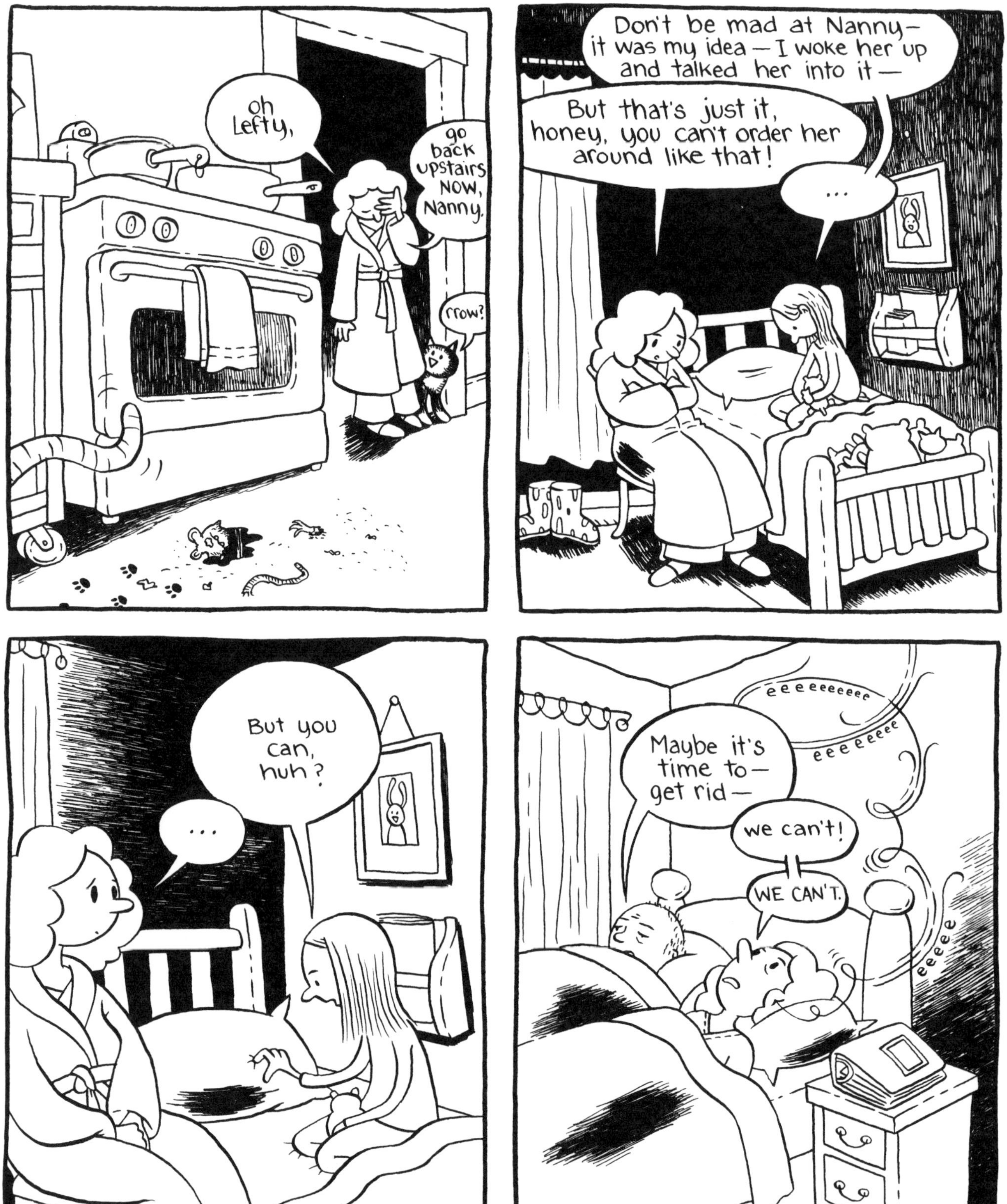
oh Lefty,
go back upstairs NOW, Nanny.
rrow?
Don't be mad at Nanny— it was my idea — I woke her up and talked her into it —
But that's just it, honey, you can't order her around like that!
. . .
. . .
But you can, huh?
eeeeeeeeee
eeeeeeee
Maybe it's time to— get rid—
we can't!
WE CAN'T.
eeeee

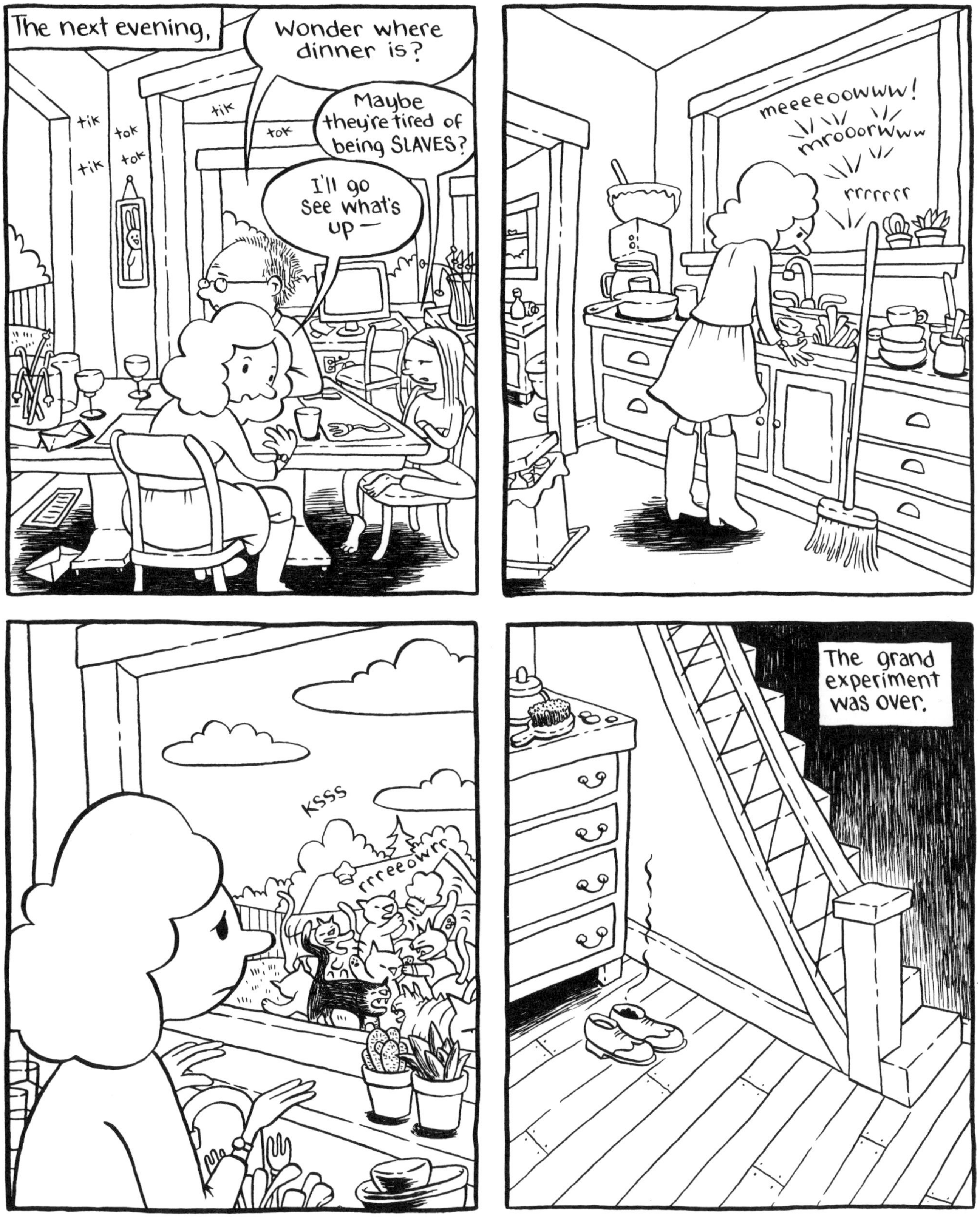
The next evening,
Wonder where dinner is?
tik
tok
tik
tok
tik
tok
Maybe they're tired of being SLAVES?
I'll go see what's up—
meeeeoowww!
mrooorwww
rrrrrrr
KSSS
rrreeowrr
The grand experiment was over.

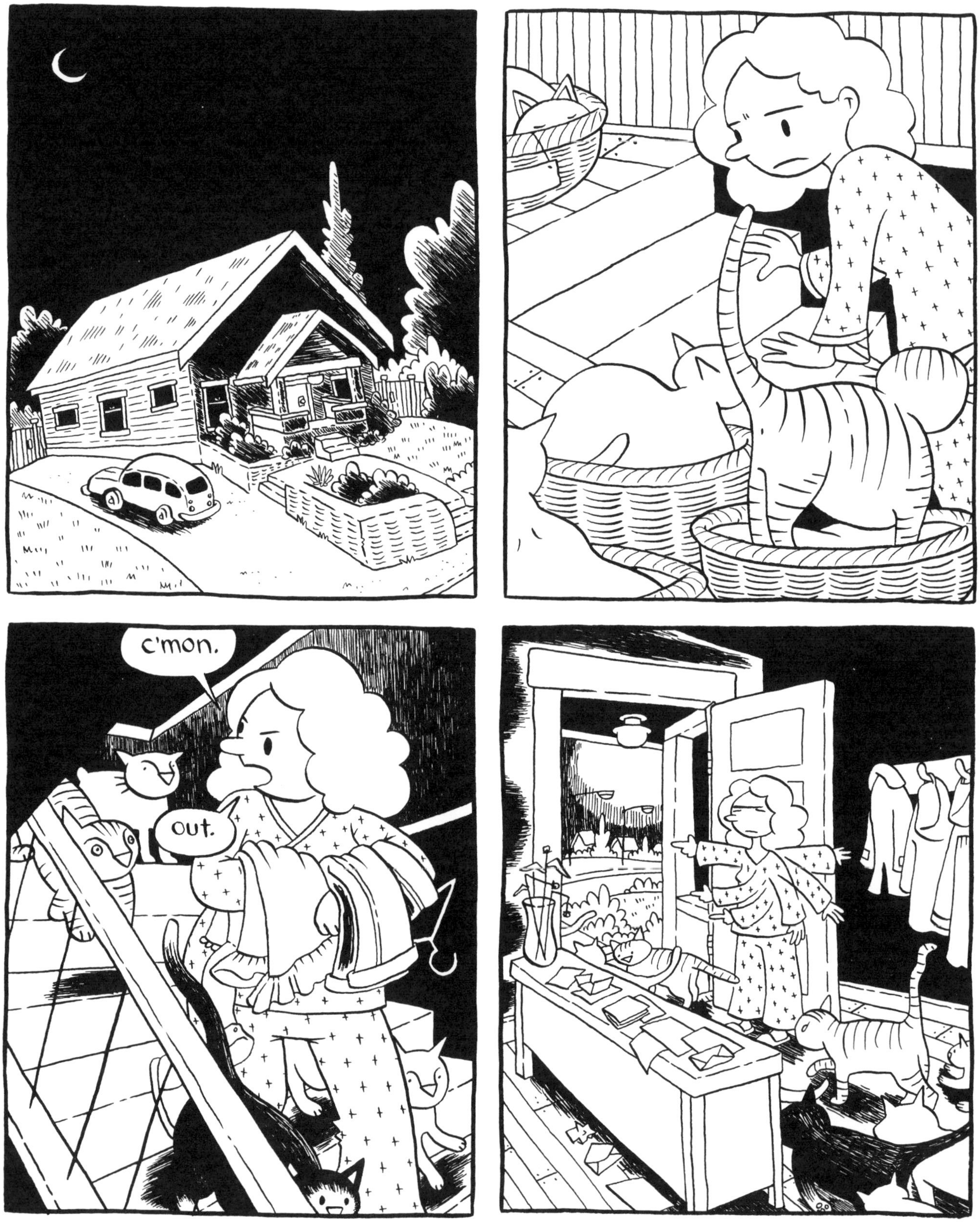
c'mon.
out.

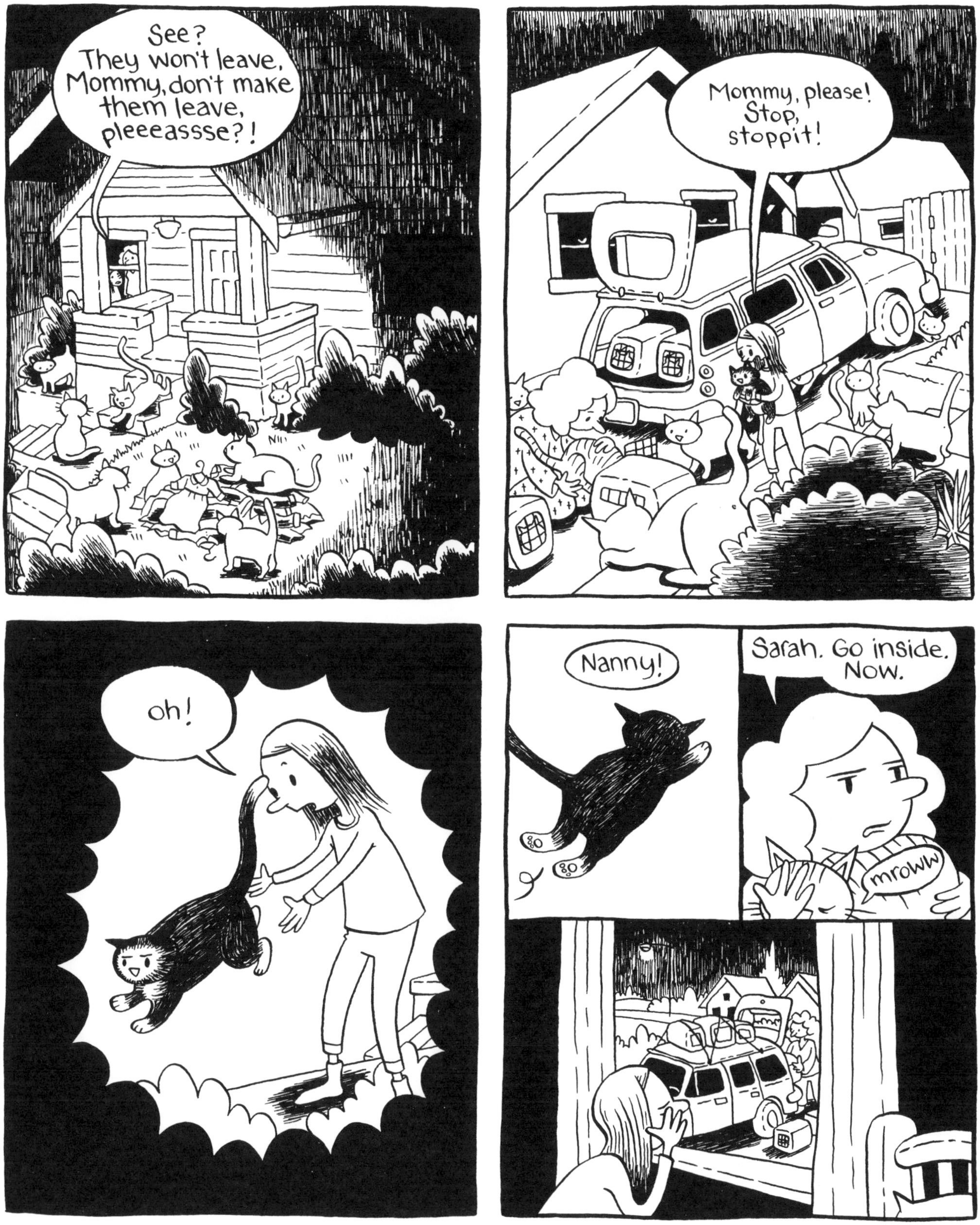
See? They won't leave. Mommy, don't make them leave, pleeeassse?!
Mommy, please! Stop, stoppit!
oh!
Nanny!
Sarah. Go inside. Now.
mroww

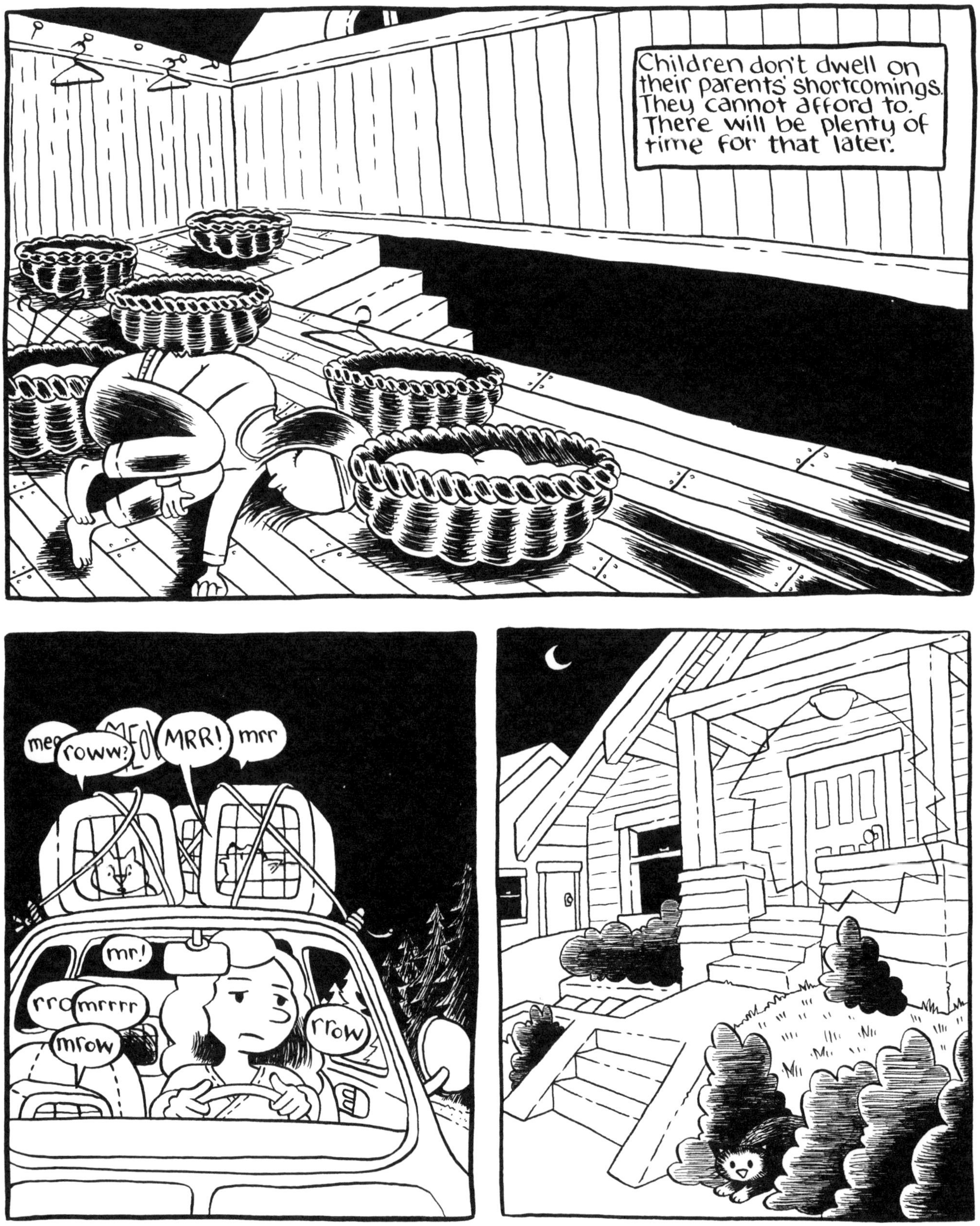
Children don't dwell on their parents' shortcomings. They cannot afford to. There will be plenty of time for that later.
roww?
MRR!
mrr
mr!
rro
mrrrrr
mrow
rrow

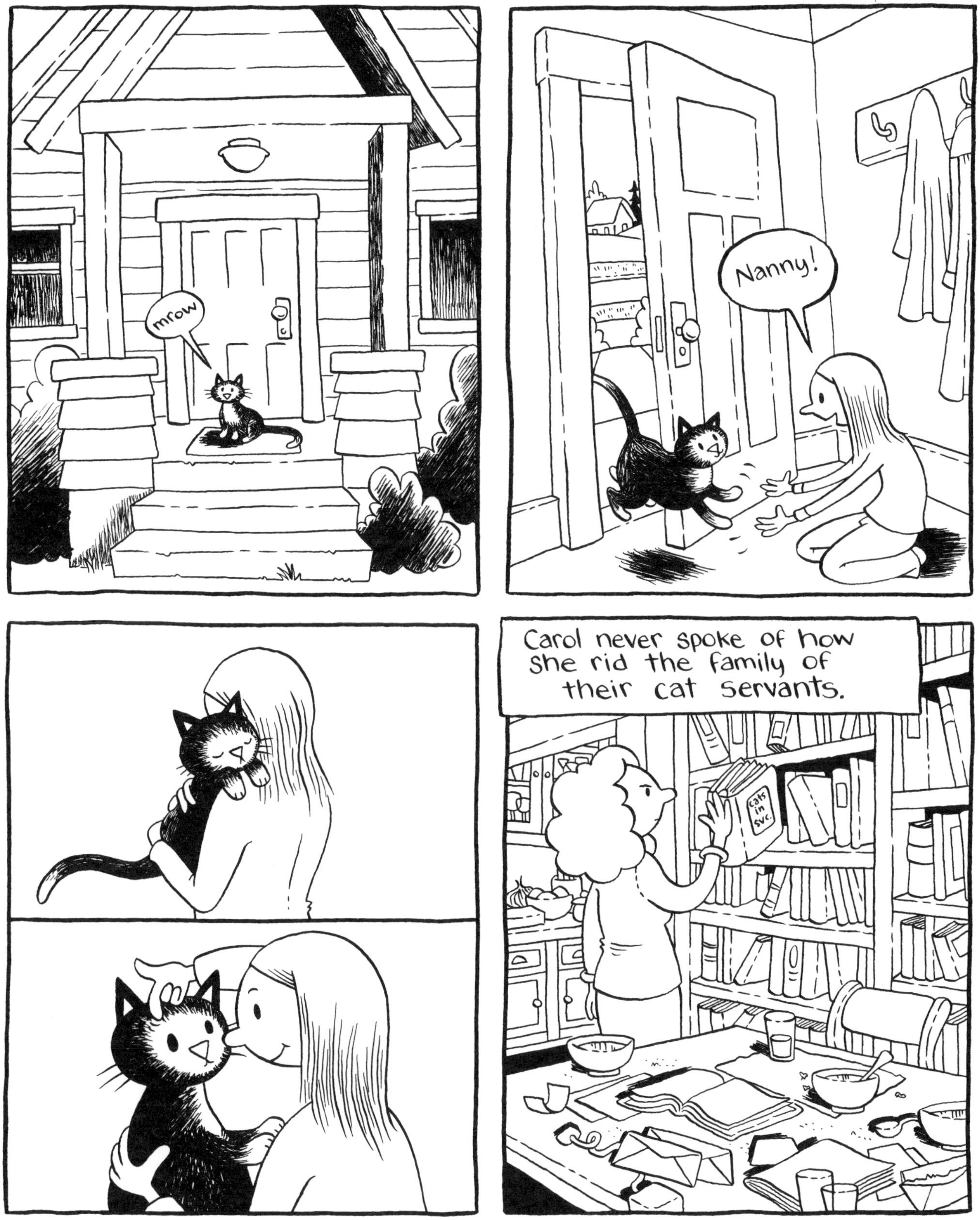
mrow
Nanny!
Carol never spoke of how she rid the family of their cat servants.
Cats in Svc.

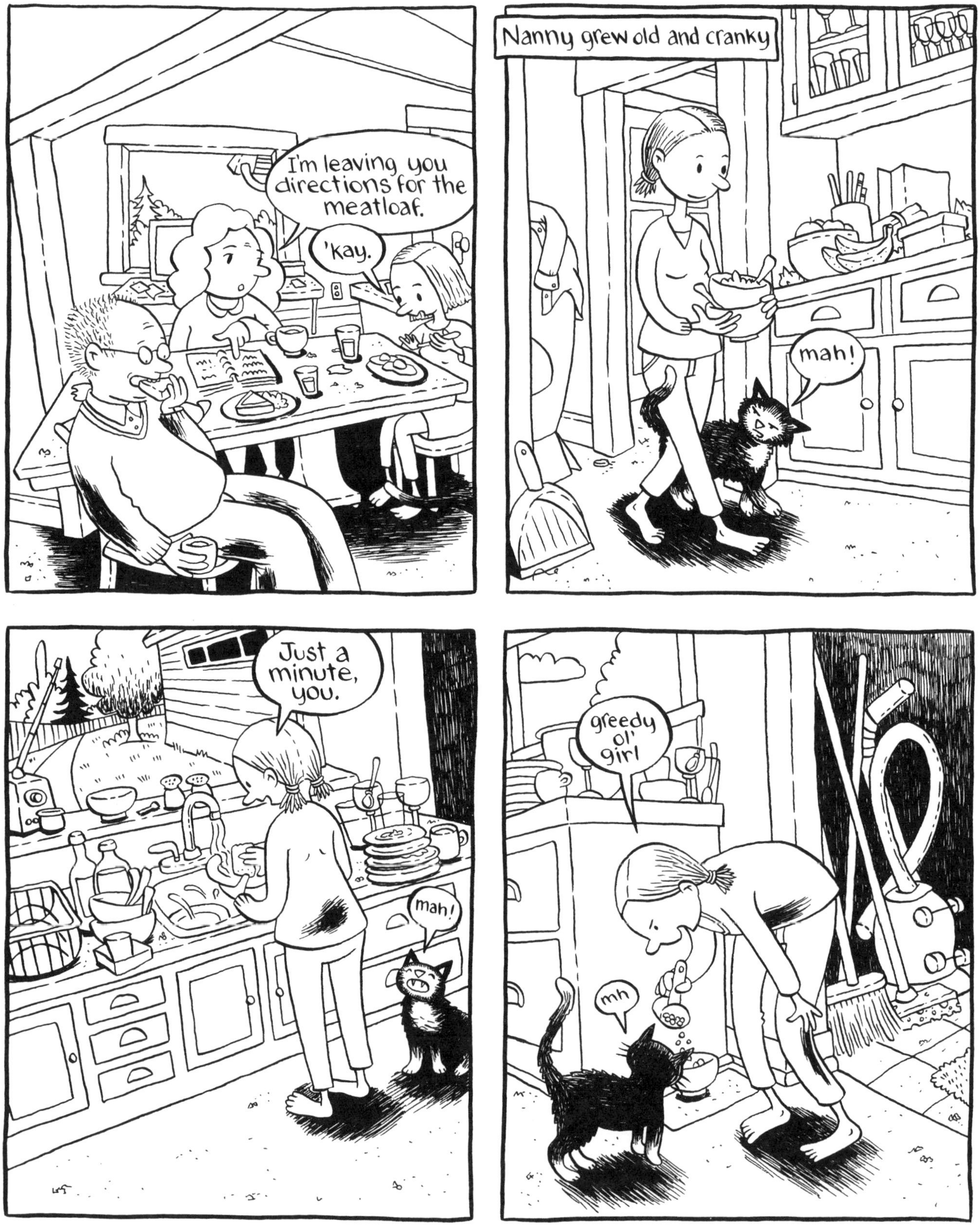
I'm leaving you directions for the meatloaf.
'kay.
Nanny grew old and cranky
mah!
Just a minute, you.
mah!
greedy ol' girl
mh

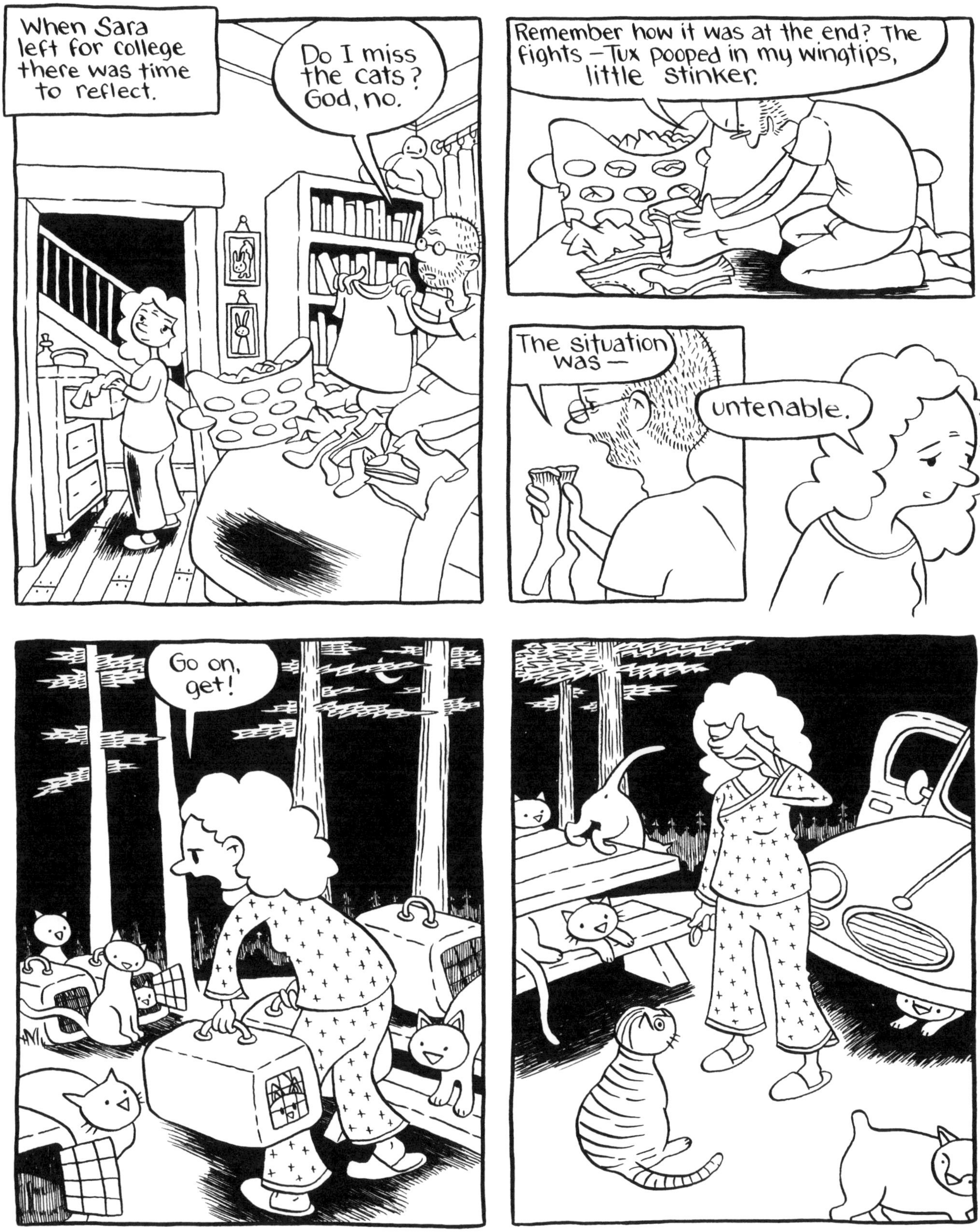
When Sara left for college there was time to reflect.
Do I miss the cats? God, no.
Remember how it was at the end? The fights —Tux pooped in my wingtips, little stinker.
The situation was —
untenable.
Go on, get!

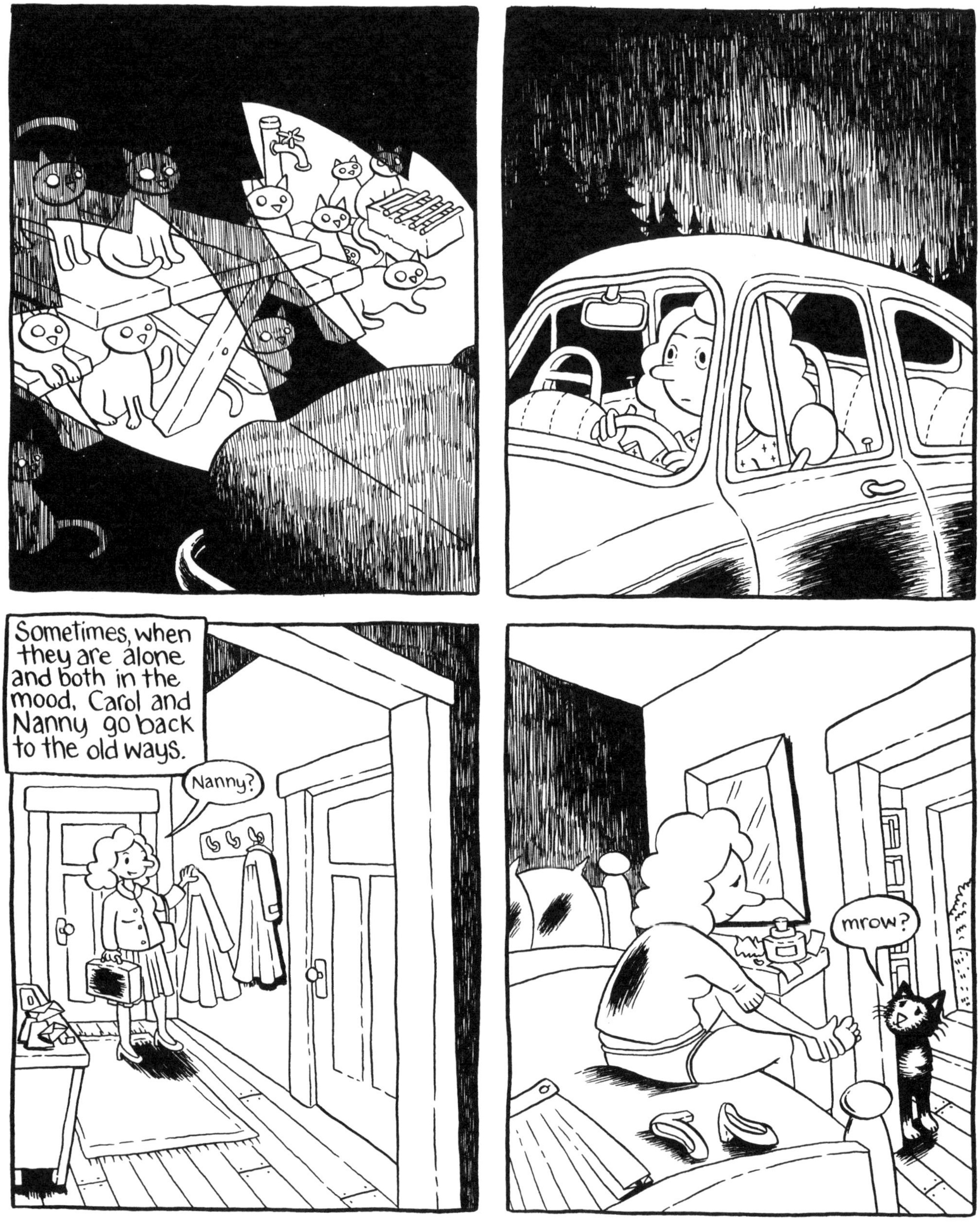
Sometimes, when they are alone and both in the mood, Carol and Nanny go back to the old ways.
Nanny?
mrow?

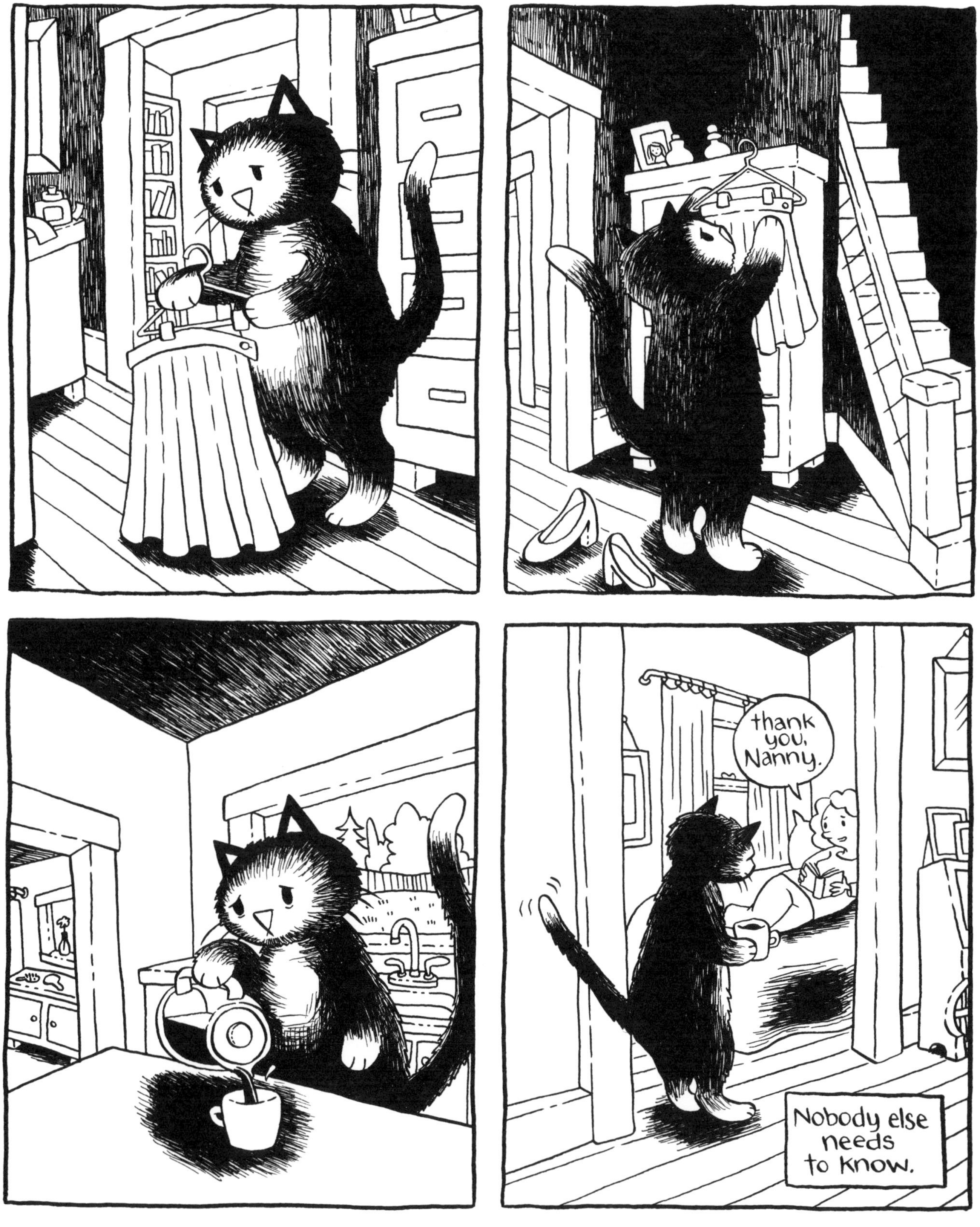
thank you, Nanny.
Nobody else needs to know.

3

The
Egg Room

MEGAN KELSO

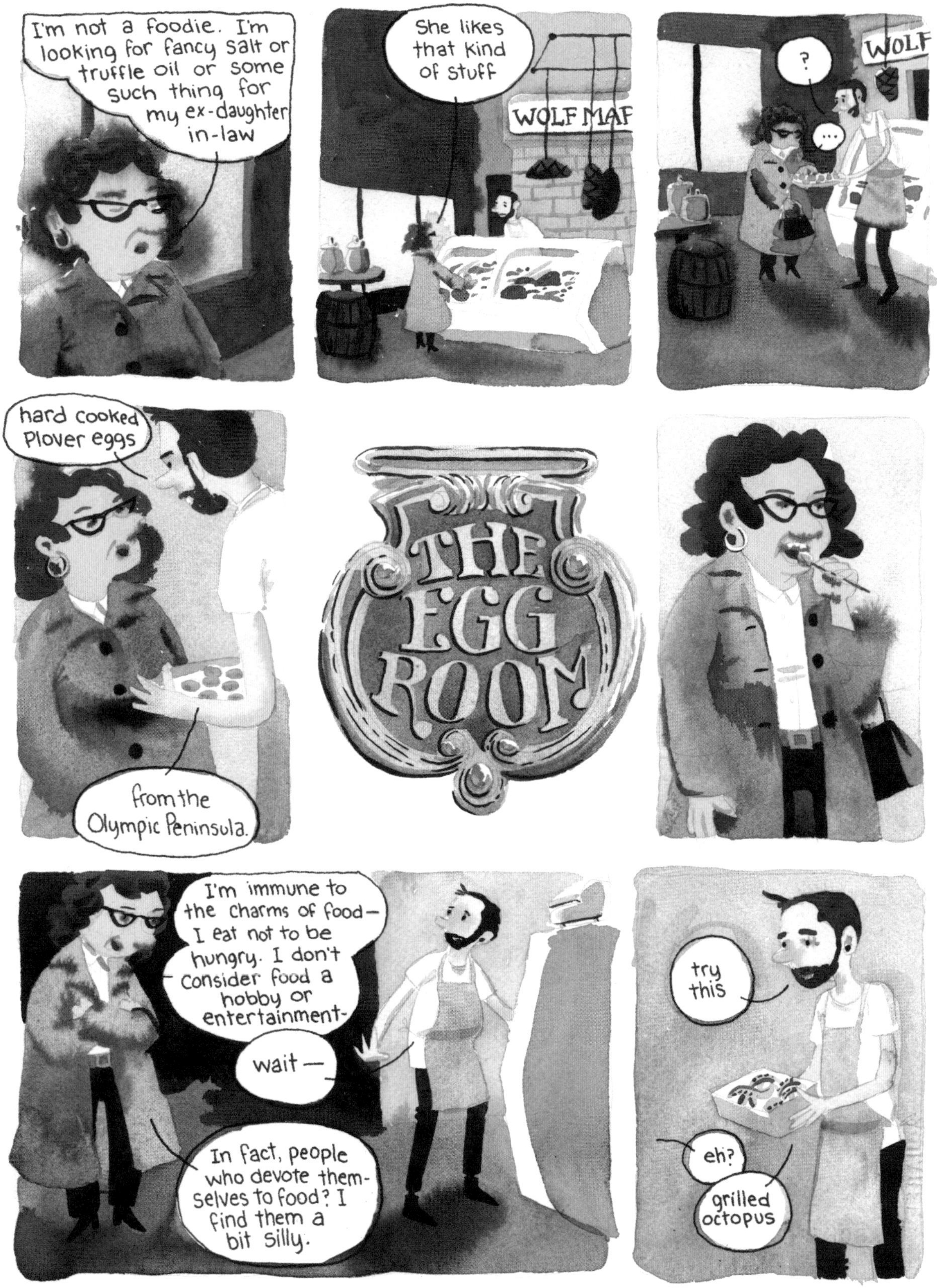
I'm not a foodie. I'm looking for fancy salt or truffle oil or some such thing for my ex-daughter in-law
She likes that kind of stuff
WOLF MAF
?
...
WOLF
hard cooked Plover eggs
from the Olympic Peninsula.
THE EGG ROOM
I'm immune to the charms of food— I eat not to be hungry. I don't consider food a hobby or entertainment-
wait—
In fact, people who devote themselves to food? I find them a bit silly.
try this
eh?
grilled octopus

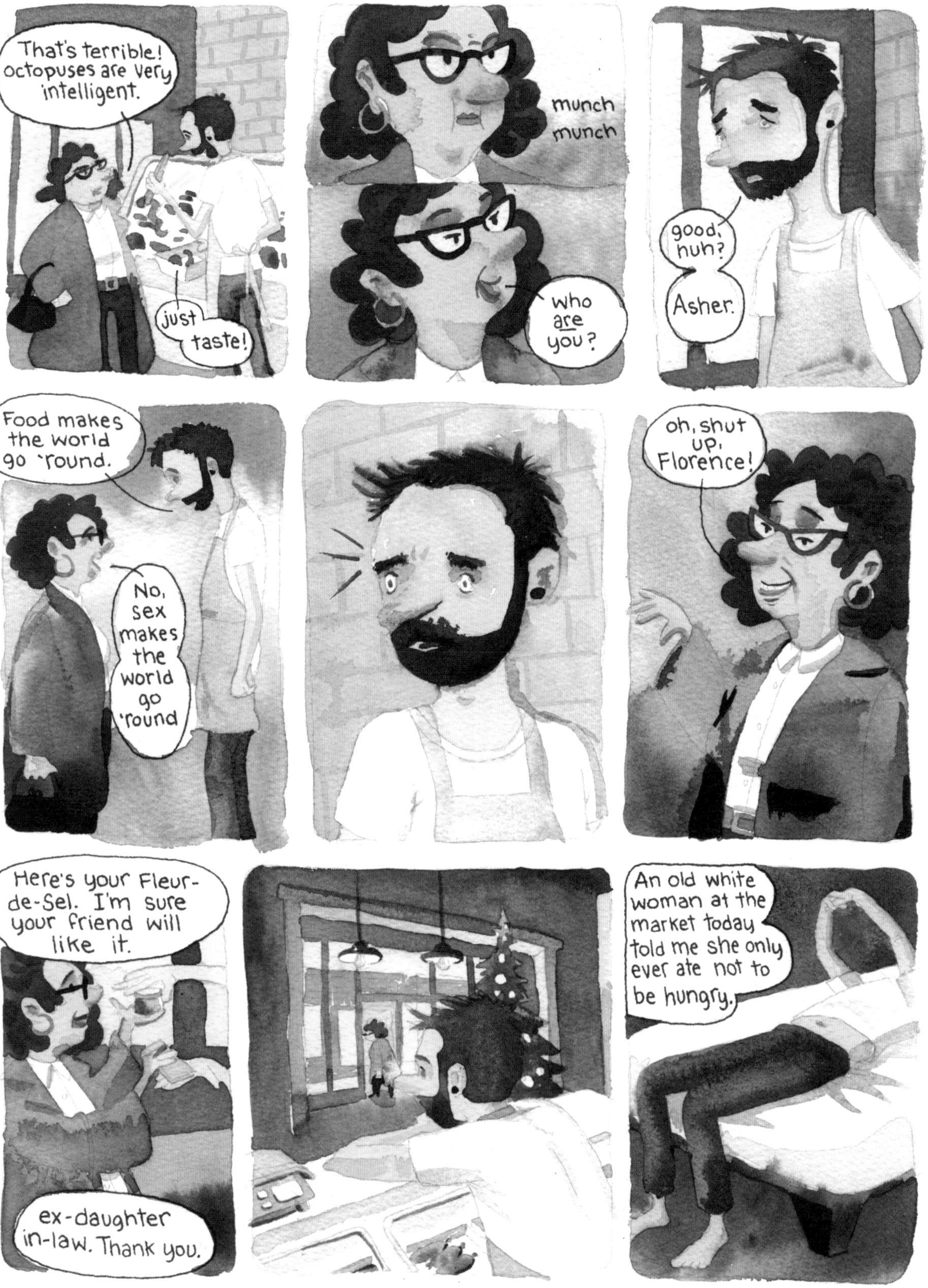
That's terrible! octopuses are very intelligent.
just taste!
munch
munch
who are you?
good, huh?
Asher.
Food makes the world go 'round.
No, sex makes the world go 'round
oh, shut up, Florence!
Here's your Fleur-de-Sel. I'm sure your friend will like it.
ex-daughter in-law. Thank you.
An old white woman at the market today told me she only ever ate not to be hungry.

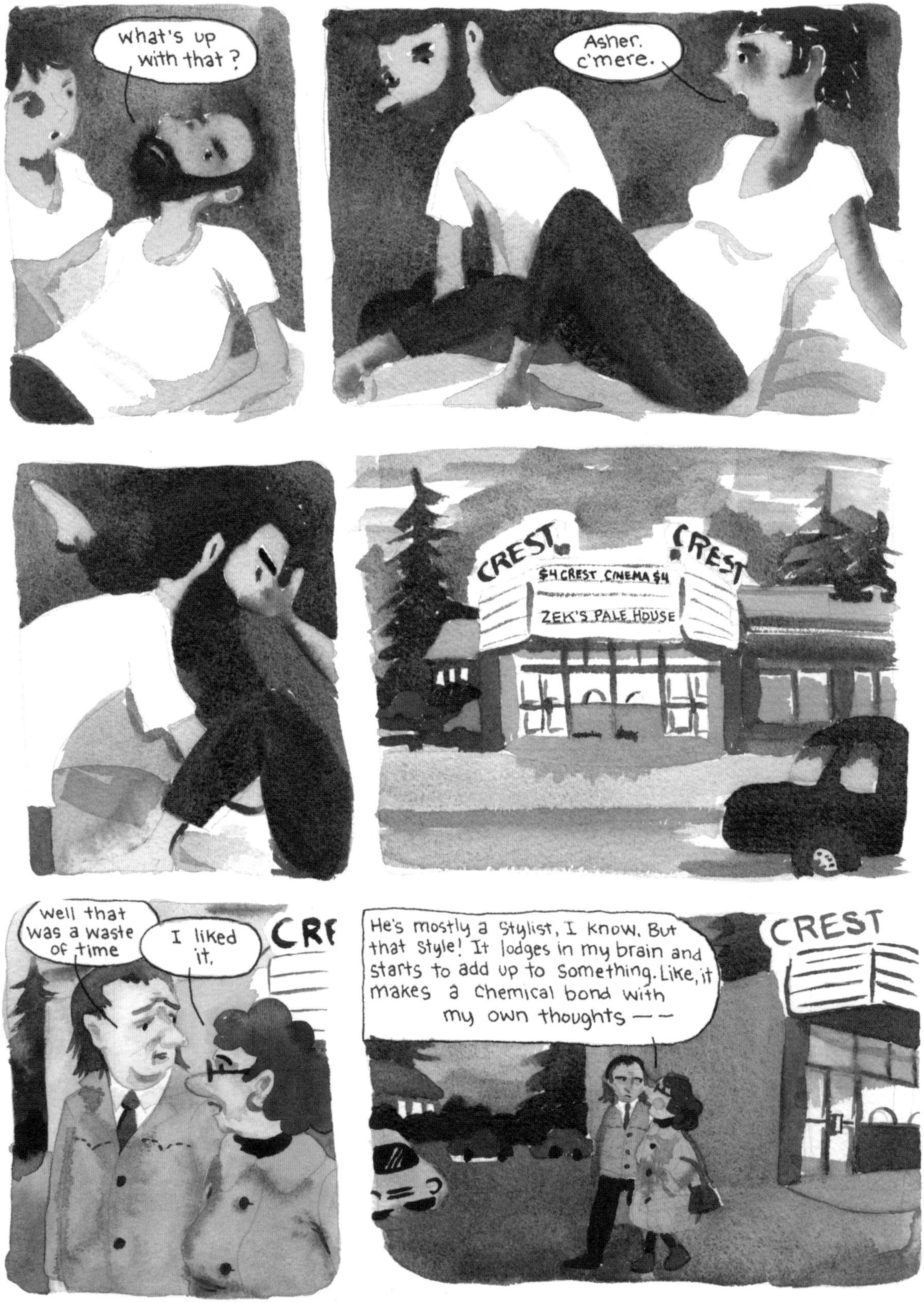
What's up with that?
Asher. c'mere.
CREST
CREST
$4 CREST CINEMA $4
ZEK'S PALE HOUSE
Well that was a waste of time
I liked it.
He's mostly a stylist, I know. But that style! It lodges in my brain and starts to add up to something. Like, it makes a chemical bond with my own thoughts — —
CREST

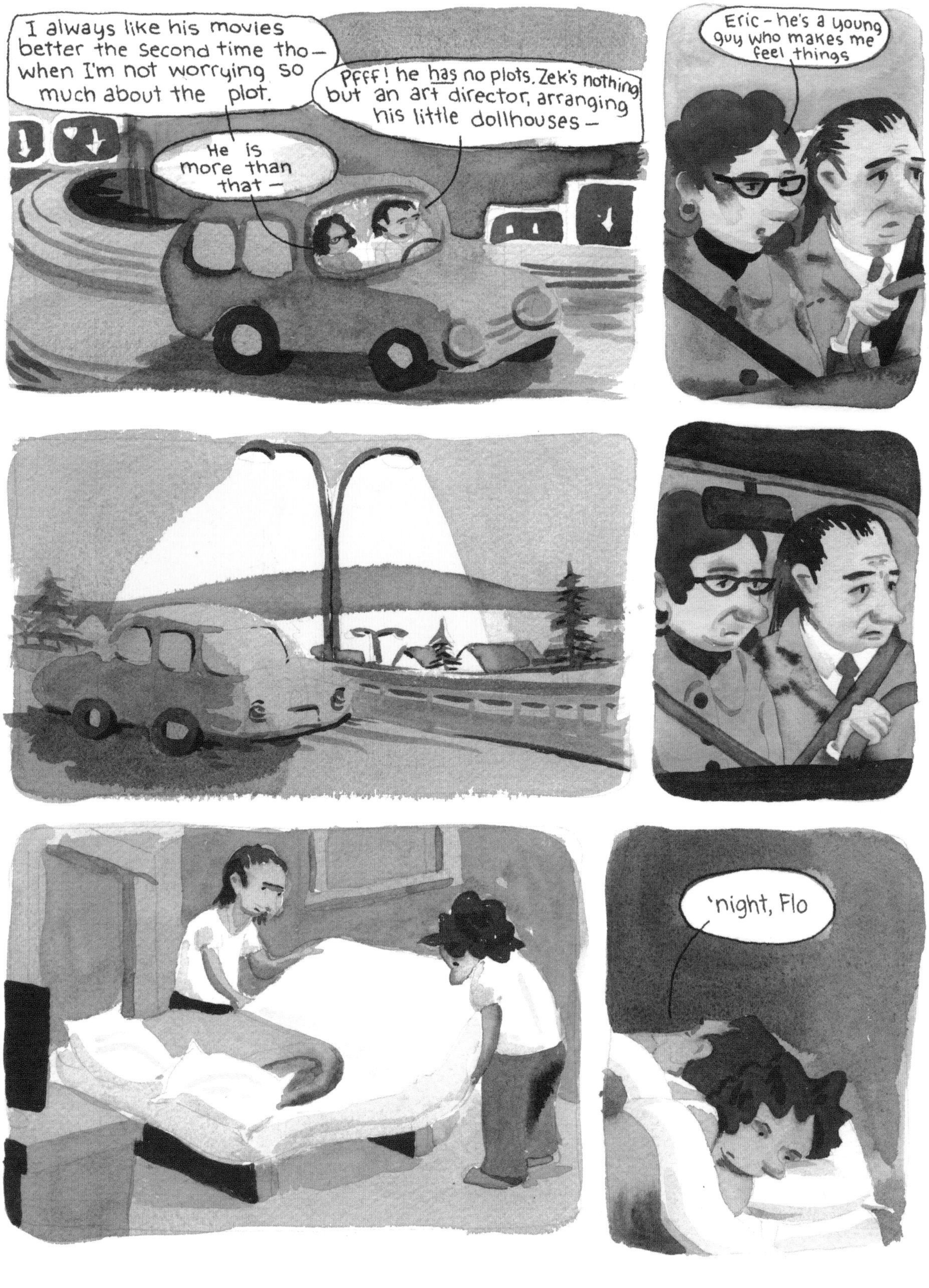
I always like his movies better the second time tho— when I'm not worrying so much about the plot.
Pfff! he has no plots. Zek's nothing but an art director, arranging his little dollhouses—
He is more than that—
Eric—he's a young guy who makes me feel things
'night, Flo

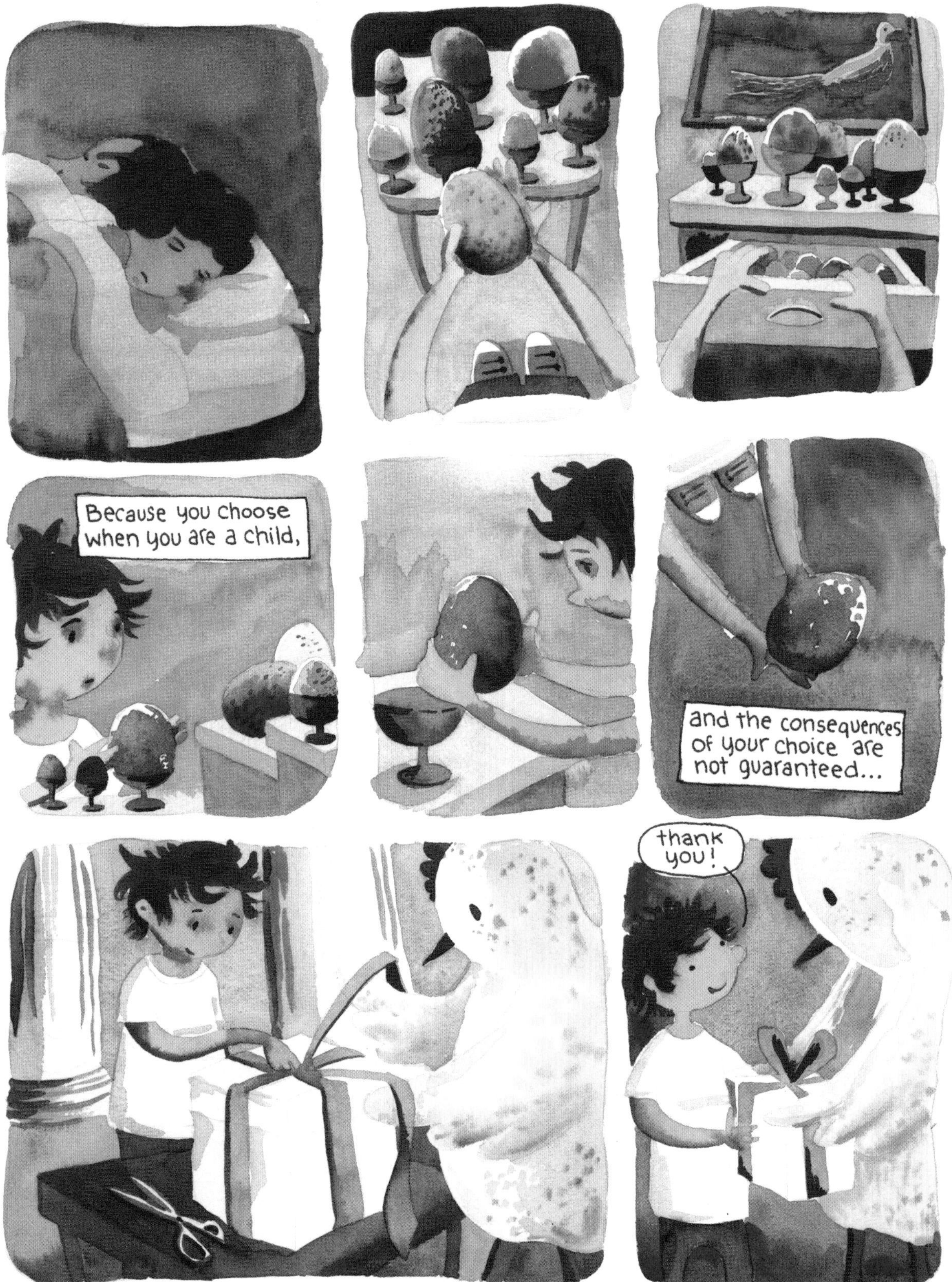
Because you choose
when you are a child,
and the consequences
of your choice are
not guaranteed...
thank
you!

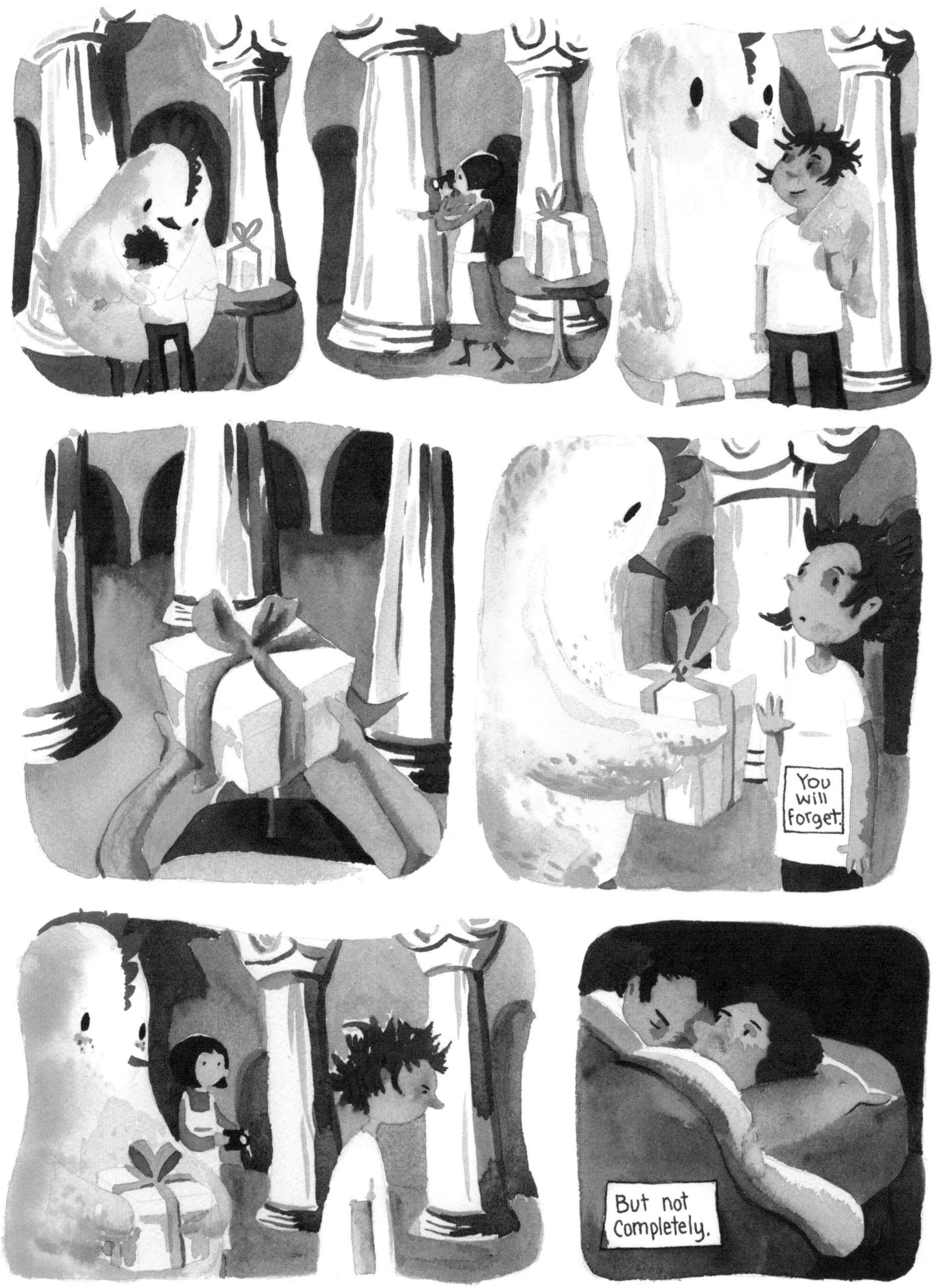
You will forget.
But not completely.

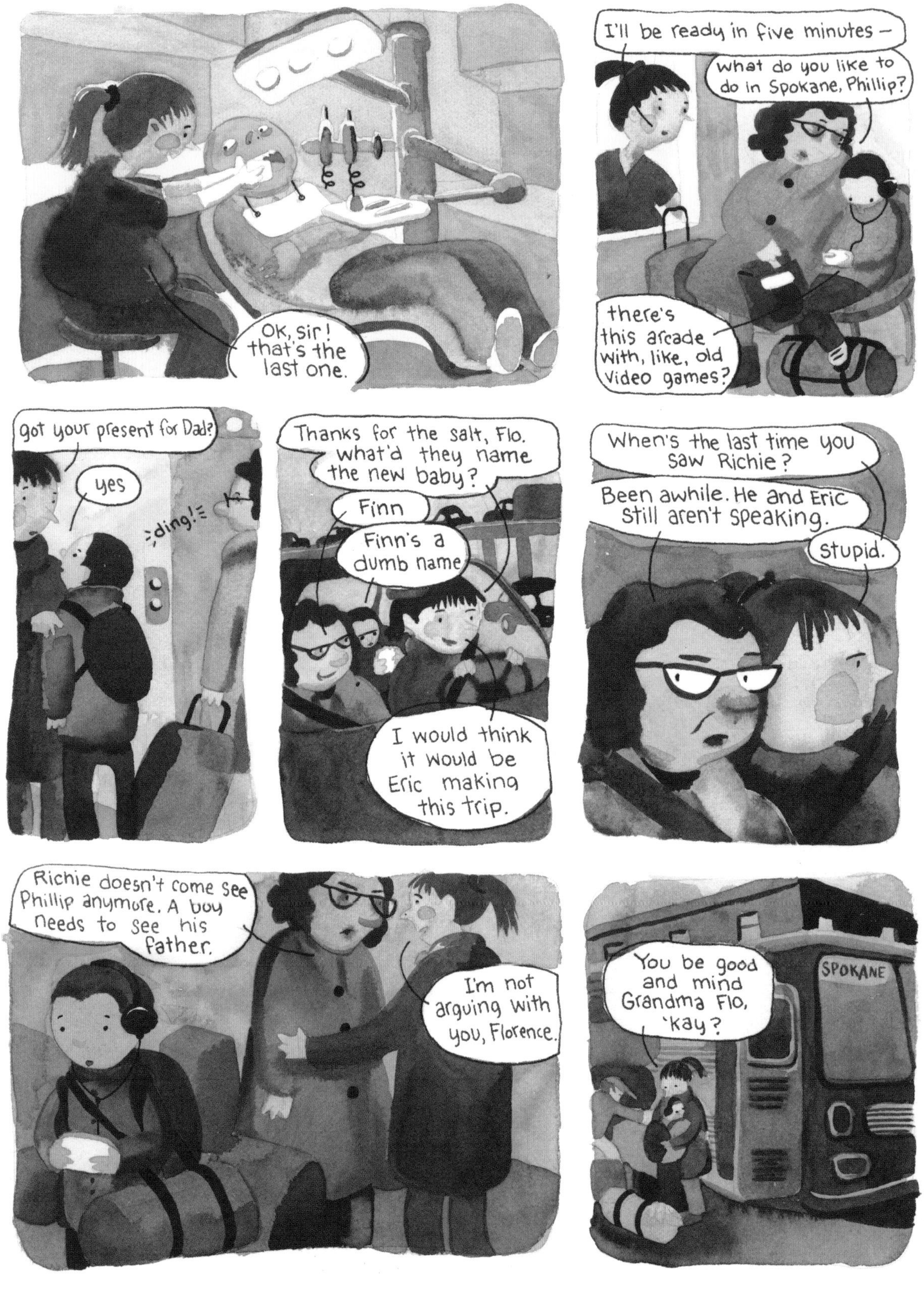
Ok, sir! that's the last one.
I'll be ready in five minutes –
what do you like to do in Spokane, Phillip?
there's this arcade with, like, old video games?
got your present for Dad?
yes
ding!
Thanks for the salt, Flo. what'd they name the new baby?
Finn
Finn's a dumb name
I would think it would be Eric making this trip.
When's the last time you saw Richie?
Been awhile. He and Eric still aren't speaking.
Stupid.
Richie doesn't come see Phillip anymore. A boy needs to see his father.
I'm not arguing with you, Florence.
SPOKANE
You be good and mind Grandma Flo, 'kay?

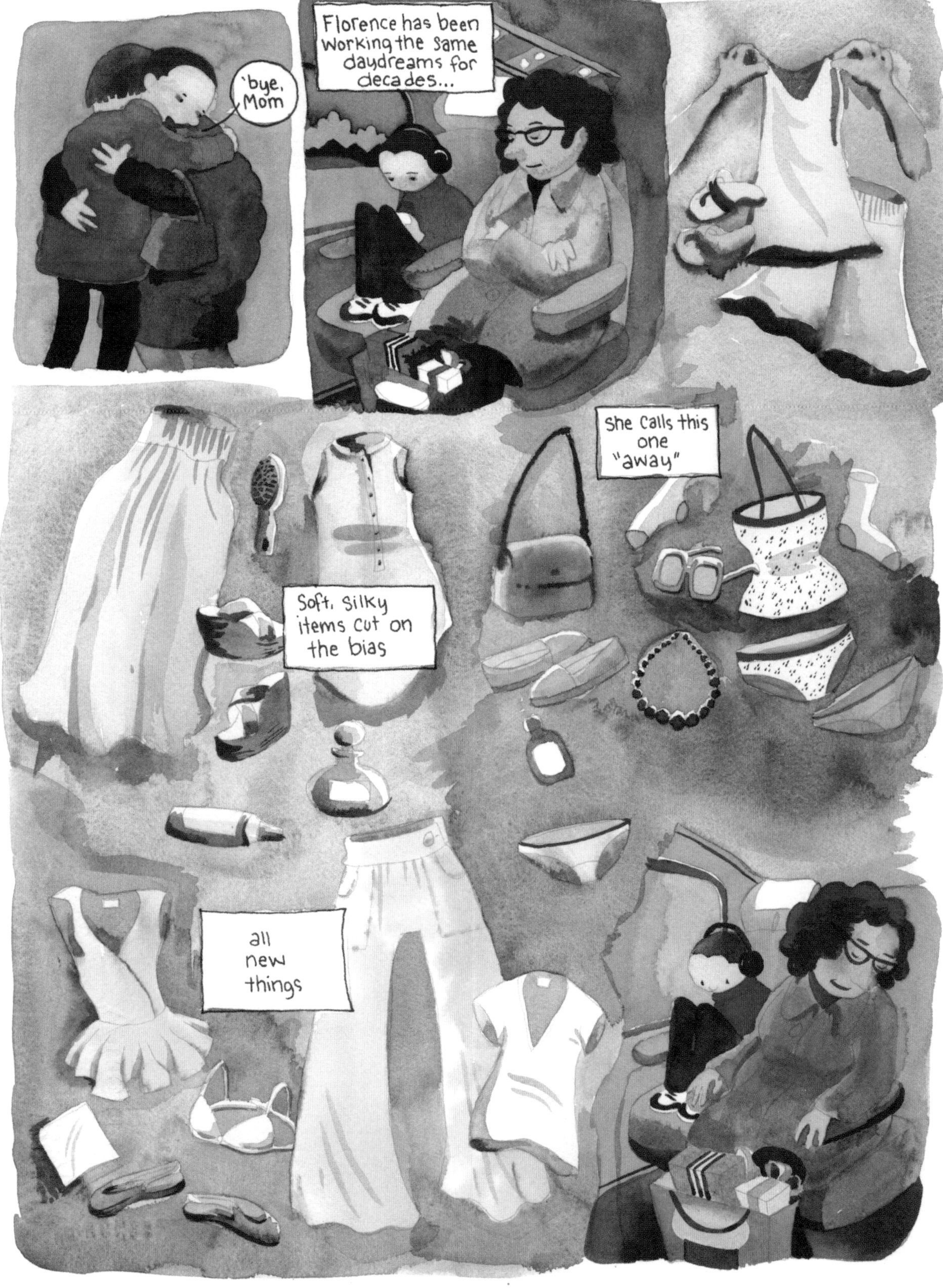
'bye, Mom
Florence has been working the same daydreams for decades...
She calls this one "away"
Soft, silky items cut on the bias
all new things

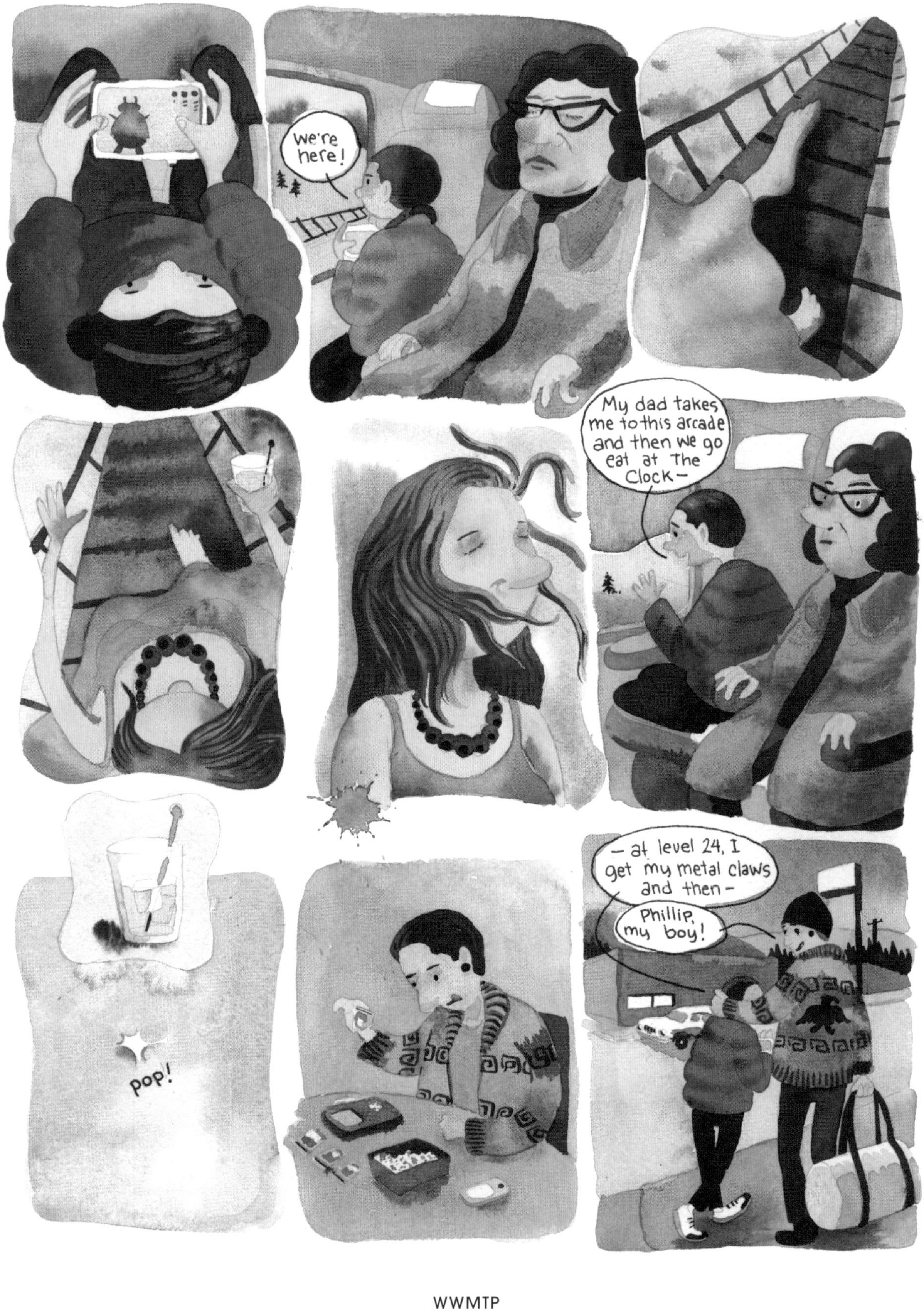
We're here!
My dad takes me to this arcade and then we go eat at The Clock—
pop!
—at level 24, I get my metal claws and then—
Phillip, my boy!

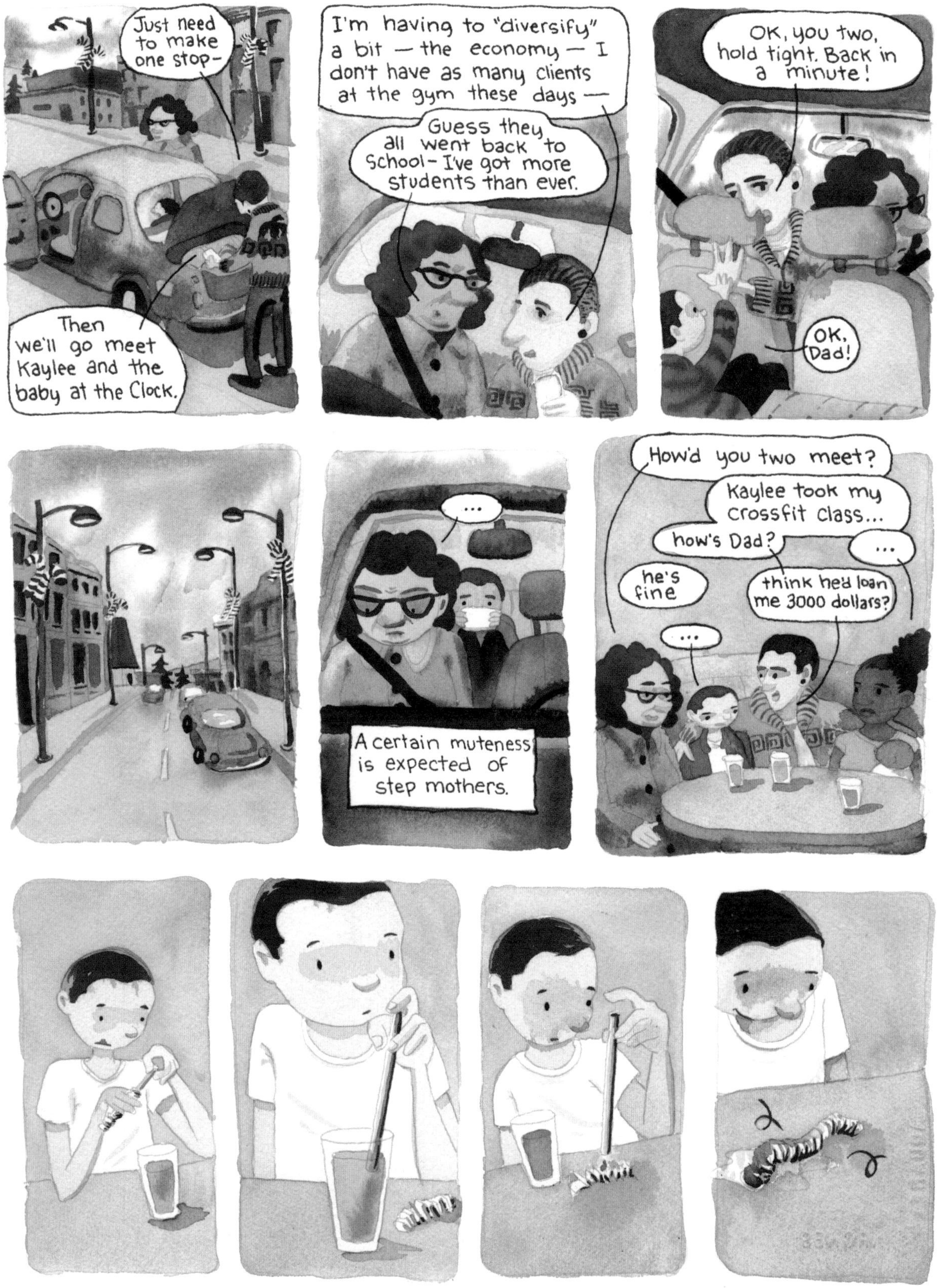

Just need to make one stop-
Then we'll go meet Kaylee and the baby at the Clock.
I'm having to "diversify" a bit — the economy — I don't have as many clients at the gym these days —
Guess they all went back to School- I've got more students than ever.
OK, you two, hold tight. Back in a minute!
OK, Dad!
...
A certain muteness is expected of step mothers.
How'd you two meet?
Kaylee took my crossfit class...
how's Dad?
...
he's fine
think he'd loan me 3000 dollars?
...

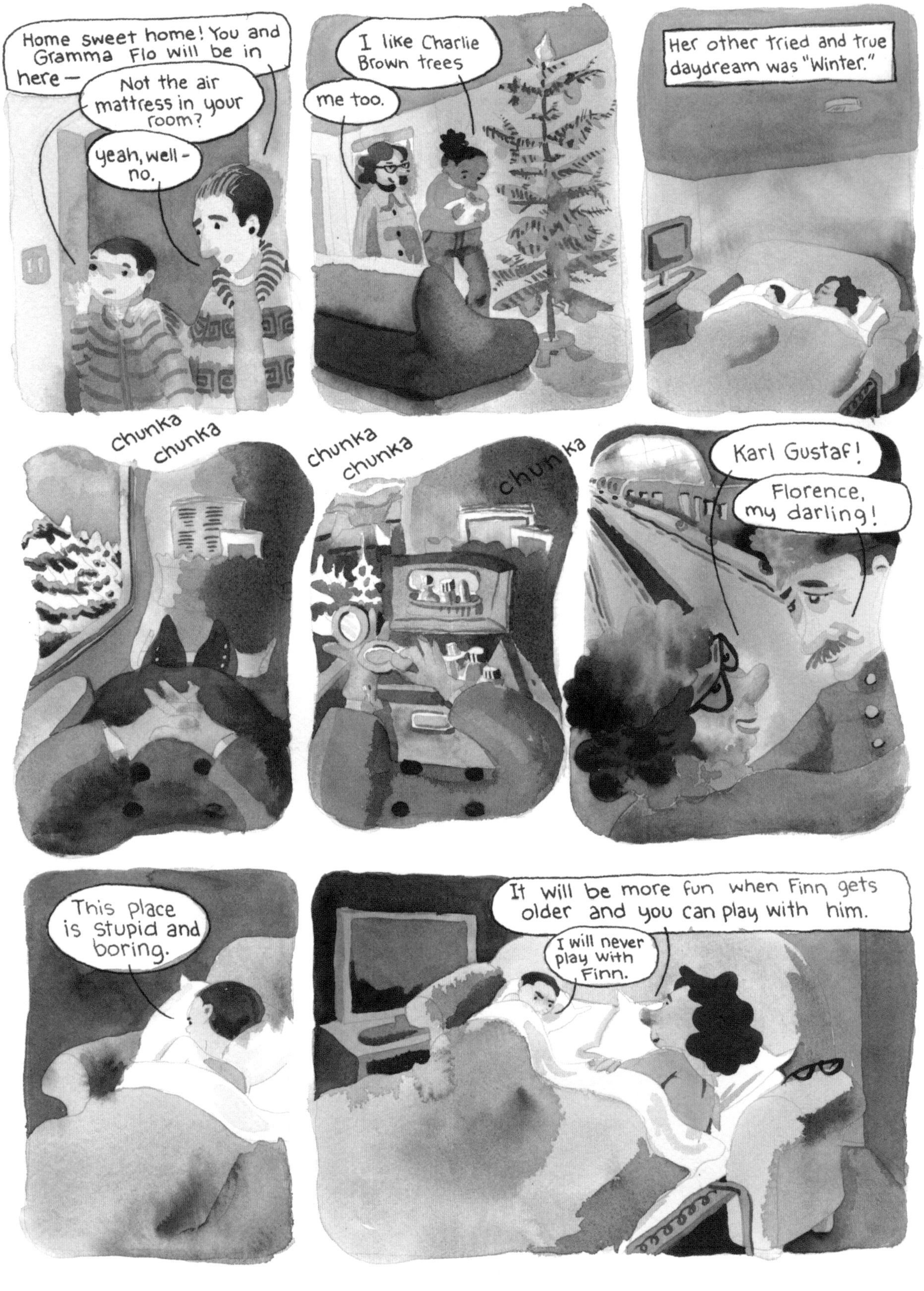
Home sweet home! You and Gramma Flo will be in here—
Not the air mattress in your room?
yeah, well-no.
I like Charlie Brown trees
me too.
Her other tried and true daydream was "Winter."
chunka chunka
chunka chunka
chunka
Karl Gustaf!
Florence, my darling!
This place is stupid and boring.
It will be more fun when Finn gets older and you can play with him.
I will never play with Finn.

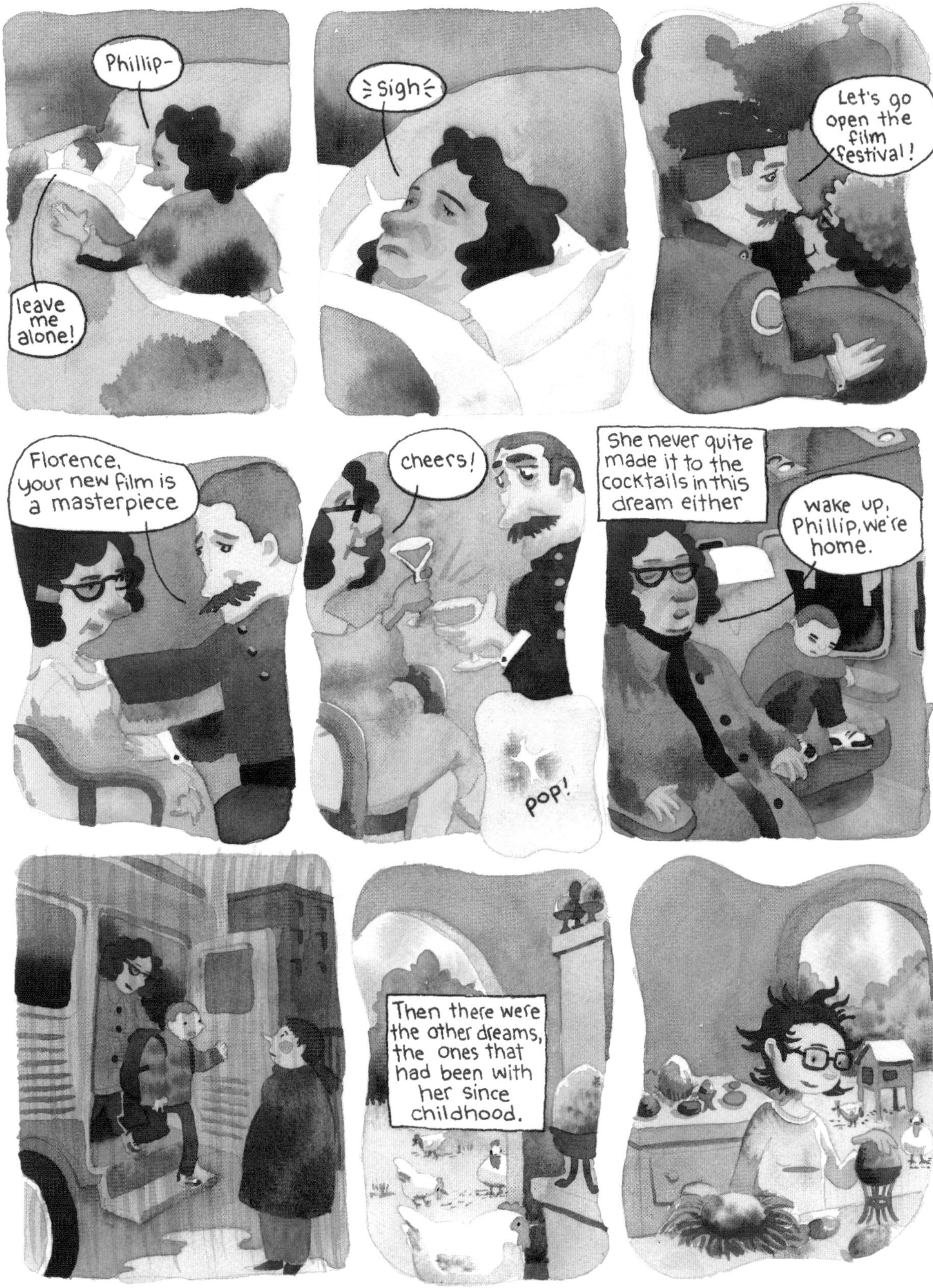
Phillip-
leave me alone!
≡sigh≡
Let's go open the film festival!
Florence, your new film is a masterpiece
cheers!
pop!
She never quite made it to the cocktails in this dream either
wake up, Phillip, we're home.
Then there were the other dreams, the ones that had been with her since childhood.

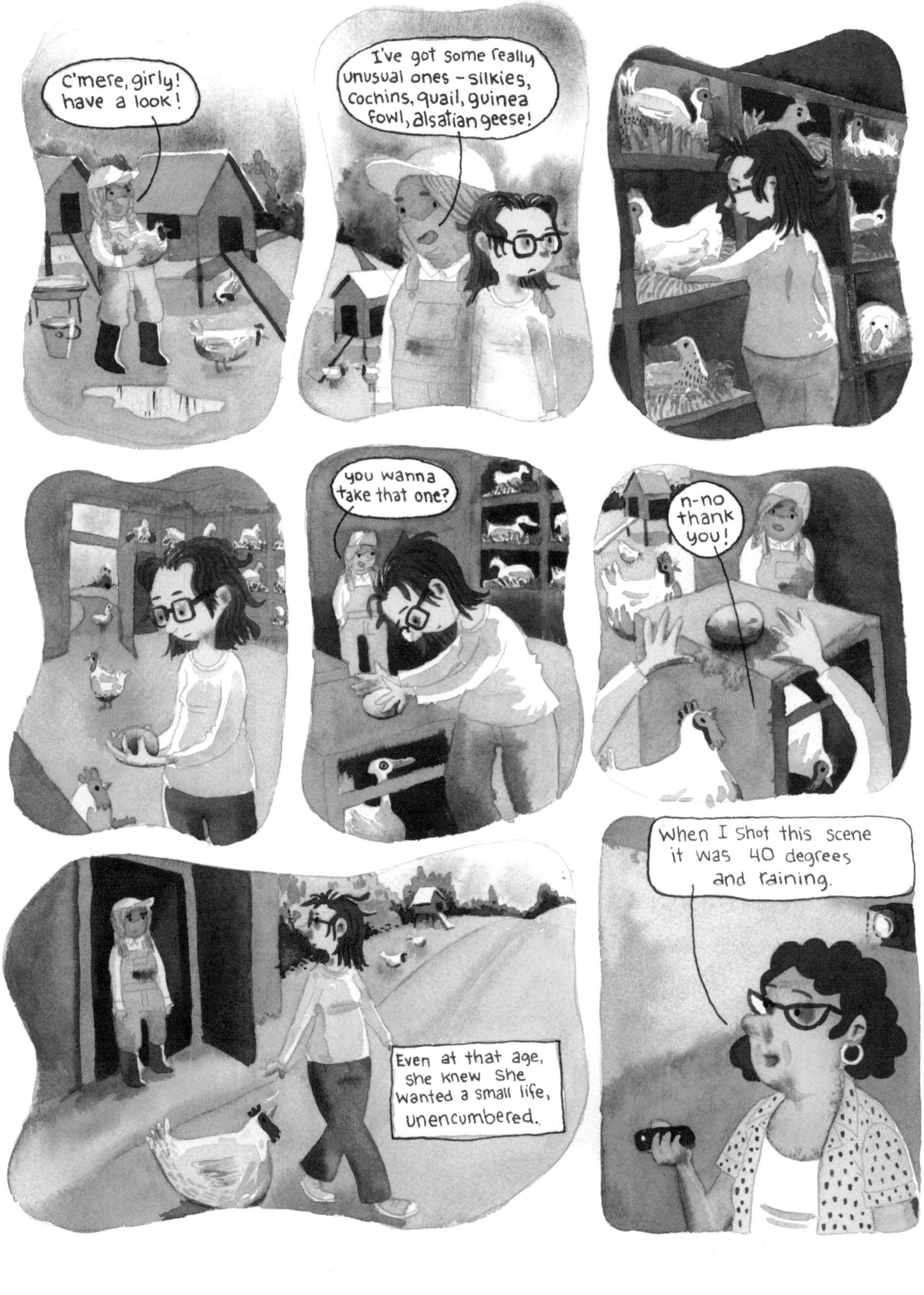
C'mere, girly! have a look!
I've got some really unusual ones - silkies, cochins, quail, guinea fowl, alsatian geese!
you wanna take that one?
n-no thank you!
Even at that age, she knew she wanted a small life, unencumbered.
When I shot this scene it was 40 degrees and raining.

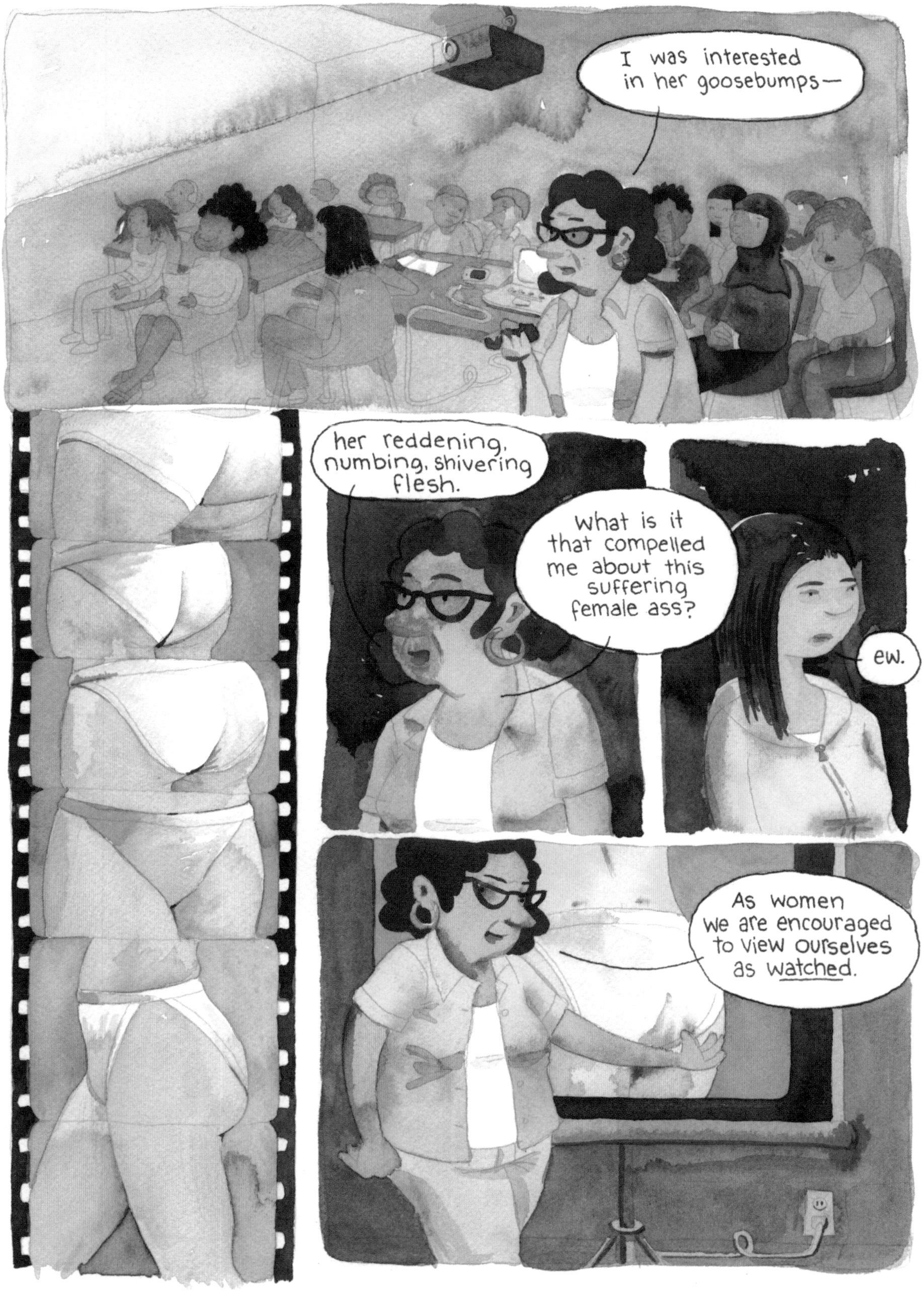
I was interested in her goosebumps—
her reddening, numbing, shivering flesh.
What is it that compelled me about this suffering female ass?
ew.
As women we are encouraged to view ourselves as watched.

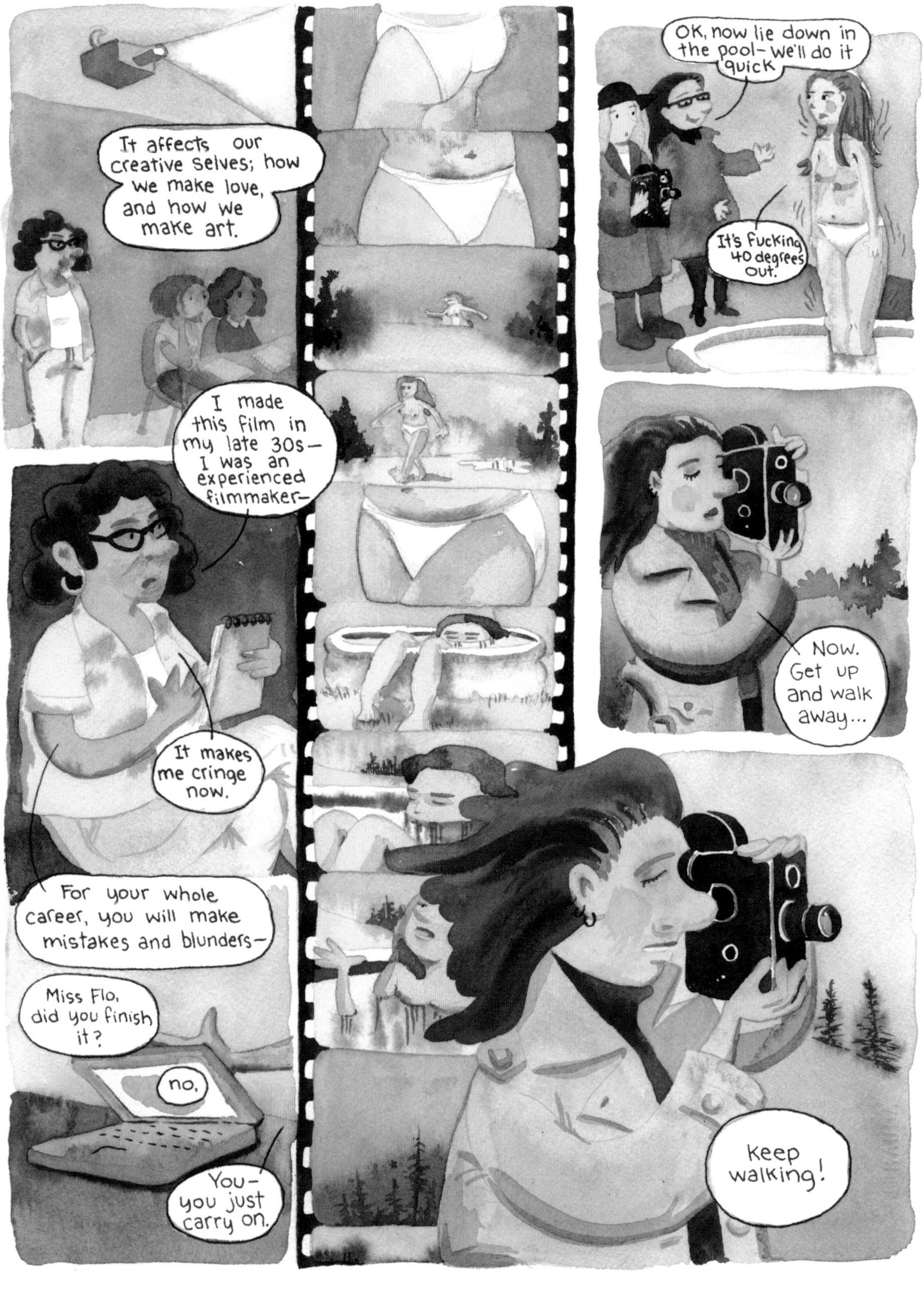
It affects our creative selves; how we make love, and how we make art.
I made this film in my late 30s— I was an experienced filmmaker—
It makes me cringe now.
For your whole career, you will make mistakes and blunders—
Miss Flo, did you finish it?
no,
You— you just carry on.
OK, now lie down in the pool— we'll do it quick
It's fucking 40 degrees out.
Now. Get up and walk away...
Keep walking!

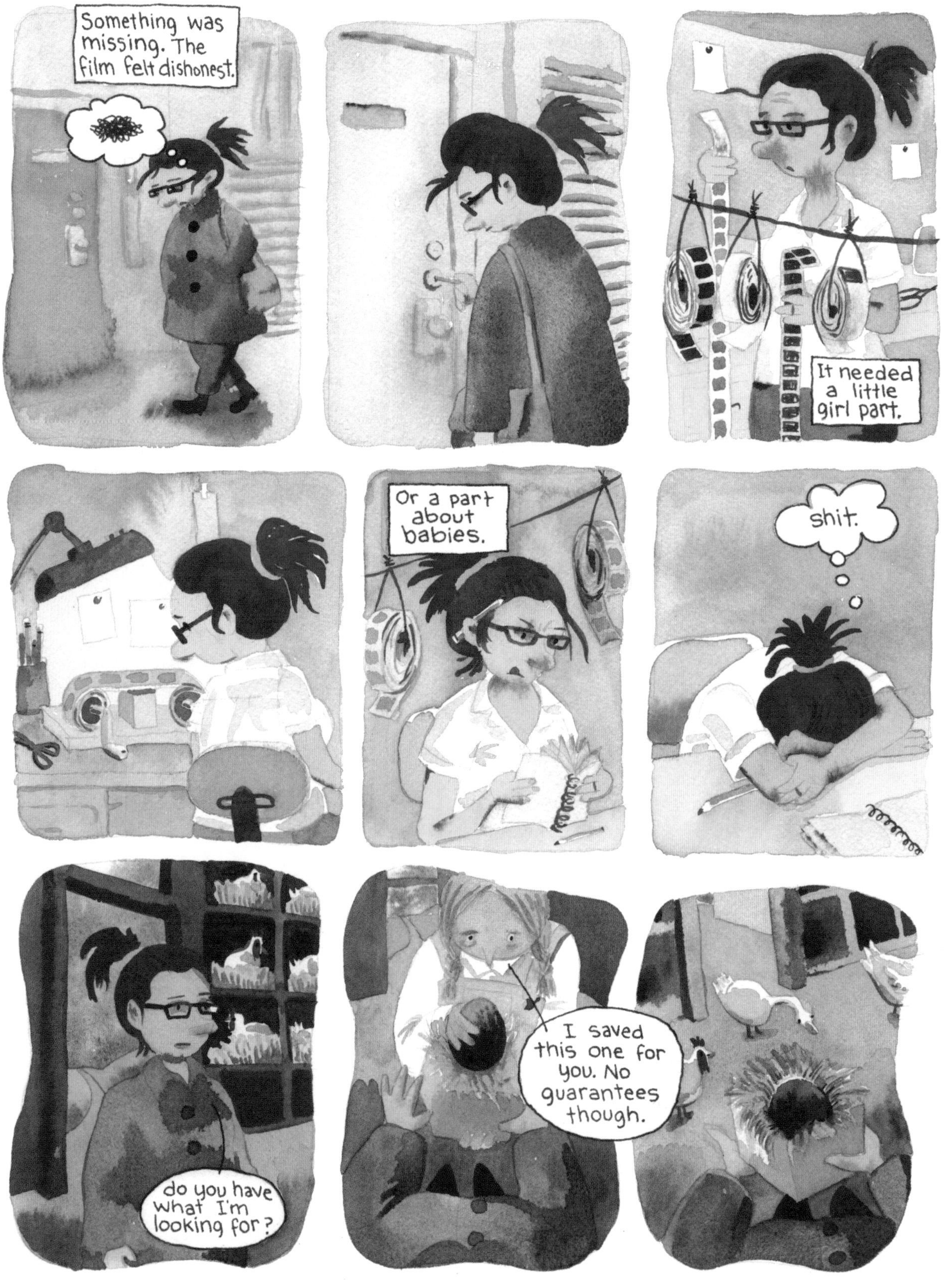

Something was missing. The film felt dishonest.
It needed a little girl part.
Or a part about babies.
shit.
do you have what I'm looking for?
I saved this one for you. No guarantees though.

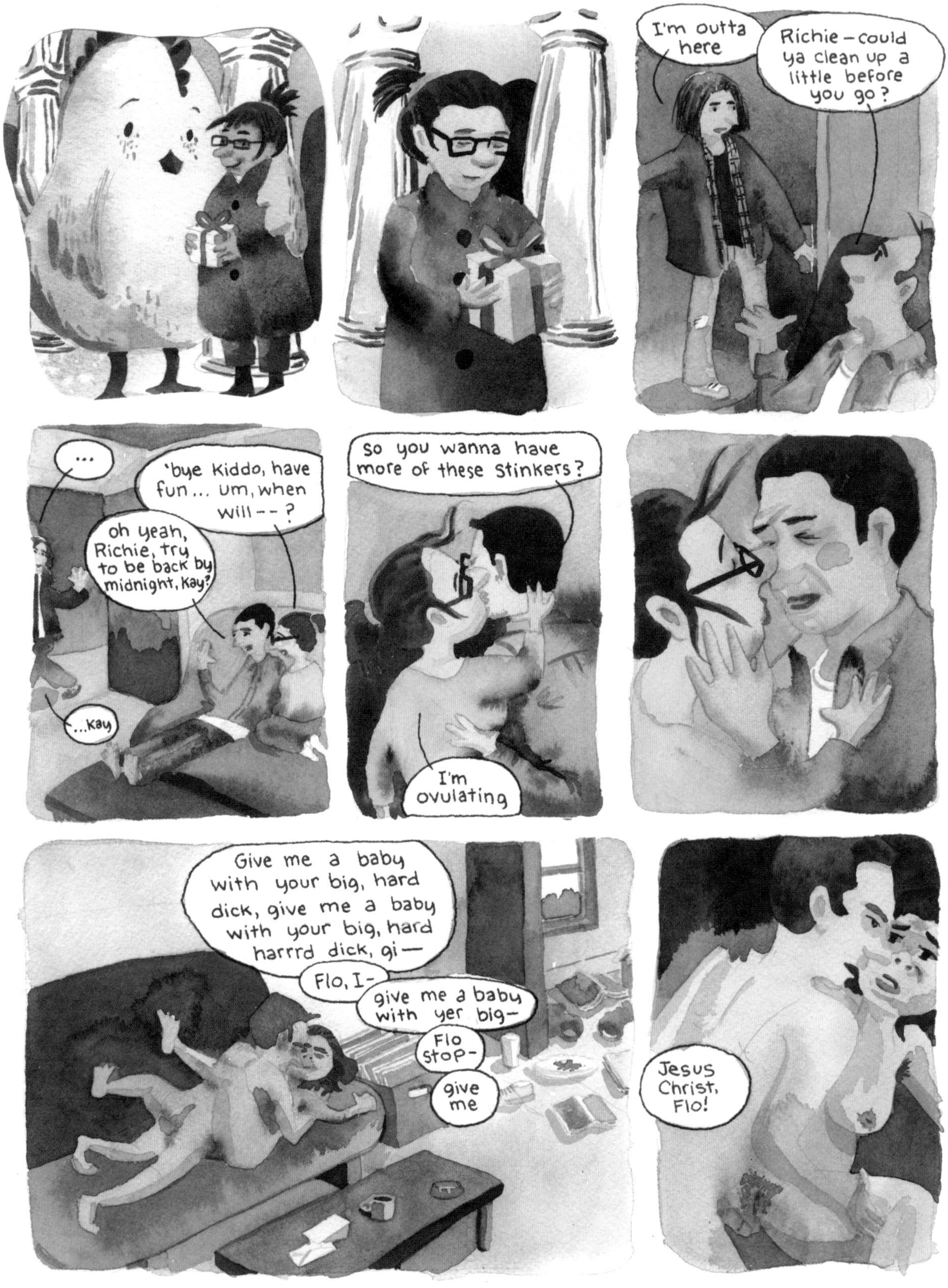
I'm outta here
Richie—could ya clean up a little before you go?
...
'bye kiddo, have fun... um, when will--?
oh yeah, Richie, try to be back by midnight, kay?
...kay
So you wanna have more of these stinkers?
I'm ovulating
Give me a baby with your big, hard dick, give me a baby with your big, hard harrrd dick, gi—
Flo, I-
give me a baby with yer big-
Flo stop-
give me
Jesus Christ, Flo!

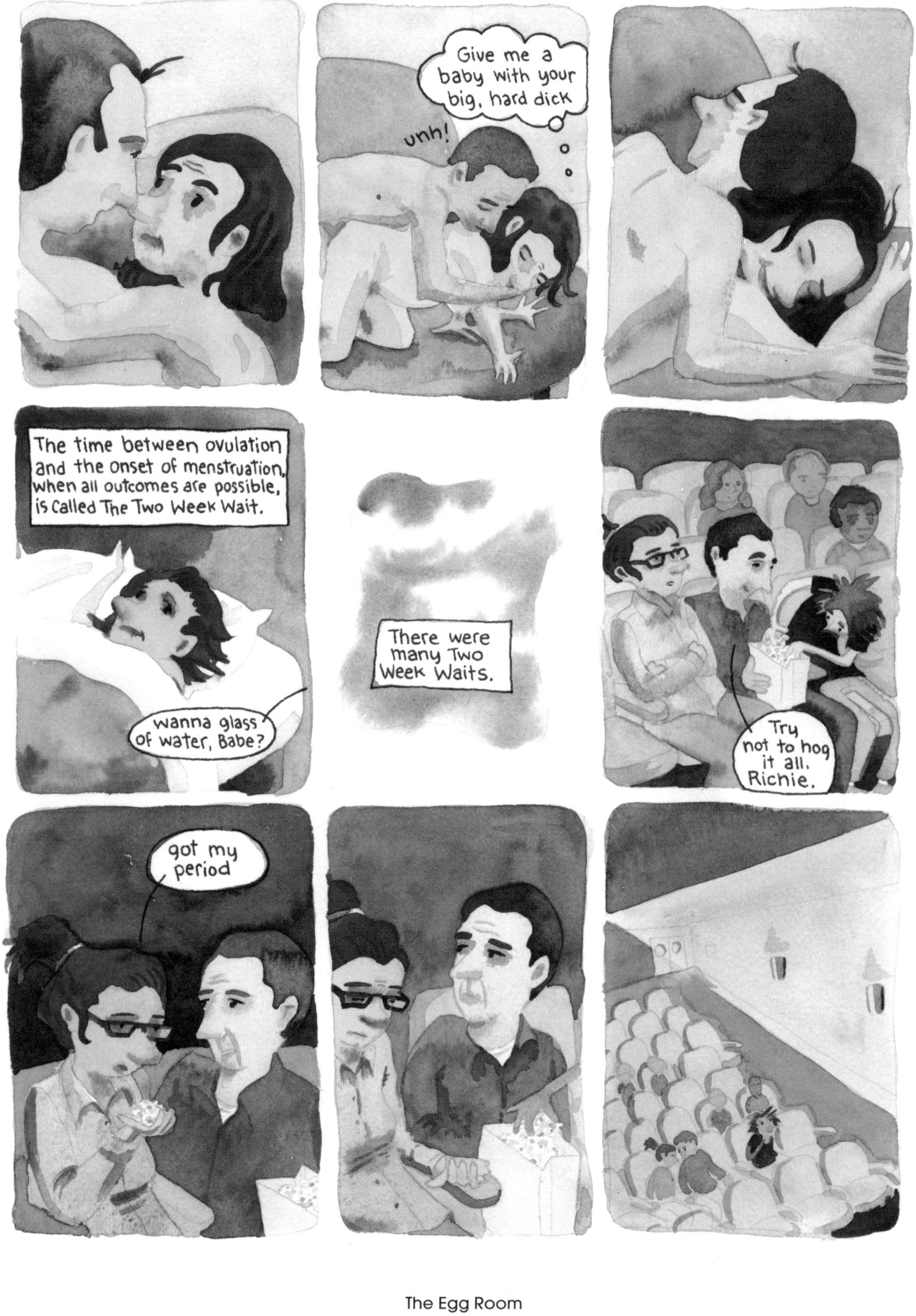

Give me a baby with your big, hard dick
unh!
The time between ovulation and the onset of menstruation, when all outcomes are possible, is called The Two Week Wait.
wanna glass of water, Babe?
There were many Two Week Waits.
Try not to hog it all, Richie.
got my period

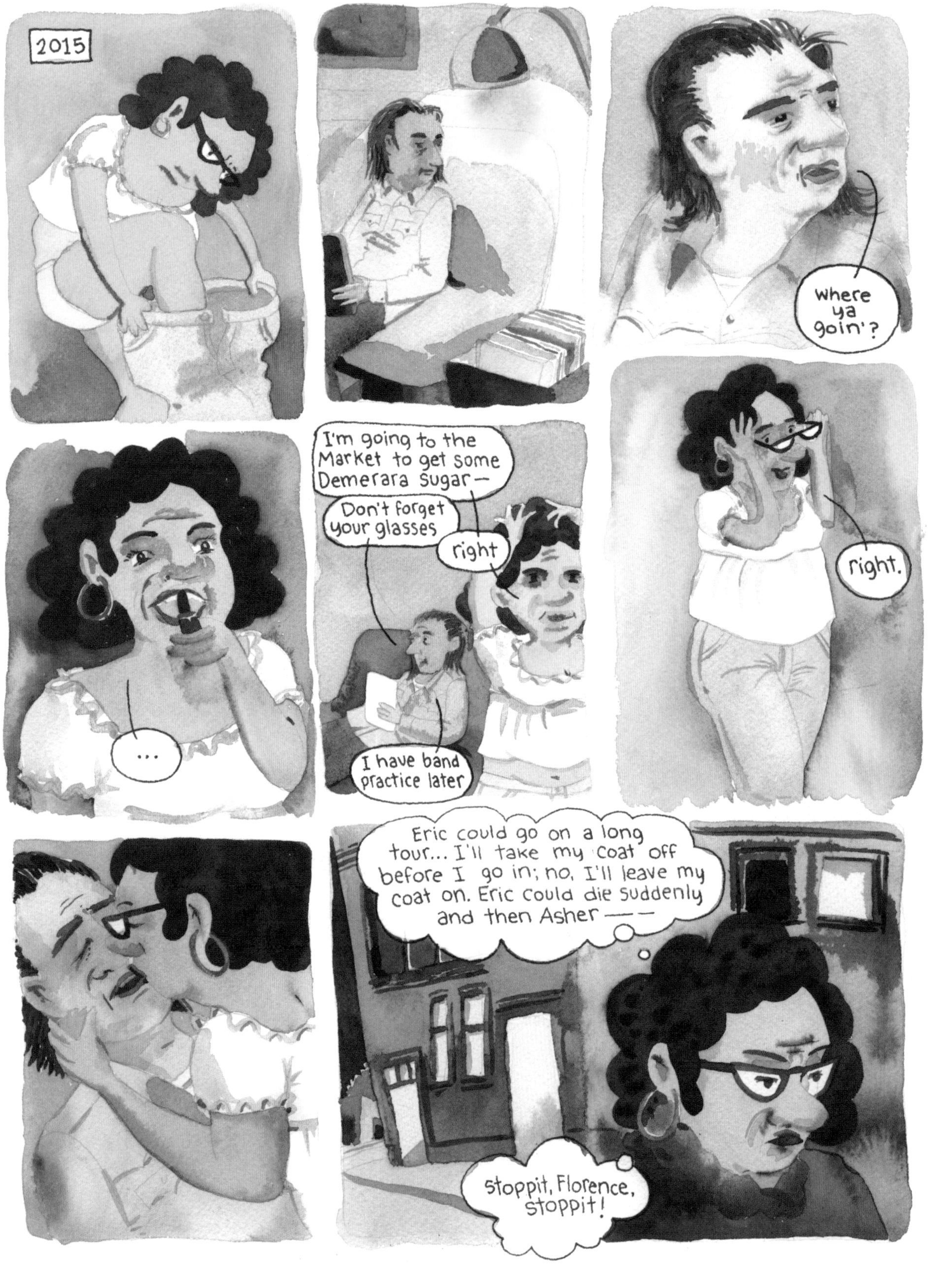
2015
Where ya goin'?
...
I'm going to the Market to get some Demerara Sugar—
Don't forget your glasses
right
I have band practice later
right.
Eric could go on a long tour... I'll take my coat off before I go in; no, I'll leave my coat on. Eric could die suddenly and then Asher ——
Stoppit, Florence, stoppit!

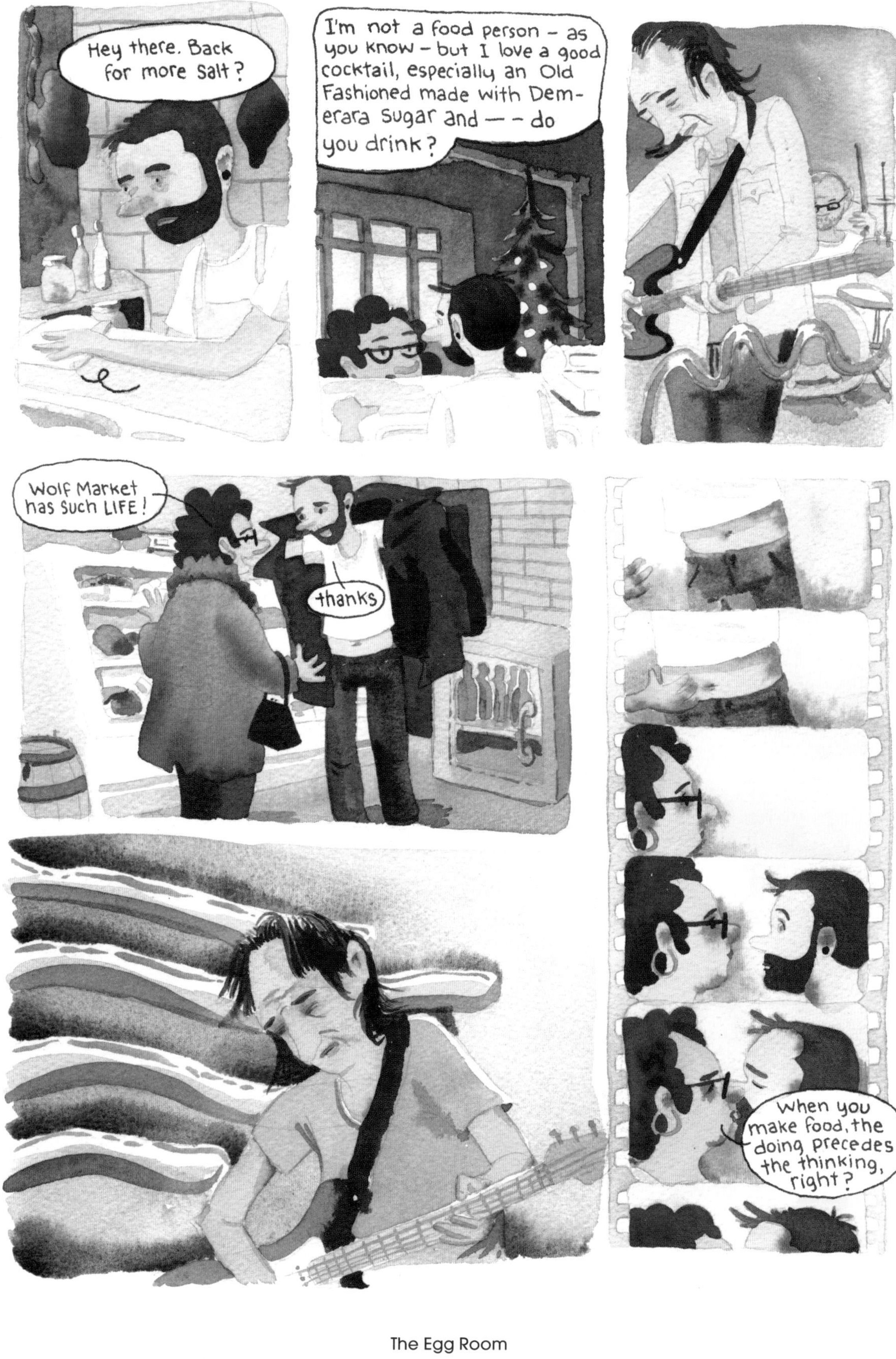
Hey there. Back for more salt?
I'm not a food person – as you know – but I love a good cocktail, especially an Old Fashioned made with Demerara Sugar and — – do you drink?
Wolf Market has such LIFE!
thanks
When you make food, the doing precedes the thinking, right?

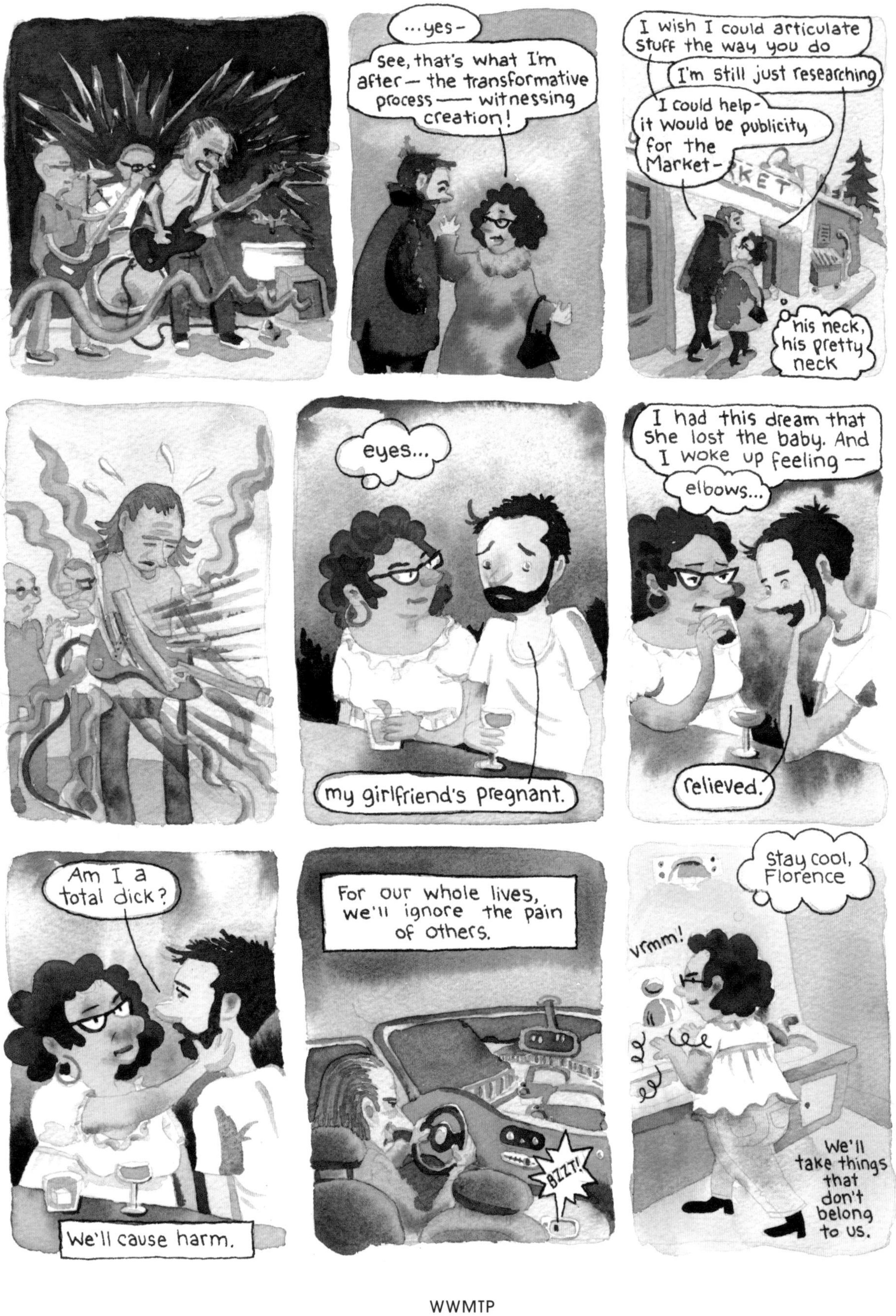

...yes-
See, that's what I'm after — the transformative process —— witnessing creation!
I wish I could articulate stuff the way you do
I'm still just researching
I could help- it would be publicity for the Market-
his neck, his pretty neck
eyes...
my girlfriend's pregnant.
I had this dream that she lost the baby. And I woke up feeling —
elbows...
relieved.
Am I a total dick?
We'll cause harm.
For our whole lives, we'll ignore the pain of others.
BZZT!
Stay cool, Florence
vrmm!
We'll take things that don't belong to us.

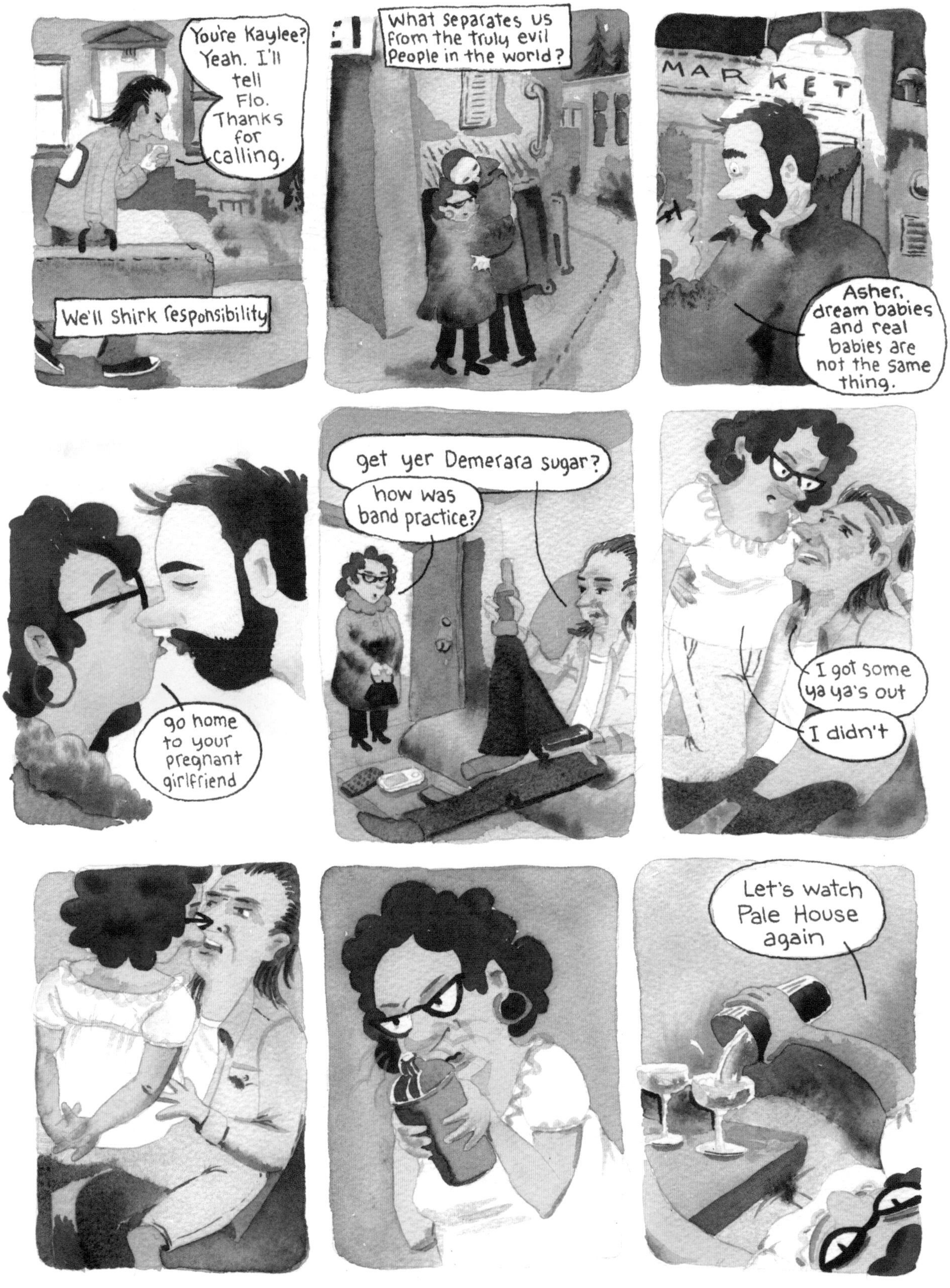
You're Kaylee? Yeah. I'll tell Flo. Thanks for calling.
We'll shirk responsibility
What separates us from the truly evil People in the world?
MARKET
Asher, dream babies and real babies are not the same thing.
go home to your pregnant girlfriend
get yer Demerara sugar?
how was band practice?
I got some ya ya's out
I didn't
Let's watch Pale House again

Zek, man. He's such a manipulator.

Shut up!

hey...

I enjoyed criticizing him back when I was younger — I figured I'd make something better than he did —

heyy...

But I didn't, Eric, I didn't!

Pshaw. Yer just like most people, barely hanging on.

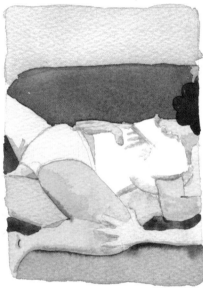

oh shit —

I just remembered — Kaylee called. Richie's in jail again

Fuck if I know what to do.

...

Sometimes a step-mother needs to speak up.

let's go to our boy.

4

Korin Voss

MEGAN KELSO

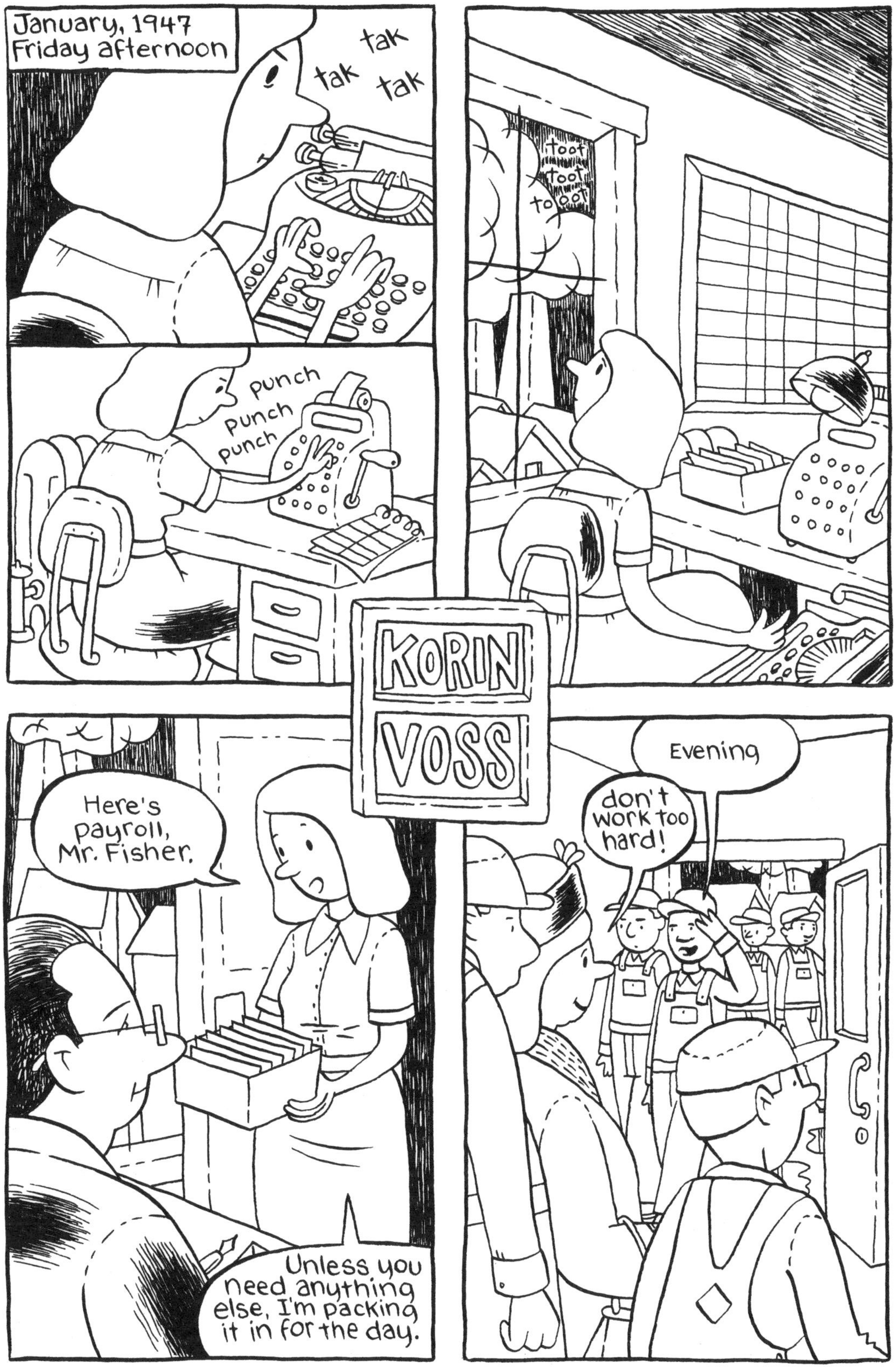
January, 1947
Friday afternoon
tak tak
tak tak
toot
toot
toot
punch
punch
punch
KORIN
VOSS
Here's payroll, Mr. Fisher.
Unless you need anything else, I'm packing it in for the day.
Evening
don't work too hard!

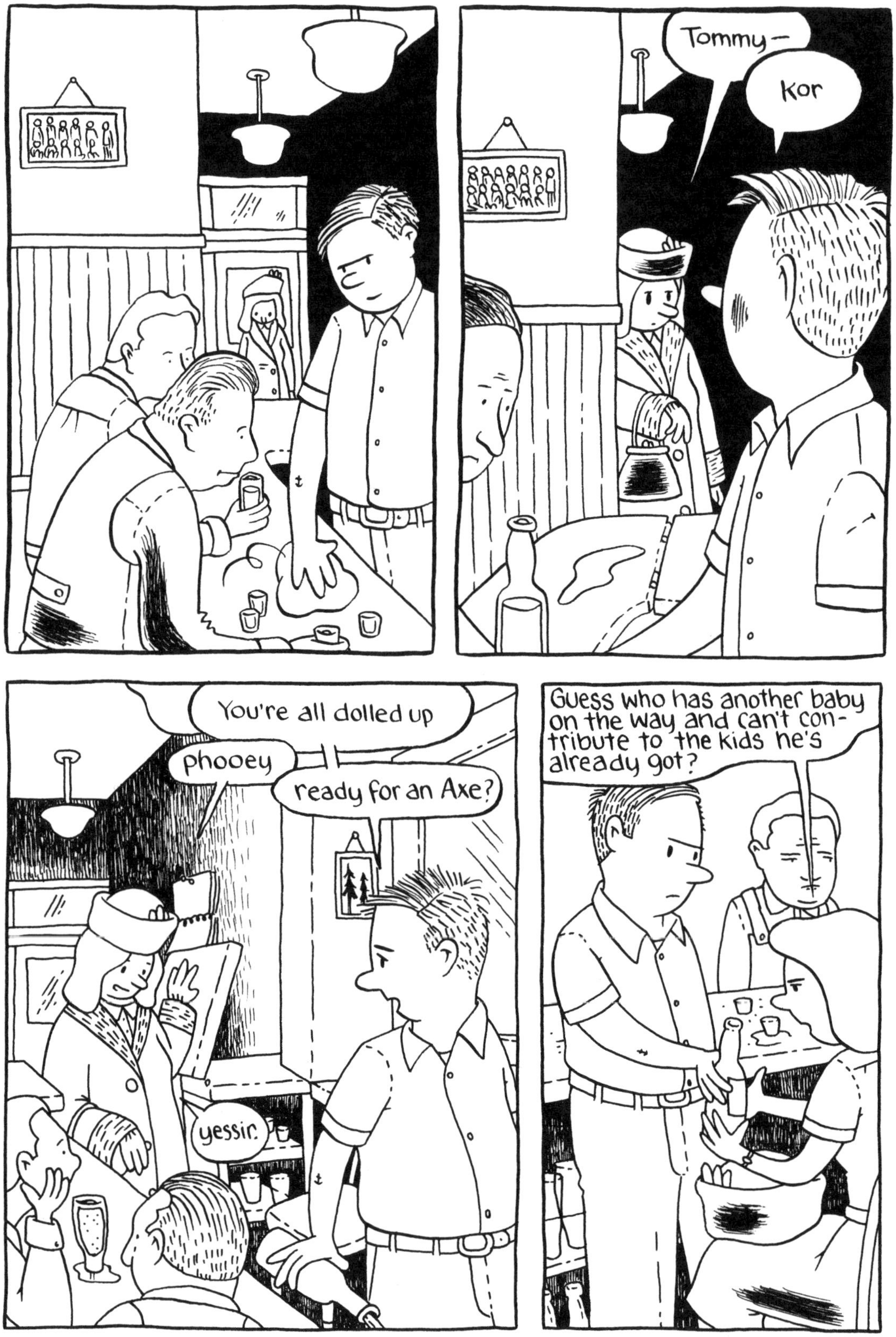
Tommy—
Kor
You're all dolled up
phooey
ready for an Axe?
yessir.
Guess who has another baby on the way and can't contribute to the kids he's already got?

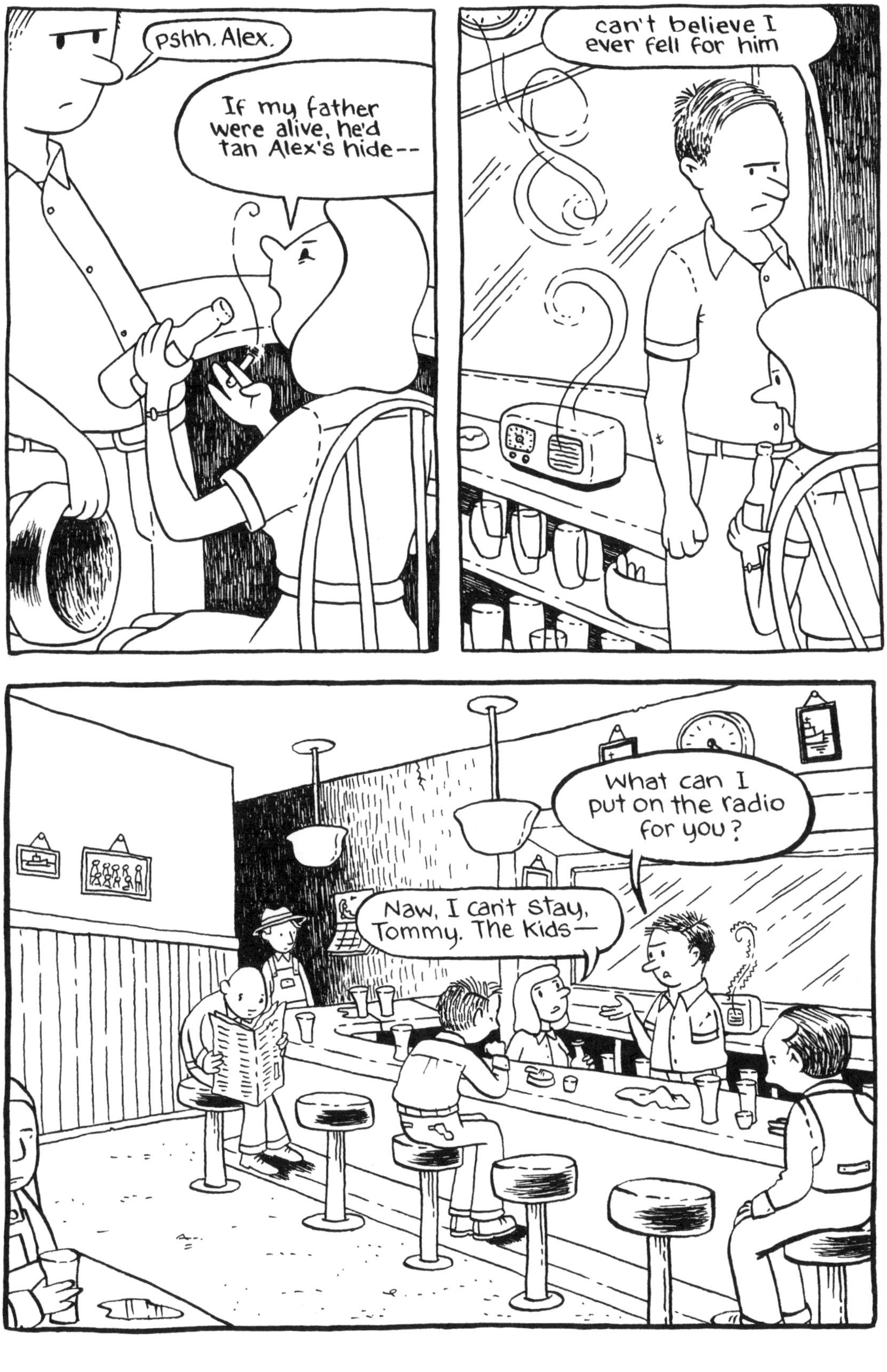
pshh. Alex.
If my father were alive, he'd tan Alex's hide--
can't believe I ever fell for him
What can I put on the radio for you?
Naw, I can't stay, Tommy. The Kids—

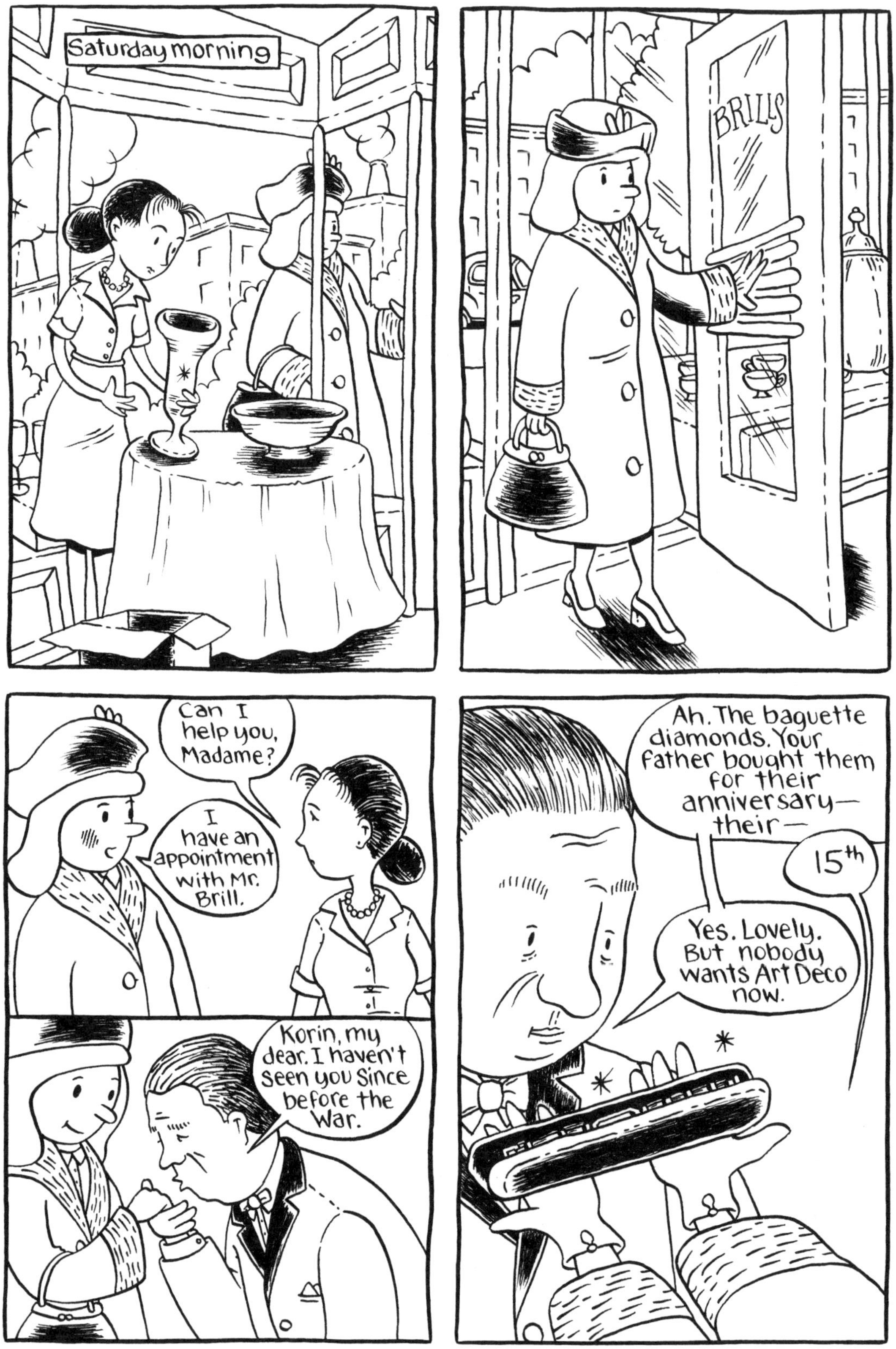
Saturday morning
BRILLS
Can I help you, Madame?
I have an appointment with Mr. Brill.
Korin, my dear. I haven't seen you since before the War.
Ah. The baguette diamonds. Your father bought them for their anniversary— their—
15th
Yes. Lovely. But nobody wants Art Deco now.

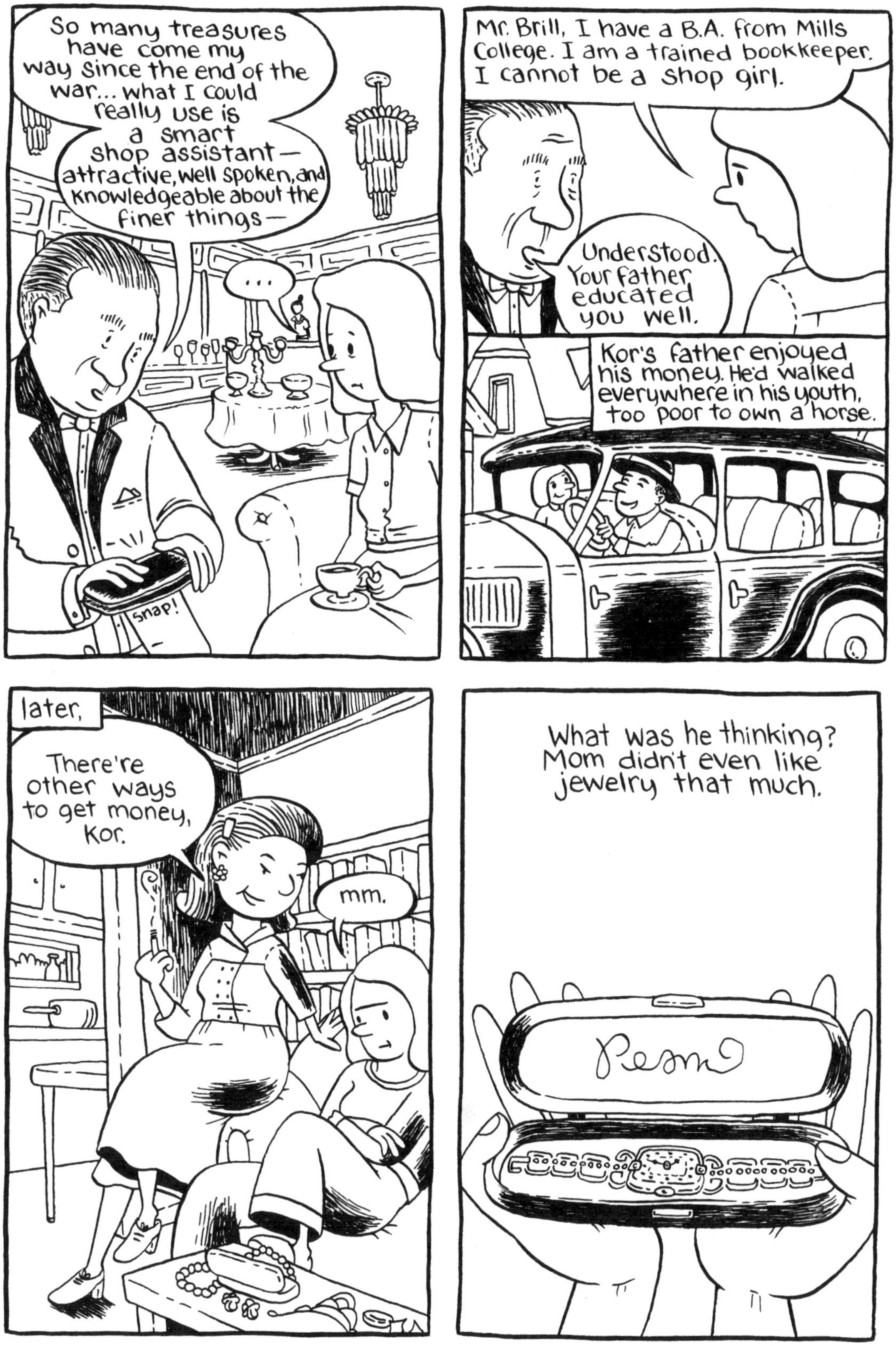
So many treasures have come my way since the end of the war... what I could really use is a smart shop assistant— attractive, well spoken, and knowledgeable about the finer things—
...
SNAP!
Mr. Brill, I have a B.A. from Mills College. I am a trained bookkeeper. I cannot be a shop girl.
Understood. Your father educated you well.
Kor's father enjoyed his money. He'd walked everywhere in his youth, too poor to own a horse.
later,
There're other ways to get money, Kor.
mm.
What was he thinking? Mom didn't even like jewelry that much.

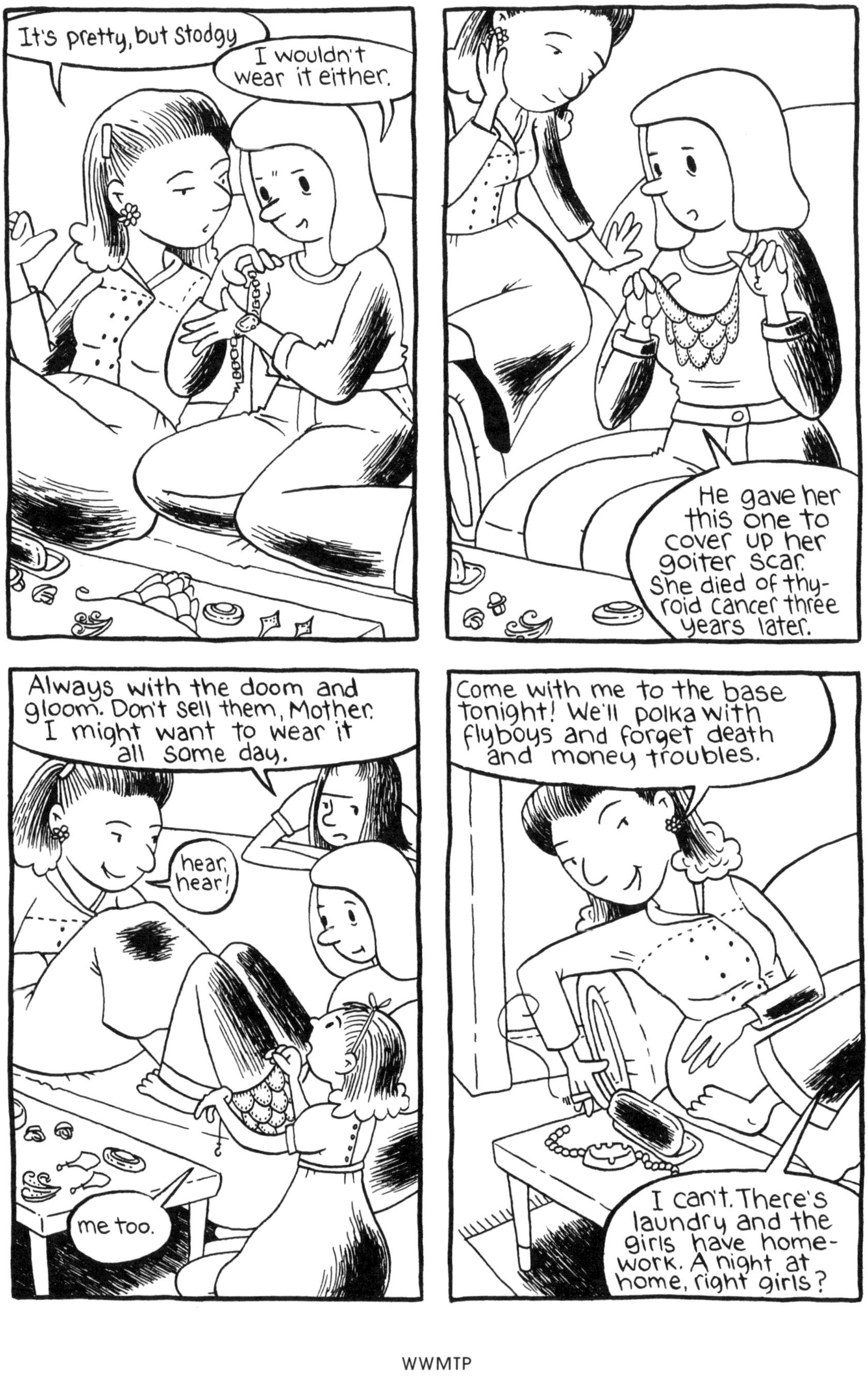
It's pretty, but stodgy
I wouldn't wear it either.
He gave her this one to cover up her goiter scar. She died of thyroid cancer three years later.
Always with the doom and gloom. Don't sell them, Mother. I might want to wear it all some day.
hear, hear!
me too.
Come with me to the base tonight! We'll polka with flyboys and forget death and money troubles.
I can't. There's laundry and the girls have homework. A night at home, right girls?

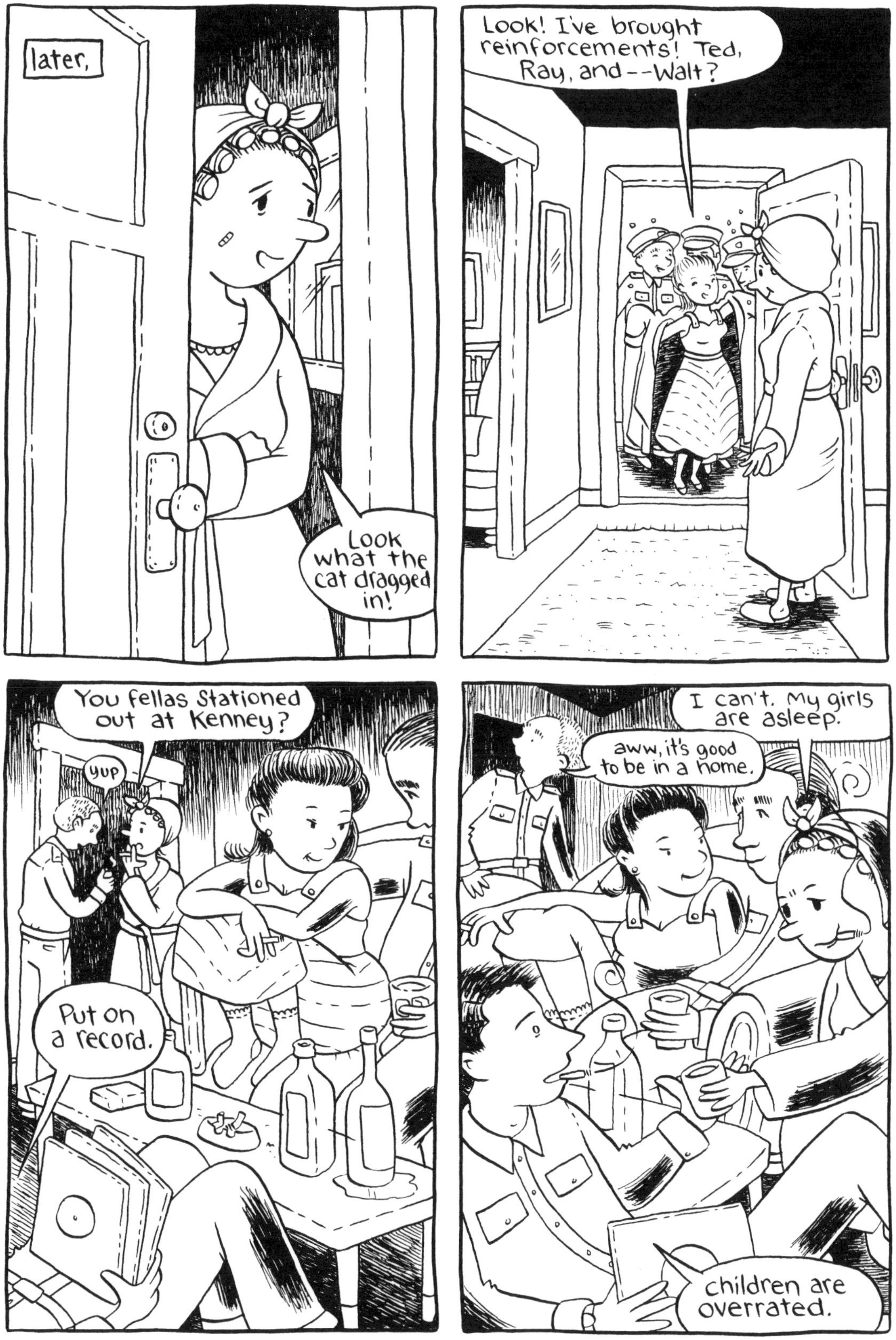

later,
Look what the cat dragged in!
Look! I've brought reinforcements! Ted, Ray, and--Walt?
You fellas stationed out at Kenney?
yup
Put on a record.
I can't. My girls are asleep.
aww, it's good to be in a home.
children are overrated.

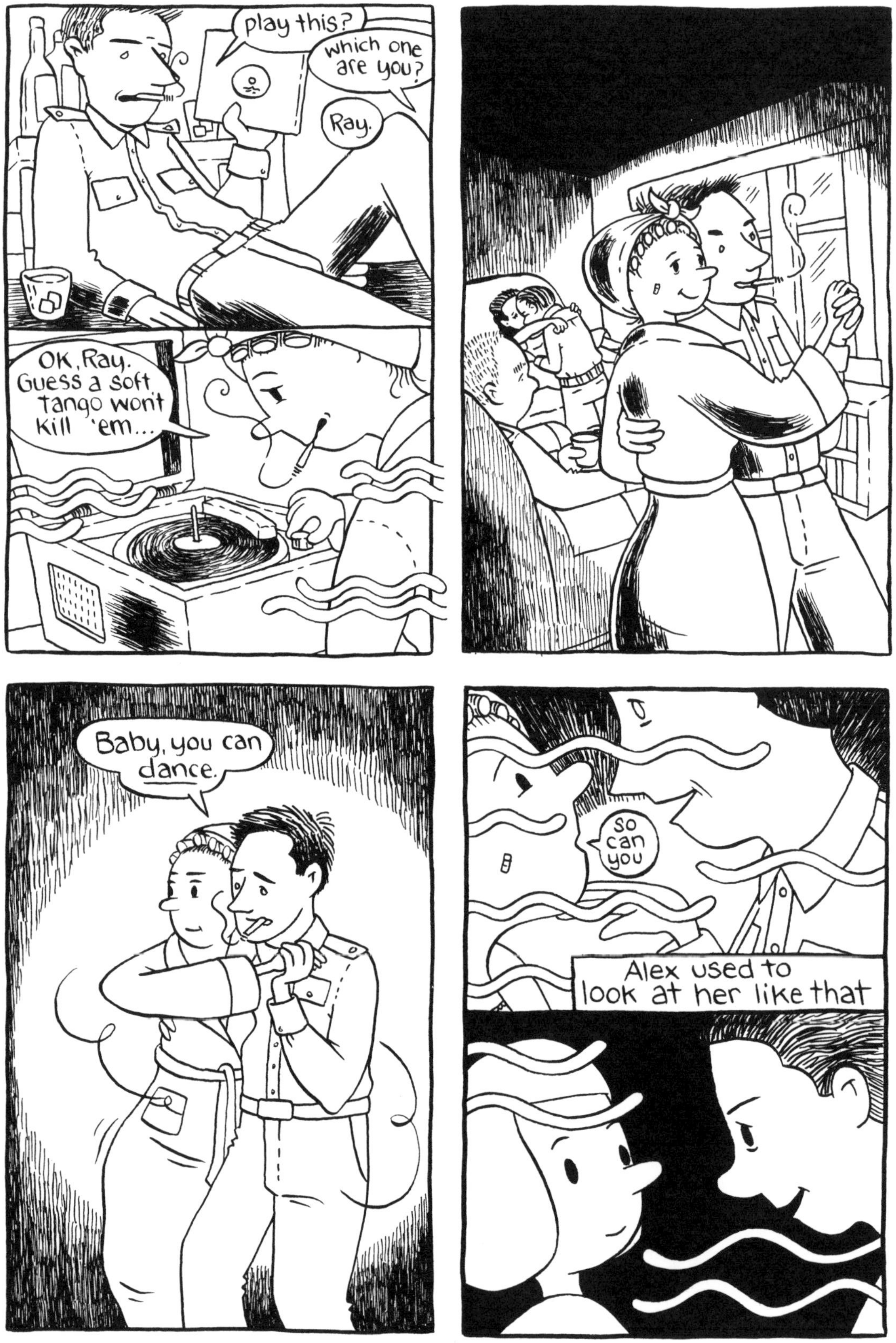
play this?
which one are you?
Ray.
OK, Ray. Guess a soft tango won't kill 'em...
Baby, you can dance.
so can you
Alex used to look at her like that

September, 1940
School had started, but they were still following the hop and apple harvests.
dance with me!
what's for dinner
potatoes!
potatoes?
poootaaaytooes

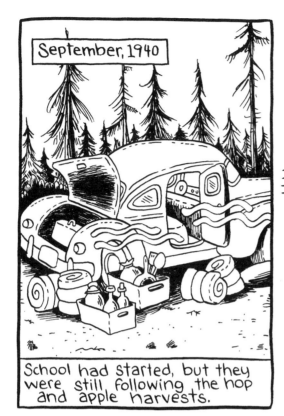

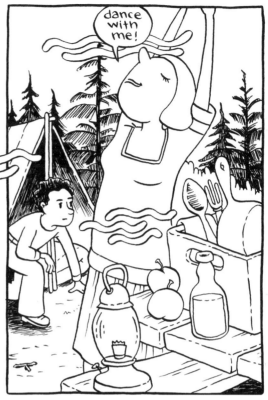

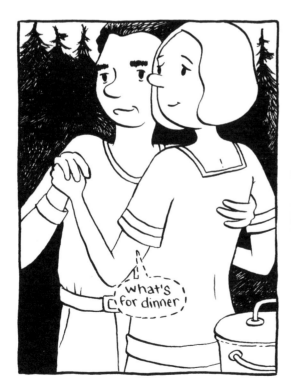

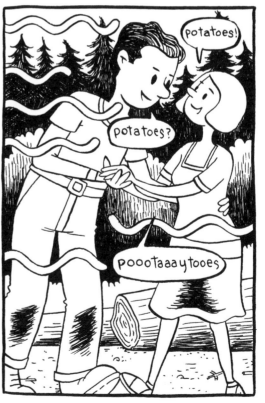

What she didn't understand was, they weren't running away together.

Pen go potty!

He was running away from _her_ — waiting for her to just give up and take the girls back to town.

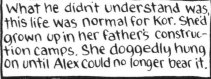

bark doesn't burn very well, Pen.

How many days of 2nd grade have you missed so far, Athena?

Daaad, it's not my fault!

What he didn't understand was, this life was normal for Kor. She'd grown up in her father's construction camps. She doggedly hung on until Alex could no longer bear it.

ZZZZ

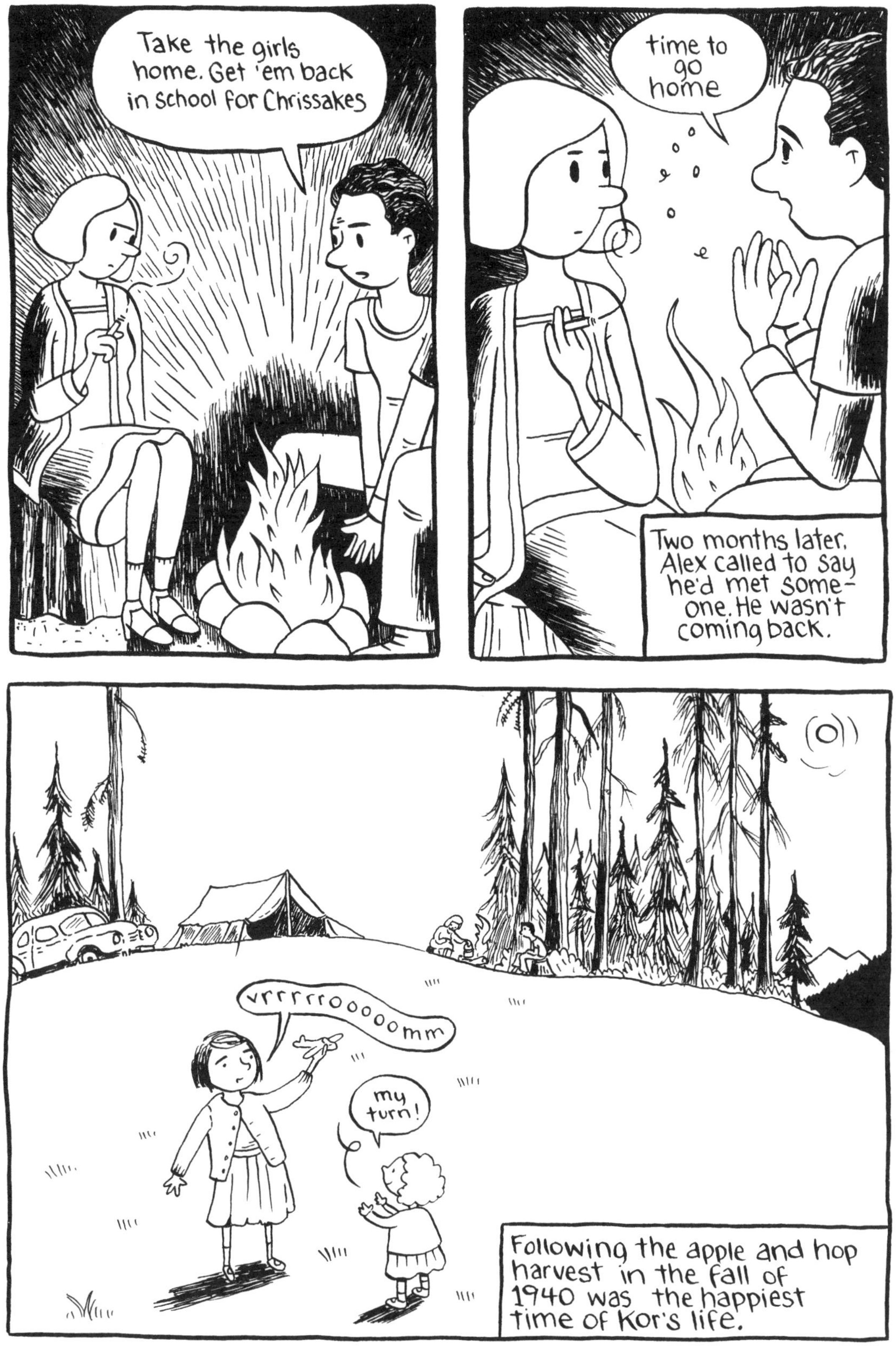
Take the girls home. Get 'em back in school for Chrissakes
time to go home
Two months later, Alex called to say he'd met someone. He wasn't coming back.
vrrrrroooooomm
my turn!
Following the apple and hop harvest in the fall of 1940 was the happiest time of Kor's life.

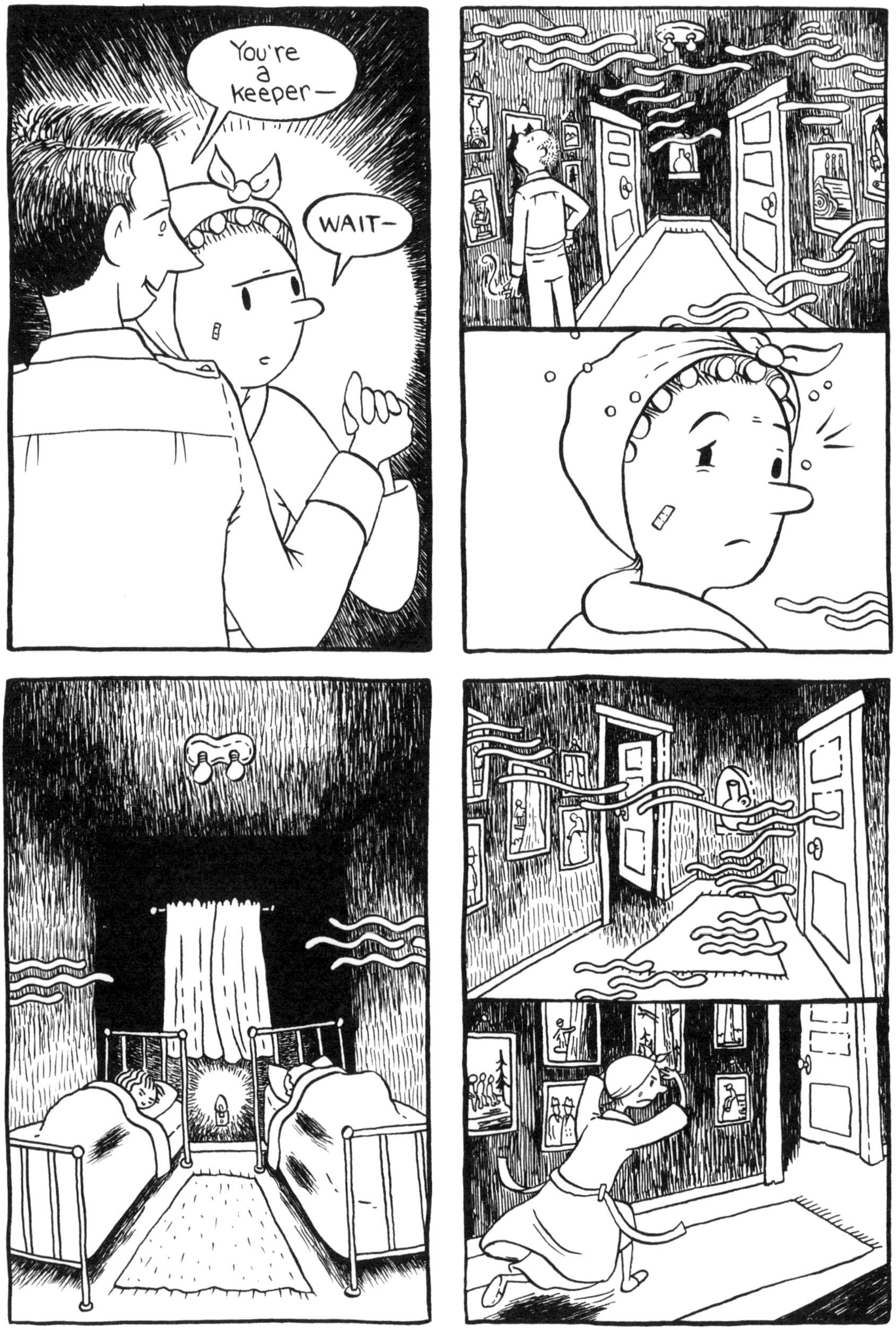
You're a keeper—
WAIT-

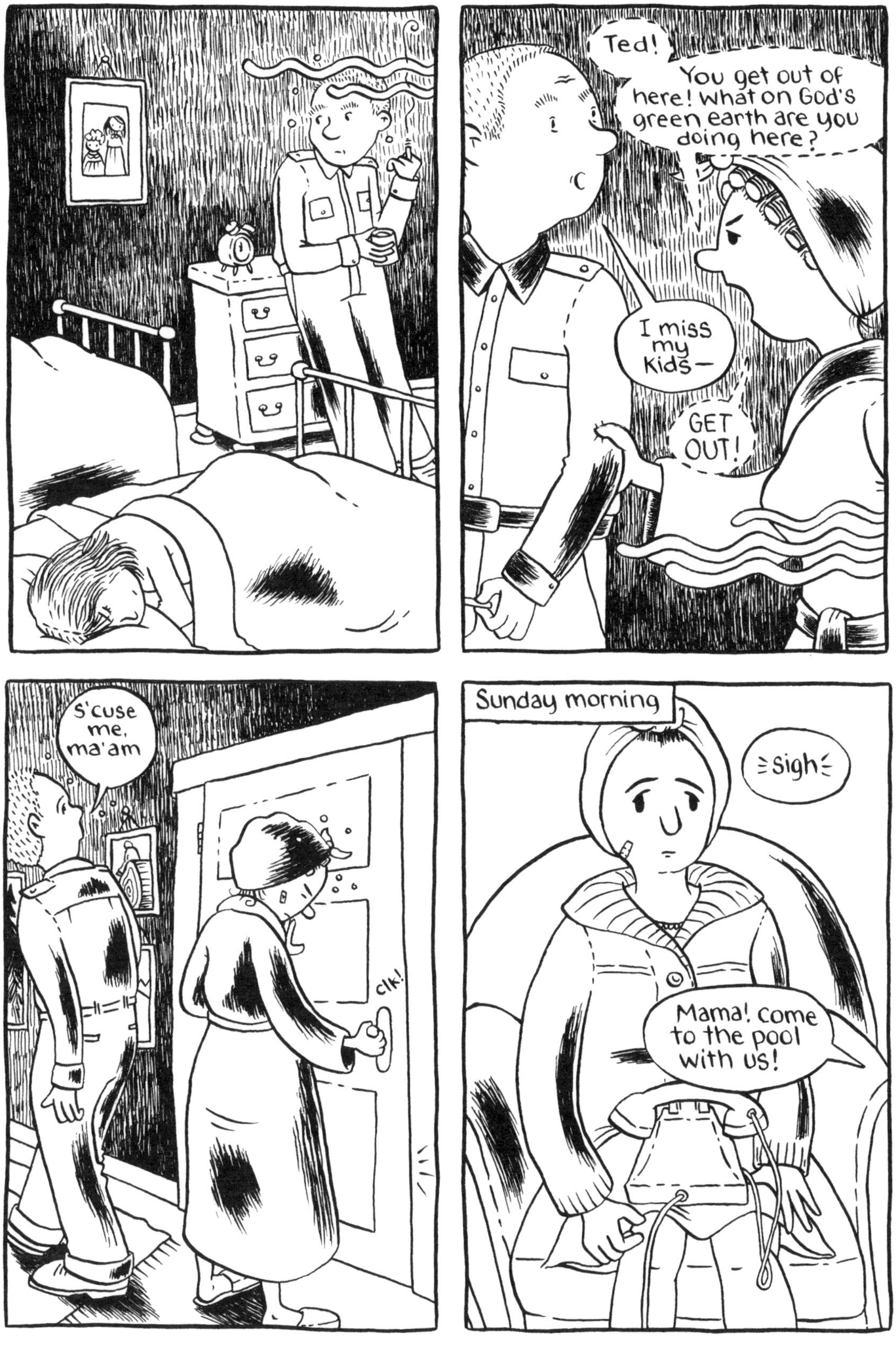
Ted!
You get out of here! What on God's green earth are you doing here?
I miss my kids—
GET OUT!
S'cuse me, ma'am
clk!
Sunday morning
Sigh
Mama! come to the pool with us!

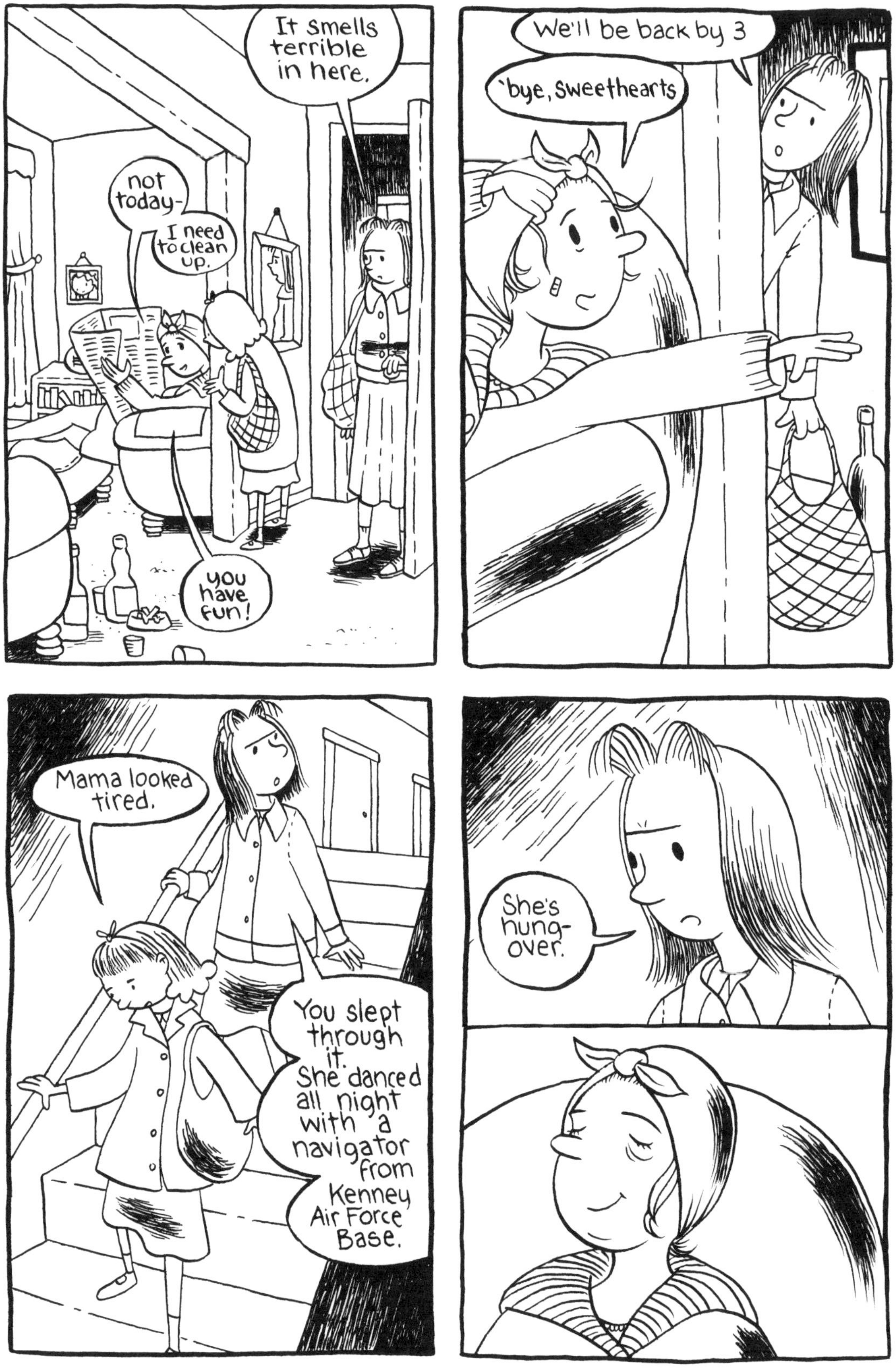
It smells terrible in here.
not today-
I need to clean up.
you have fun!
We'll be back by 3
`bye, sweethearts
Mama looked tired.
You slept through it. She danced all night with a navigator from Kenney Air Force Base.
She's hung-over.

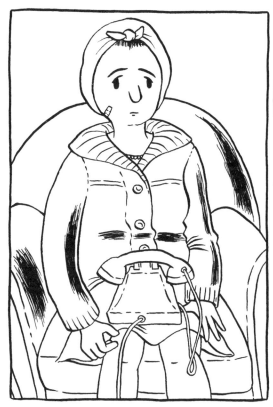

Hi. They're fine. Alex? It's been tight at the end of the month lately. Haven't gotten any money from you since—

Alex?

Oh, Korrr... It's just plain bad timing! Got expenses up the wazoo. Spring will be better. Can you hold on?

Her father had built roads, traded horses, mined coal, and distilled his own gin. He made and lost a fortune, then died when she was nineteen.

His final words to her were, "be a good girl"

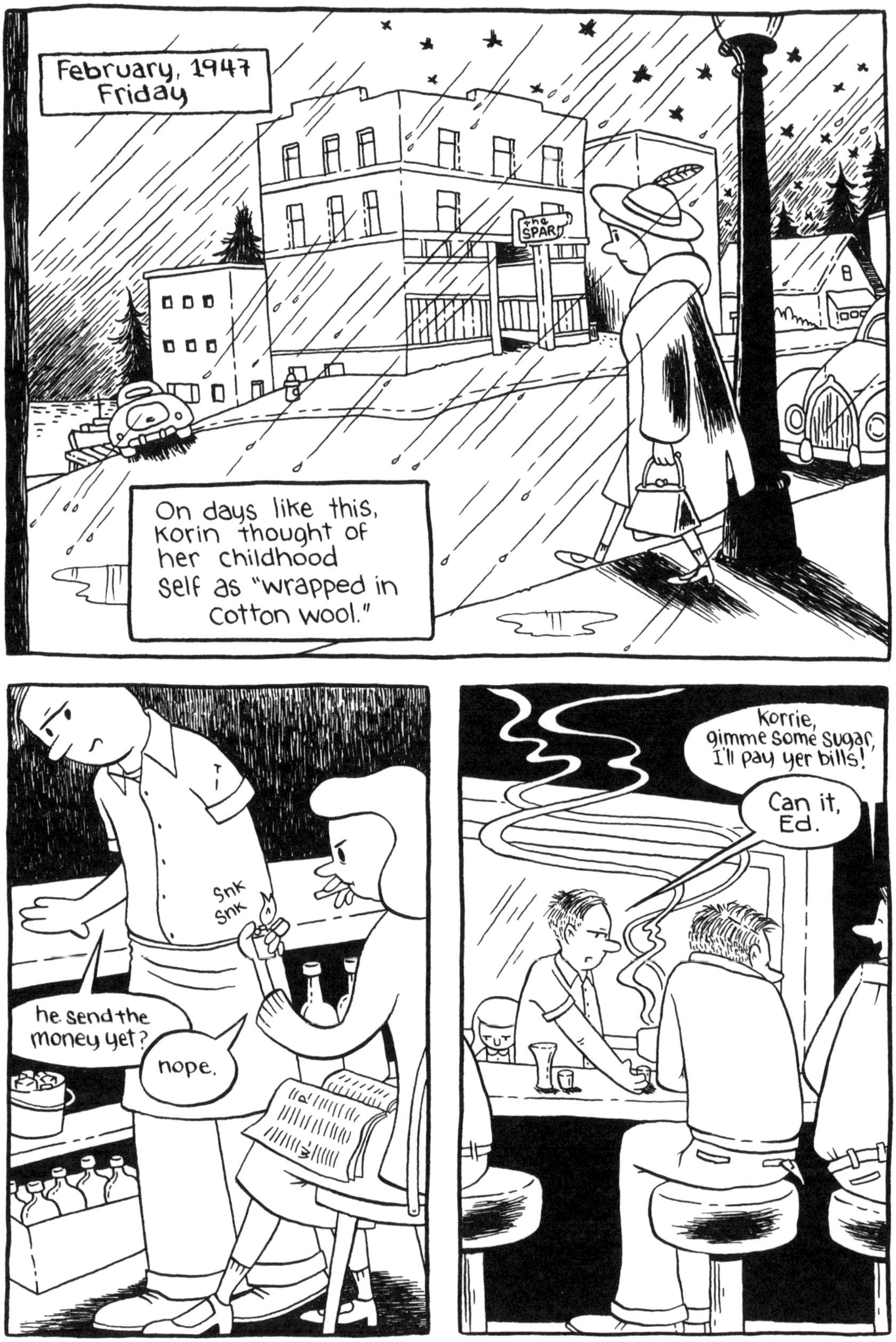
February, 1947
Friday
the SPAR
On days like this, Korin thought of her childhood self as "wrapped in cotton wool."
snk
snk
he send the money yet?
nope.
Korrie, gimme some sugar, I'll pay yer bills!
Can it, Ed.

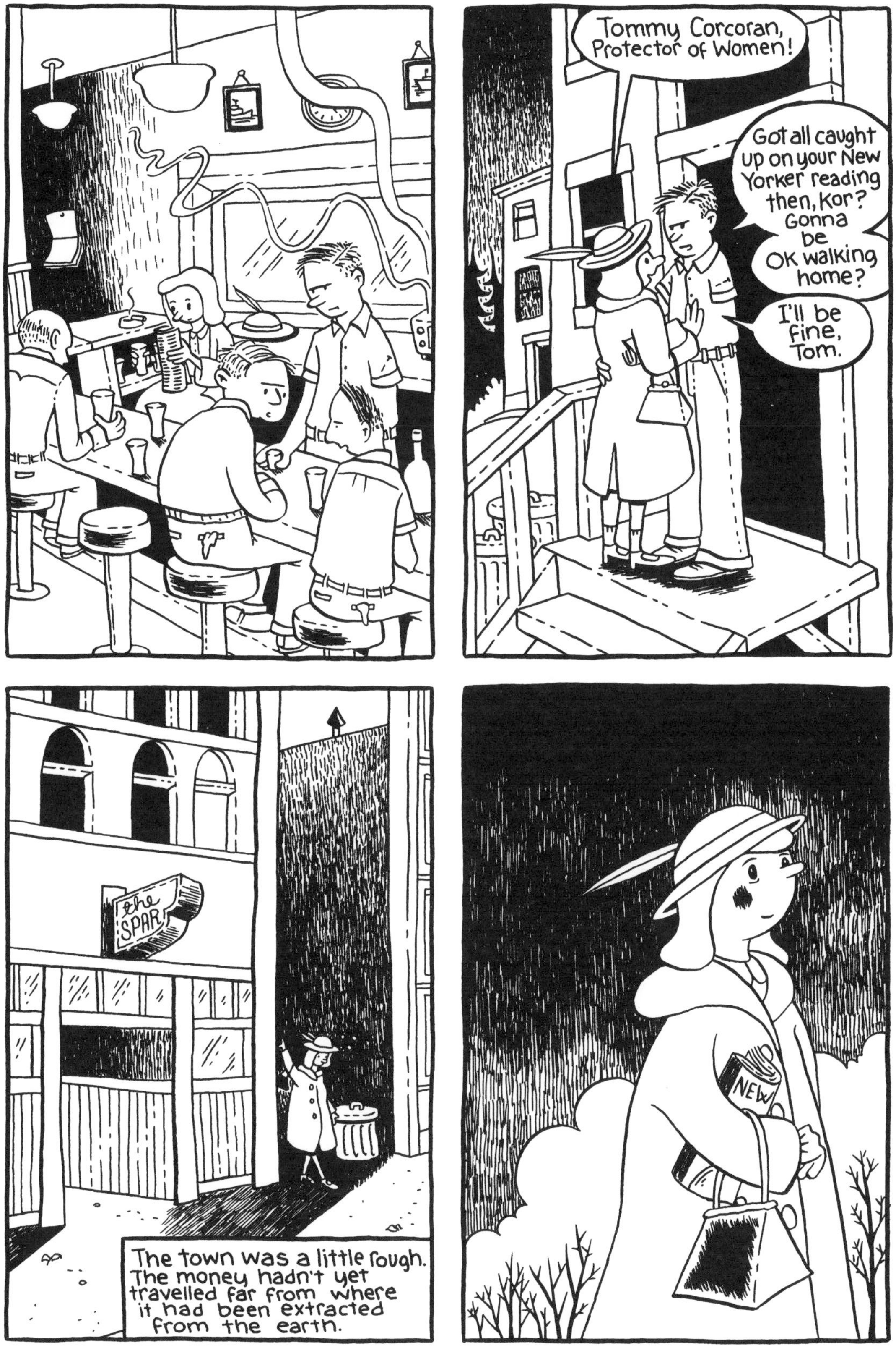
Tommy Corcoran, Protector of Women!
Got all caught up on your New Yorker reading then, Kor? Gonna be OK walking home?
I'll be fine, Tom.
the SPAR
The town was a little rough. The money hadn't yet travelled far from where it had been extracted from the earth.
NEW

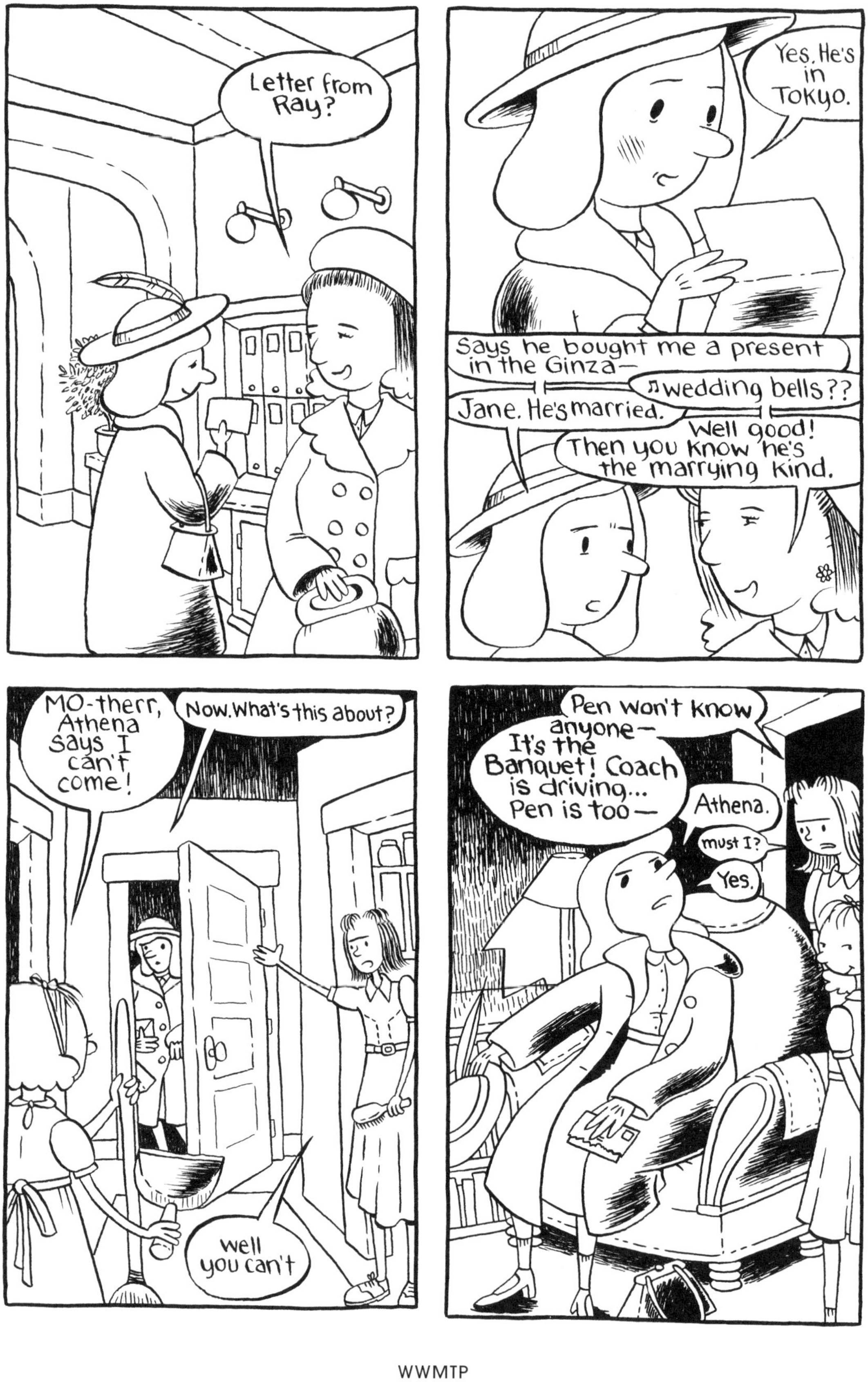
Letter from Ray?
Yes. He's in Tokyo.
Says he bought me a present in the Ginza—
♫ wedding bells??
Jane. He's married.
Well good! Then you know he's the marrying kind.
MO-therr, Athena says I can't come!
Now. What's this about?
well you can't
Pen won't know anyone—
It's the Banquet! Coach is driving... Pen is too—
Athena.
must I?
Yes.

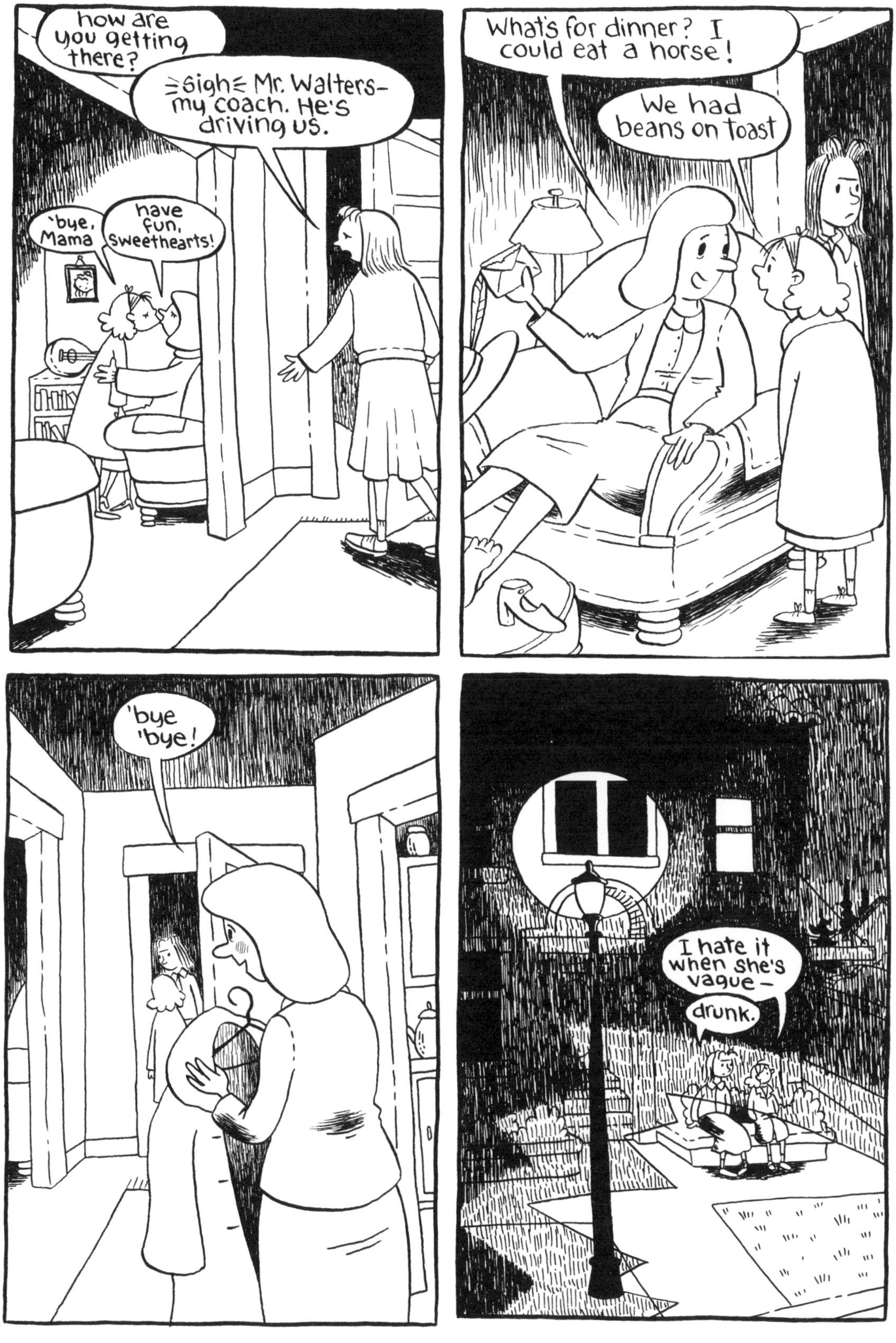
how are you getting there?
≡sigh≡ Mr. Walters- my coach. He's driving us.
'bye, Mama
have fun, sweethearts!
What's for dinner? I could eat a horse!
We had beans on toast
'bye 'bye!
I hate it when she's vague-
drunk.

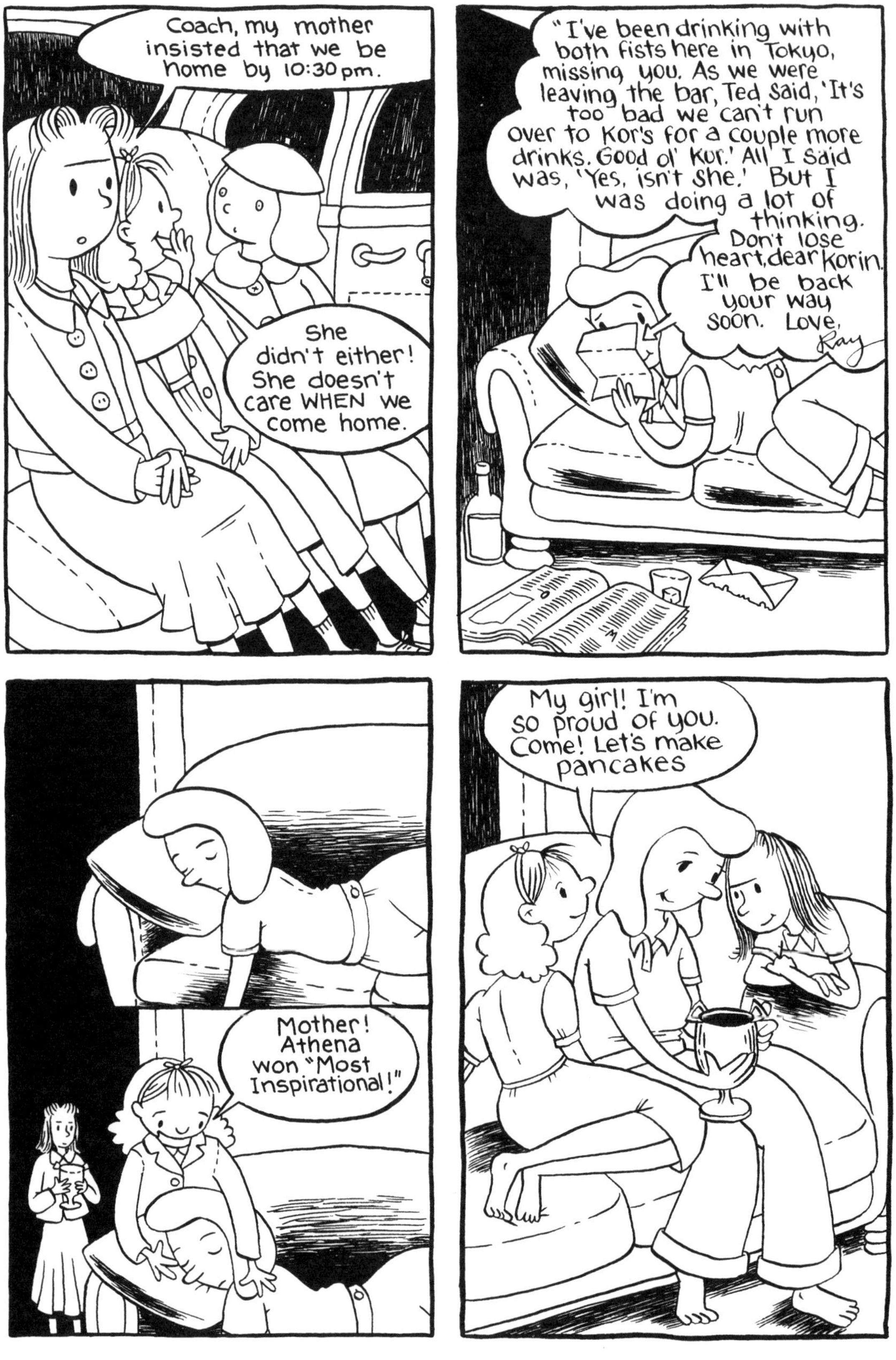
Coach, my mother insisted that we be home by 10:30 pm.
She didn't either! She doesn't care WHEN we come home.
"I've been drinking with both fists here in Tokyo, missing you. As we were leaving the bar, Ted said, 'It's too bad we can't run over to Kor's for a couple more drinks. Good ol' Kor.' All I said was, 'Yes, isn't she.' But I was doing a lot of thinking.
Don't lose heart, dear Korin. I'll be back your way soon. Love, Ray
Mother! Athena won "Most Inspirational!"
My girl! I'm so proud of you. Come! Let's make pancakes

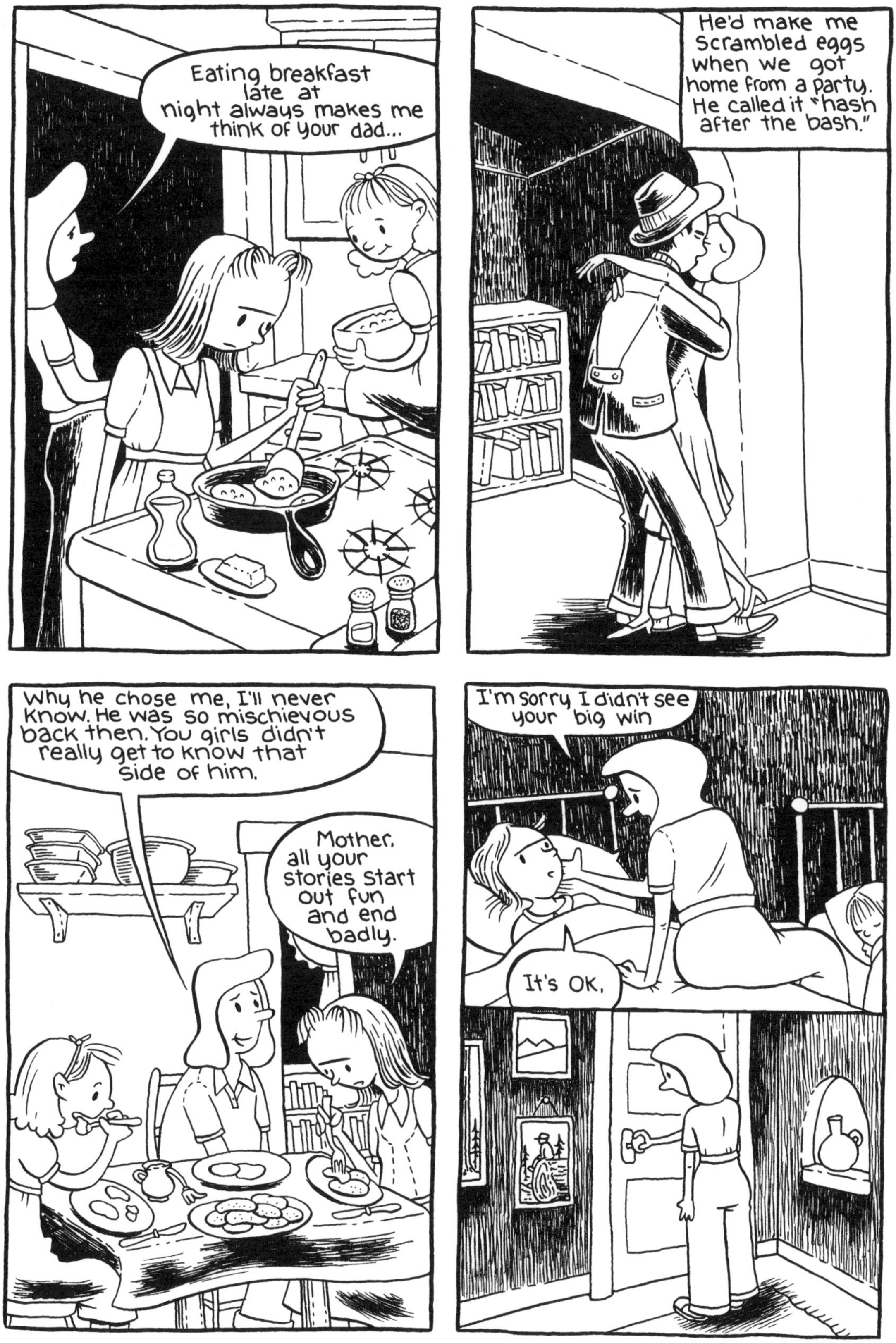
Eating breakfast late at night always makes me think of your dad...
He'd make me scrambled eggs when we got home from a party. He called it "hash after the bash."
Why he chose me, I'll never know. He was so mischievous back then. You girls didn't really get to know that side of him.
Mother, all your stories start out fun and end badly.
I'm sorry I didn't see your big win
It's OK,

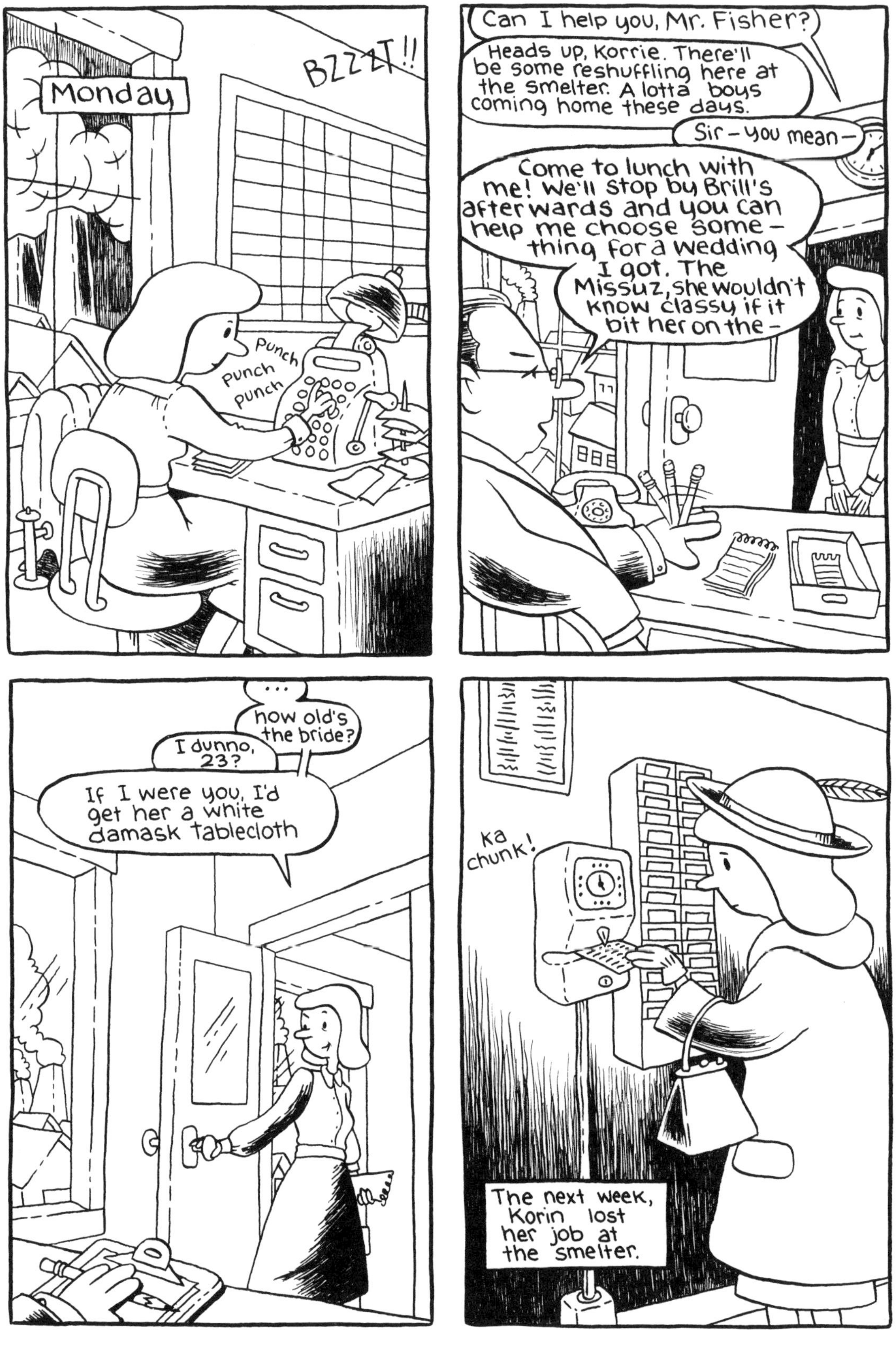
Monday
BZZZT!!
Punch
punch
punch
Can I help you, Mr. Fisher?
Heads up, Korrie. There'll be some reshuffling here at the smelter. A lotta boys coming home these days.
Sir – you mean–
Come to lunch with me! We'll stop by Brill's afterwards and you can help me choose some-thing for a wedding I got. The Missuz, she wouldn't know classy if it bit her on the–
...
how old's the bride?
I dunno, 23?
If I were you, I'd get her a white damask tablecloth
Ka chunk!
The next week, Korin lost her job at the smelter.

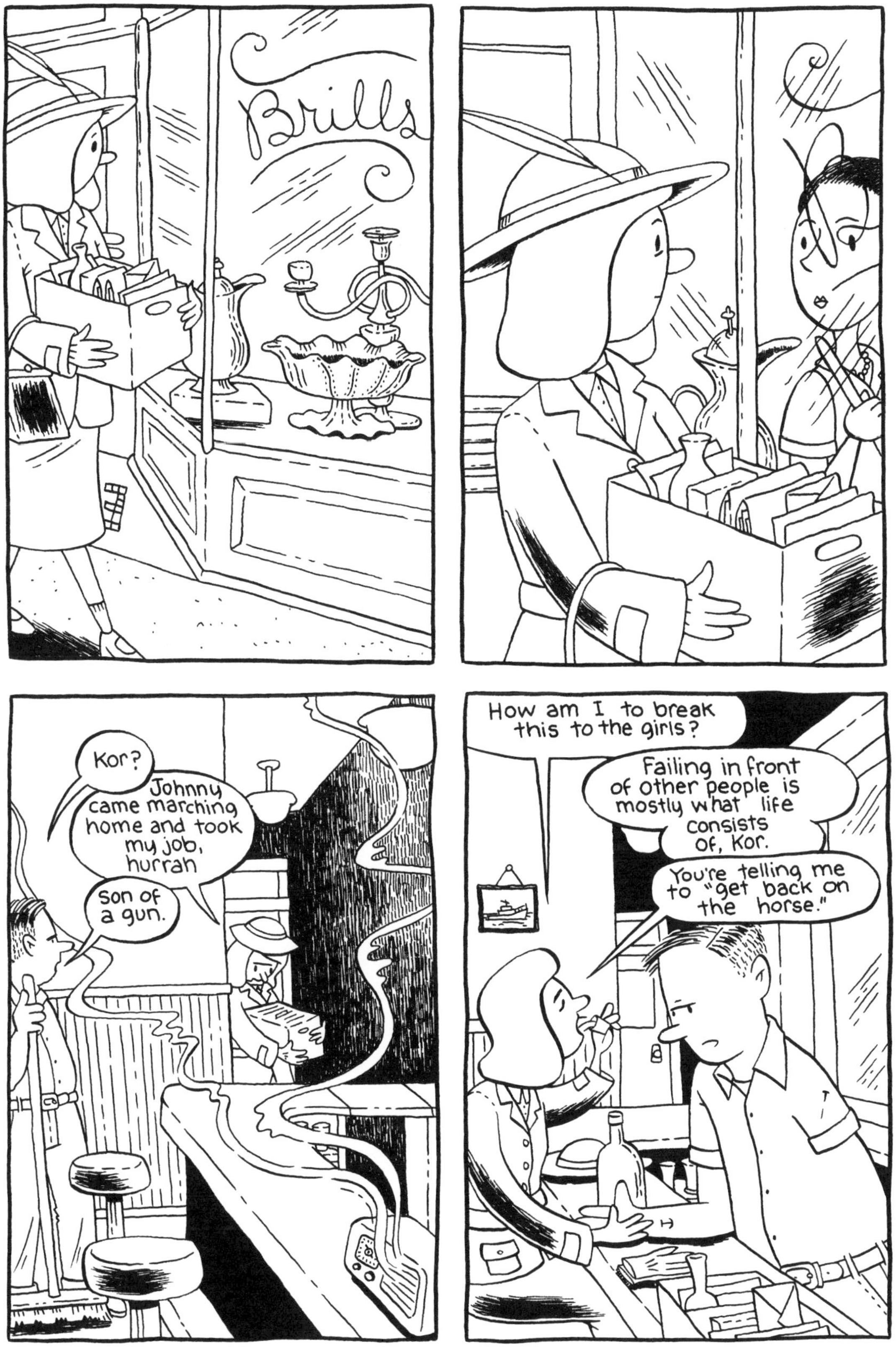
Brills
Kor?
Johnny came marching home and took my job, hurrah
Son of a gun.
How am I to break this to the girls?
Failing in front of other people is mostly what life consists of, Kor.
You're telling me to "get back on the horse."

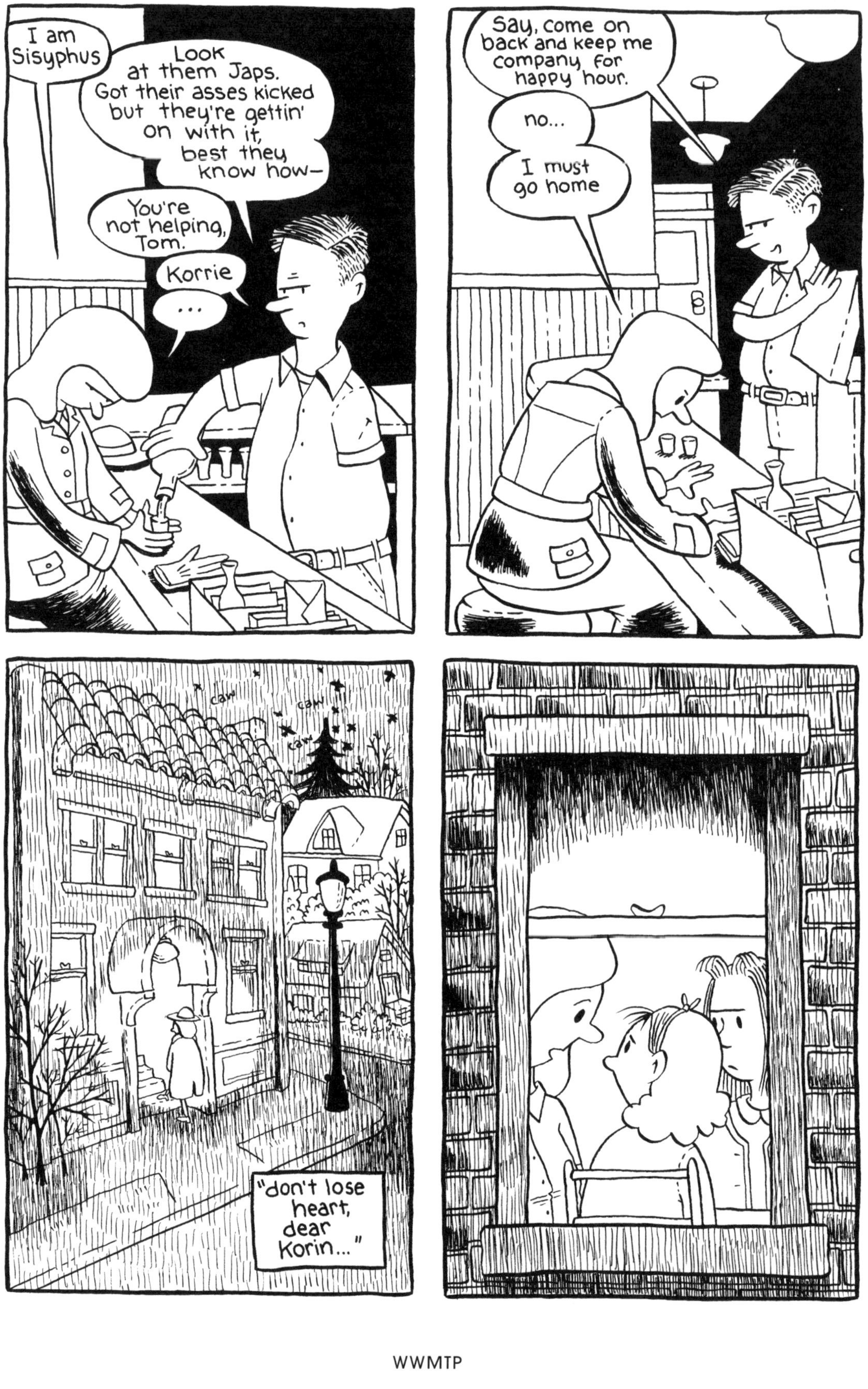

I am Sisyphus
Look at them Japs. Got their asses kicked but they're gettin' on with it, best they know how—
You're not helping, Tom.
Korrie
...
Say, come on back and keep me company for happy hour.
no...
I must go home
caw
caw
caw
"don't lose heart, dear Korin..."

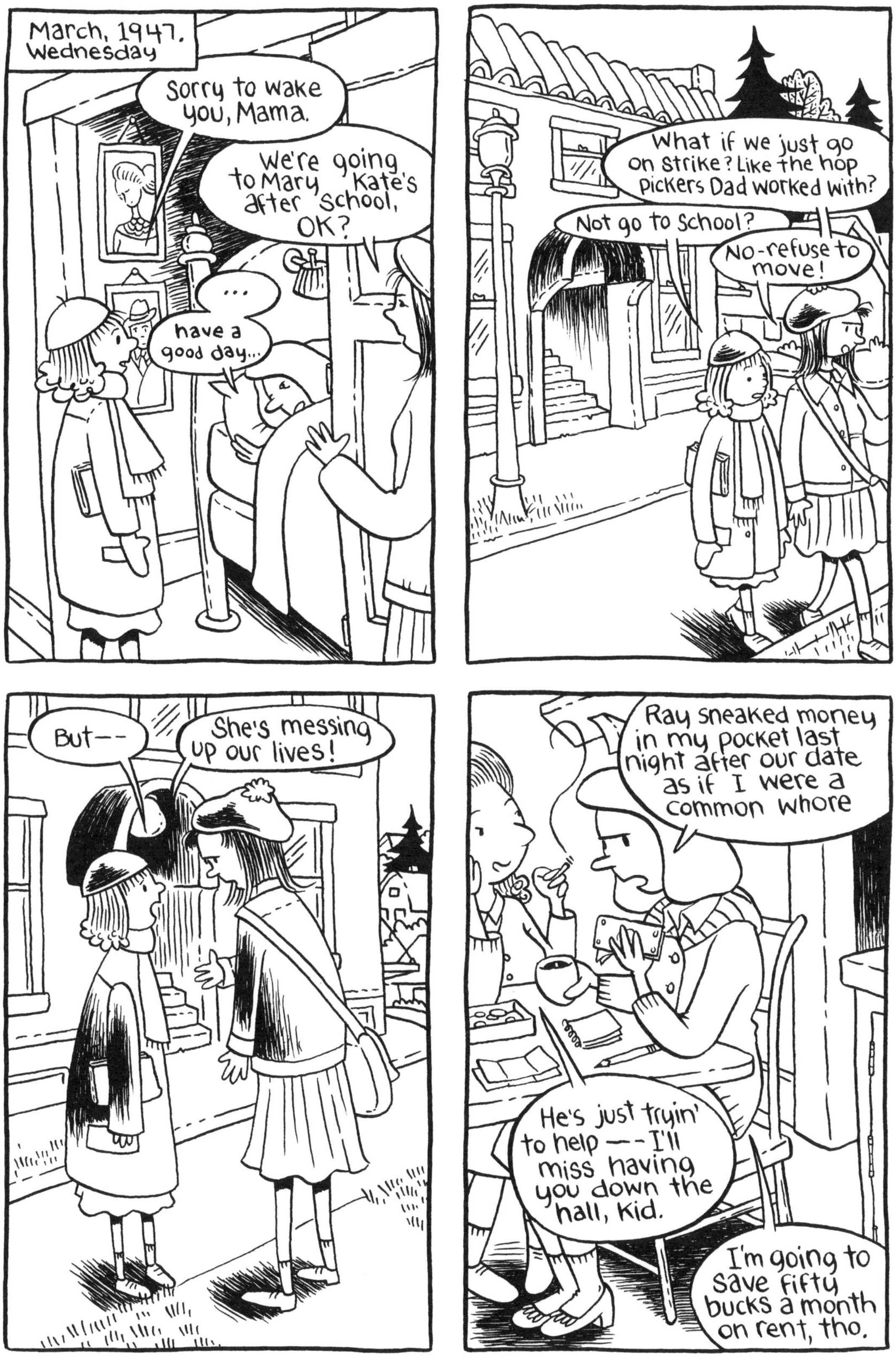
March, 1947. Wednesday
Sorry to wake you, Mama.
We're going to Mary Kate's after School, OK?
...
have a good day...
What if we just go on strike? Like the hop pickers Dad worked with?
Not go to School?
No-refuse to move!
But--
She's messing up our lives!
Ray sneaked money in my pocket last night after our date as if I were a common whore
He's just tryin' to help --- I'll miss having you down the hall, Kid.
I'm going to Save fifty bucks a month on rent, tho.

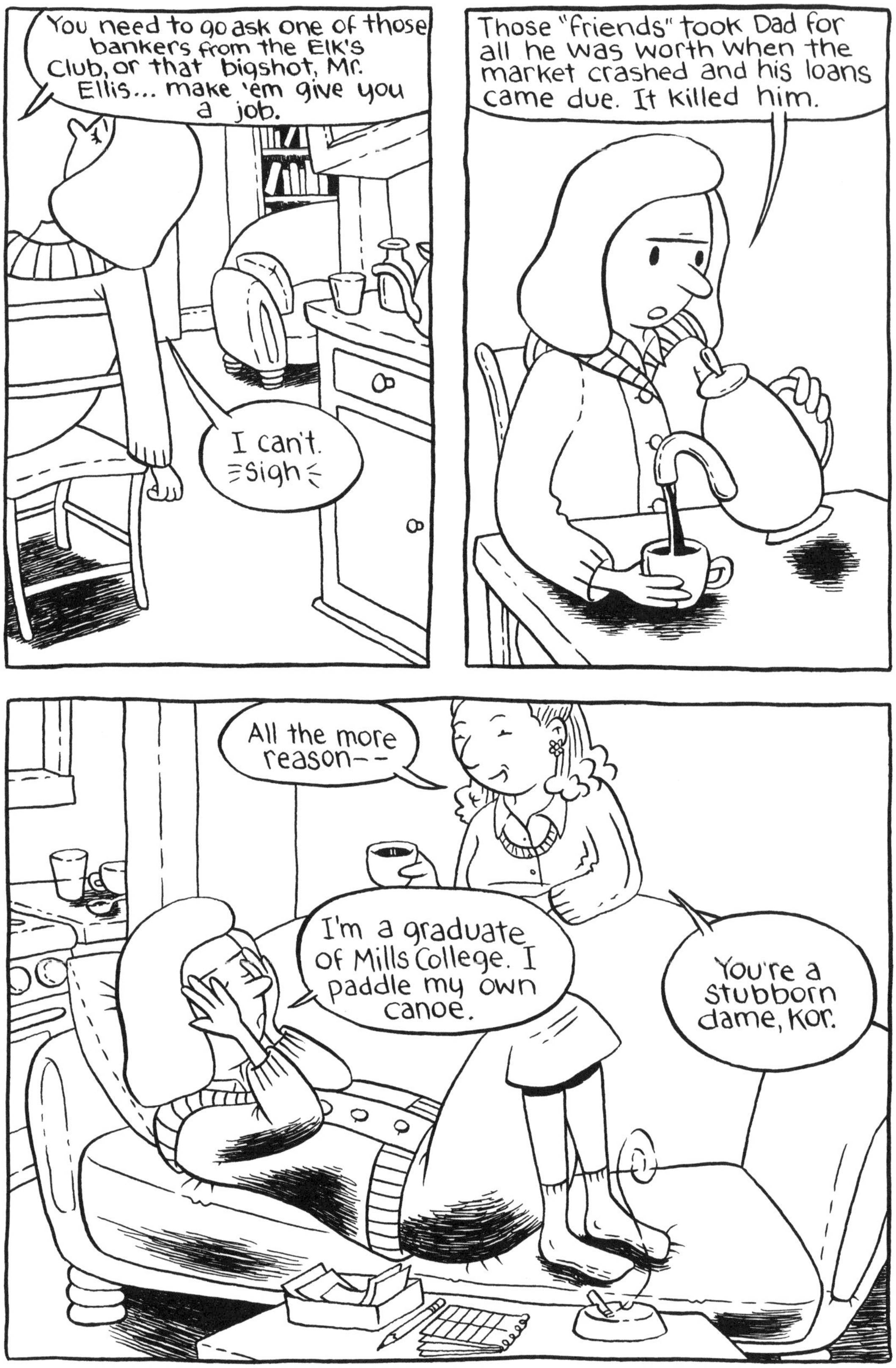
You need to go ask one of those bankers from the Elk's Club, or that bigshot, Mr. Ellis... make 'em give you a job.
I can't. ≡sigh≡
Those "friends" took Dad for all he was worth when the market crashed and his loans came due. It killed him.
All the more reason--
I'm a graduate of Mills College. I paddle my own canoe.
You're a stubborn dame, Kor.

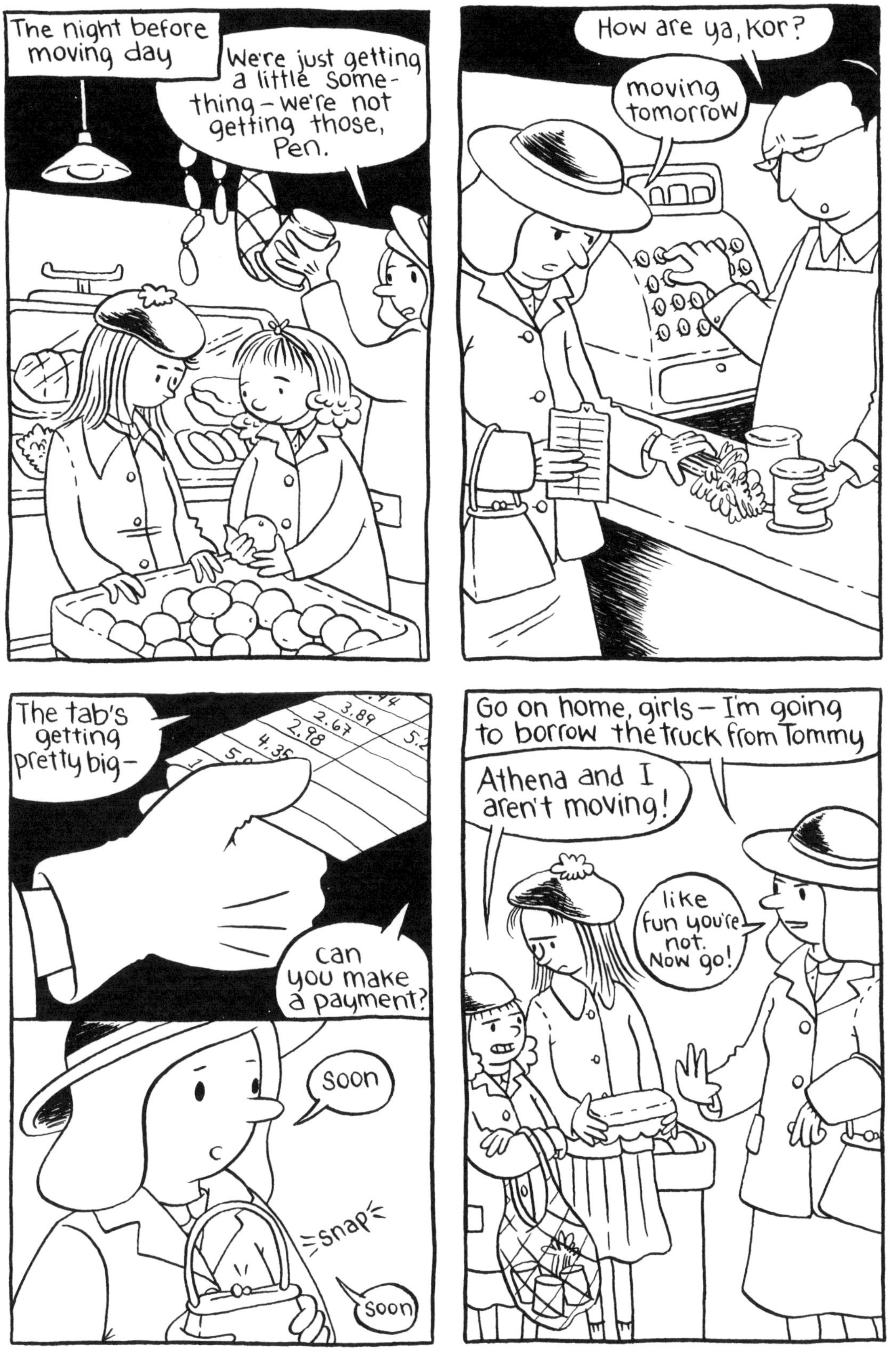

The night before moving day
We're just getting a little some-thing – we're not getting those, Pen.
How are ya, Kor?
moving tomorrow
The tab's getting pretty big–
3.89
2.67
2.98
4.35
can you make a payment?
Soon
snap
Soon
Go on home, girls – I'm going to borrow the truck from Tommy
Athena and I aren't moving!
like fun you're not. Now go!

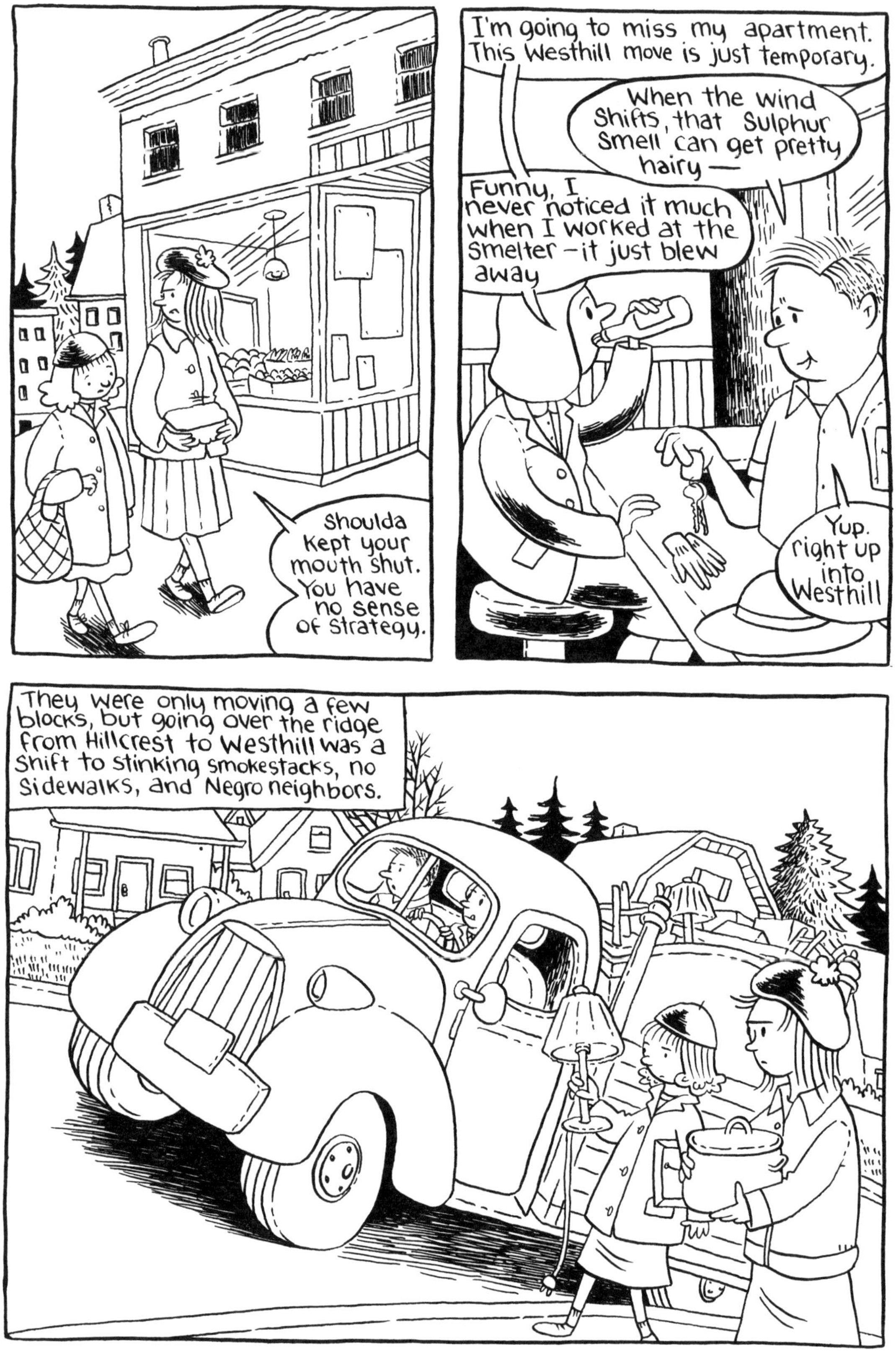
Shoulda kept your mouth shut. You have no sense of strategy.
I'm going to miss my apartment. This Westhill move is just temporary.
When the wind shifts, that sulphur smell can get pretty hairy —
Funny, I never noticed it much when I worked at the smelter — it just blew away
Yup. right up into Westhill
They were only moving a few blocks, but going over the ridge from Hillcrest to Westhill was a shift to stinking smokestacks, no sidewalks, and Negro neighbors.

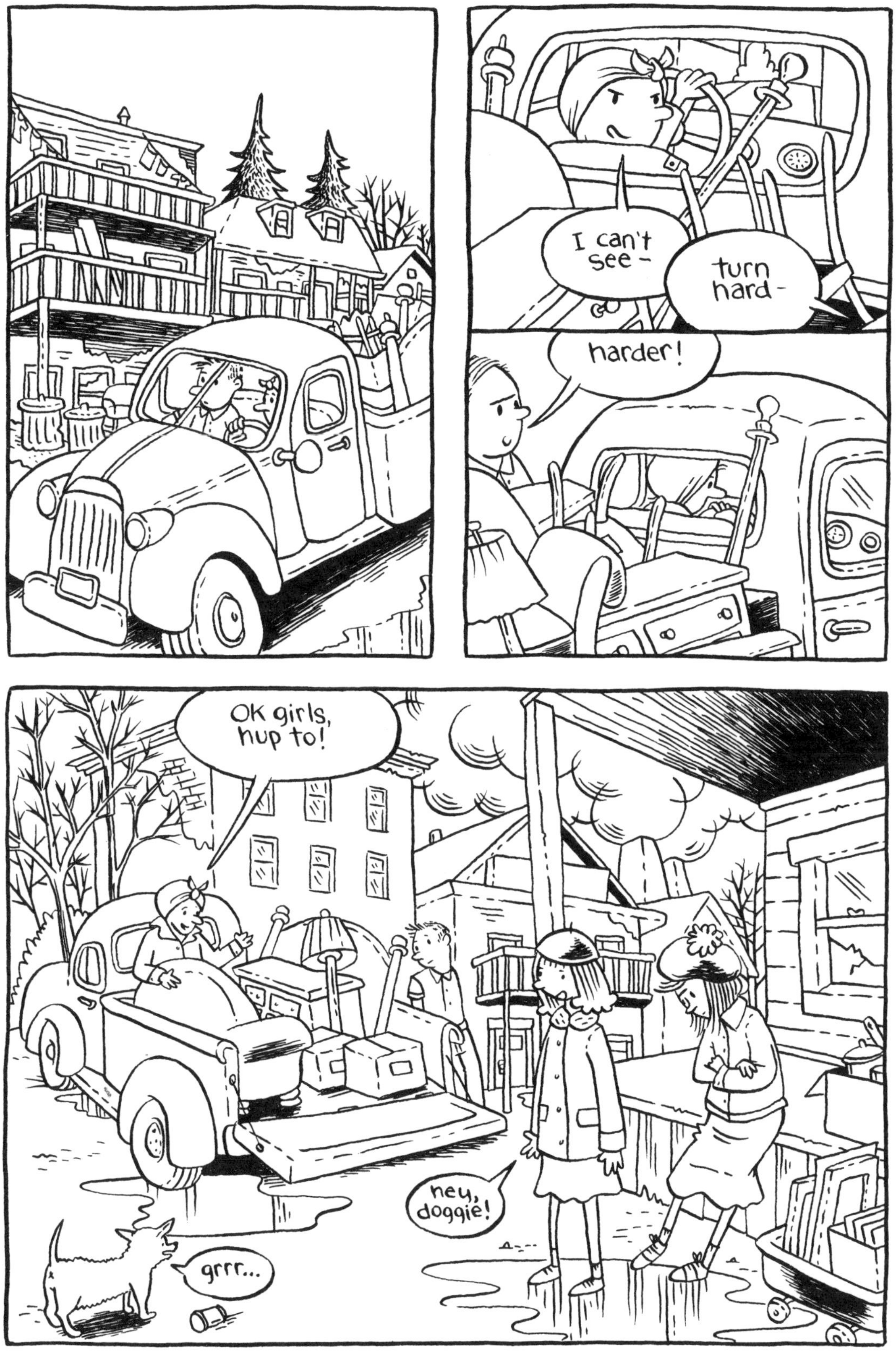
I can't see -
turn hard -
harder!
OK girls, hup to!
grrr...
hey, doggie!

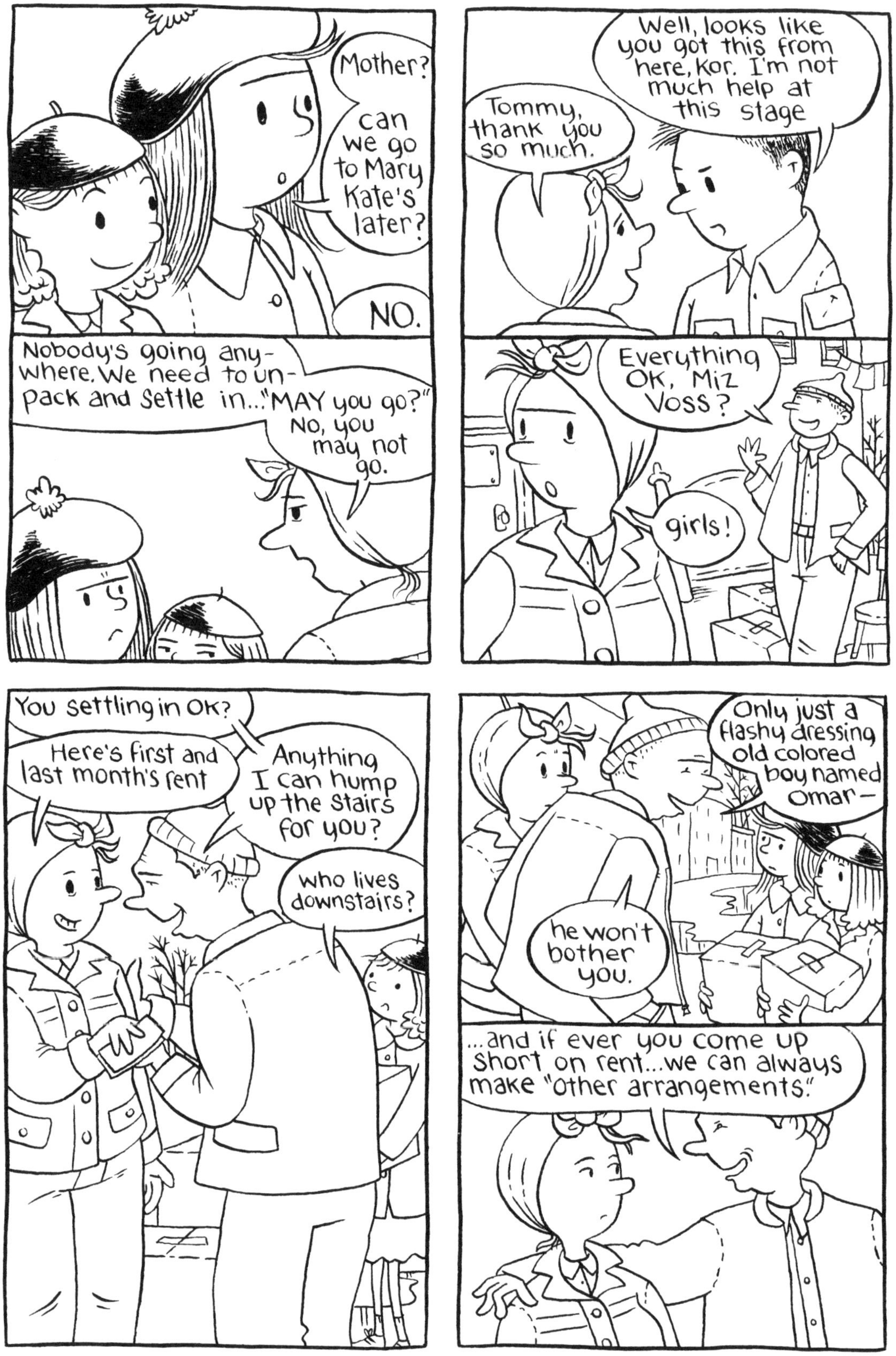
Mother?
can we go to Mary Kate's later?
NO.
Tommy, thank you so much.
Well, looks like you got this from here, Kor. I'm not much help at this stage
Nobody's going anywhere. We need to unpack and settle in..."MAY you go?"
No, you may not go.
Everything OK, Miz Voss?
girls!
You settling in OK?
Here's first and last month's rent
Anything I can hump up the stairs for you?
who lives downstairs?
Only just a flashy dressing old colored boy named Omar—
he won't bother you.
...and if ever you come up short on rent...we can always make "other arrangements."

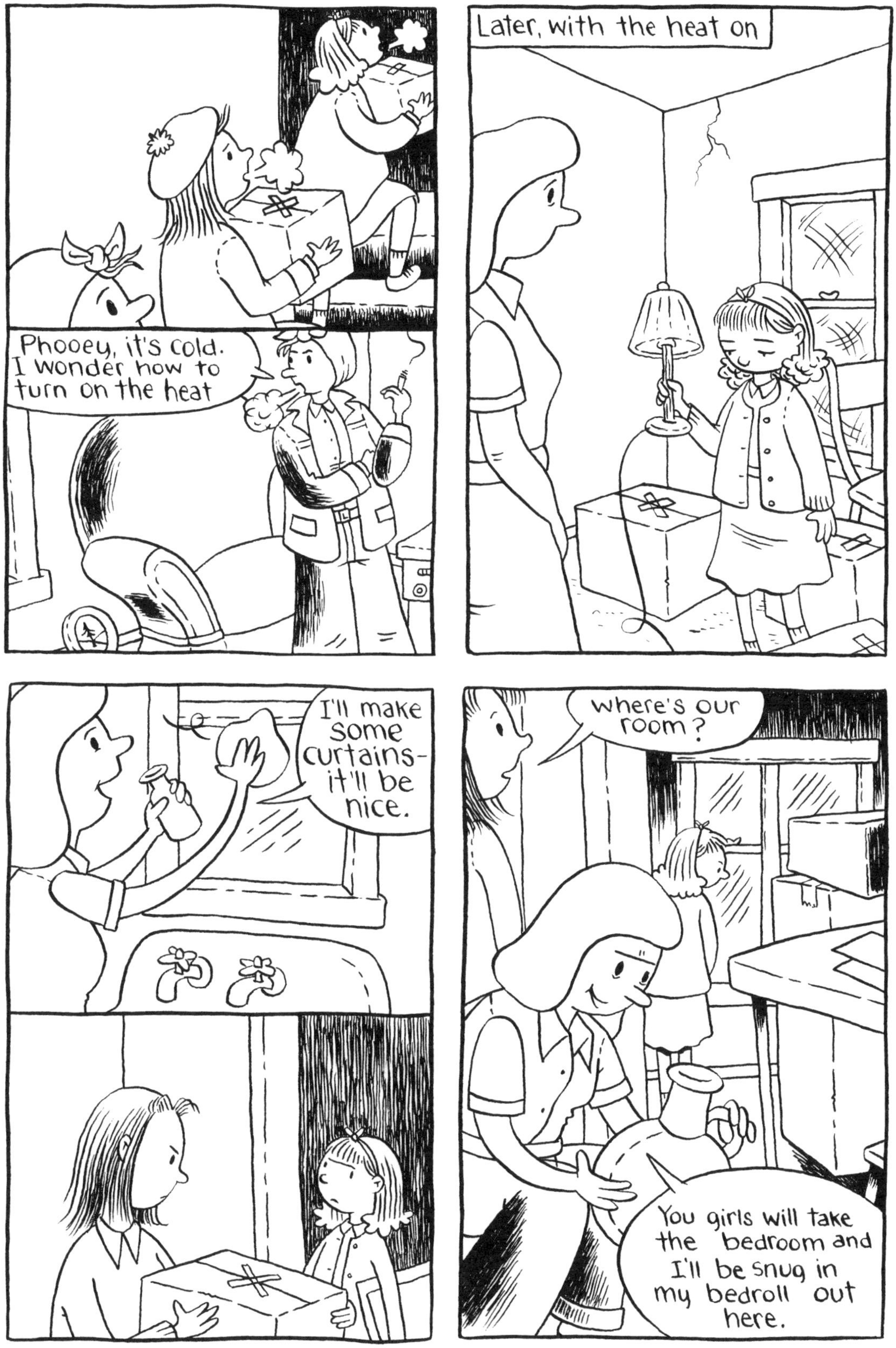
Phooey, it's cold. I wonder how to turn on the heat
Later, with the heat on
I'll make some curtains- it'll be nice.
where's our room?
You girls will take the bedroom and I'll be snug in my bedroll out here.

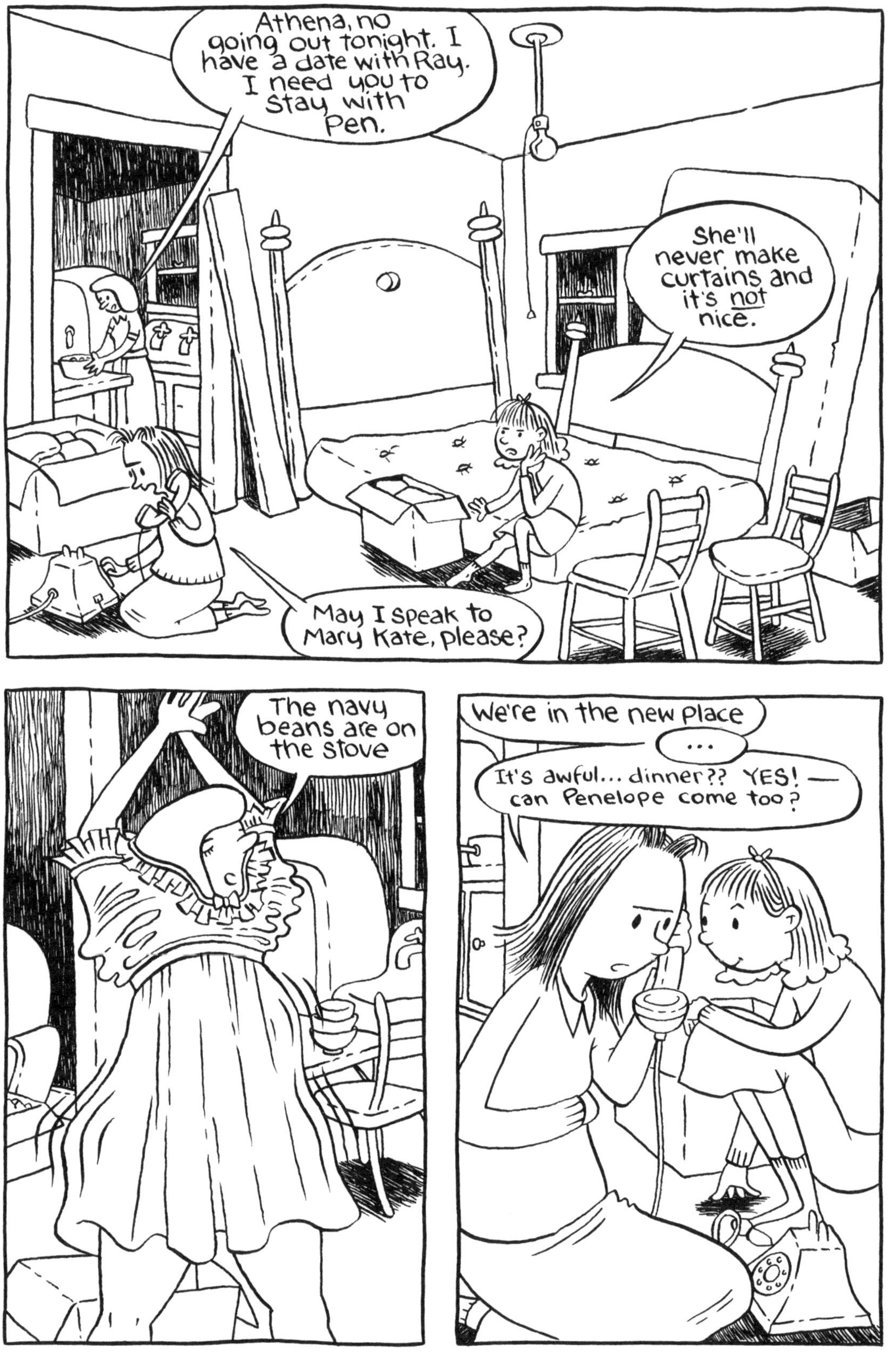
Athena, no going out tonight. I have a date with Ray. I need you to stay with Pen.
She'll never make curtains and it's not nice.
May I speak to Mary Kate, please?
The navy beans are on the stove
We're in the new place
...
It's awful... dinner?? YES! — can Penelope come too?

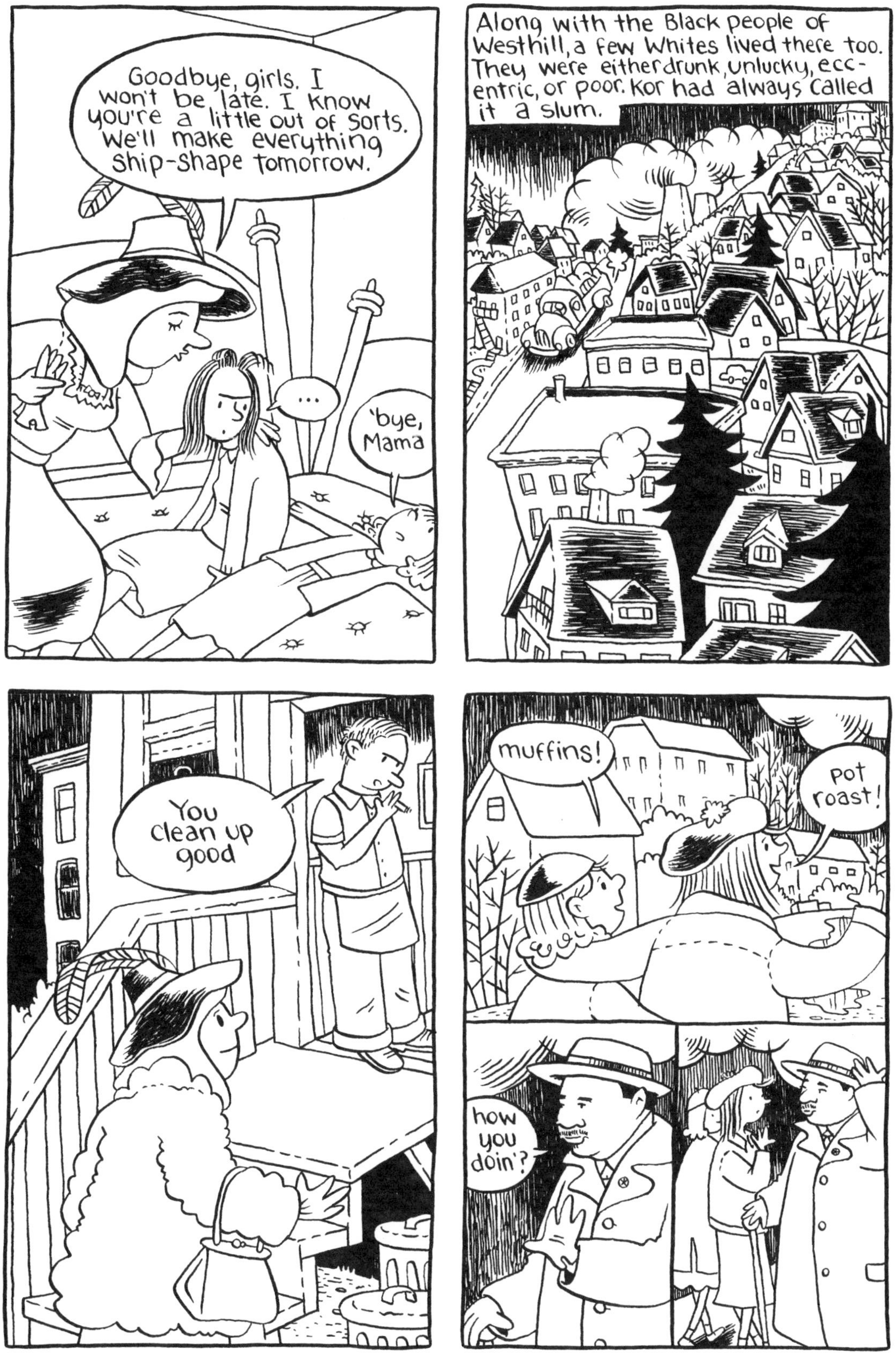
Goodbye, girls. I won't be late. I know you're a little out of sorts. We'll make everything ship-shape tomorrow.
...
'bye, Mama
Along with the Black people of Westhill, a few Whites lived there too. They were either drunk, unlucky, ecc-entric, or poor. Kor had always called it a slum.
You clean up good
muffins!
pot roast!
how you doin'?

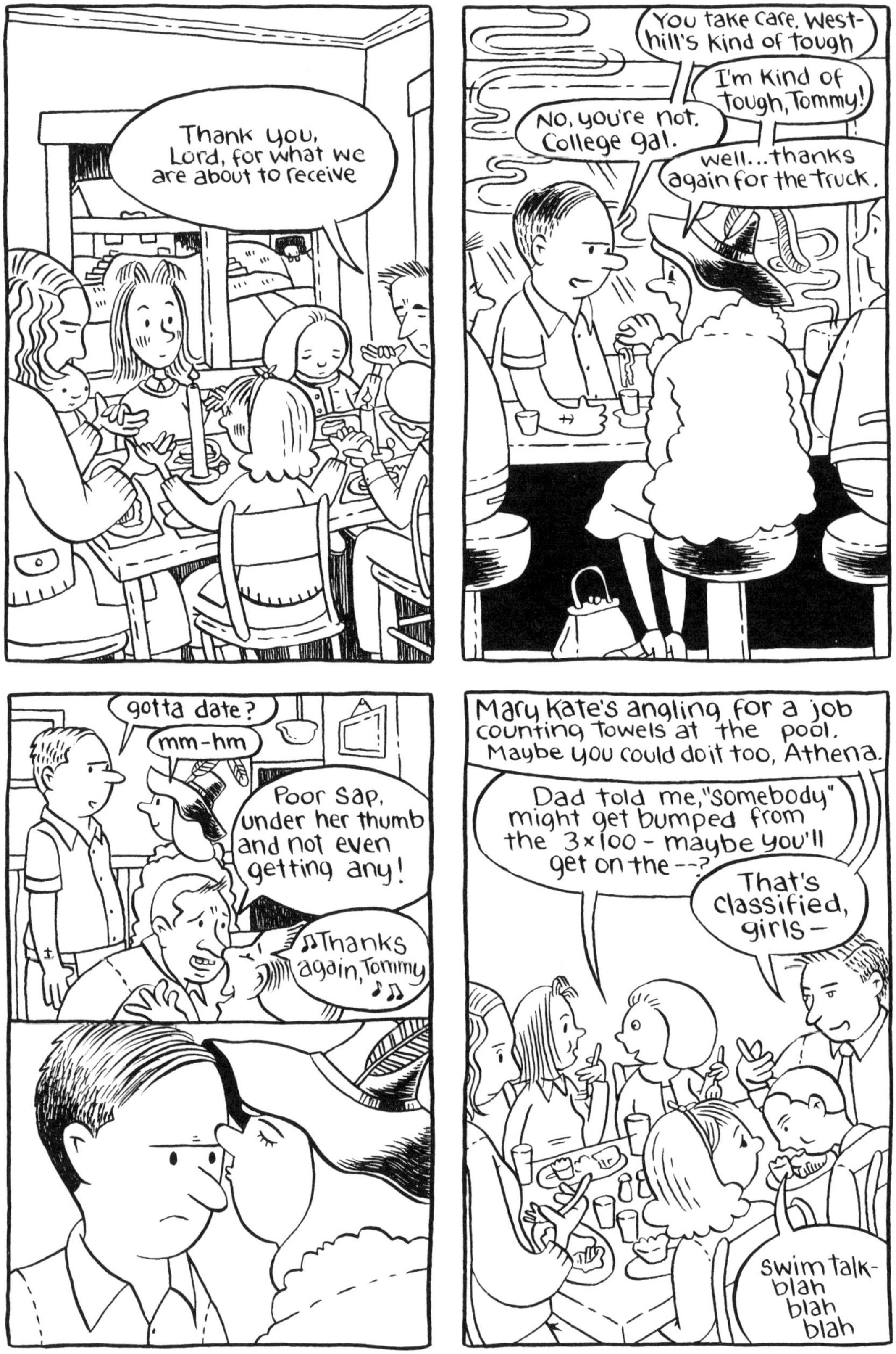
Thank you, Lord, for what we are about to receive
You take care. West-hill's kind of tough
I'm kind of tough, Tommy!
No, you're not. College gal.
well... thanks again for the truck.
gotta date?
mm-hm
Poor sap, under her thumb and not even getting any!
♫Thanks again, Tommy ♪♫
Mary Kate's angling for a job counting towels at the pool. Maybe you could do it too, Athena.
Dad told me, "somebody" might get bumped from the 3×100 - maybe you'll get on the --?
That's classified, girls—
swim talk-blah blah blah

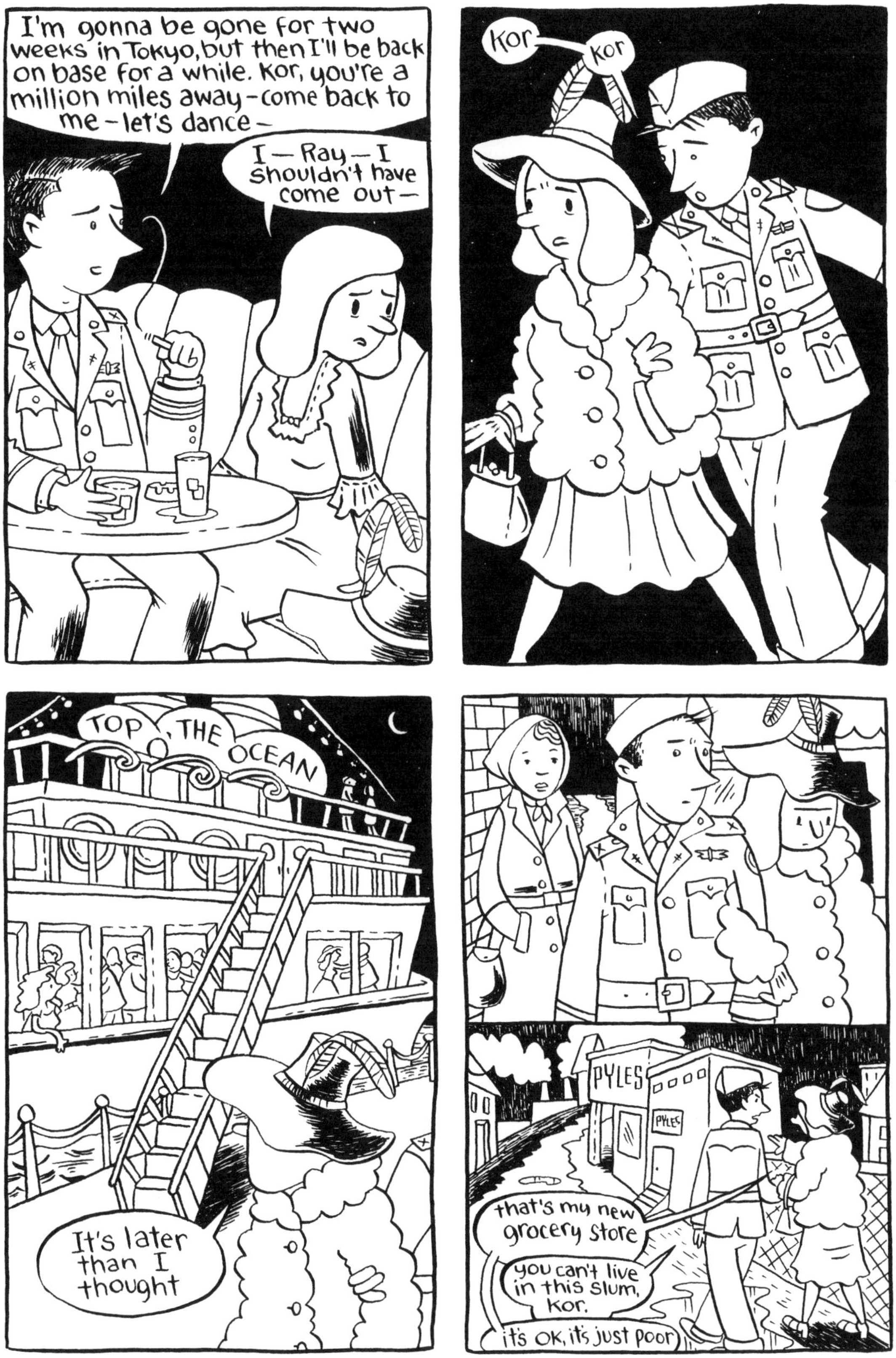
I'm gonna be gone for two weeks in Tokyo, but then I'll be back on base for a while. Kor, you're a million miles away - come back to me - let's dance -
I — Ray — I shouldn't have come out —
Kor
Kor
TOP THE OCEAN
It's later than I thought
PYLES
PYLES
that's my new grocery store
you can't live in this slum, Kor.
it's OK, it's just poor

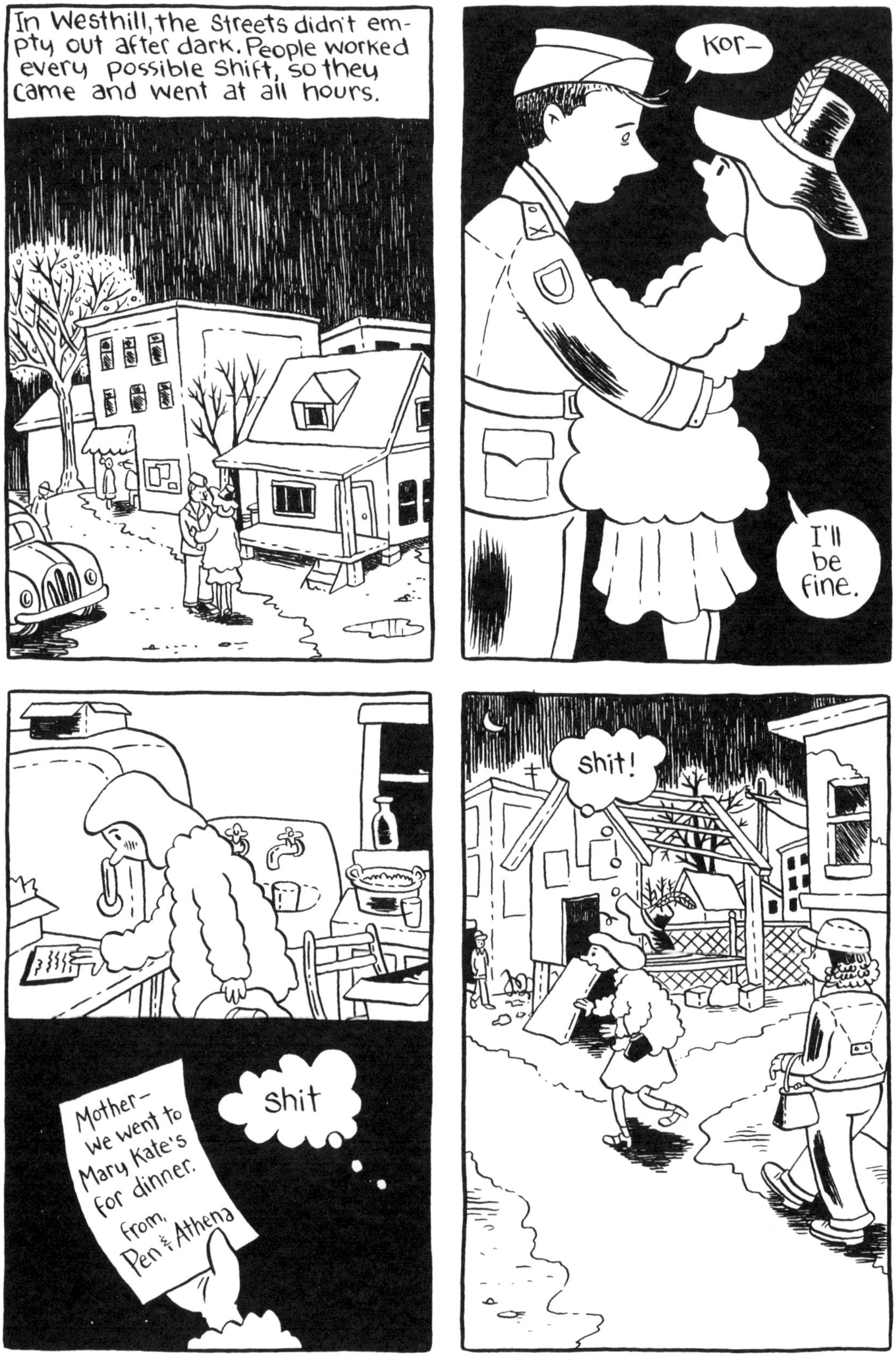
In Westhill, the streets didn't empty out after dark. People worked every possible shift, so they came and went at all hours.
Kor–
I'll be fine.
Mother– We went to Mary Kate's for dinner. from, Pen & Athena
shit
shit!

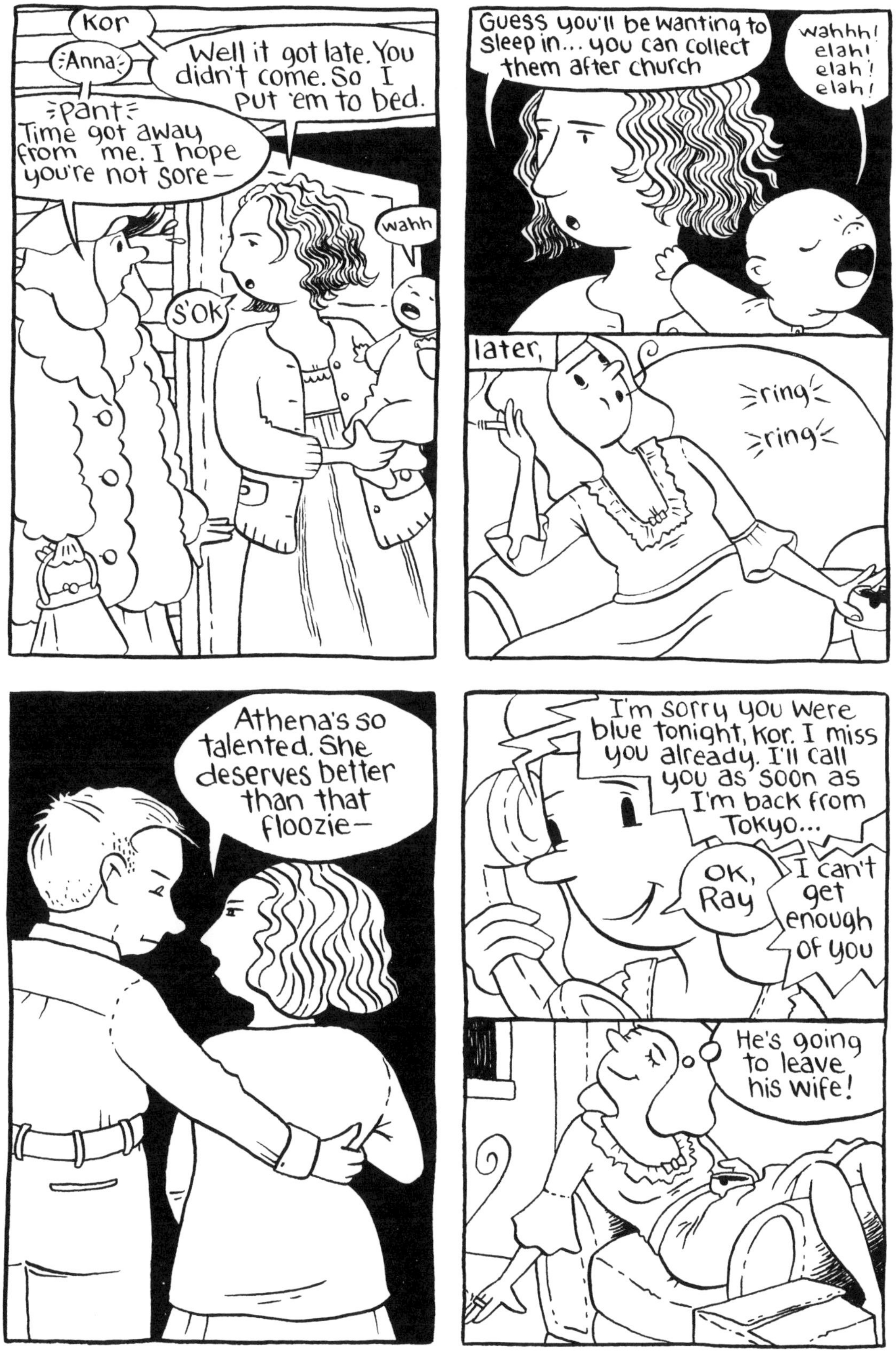
Kor
Anna
Well it got late. You didn't come. So I put 'em to bed.
pant
Time got away from me. I hope you're not sore—
S'OK
wahh
Guess you'll be wanting to sleep in... you can collect them after church
wahhh! elah! elah! elah!
later,
ring
ring
Athena's so talented. She deserves better than that floozie—
I'm sorry you were blue tonight, Kor. I miss you already. I'll call you as soon as I'm back from Tokyo...
OK, Ray
I can't get enough of you
He's going to leave his wife!

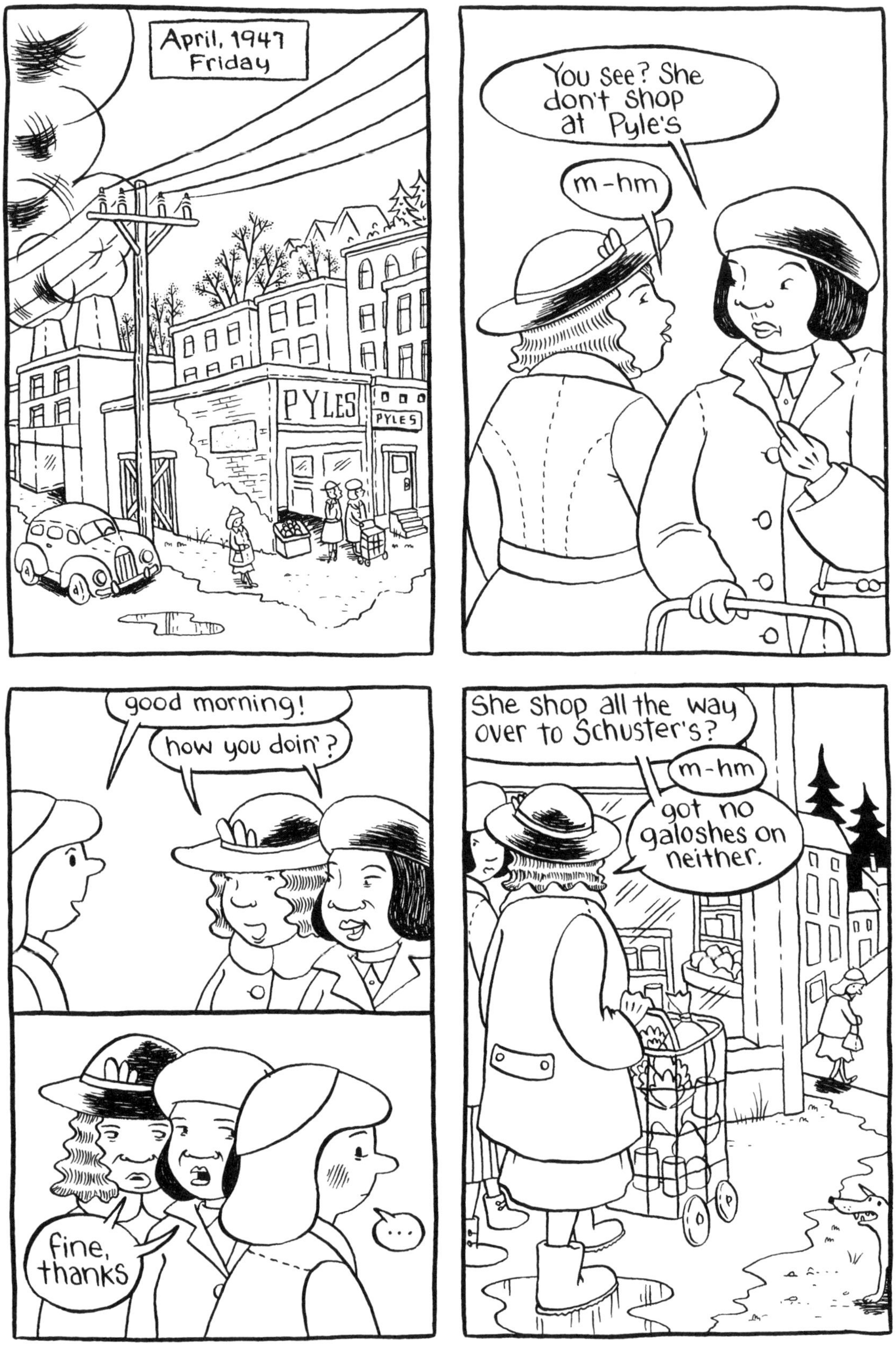
April, 1947
Friday
PYLES
PYLES
You see? She don't shop at Pyle's
m-hm
good morning!
how you doin'?
fine, thanks
...
She shop all the way over to Schuster's?
m-hm
got no galoshes on neither.

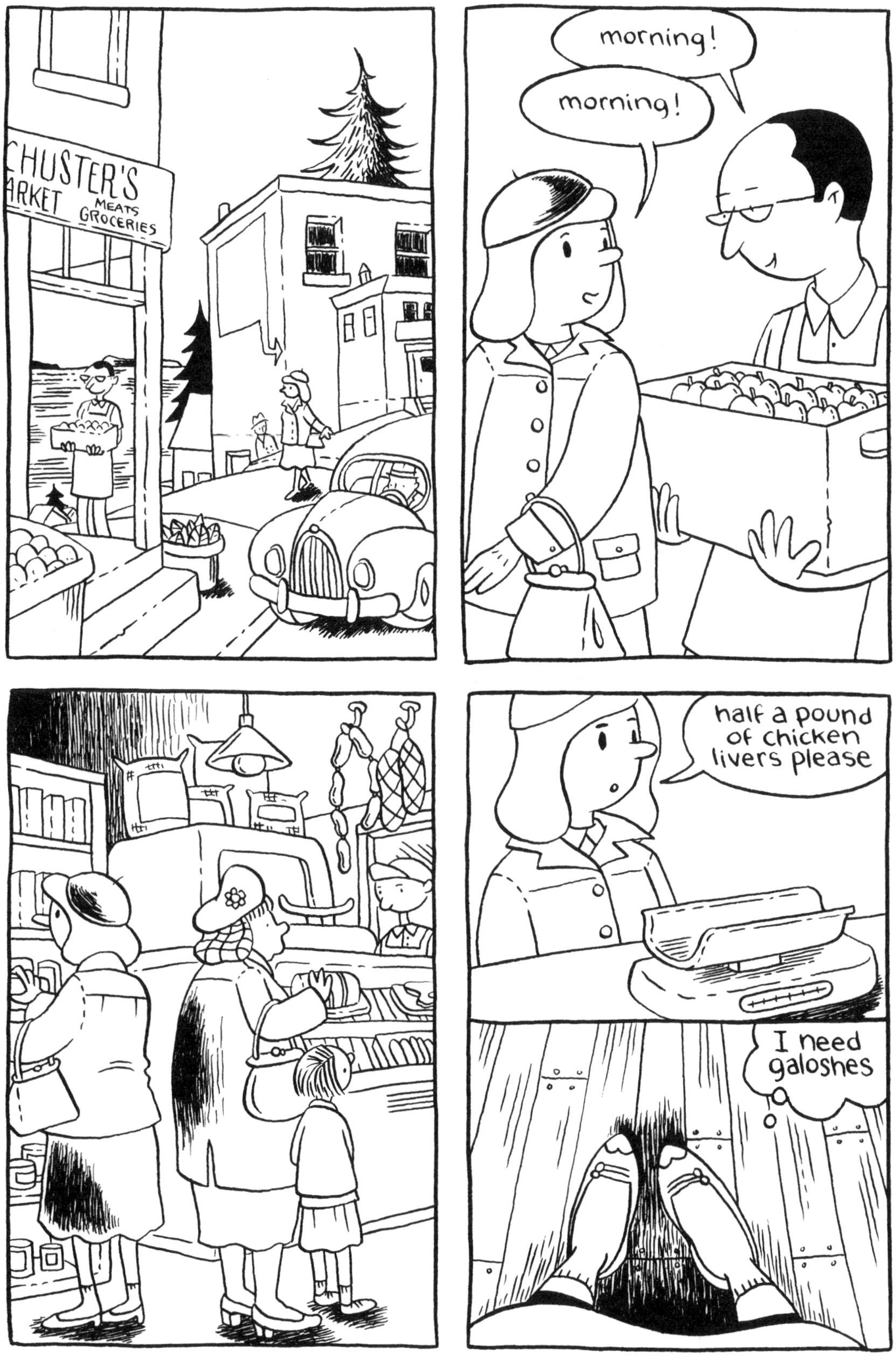
CHUSTER'S
ARKET MEATS GROCERIES
morning!
morning!
half a pound of chicken livers please
I need galoshes

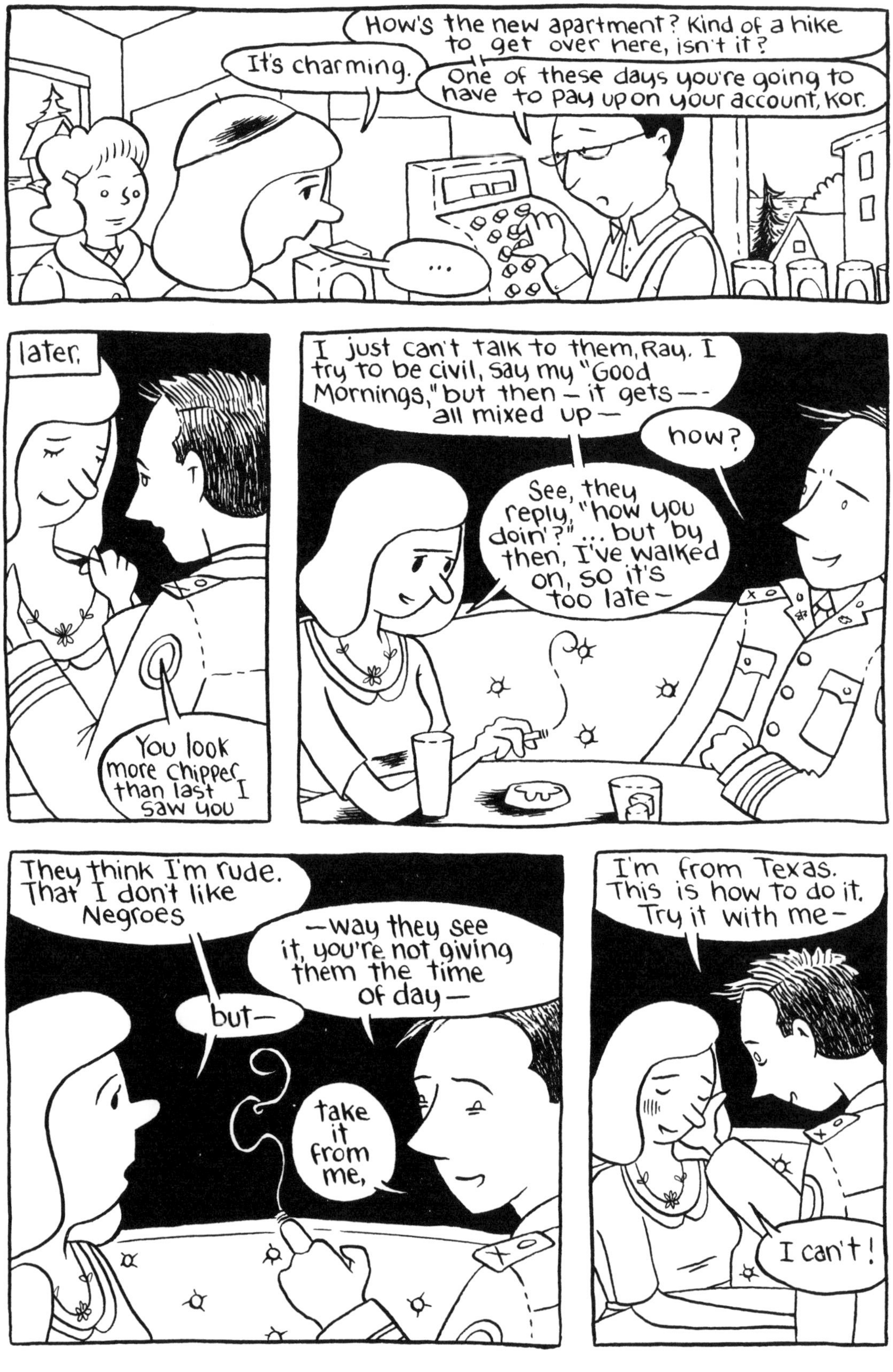
How's the new apartment? Kind of a hike to get over here, isn't it?
It's charming.
One of these days you're going to have to pay up on your account, Kor.
...
later.
You look more chipper than last I saw you
I just can't talk to them, Ray. I try to be civil, say my "Good Mornings," but then — it gets — - all mixed up —
how?
See, they reply, "how you doin'?" ... but by then, I've walked on, so it's too late —
They think I'm rude. That I don't like Negroes
—way they see it, you're not giving them the time of day —
but—
take it from me,
I'm from Texas. This is how to do it. Try it with me —
I can't!

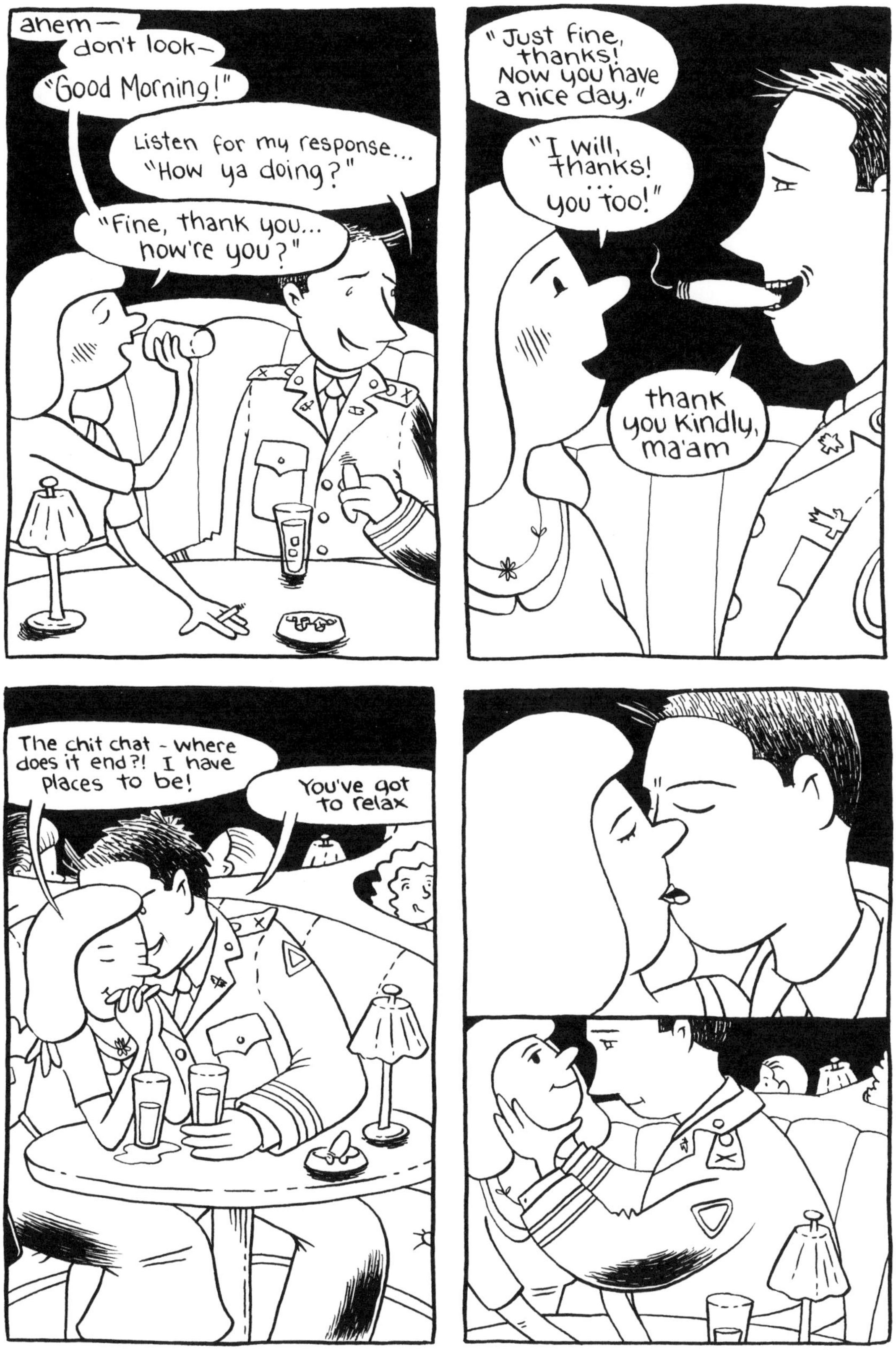
anem—
don't look—
"Good Morning!"
Listen for my response... "How ya doing?"
"Fine, thank you... how're you?"
"Just fine, thanks! Now you have a nice day."
"I will, thanks! ... you too!"
thank you kindly, ma'am
The chit chat - where does it end?! I have places to be!
You've got to relax

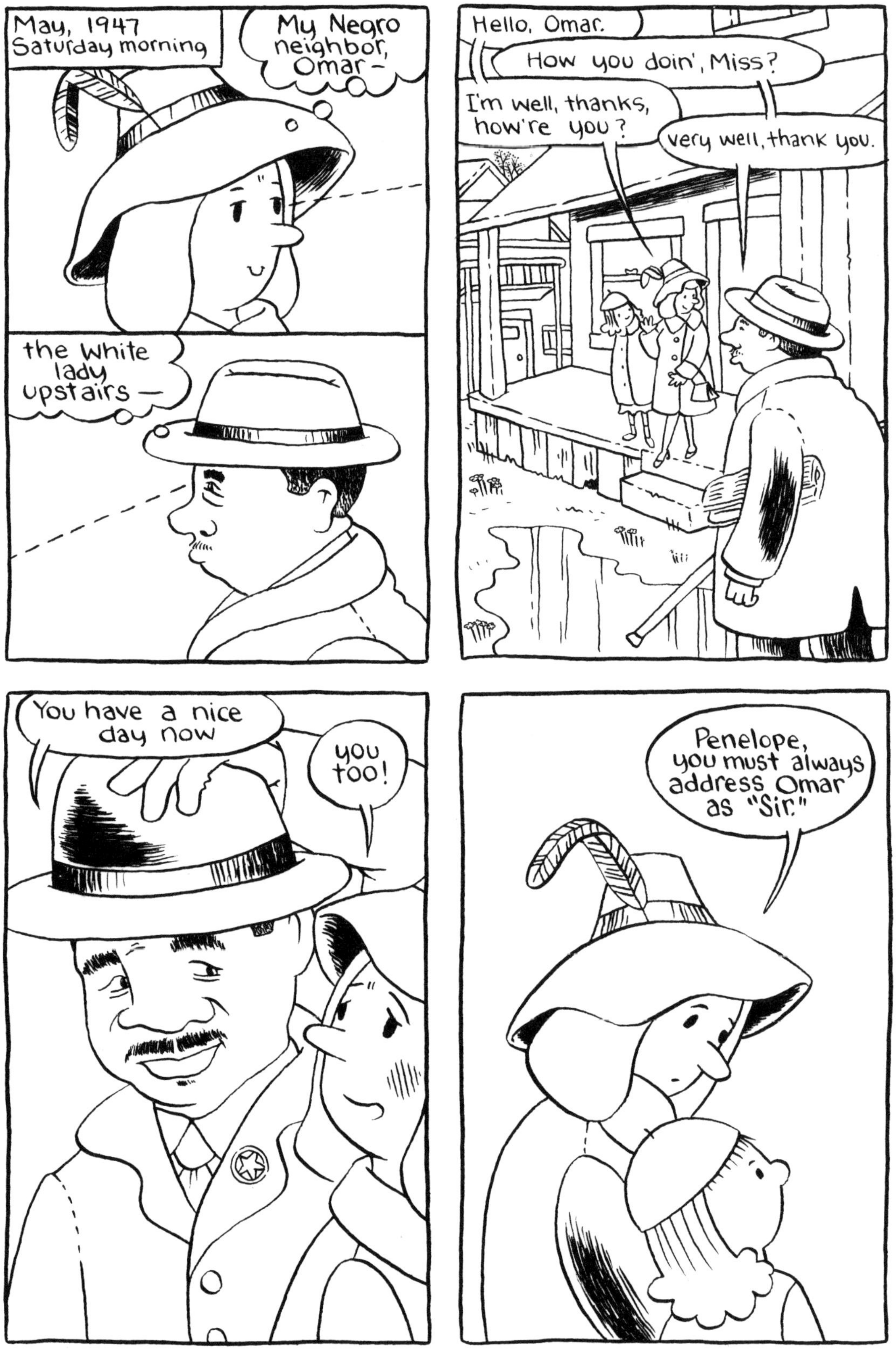
May, 1947
Saturday morning
My Negro neighbor, Omar –
the White lady upstairs –
Hello, Omar.
How you doin', Miss?
I'm well, thanks, how're you?
very well, thank you.
You have a nice day now
you too!
Penelope, you must always address Omar as "Sir."

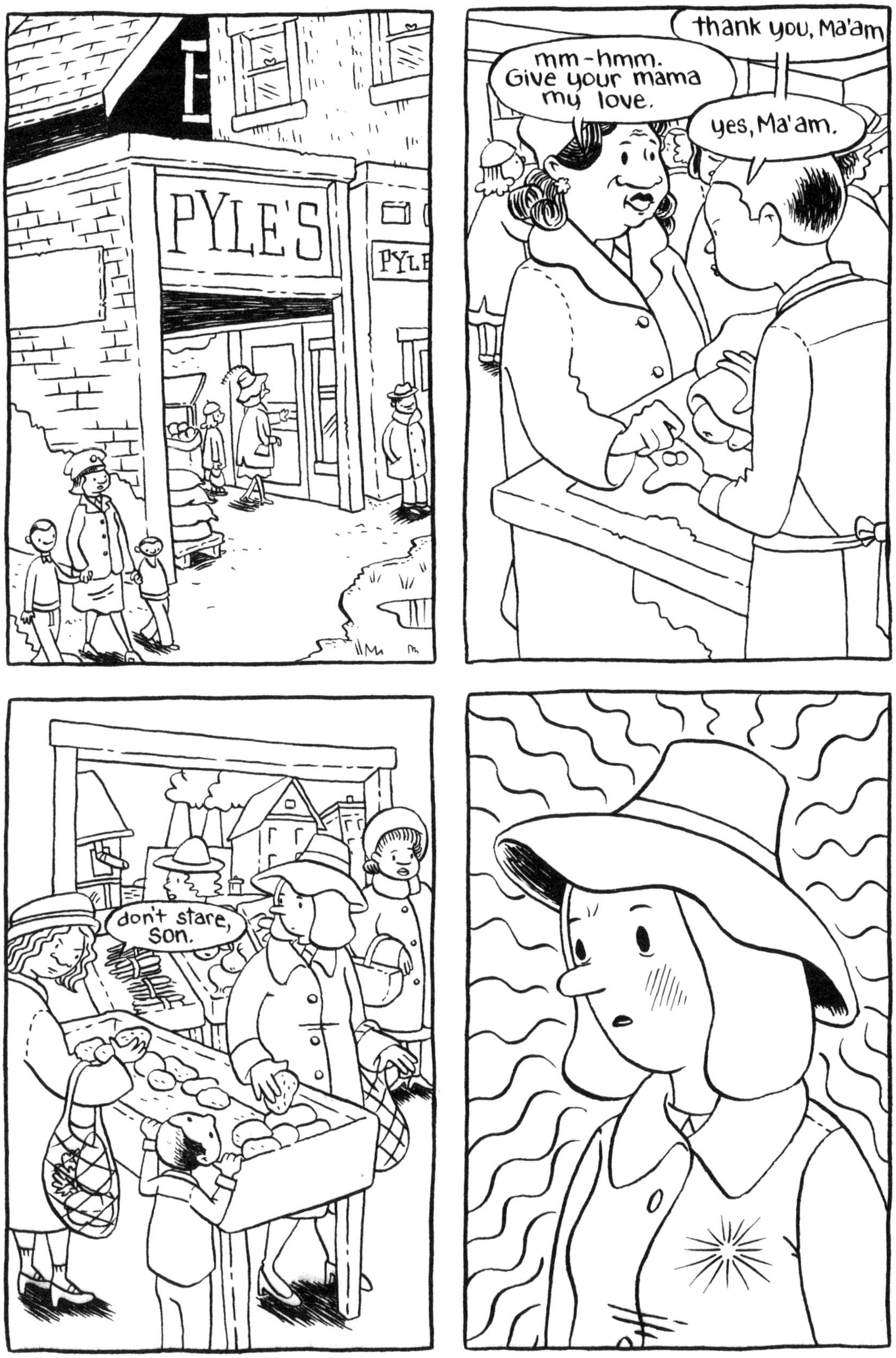
PYLE'S
PYLE
thank you, Ma'am
mm-hmm. Give your mama my love.
yes, Ma'am.
don't stare, son.

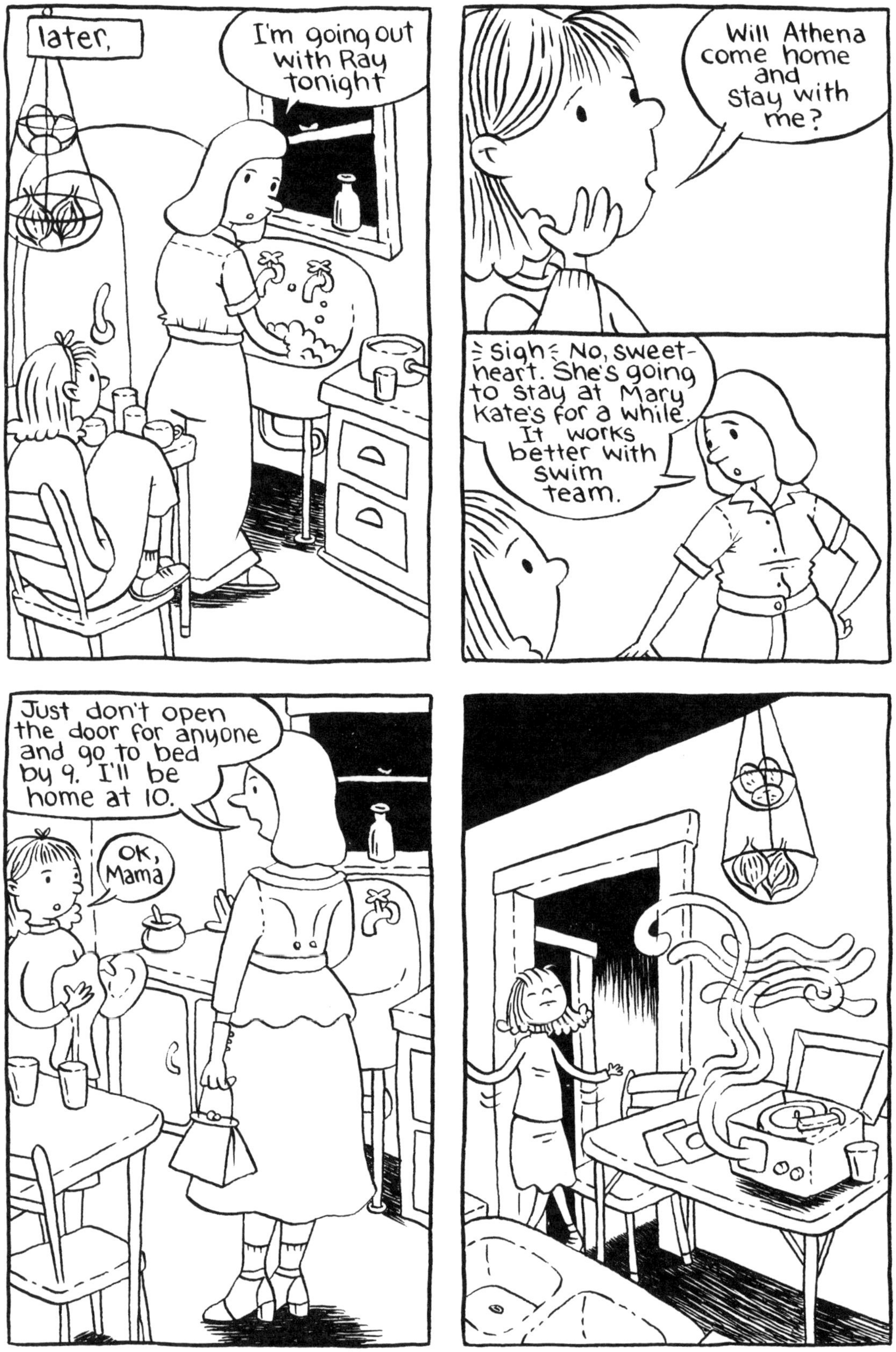
later,
I'm going out with Ray tonight
Will Athena come home and stay with me?
≡Sigh≡ No, sweet-heart. She's going to stay at Mary Kate's for a while. It works better with swim team.
Just don't open the door for anyone and go to bed by 9. I'll be home at 10.
OK, Mama

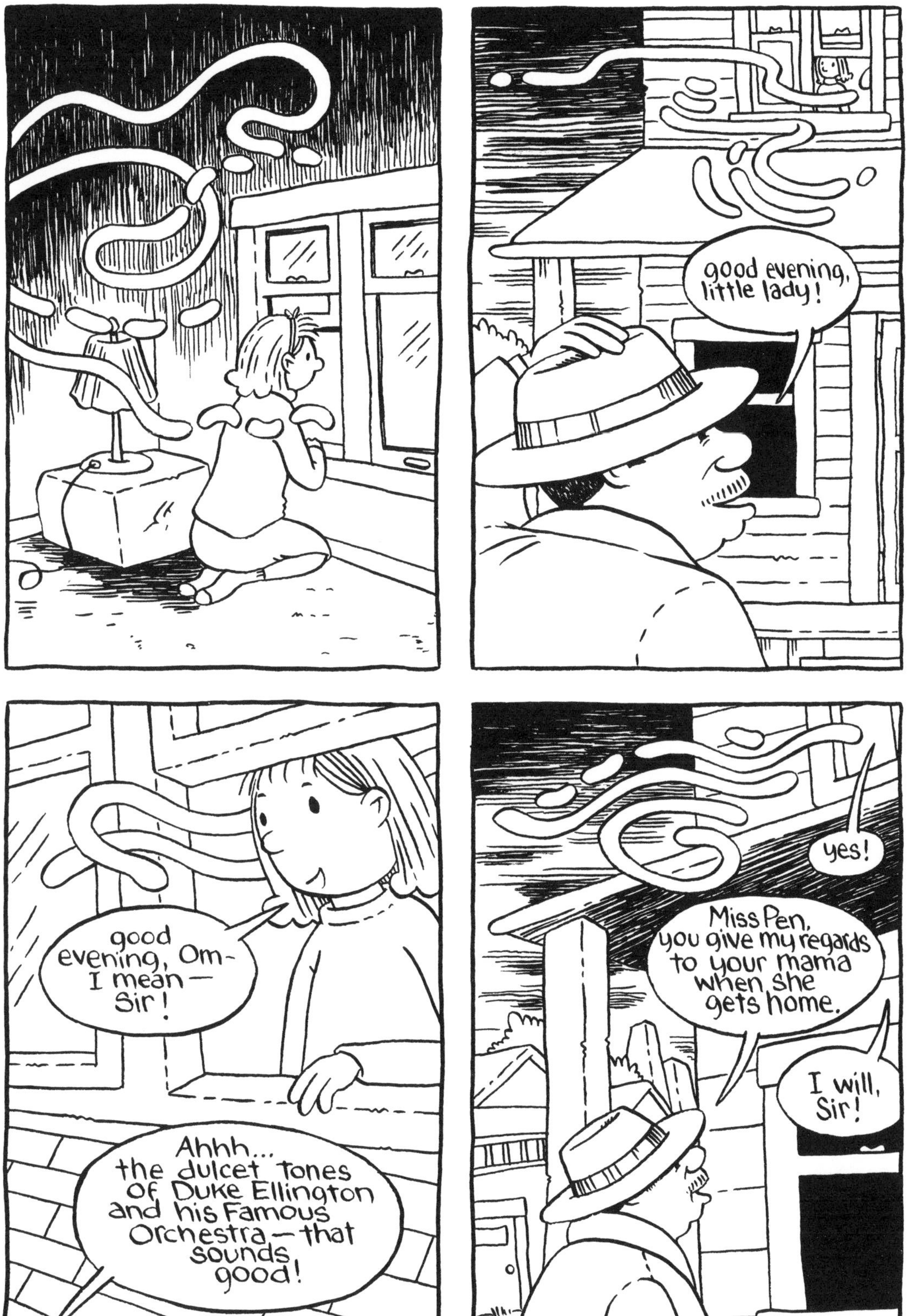
good evening, little lady!
good evening, Om- I mean — Sir!
Ahhh... the dulcet tones of Duke Ellington and his Famous Orchestra — that sounds good!
yes!
Miss Pen, you give my regards to your mama when she gets home.
I will, Sir!

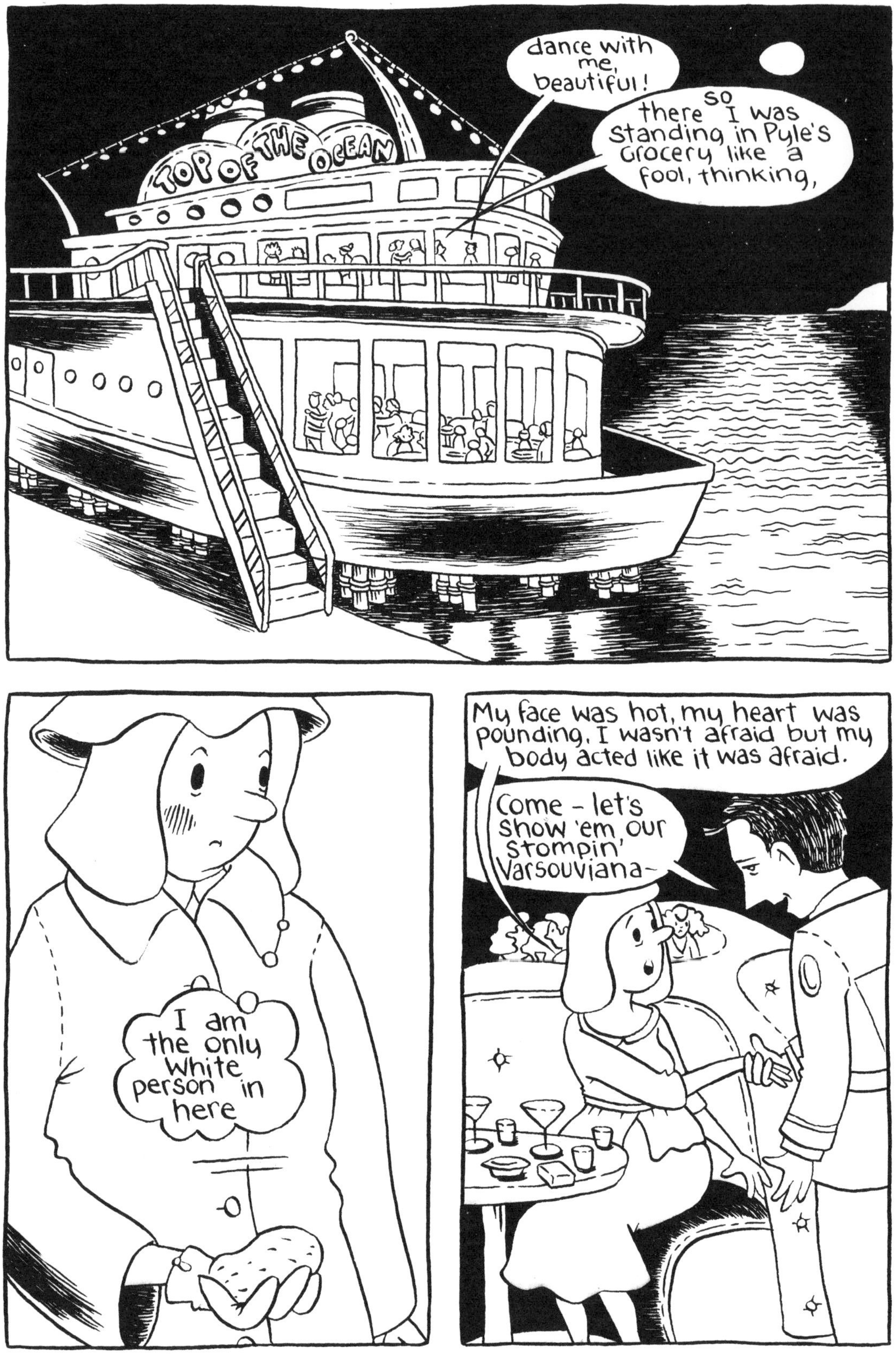
TOP OF THE OCEAN
dance with me, beautiful!
so there I was standing in Pyle's grocery like a fool, thinking,
I am the only white person in here
My face was hot, my heart was pounding. I wasn't afraid but my body acted like it was afraid.
Come - let's show 'em our stompin' Varsouviana-

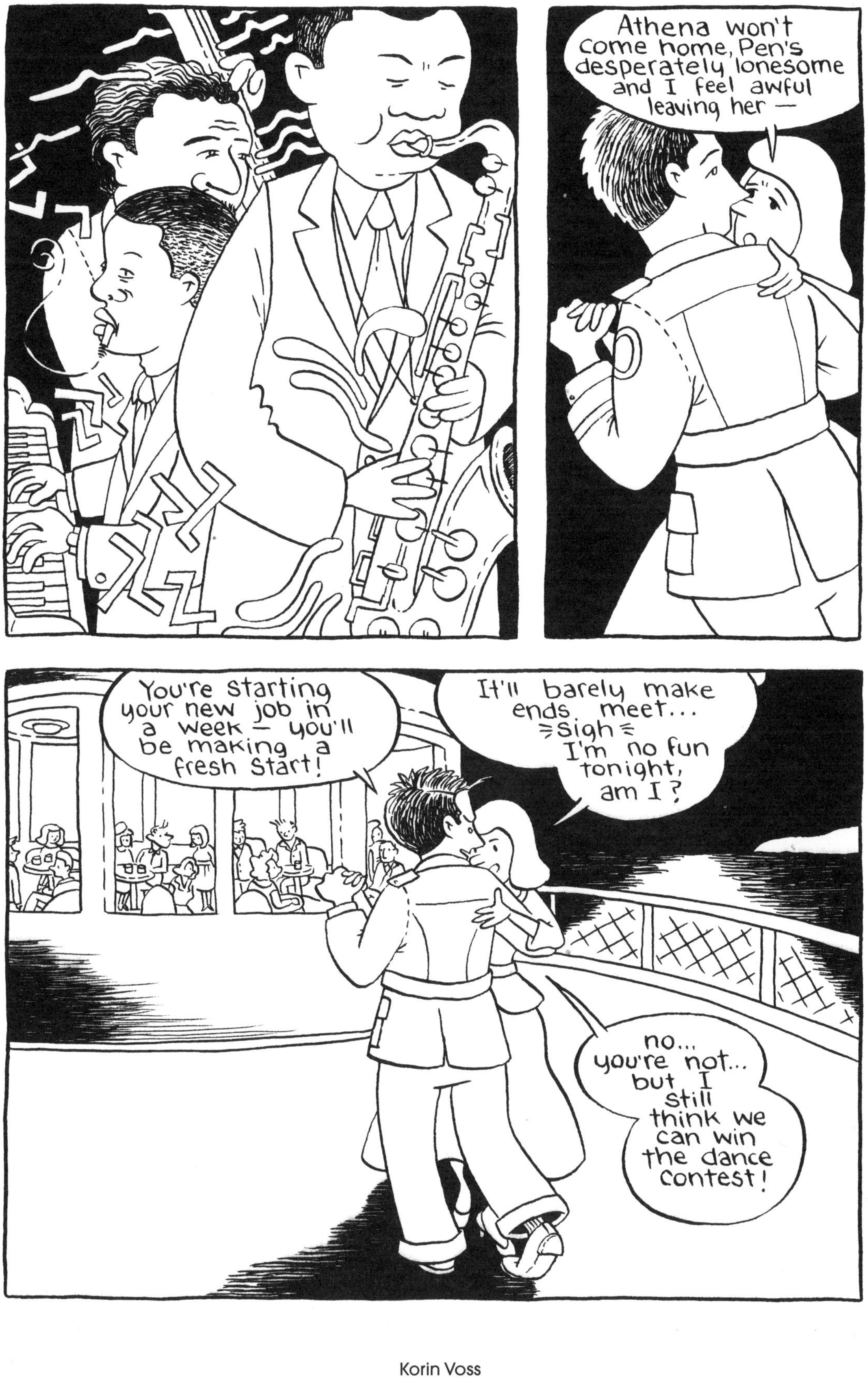
Athena won't come home, Pen's desperately lonesome and I feel awful leaving her —
You're starting your new job in a week — you'll be making a fresh start!
It'll barely make ends meet...
≈sigh≈
I'm no fun tonight, am I?
no... you're not... but I still think we can win the dance contest!

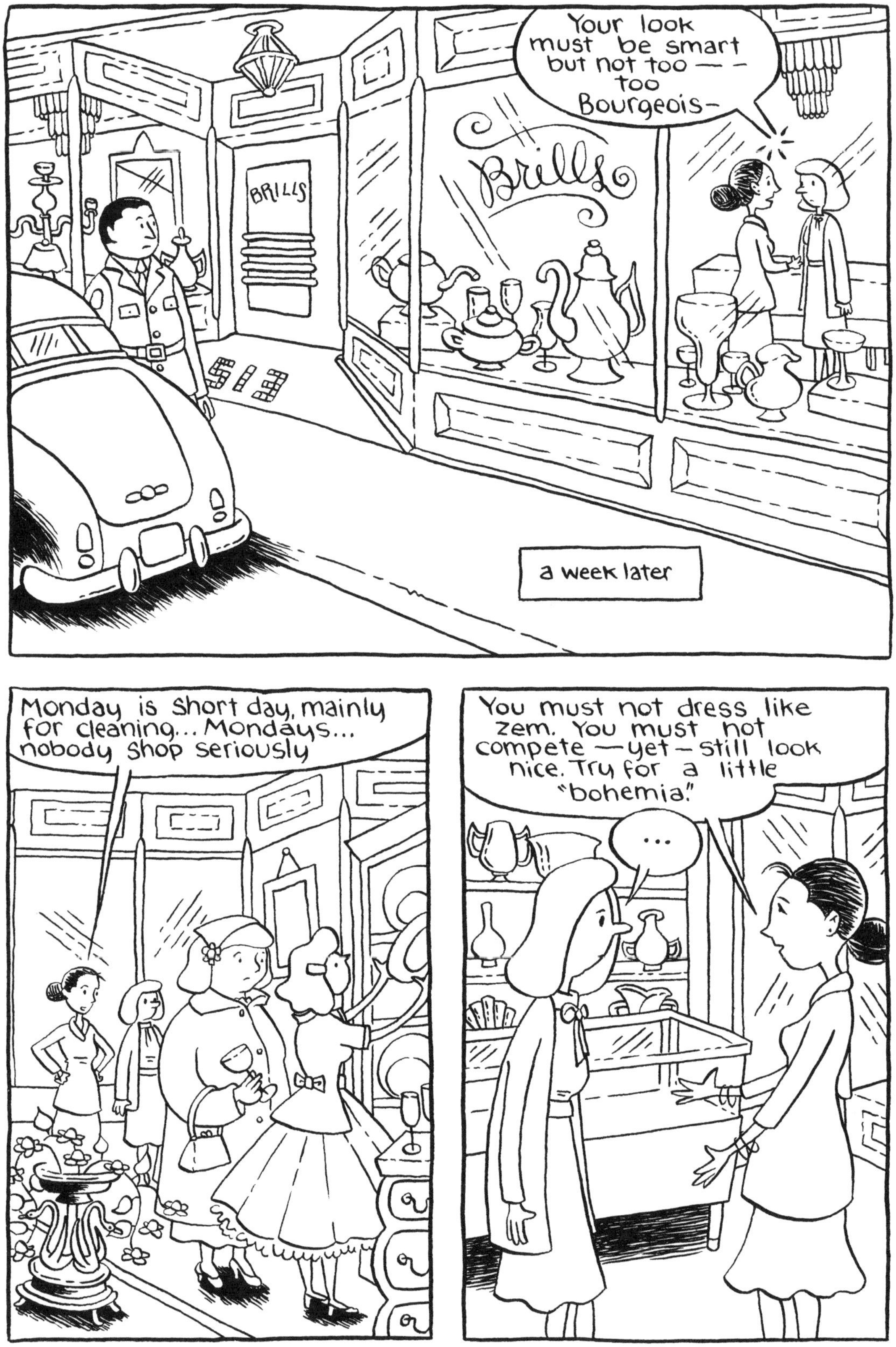
Your look must be smart but not too — — too Bourgeois-
BRILLS
Brills
513
a week later
Monday is short day, mainly for cleaning... Mondays... nobody shop seriously
You must not dress like zem. You must not compete —yet— still look nice. Try for a little "bohemia."
...

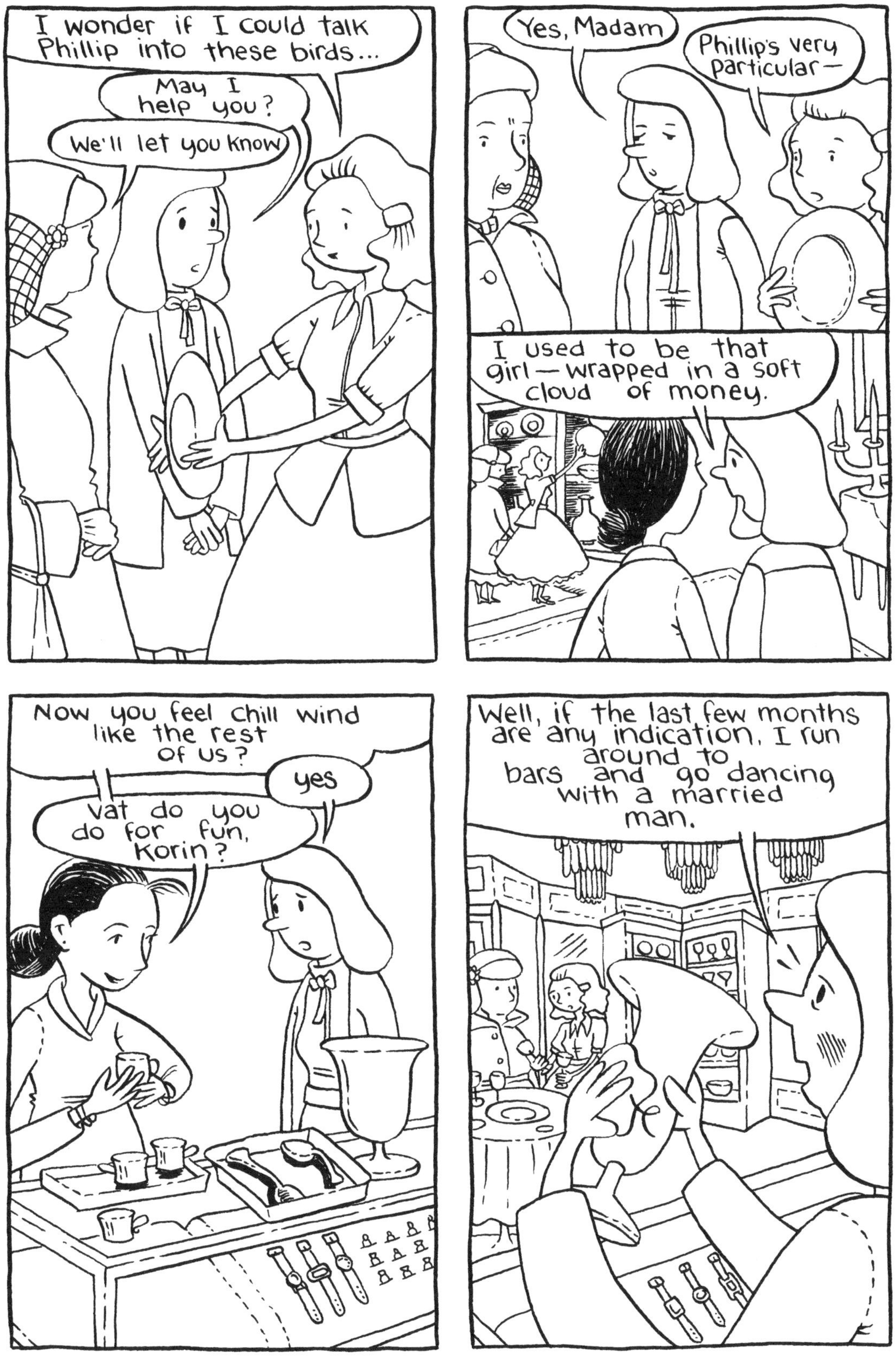
I wonder if I could talk Phillip into these birds...
May I help you?
We'll let you know
Yes, Madam
Phillip's very particular—
I used to be that girl—wrapped in a soft cloud of money.
Now you feel chill wind like the rest of us?
yes
Vat do you do for fun, Korin?
Well, if the last few months are any indication, I run around to bars and go dancing with a married man.

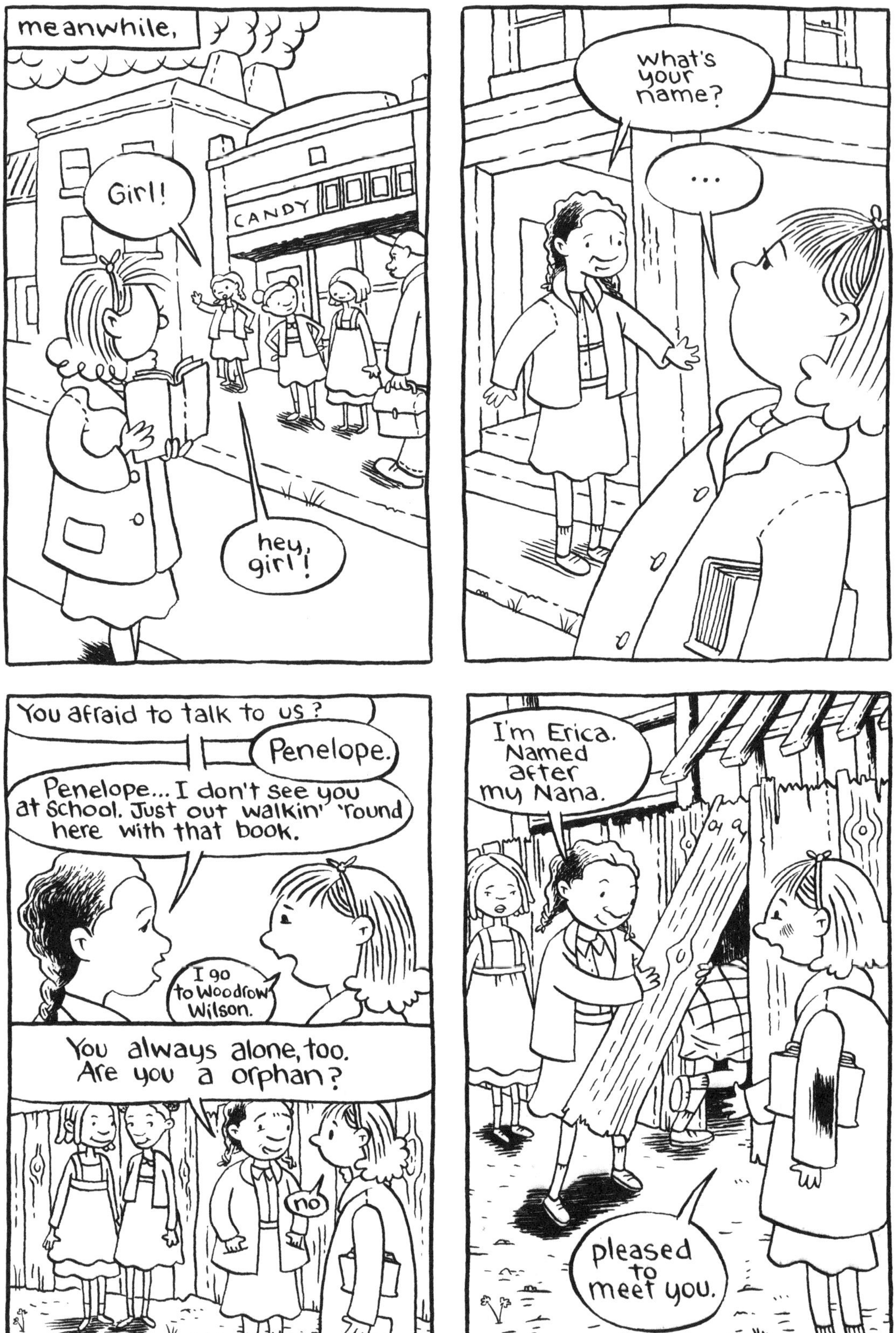
meanwhile,
Girl!
hey, girl!
What's your name?
...
You afraid to talk to us?
Penelope.
Penelope... I don't see you at School. Just out walkin' 'round here with that book.
I go to Woodrow Wilson.
You always alone, too. Are you a orphan?
no
I'm Erica. Named after my Nana.
pleased to meet you.

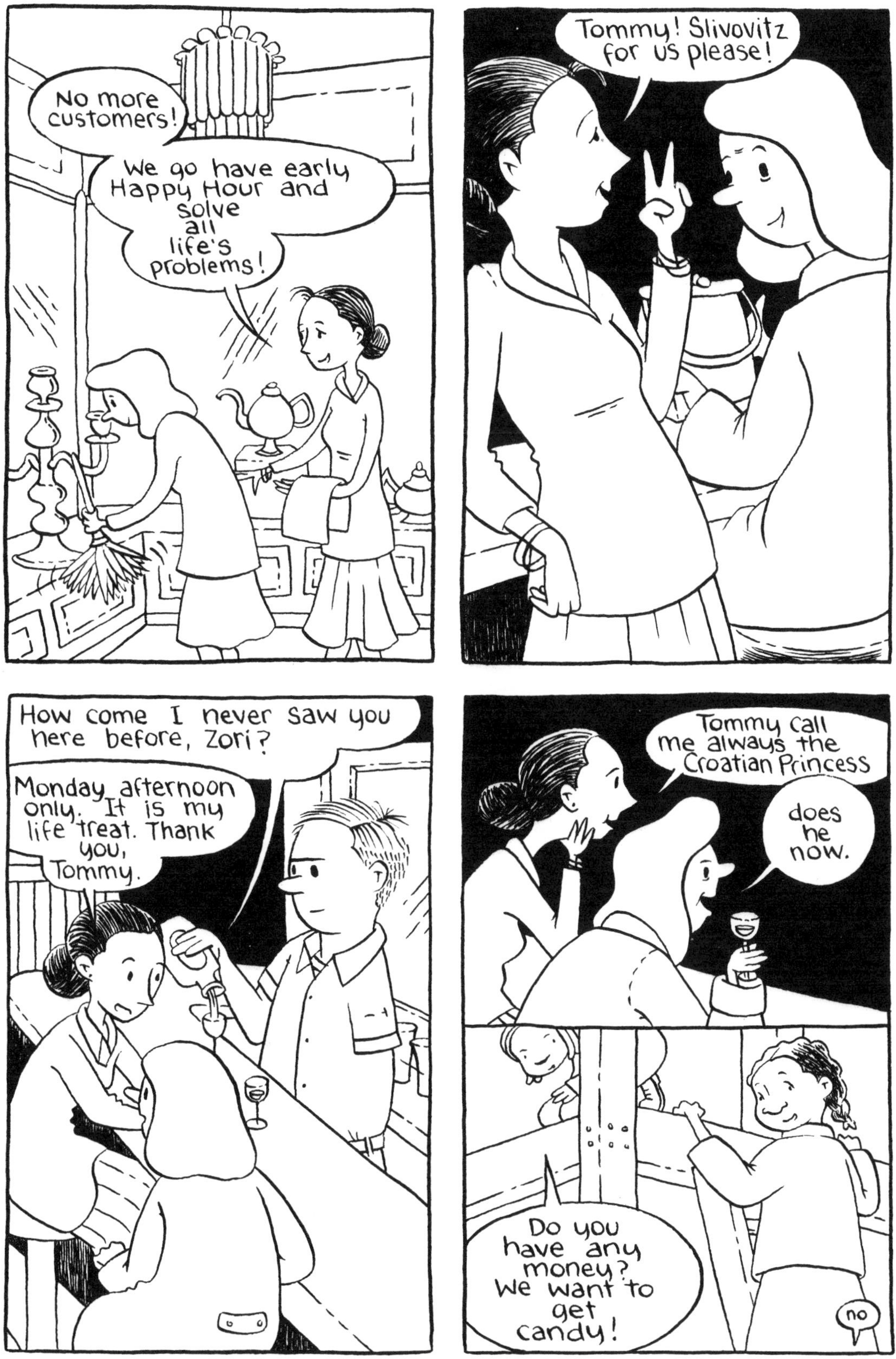
No more customers!
We go have early Happy Hour and solve all life's problems!
Tommy! Slivovitz for us please!
How come I never saw you here before, Zori?
Monday afternoon only. It is my life treat. Thank you, Tommy.
Tommy call me always the Croatian Princess
does he now.
Do you have any money? We want to get candy!
no

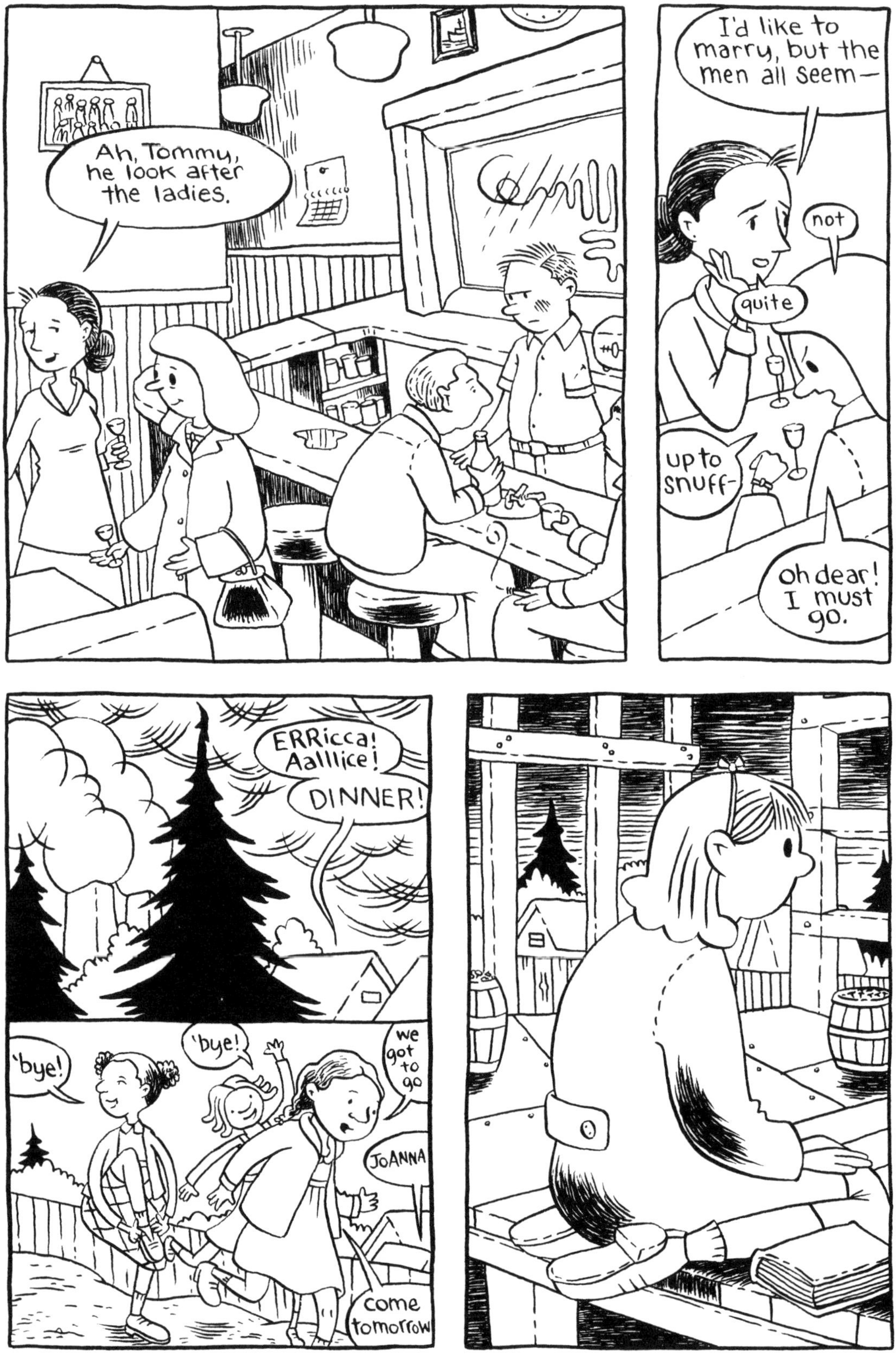

Ah, Tommy, he look after the ladies.
I'd like to marry, but the men all seem—
not
quite
up to snuff-
Oh dear! I must go.
ERRicca! Aalllice!
DINNER!
`bye!
'bye!
we got to go
JoANNA
come tomorrow

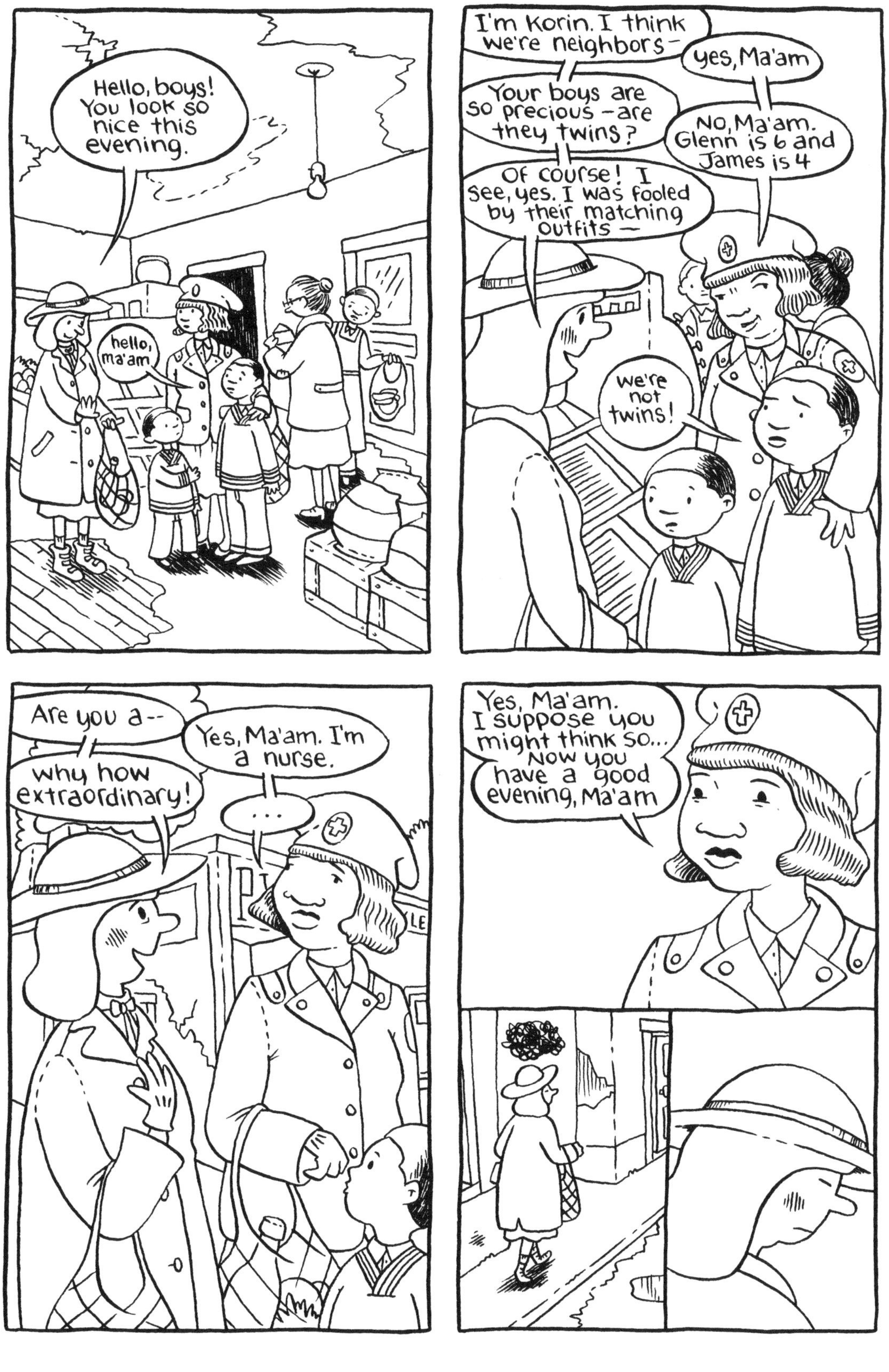
Hello, boys! You look so nice this evening.
hello, ma'am
I'm Korin. I think we're neighbors-
yes, Ma'am
Your boys are so precious -are they twins?
No, Ma'am. Glenn is 6 and James is 4
Of course! I see, yes. I was fooled by their matching outfits —
We're not twins!
Are you a--
why how extraordinary!
Yes, Ma'am. I'm a nurse.
...
Yes, Ma'am. I suppose you might think so... Now you have a good evening, Ma'am

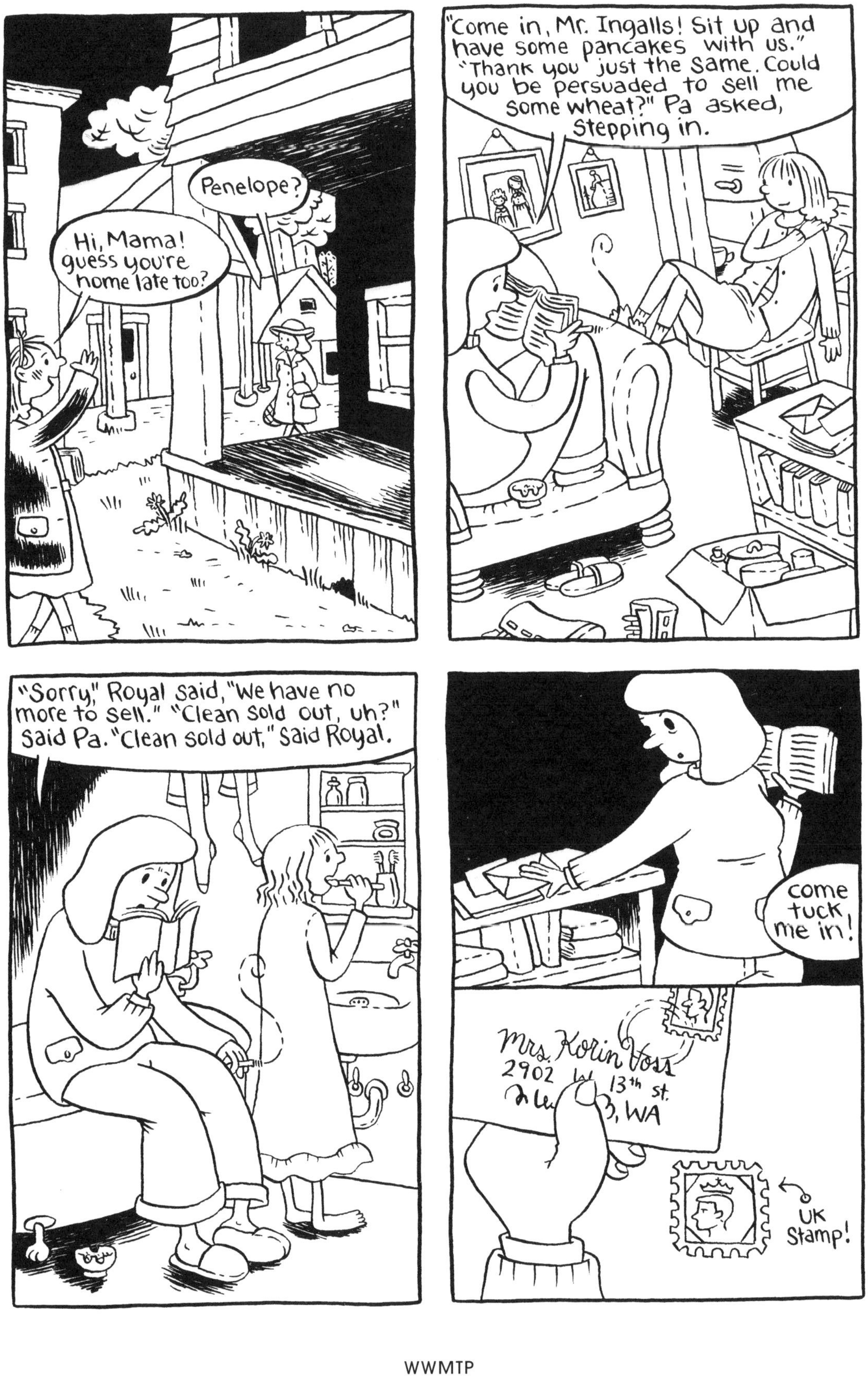
Penelope?
Hi, Mama! guess you're home late too?
"Come in, Mr. Ingalls! Sit up and have some pancakes with us." "Thank you just the same. Could you be persuaded to sell me some wheat?" Pa asked, stepping in.
"Sorry," Royal said, "We have no more to sell." "Clean sold out, uh?" said Pa. "Clean sold out," said Royal.
come tuck me in!
Mrs. Korin Voss
2902 W. 13th st.
UK Stamp!

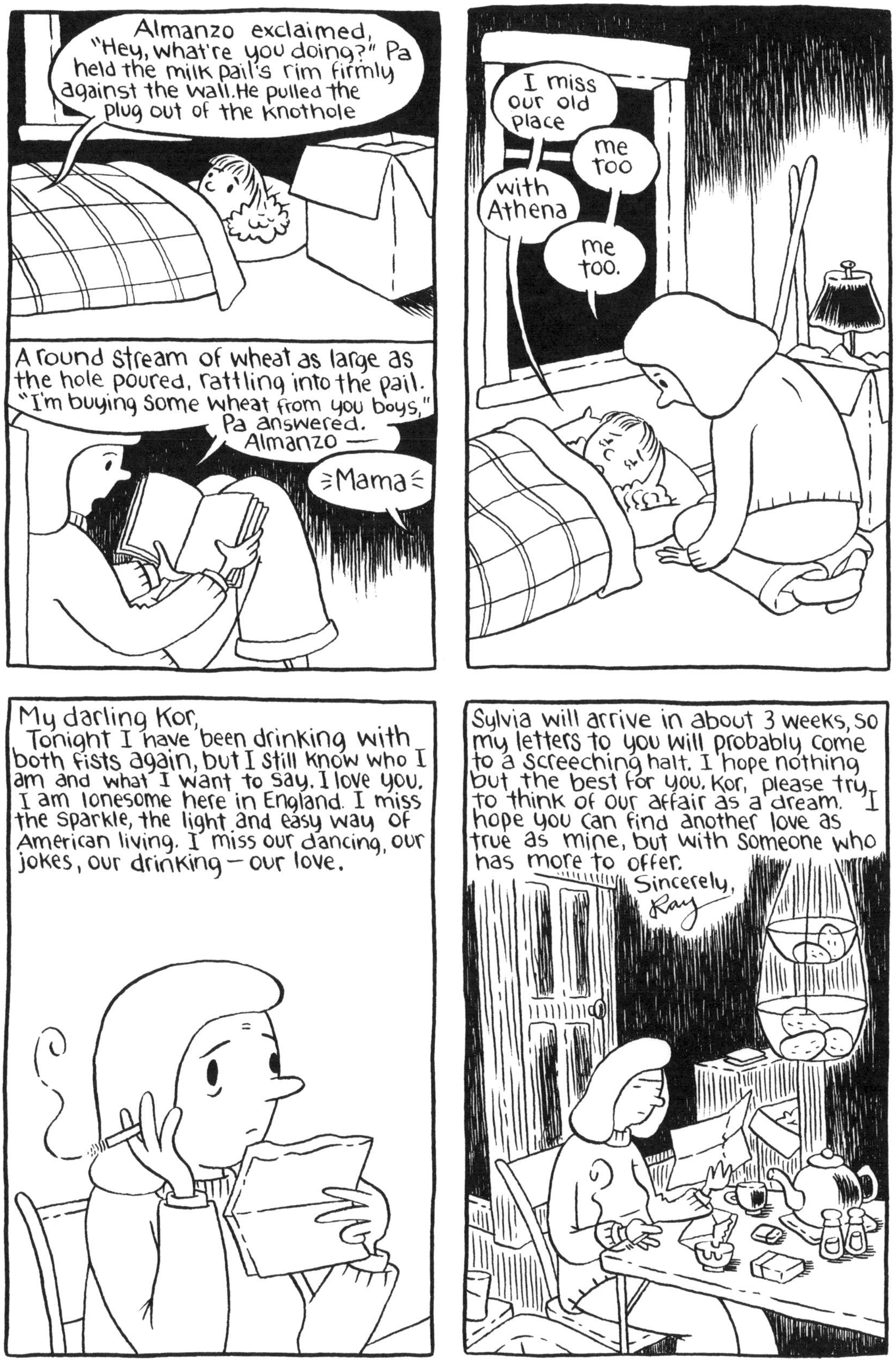

Almanzo exclaimed, "Hey, what're you doing?" Pa held the milk pail's rim firmly against the wall. He pulled the plug out of the knothole
I miss our old place
me too
with Athena
me too.
A round stream of wheat as large as the hole poured, rattling into the pail. "I'm buying some wheat from you boys," Pa answered.
Almanzo —
Mama
My darling Kor, Tonight I have been drinking with both fists again, but I still know who I am and what I want to say. I love you. I am lonesome here in England. I miss the sparkle, the light and easy way of American living. I miss our dancing, our jokes, our drinking — our love.
Sylvia will arrive in about 3 weeks, so my letters to you will probably come to a screeching halt. I hope nothing but the best for you. Kor, please try to think of our affair as a dream. I hope you can find another love as true as mine, but with someone who has more to offer.
Sincerely, Ray

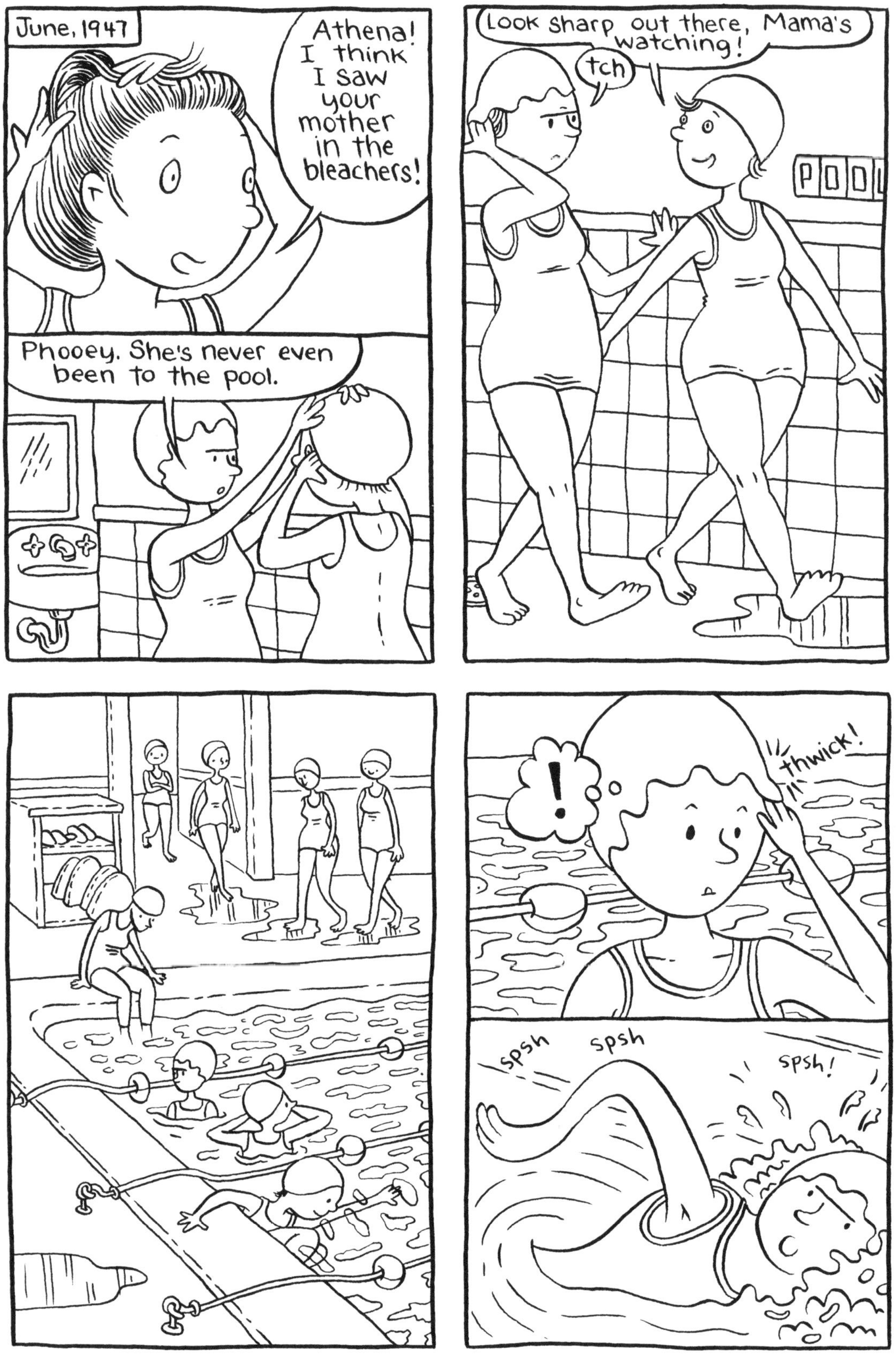
June, 1947
Athena! I think I saw your mother in the bleachers!
Phooey. She's never even been to the pool.
Look sharp out there, Mama's watching!
tch
POOL
!
thwick!
spsh
spsh
spsh!

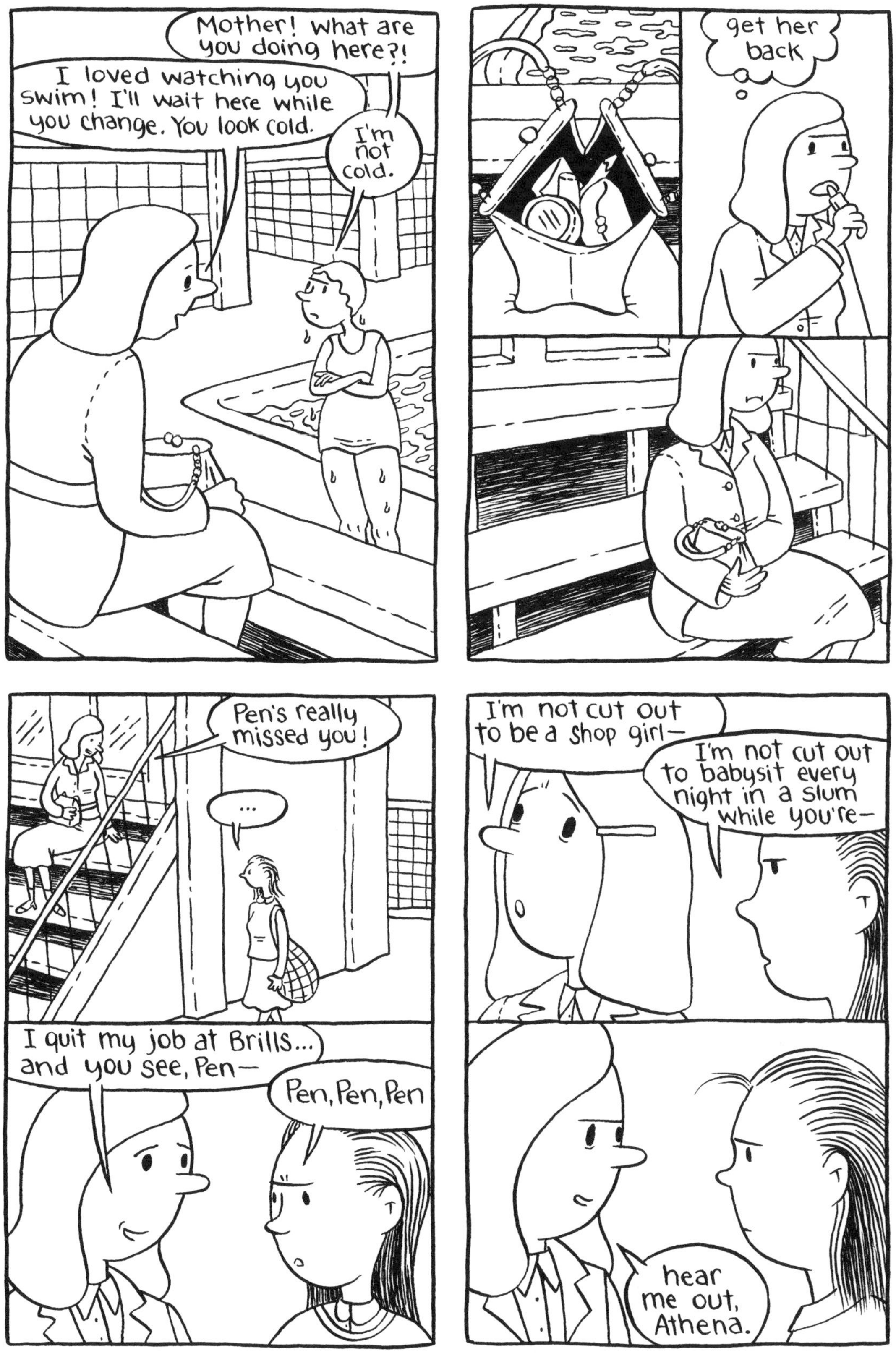
Mother! What are you doing here?!
I loved watching you swim! I'll wait here while you change. You look cold.
I'm not cold.
get her back
Pen's really missed you!
...
I'm not cut out to be a shop girl—
I'm not cut out to babysit every night in a slum while you're—
I quit my job at Brills... and you see, Pen—
Pen, Pen, Pen
hear me out, Athena.

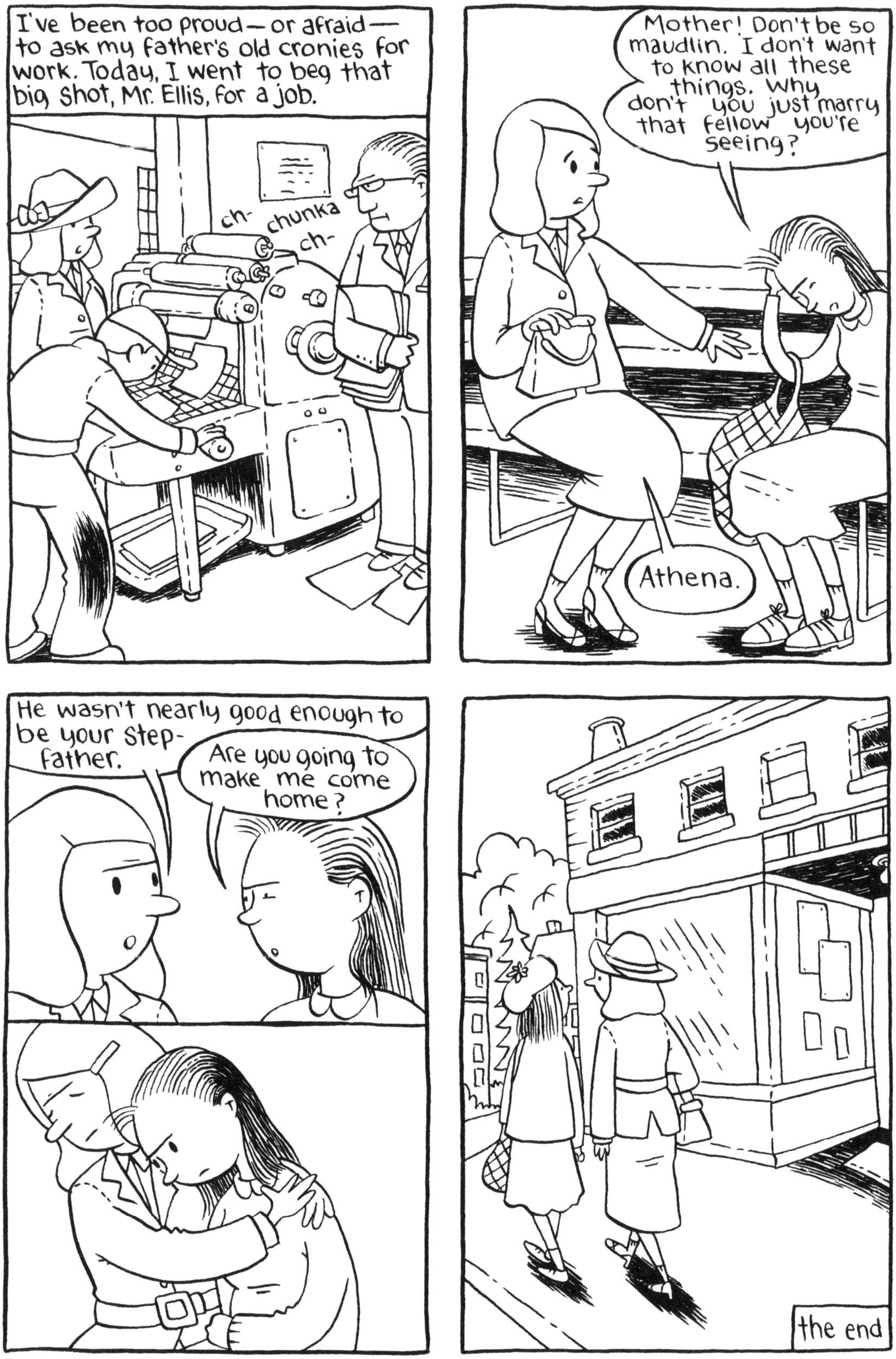
I've been too proud—or afraid—to ask my father's old cronies for work. Today, I went to beg that big shot, Mr. Ellis, for a job.
ch- chunka ch-
Mother! Don't be so maudlin. I don't want to know all these things. Why don't you just marry that fellow you're seeing?
Athena.
He wasn't nearly good enough to be your step-father.
Are you going to make me come home?
the end

5

The Golden Lasso

MEGAN KELSO

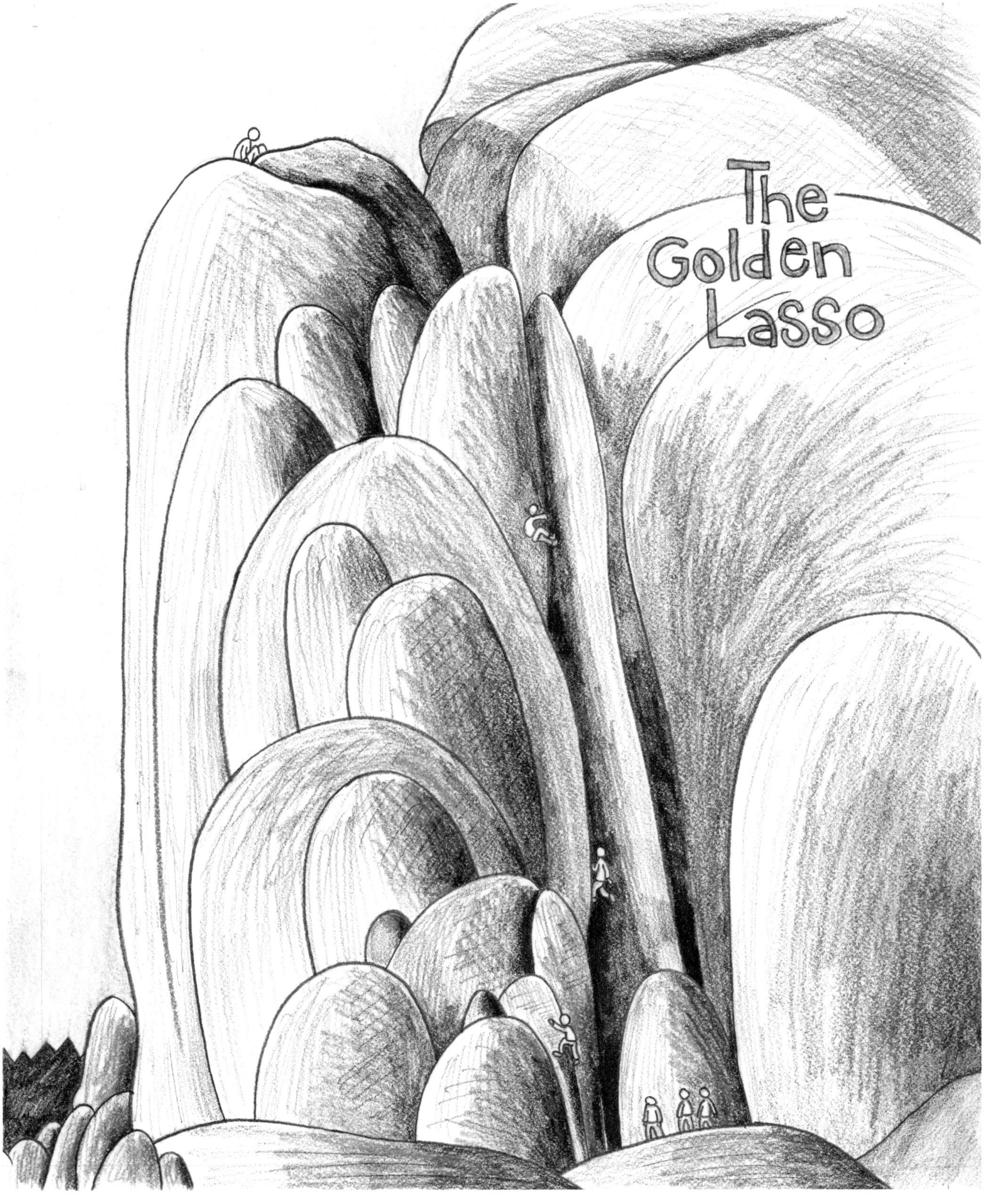
The Golden Lasso

Bastille Tower · Spring, 1980

This is Hector Peralta, cutest boy at Forest Day School.

Hector was in Upper School, but he helped Mr. Pete lead on Middle School trips.

Slack!

You girls OK with Hector? I'm going to take the beginners down to the slabs

yup

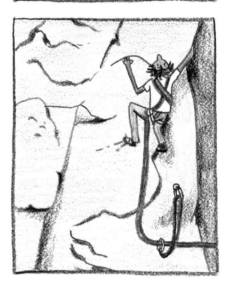

off belay!

You go next, Diana

OK

belay on!

Climbing

climb on!

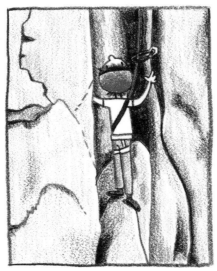

None of us could lead yet, so Hector took us up routes that were easy for him but challenging for us.

welcome!

yikes

you're over the hardest

OK, you're clipped in, now un-tie the rope

Now just sit tight and I'll be-lay the other girls up

pling!

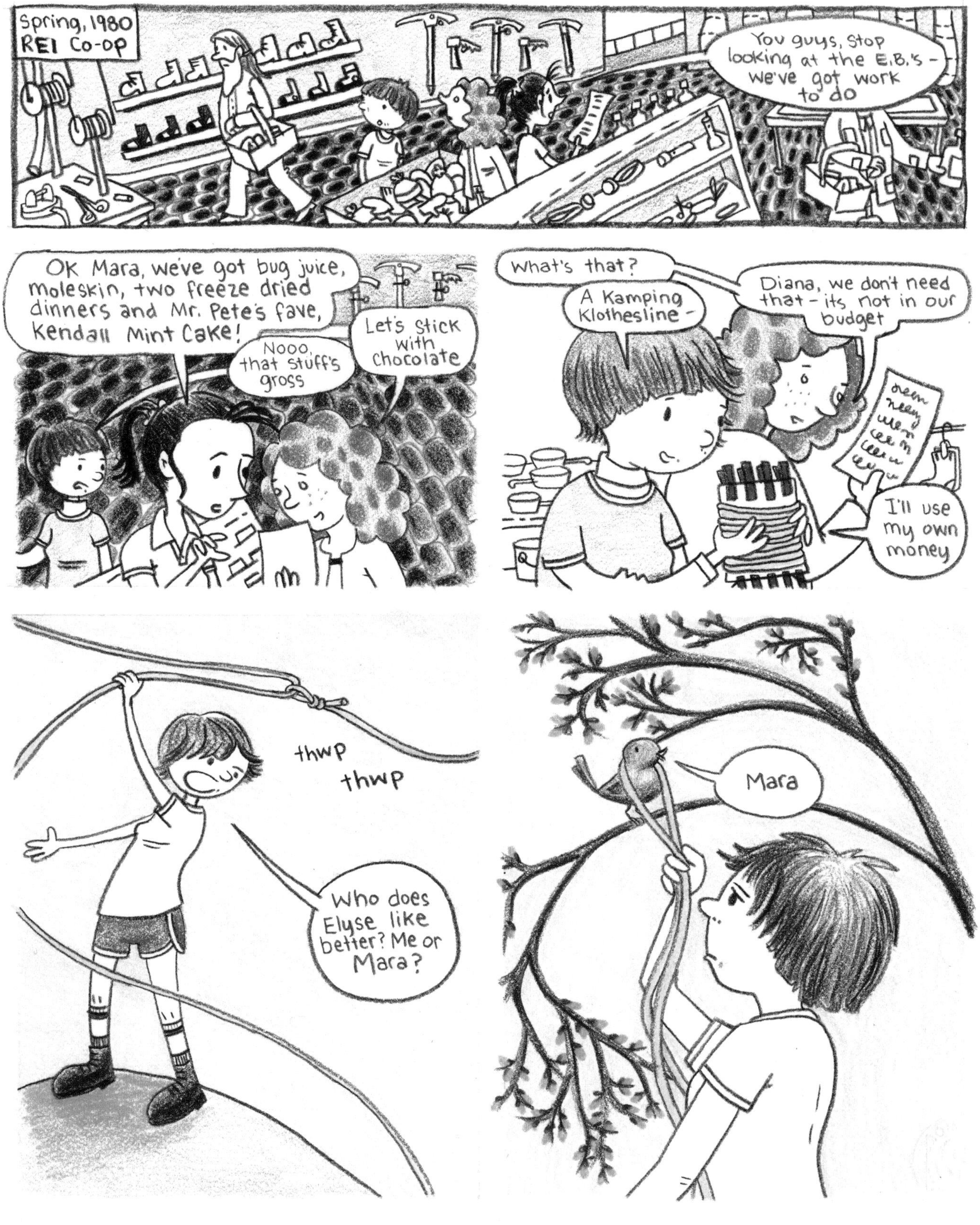

Spring, 1980
REI Co-op
You guys, stop looking at the E.B.'s - we've got work to do
OK Mara, we've got bug juice, moleskin, two freeze dried dinners and Mr. Pete's fave, Kendall Mint Cake!
Nooo, that stuff's gross
Let's stick with chocolate
What's that?
A Kamping Klothesline -
Diana, we don't need that - its not in our budget
I'll use my own money
thwp
thwp
Who does Elyse like better? Me or Mara?
Mara

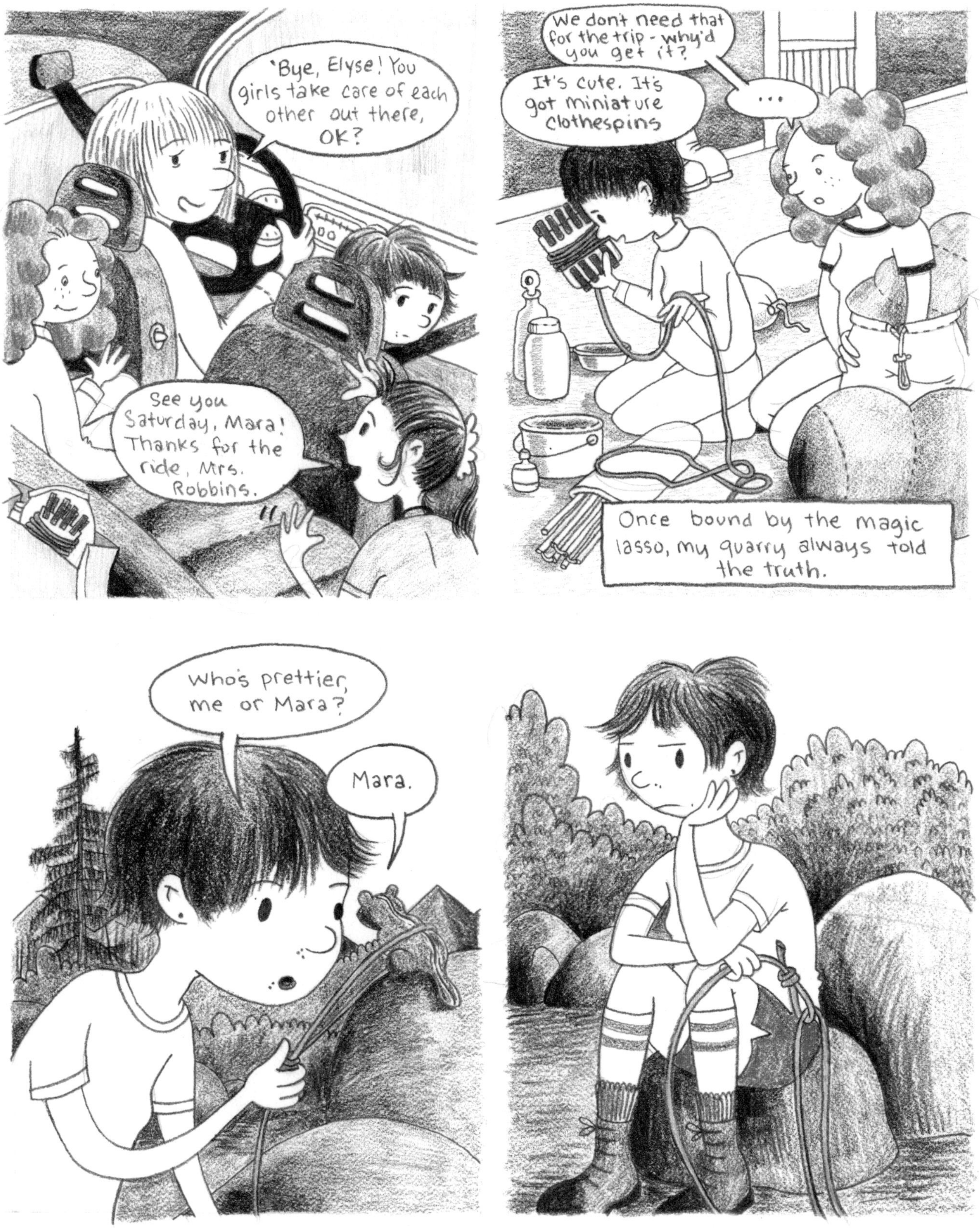
'Bye, Elyse! You girls take care of each other out there, OK?
See you Saturday, Mara! Thanks for the ride, Mrs. Robbins.
We don't need that for the trip - why'd you get it?
It's cute. It's got miniature clothespins
...
Once bound by the magic lasso, my quarry always told the truth.
Who's prettier, me or Mara?
Mara.

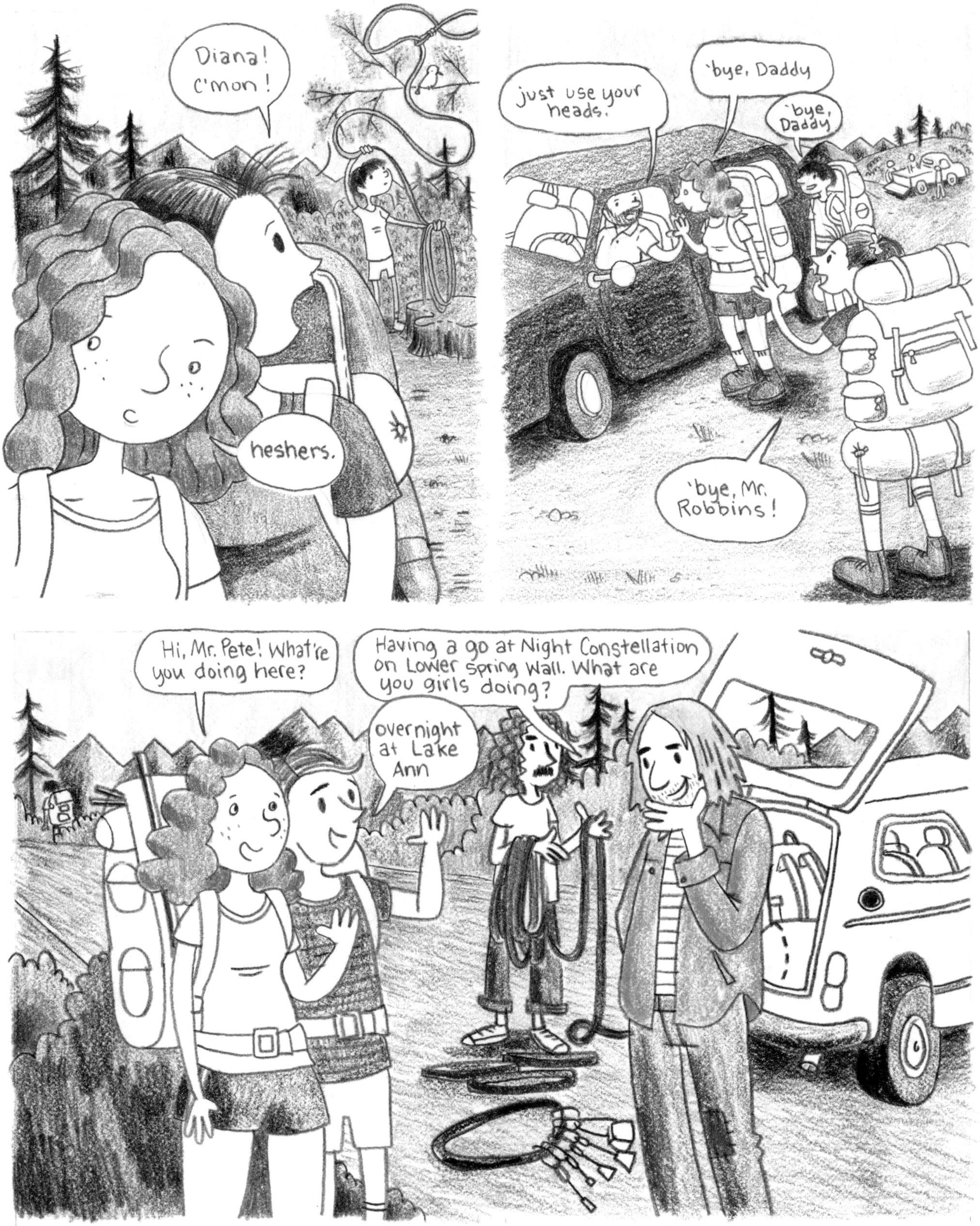
Diana! C'mon!
heshers.
just use your heads.
`bye, Daddy
`bye, Daddy
`bye, Mr. Robbins!
Hi, Mr. Pete! What're you doing here?
Having a go at Night Constellation on Lower Spring Wall. What are you girls doing?
overnight at Lake Ann

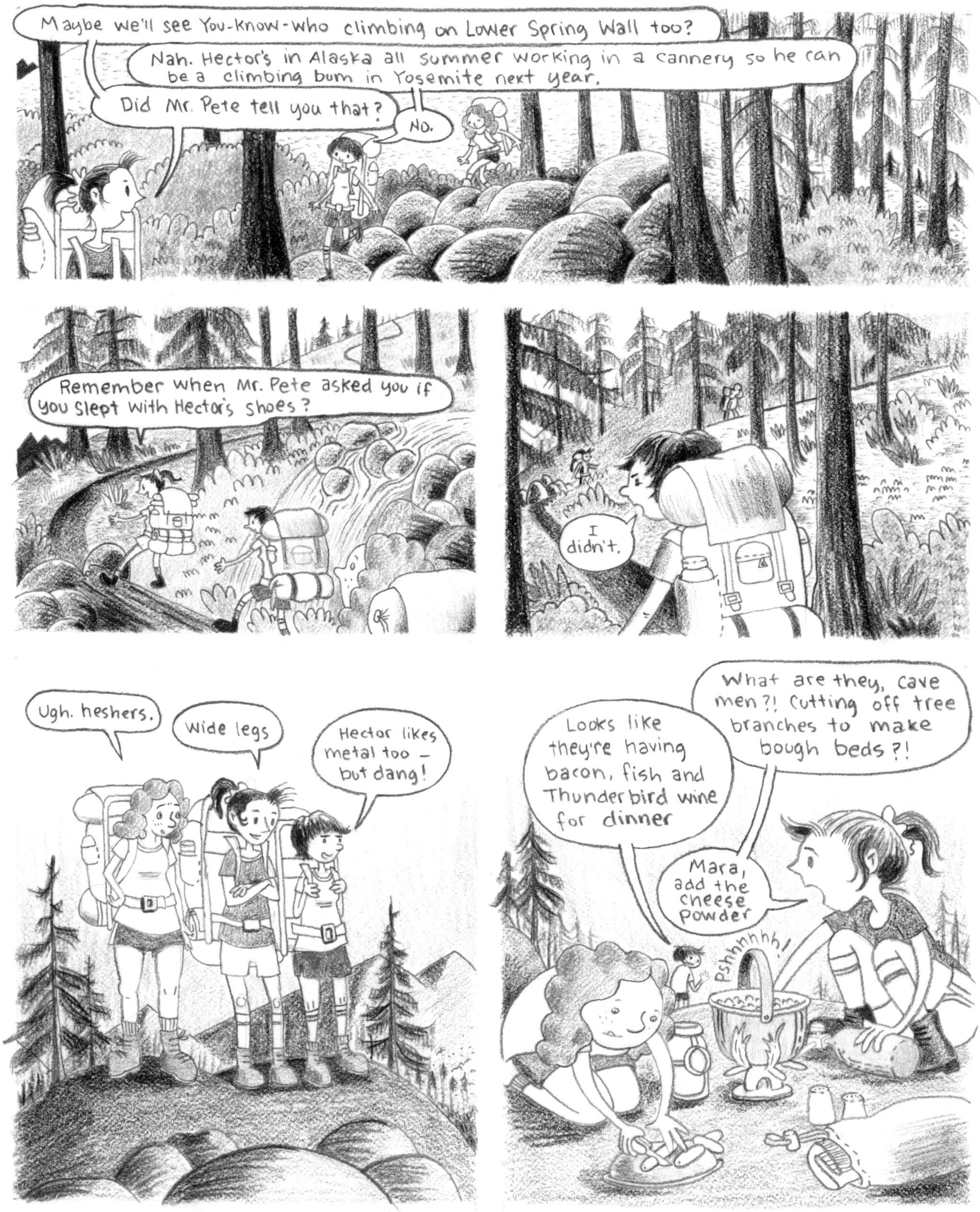
Maybe we'll see You-Know-Who climbing on Lower Spring Wall too?
Nah. Hector's in Alaska all summer working in a cannery so he can be a climbing bum in Yosemite next year.
Did Mr. Pete tell you that?
No.
Remember when Mr. Pete asked you if you slept with Hector's shoes?
I didn't.
Ugh. heshers.
Wide legs
Hector likes metal too — but dang!
Looks like they're having bacon, fish and Thunderbird wine for dinner
What are they, cave men?! Cutting off tree branches to make bough beds?!
Mara, add the cheese powder
Pshhhhhh!

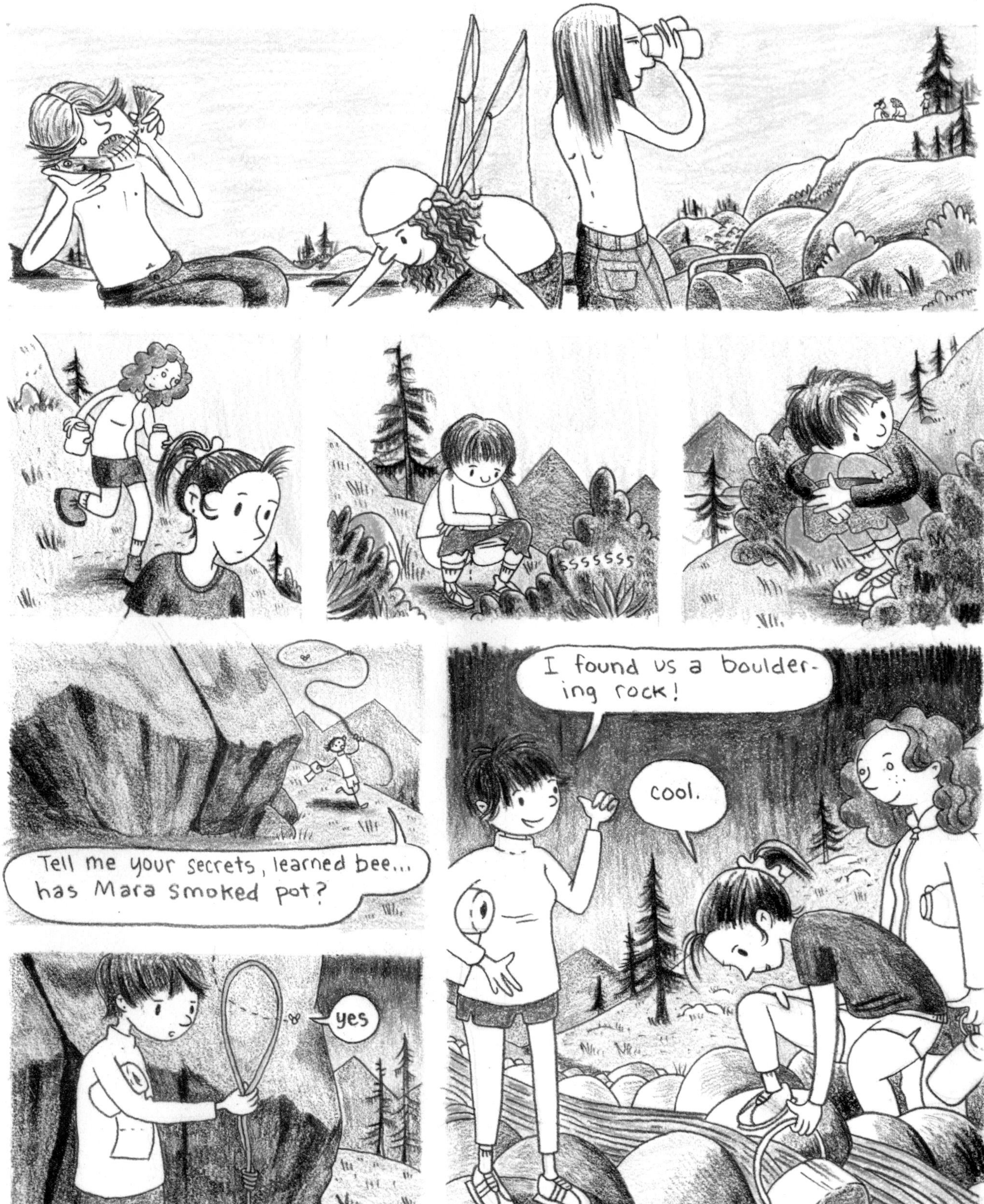
SSSSSSS
Tell me your secrets, learned bee... has Mara smoked pot?
yes
I found us a boulder-ing rock!
cool.

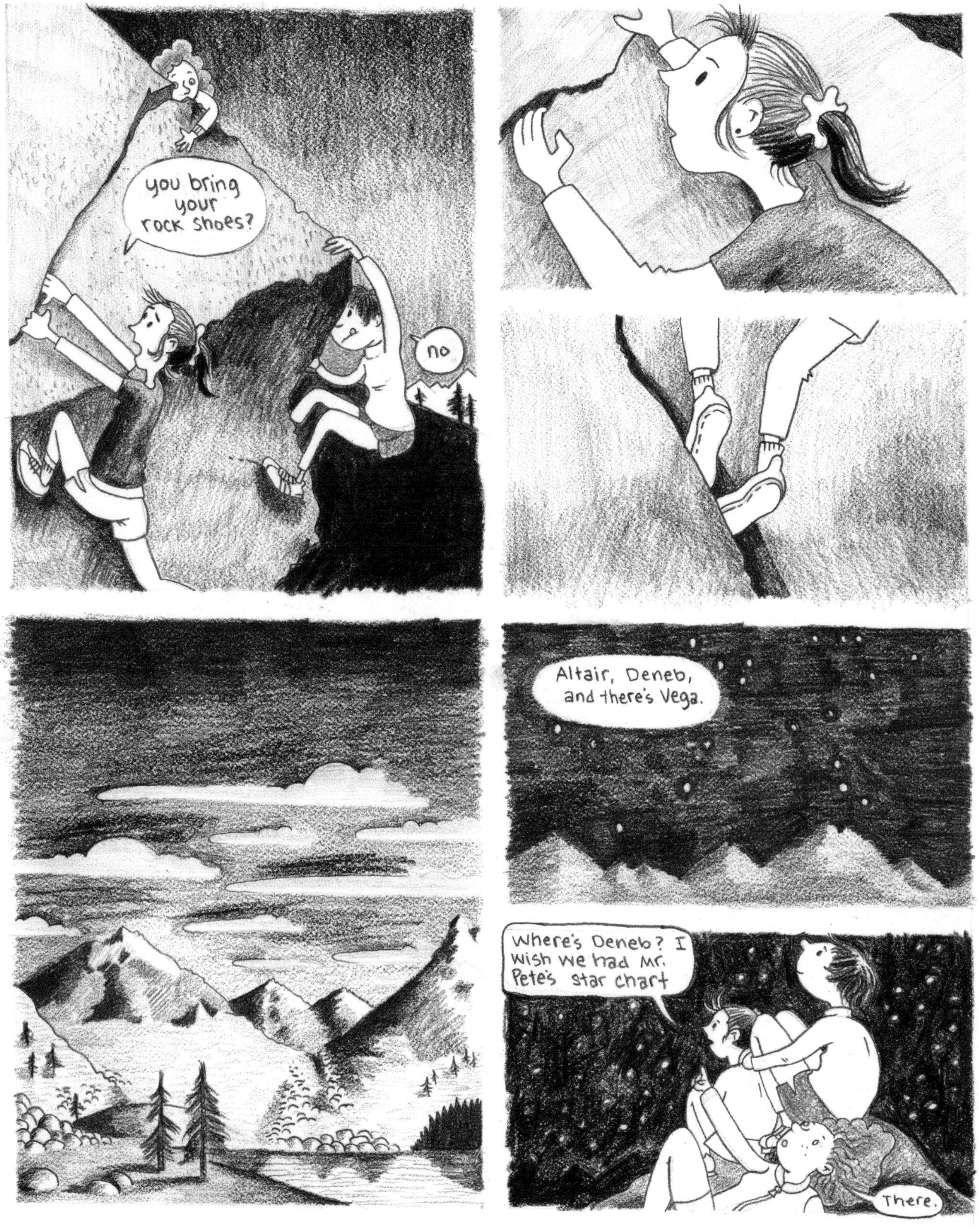
you bring your rock shoes?
no
Altair, Deneb, and there's Vega.
Where's Deneb? I wish we had Mr. Pete's star chart
There.

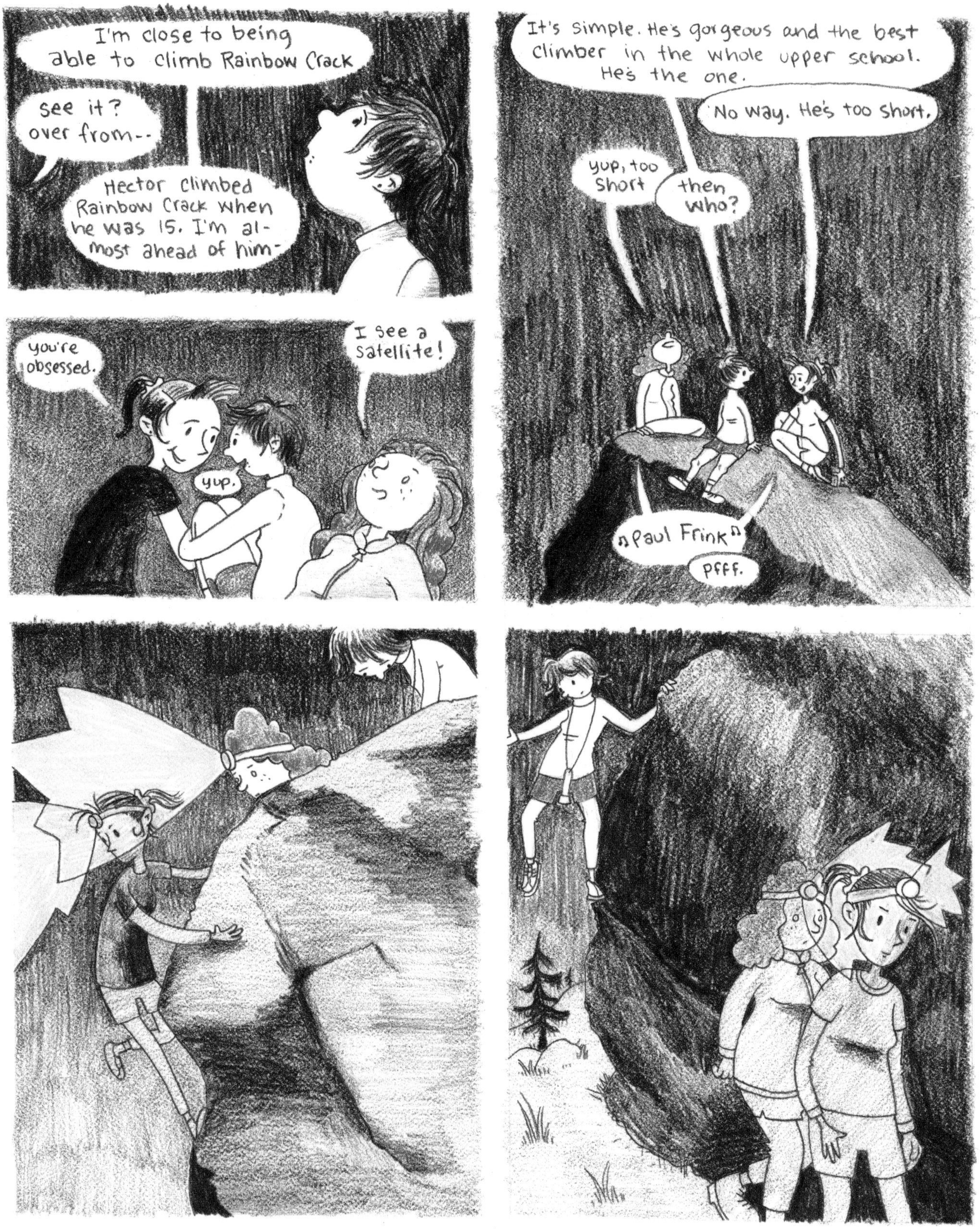
I'm close to being able to climb Rainbow Crack
see it? over from--
Hector climbed Rainbow Crack when he was 15. I'm almost ahead of him-
It's simple. He's gorgeous and the best climber in the whole upper school. He's the one.
No way. He's too short.
yup, too short
then who?
♫Paul Frink♫
pfff.
you're obsessed.
I see a satellite!
yup.

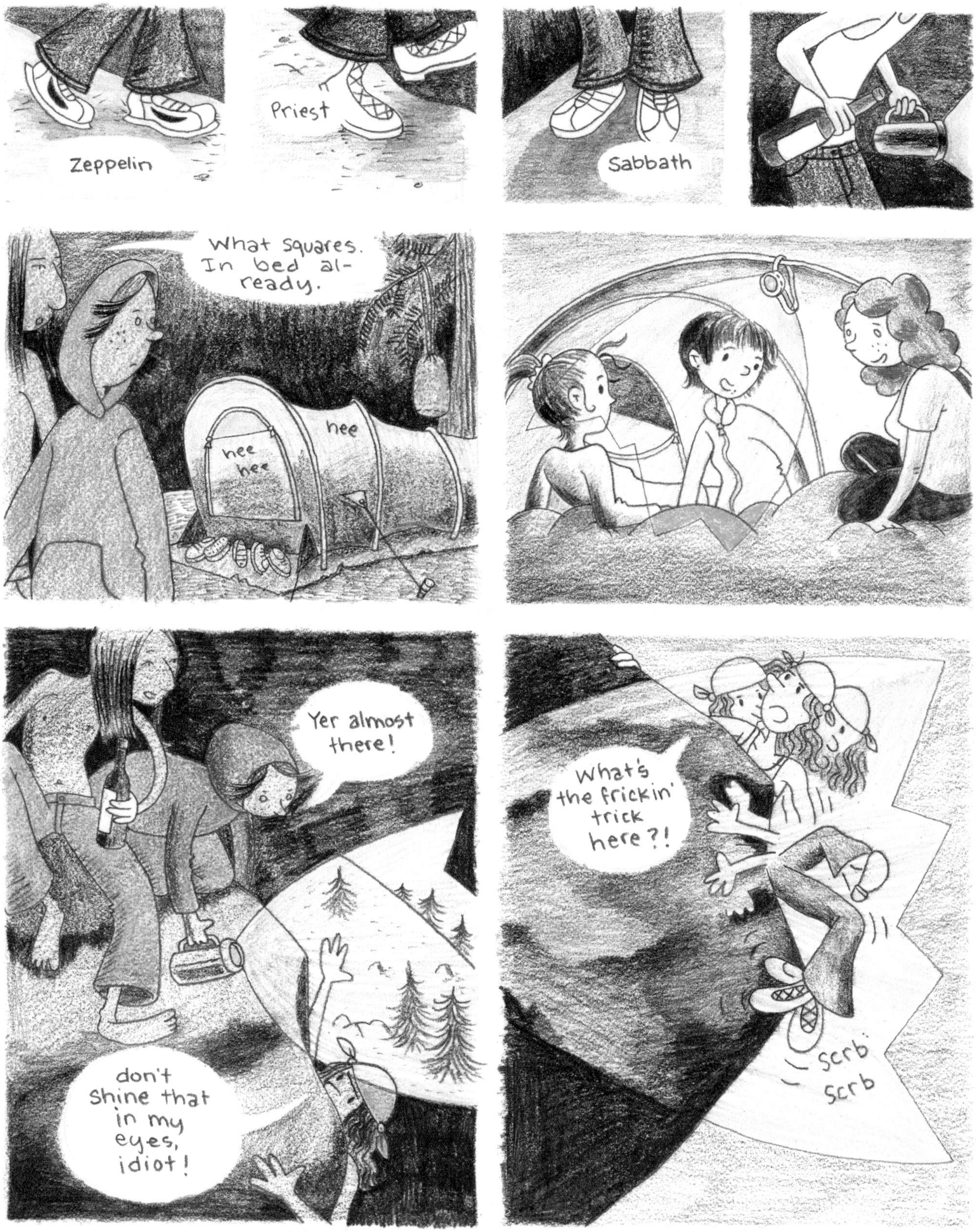
Zeppelin
Priest
Sabbath
What squares. In bed al-ready.
hee
hee hee
Yer almost there!
don't shine that in my eyes, idiot!
What's the frickin' trick here?!
scrb scrb

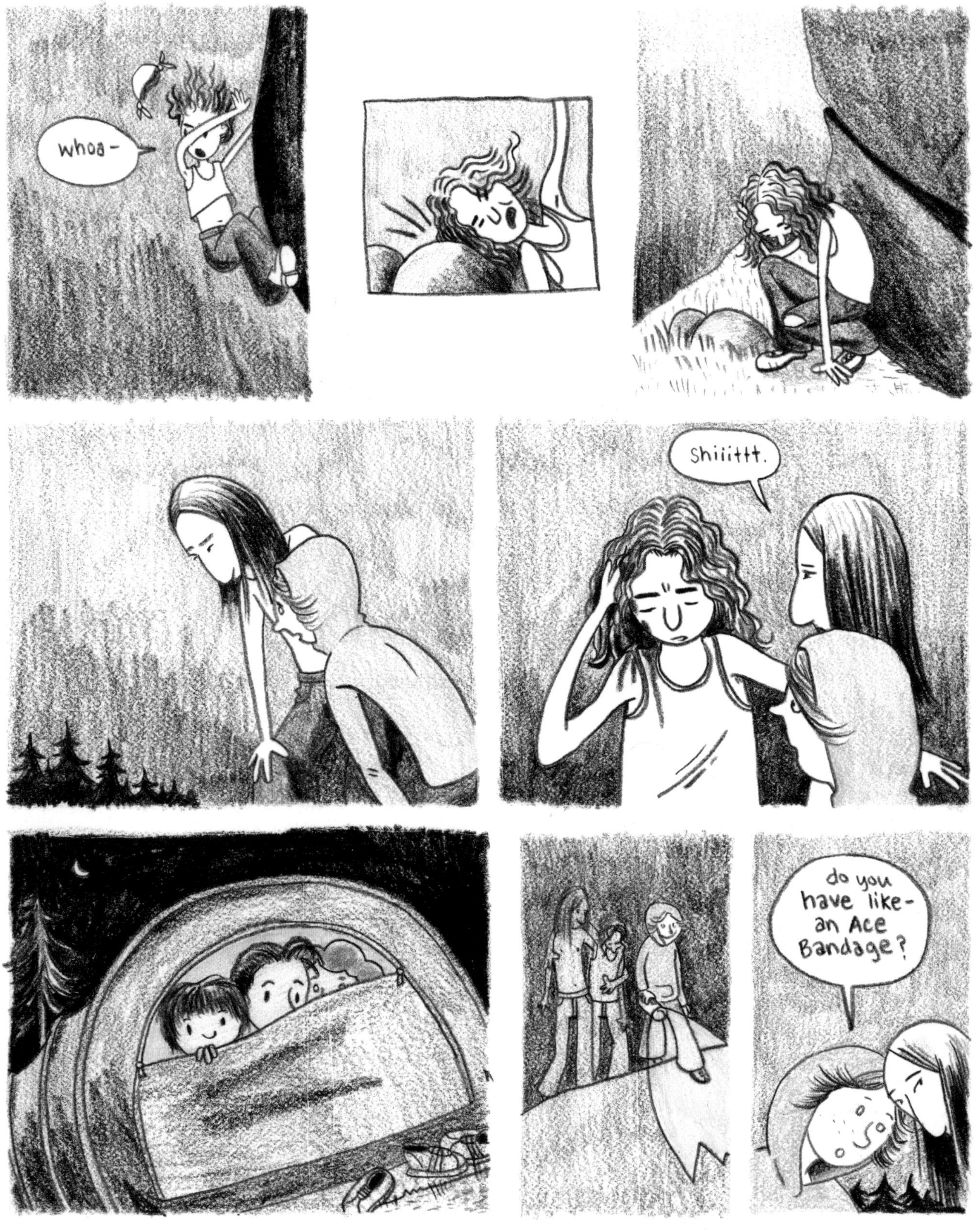
whoa-
Shiiittt.
do you have like- an Ace Bandage?

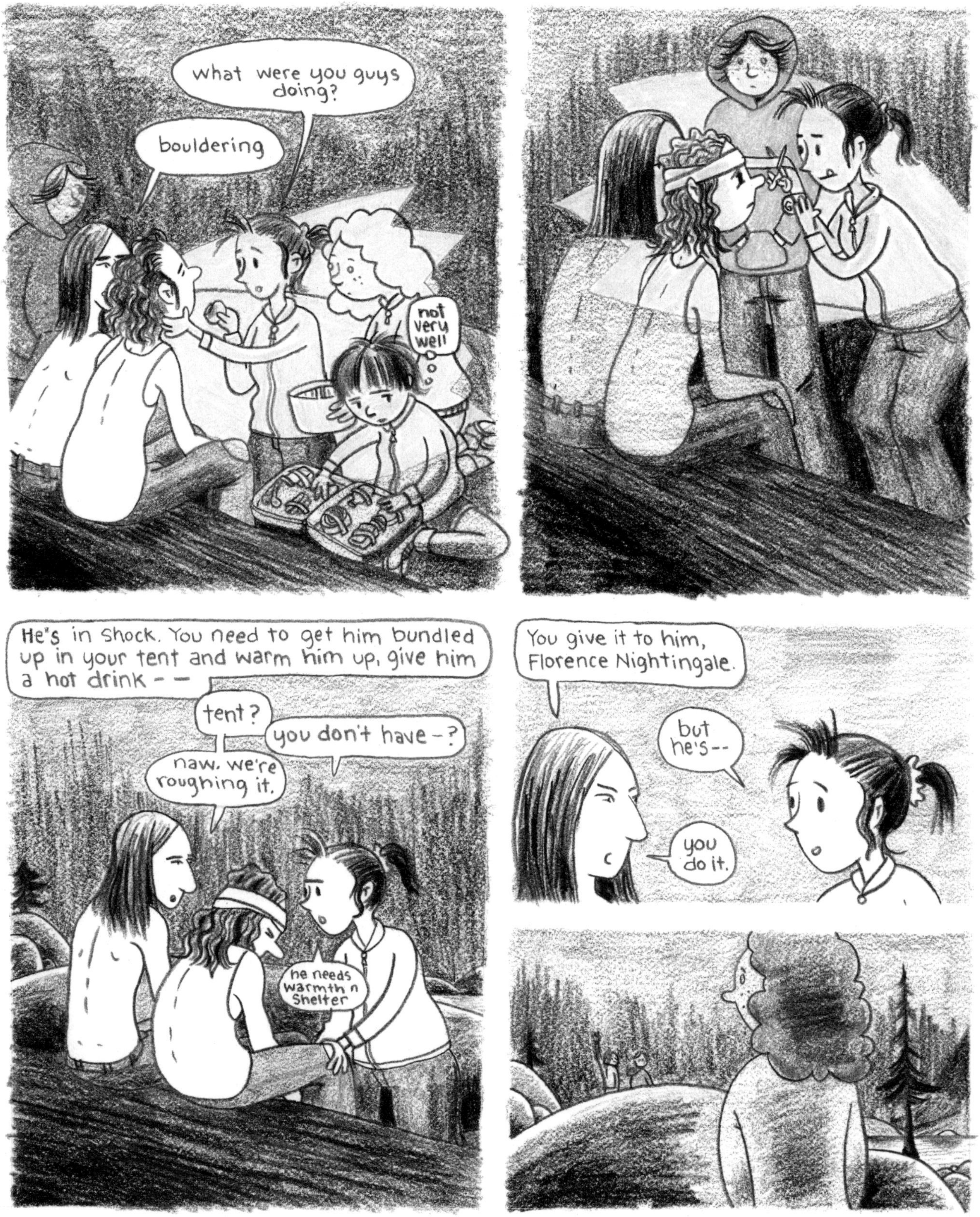

what were you guys doing?
bouldering
not very well
He's in shock. You need to get him bundled up in your tent and warm him up, give him a hot drink --
tent?
you don't have -?
naw, we're roughing it.
he needs warmth n shelter
You give it to him, Florence Nightingale.
but he's--
you do it.

I've seen my parents do this...

he smells funny

go to sleep, Diana...

Someday you'll like the way boys smell

zzzz

you gotta know how to bivouac if you're going to be a big wall climber—

I will go to Yosemite and live at Camp 4. I will climb El Capitan.

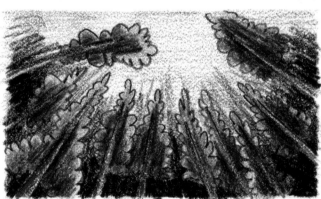

Oh, mighty second growth Douglas Fir, is Elyse a virgin?

how about Mara?

no

Nope.

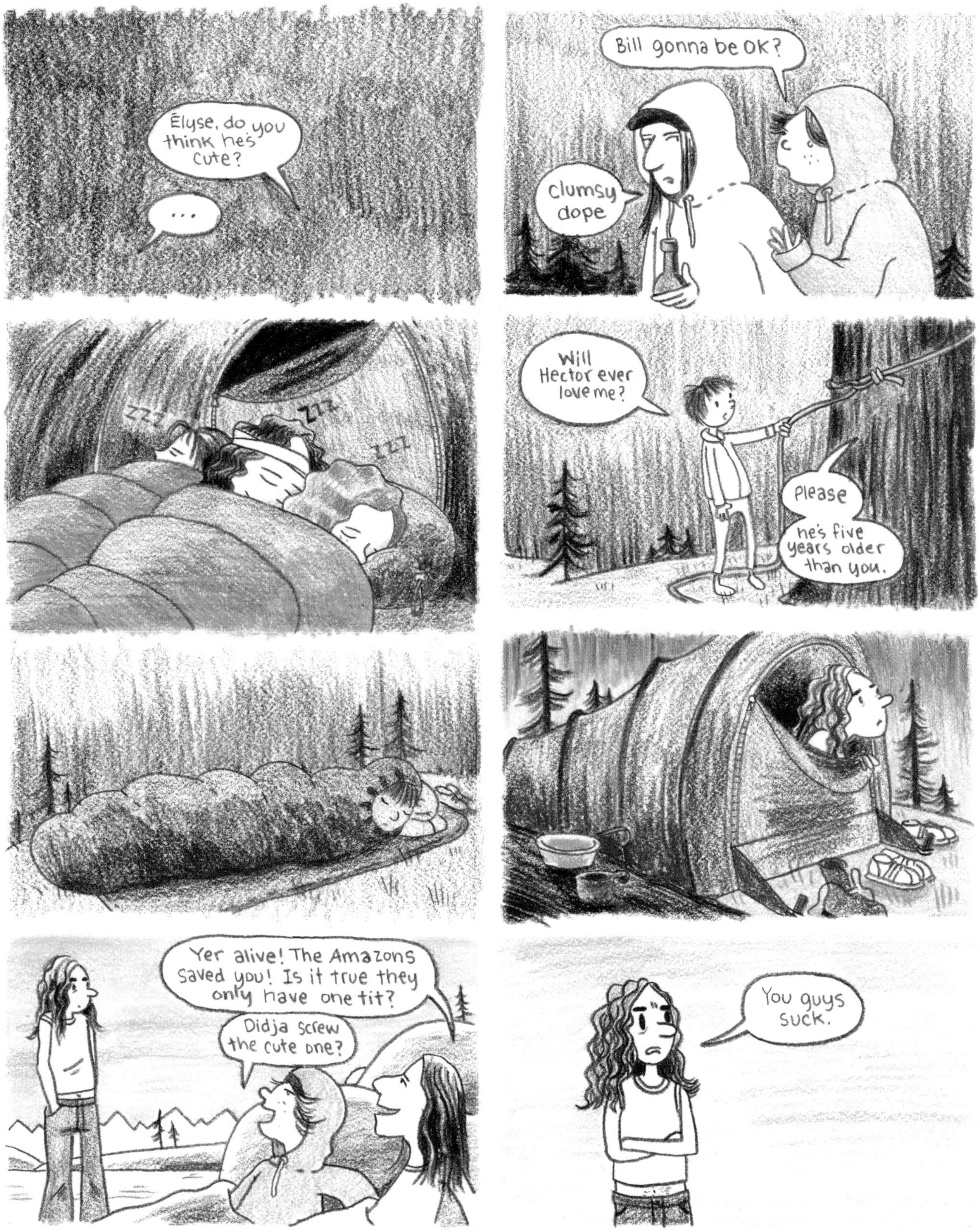
Élyse, do you think he's cute?
...
Bill gonna be OK?
clumsy dope
Will Hector ever love me?
Please
he's five years older than you.
Yer alive! The Amazons saved you! Is it true they only have one tit?
Didja screw the cute one?
You guys suck.

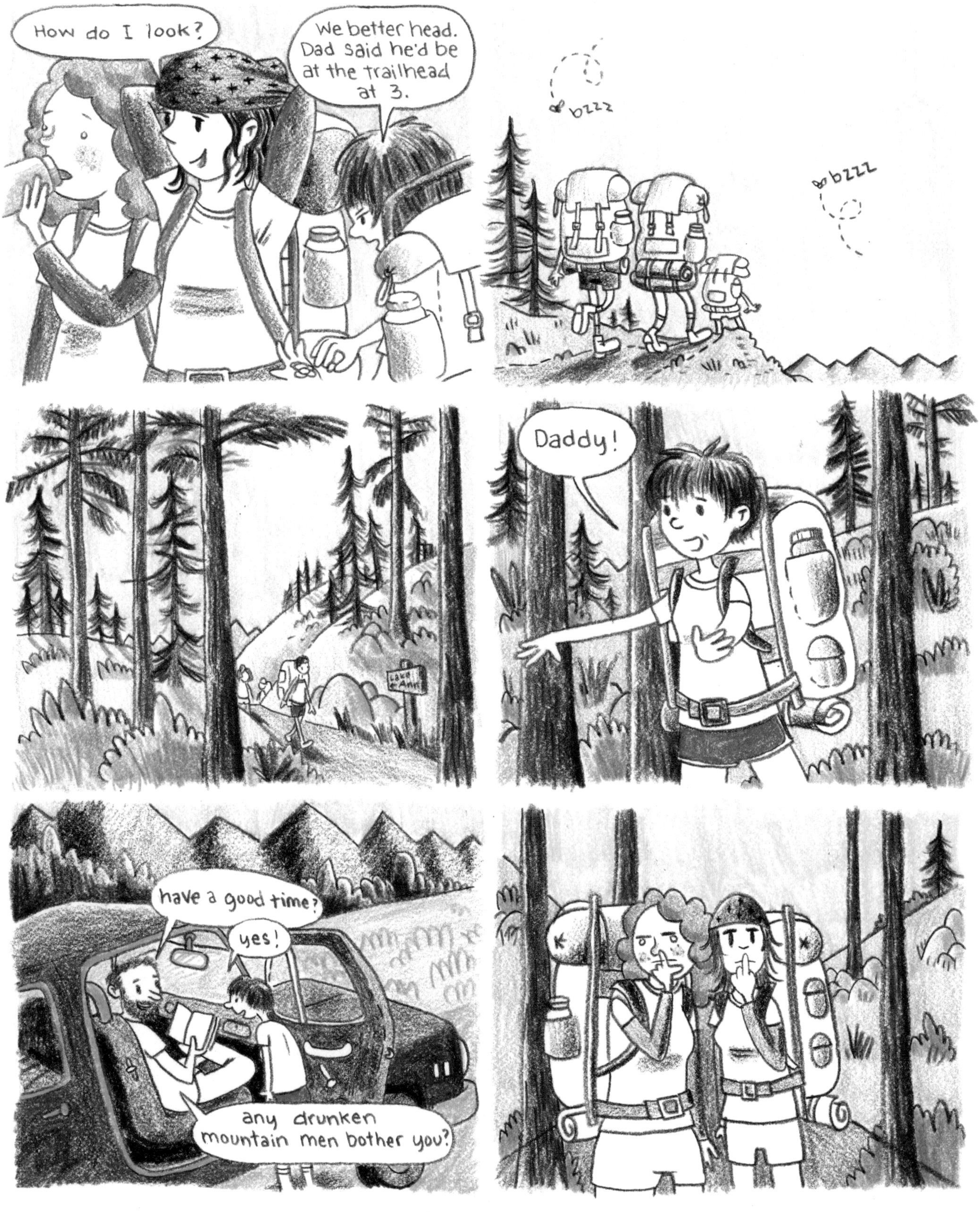
How do I look?
We better head. Dad said he'd be at the trailhead at 3.
bzzz
bzzz
Daddy!
have a good time?
yes!
any drunken mountain men bother you?

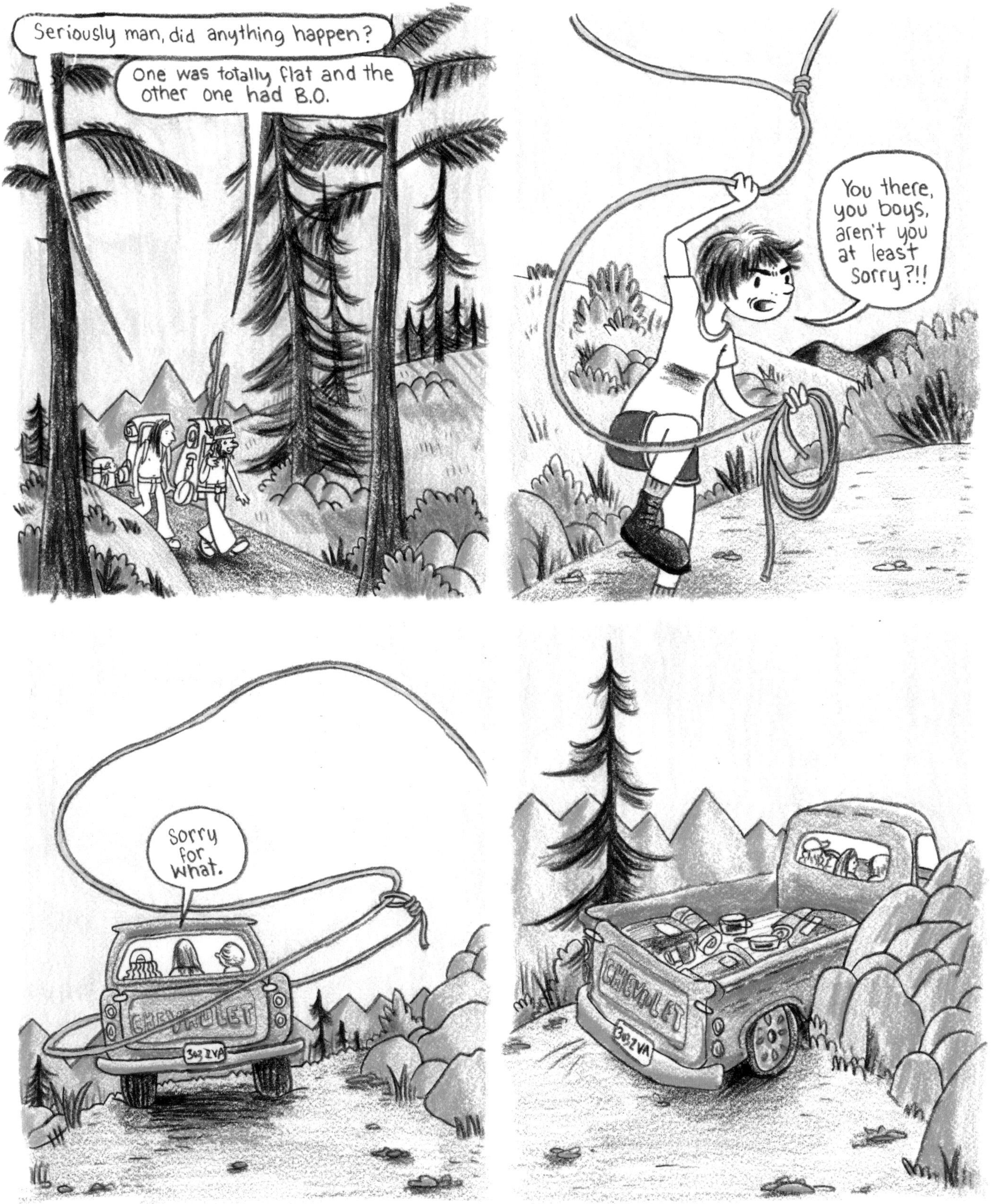
Seriously man, did anything happen?
One was totally flat and the other one had B.O.
You there, you boys, aren't you at least sorry?!!
Sorry for what.
CHEVROLET
343 ZVA
CHEVROLET
343 ZVA

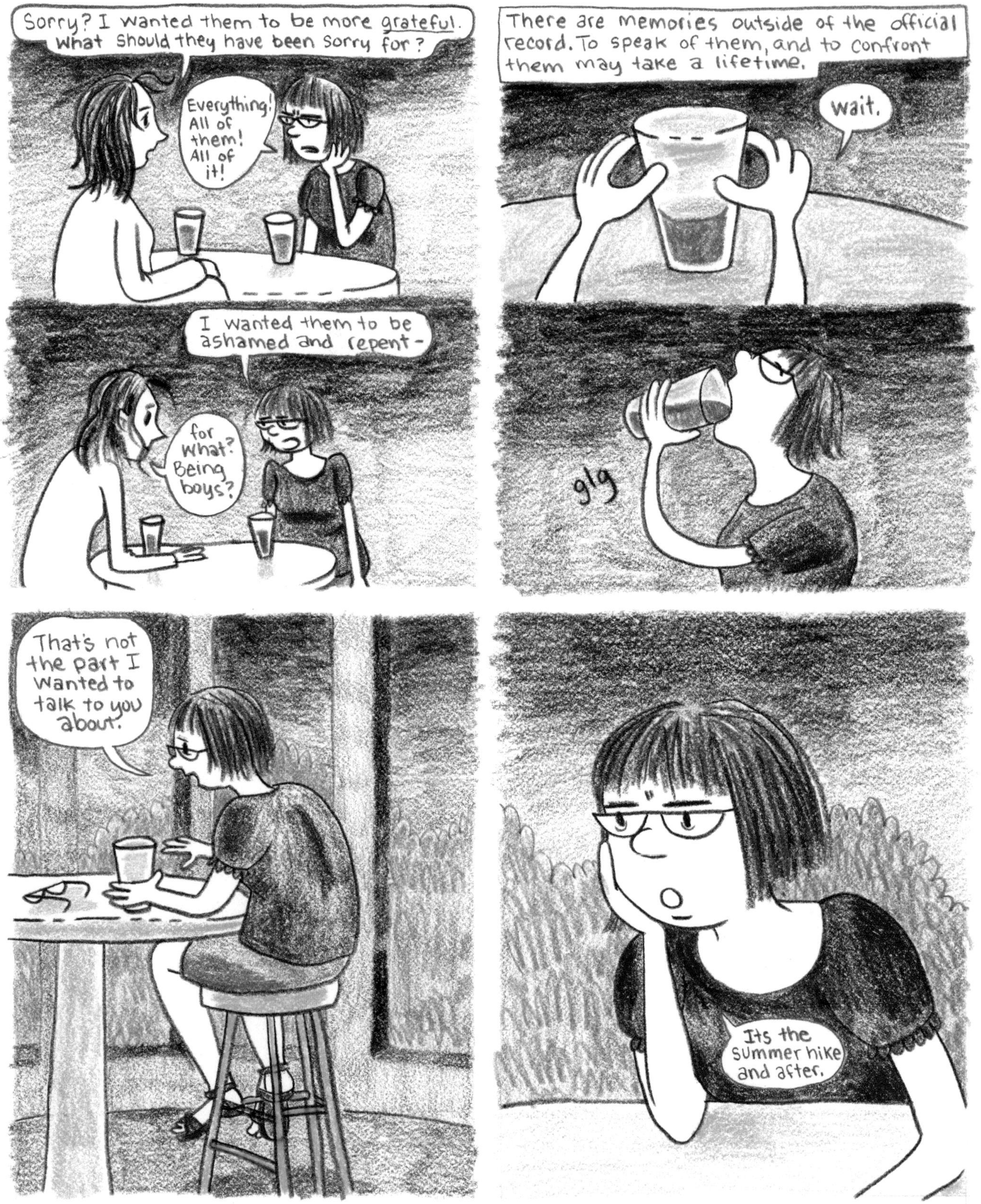
Sorry? I wanted them to be more grateful. What should they have been sorry for?
Everything! All of them! All of it!
There are memories outside of the official record. To speak of them, and to confront them may take a lifetime.
wait.
I wanted them to be ashamed and repent-
for what? Being boys?
glg
That's not the part I wanted to talk to you about.
Its the summer hike and after.

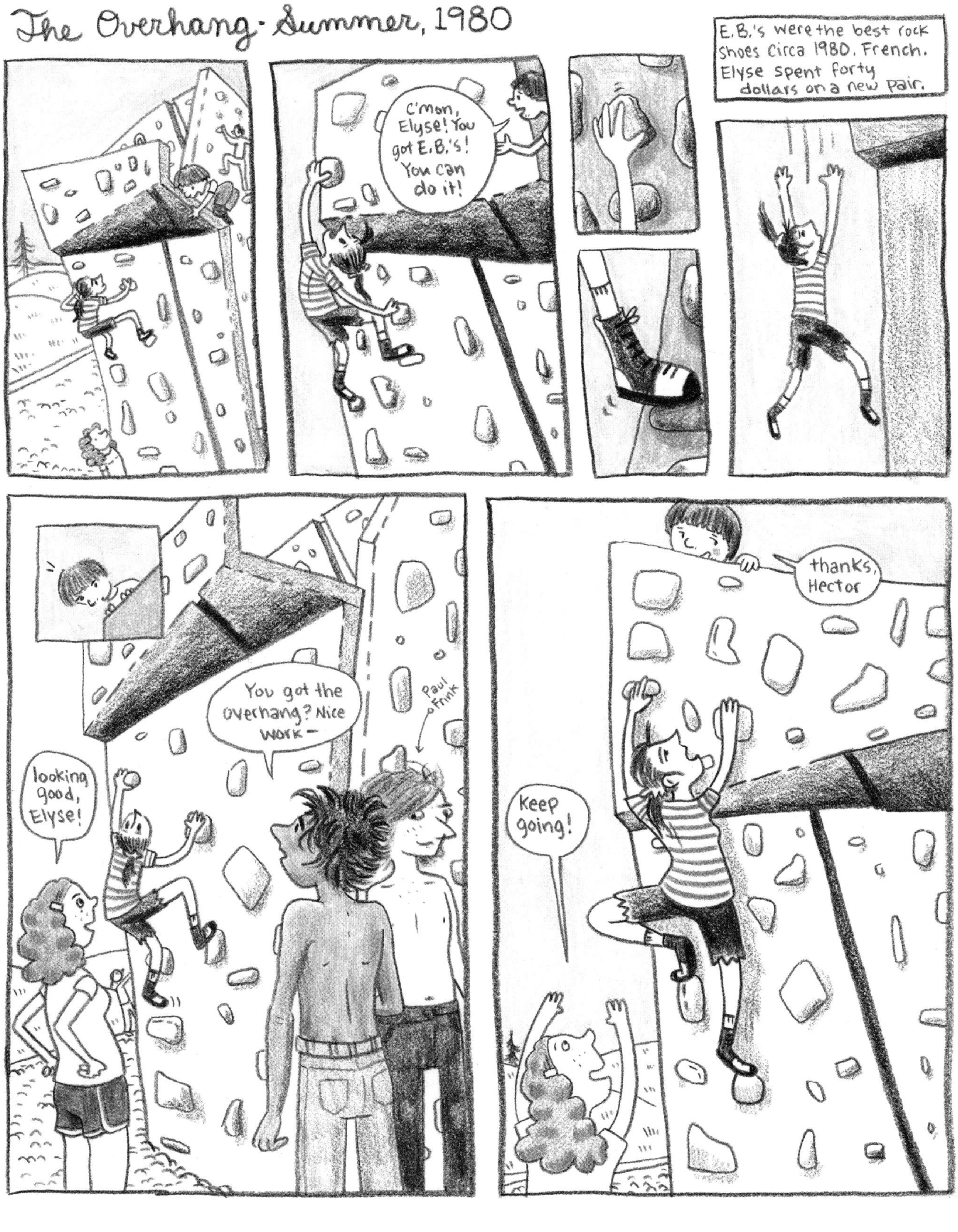
The Overhang - Summer, 1980
C'mon, Elyse! You got E.B.'s! You can do it!
E.B.'s were the best rock shoes circa 1980. French. Elyse spent forty dollars on a new pair.
looking good, Elyse!
You got the overhang? Nice work—
Paul Frink
Keep going!
thanks, Hector

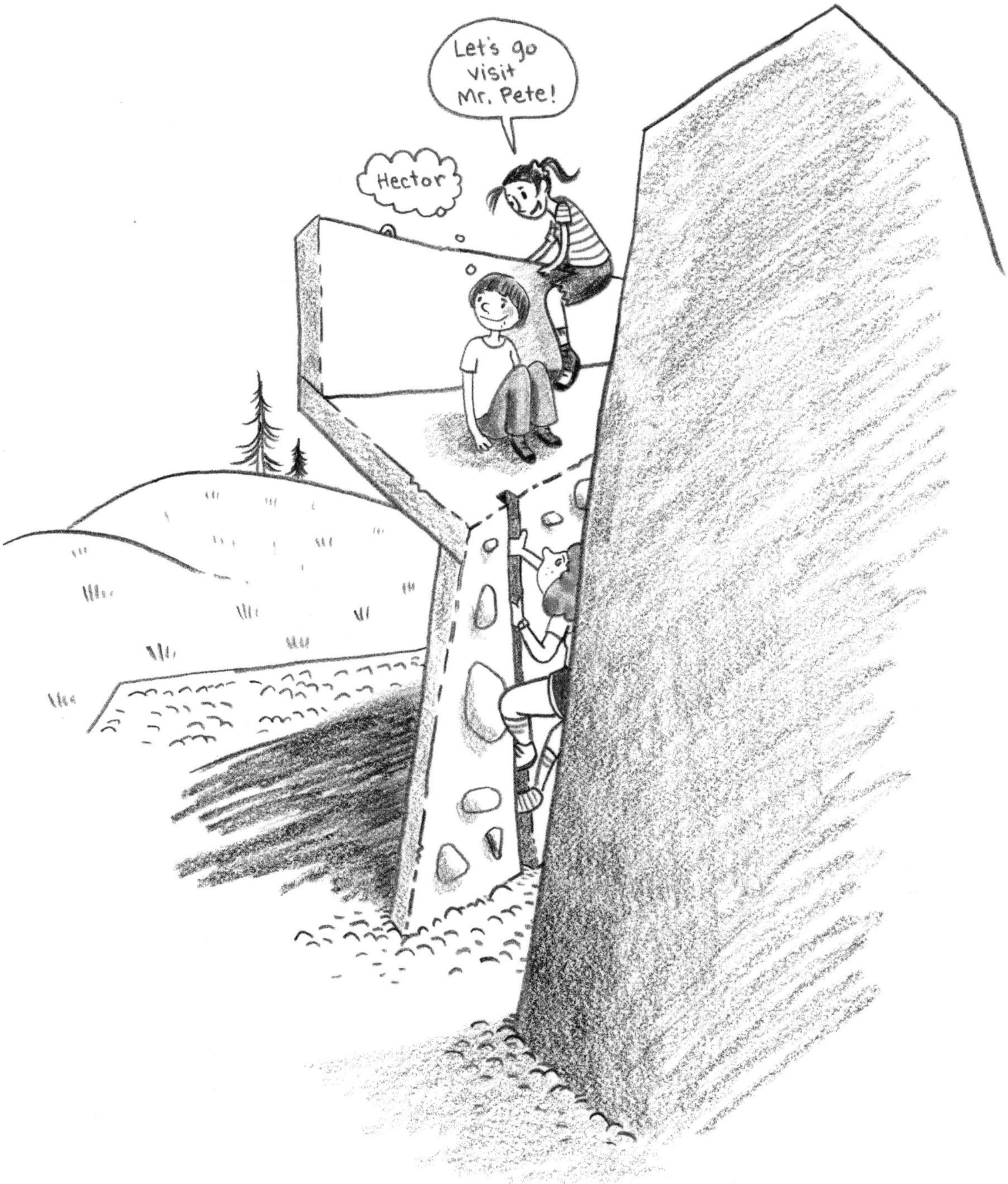
Hector
Let's go visit Mr. Pete!

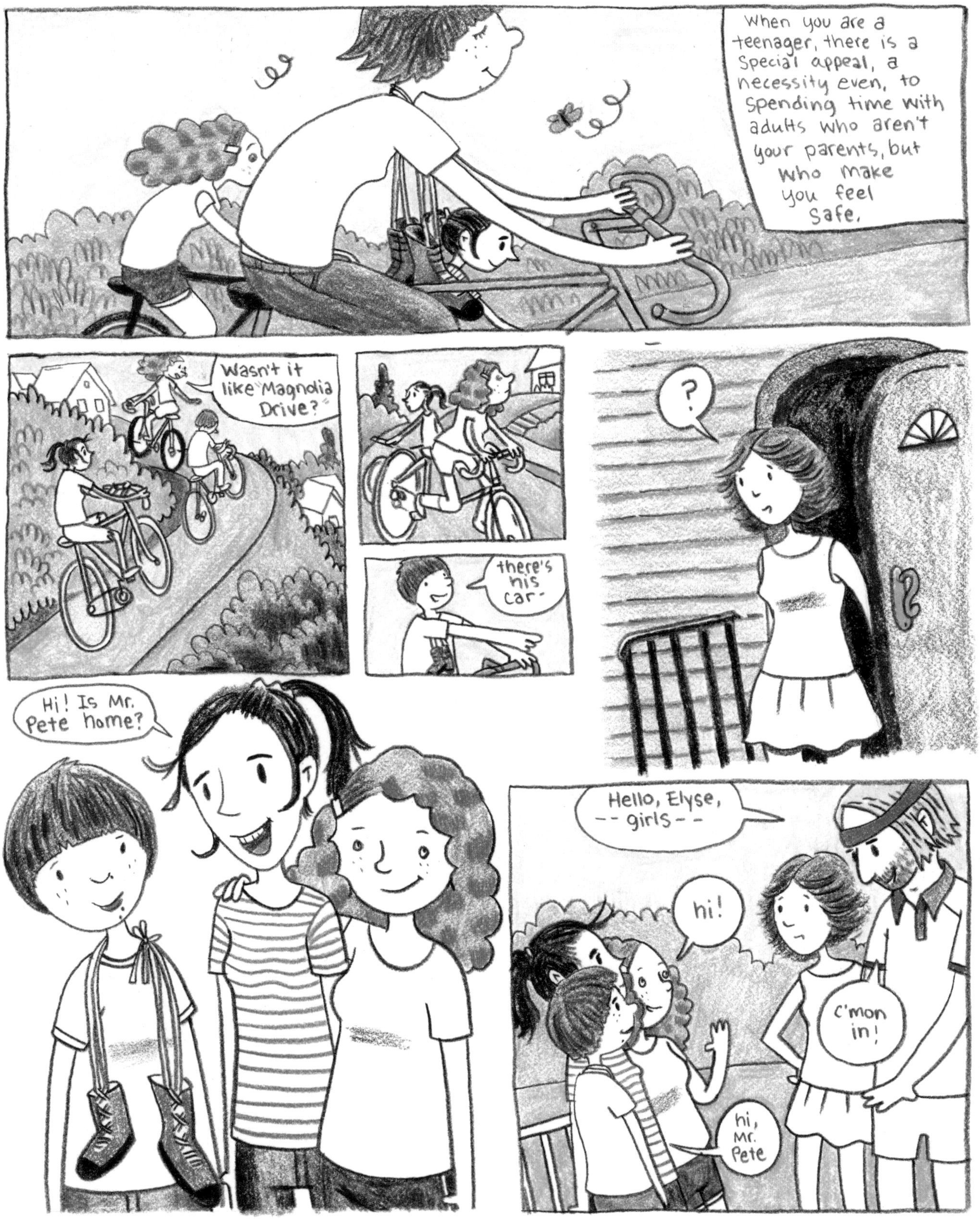
When you are a teenager, there is a special appeal, a necessity even, to spending time with adults who aren't your parents, but who make you feel safe.
Wasn't it like Magnolia Drive?
there's his car-
?
Hi! Is Mr. Pete home?
Hello, Elyse, -- girls --
hi!
C'mon in!
hi, Mr. Pete

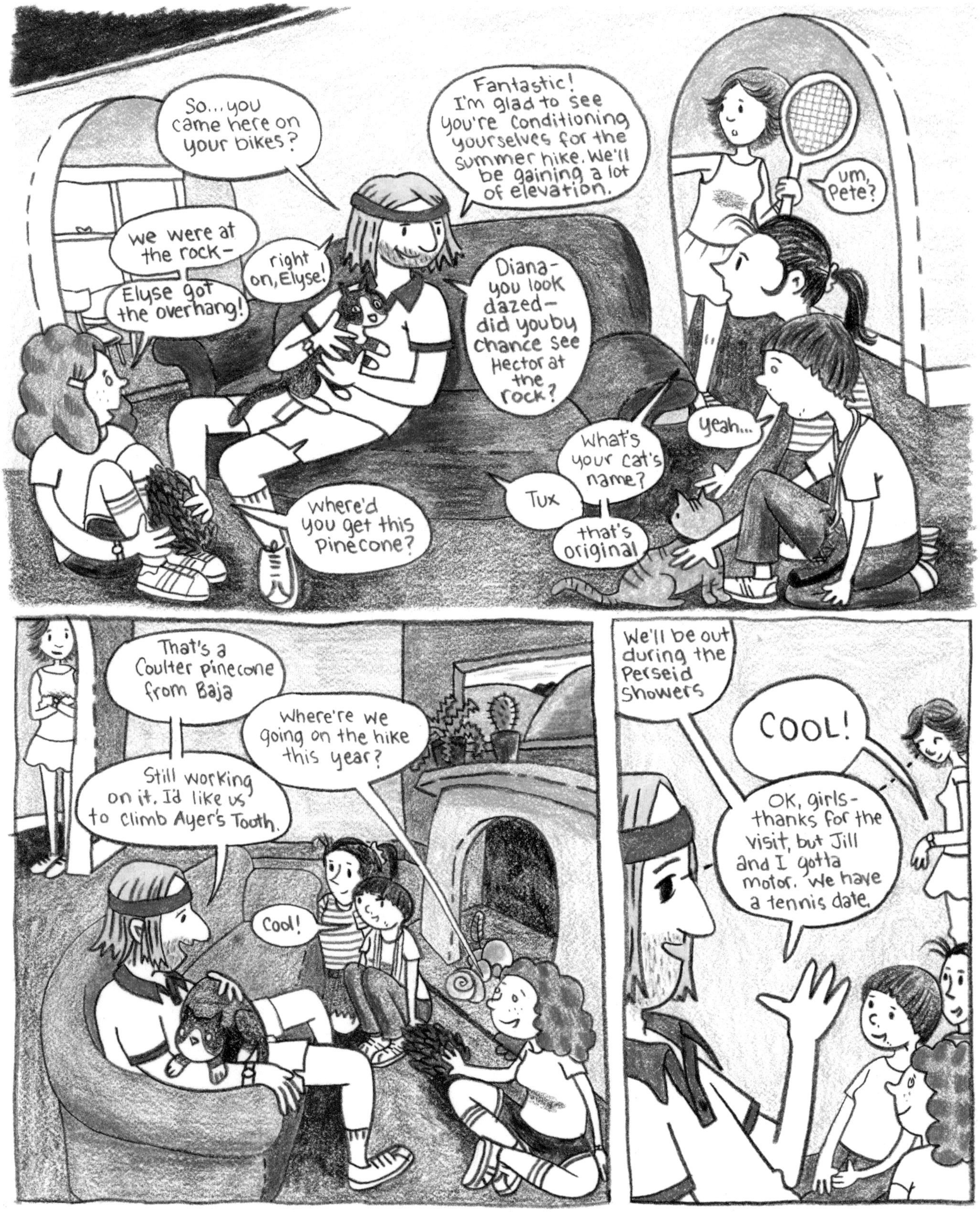
So... you came here on your bikes?
Fantastic! I'm glad to see you're conditioning yourselves for the summer hike. We'll be gaining a lot of elevation.
um, Pete?
we were at the rock-
Elyse got the overhang!
right on, Elyse!
Diana- you look dazed- did you by chance see Hector at the rock?
yeah...
What's your cat's name?
Tux
that's original
Where'd you get this Pinecone?
That's a Coulter pinecone from Baja
Where're we going on the hike this year?
Still working on it. I'd like us to climb Ayer's Tooth.
Cool!
We'll be out during the Perseid Showers
COOL!
OK, girls- thanks for the visit, but Jill and I gotta motor. We have a tennis date.

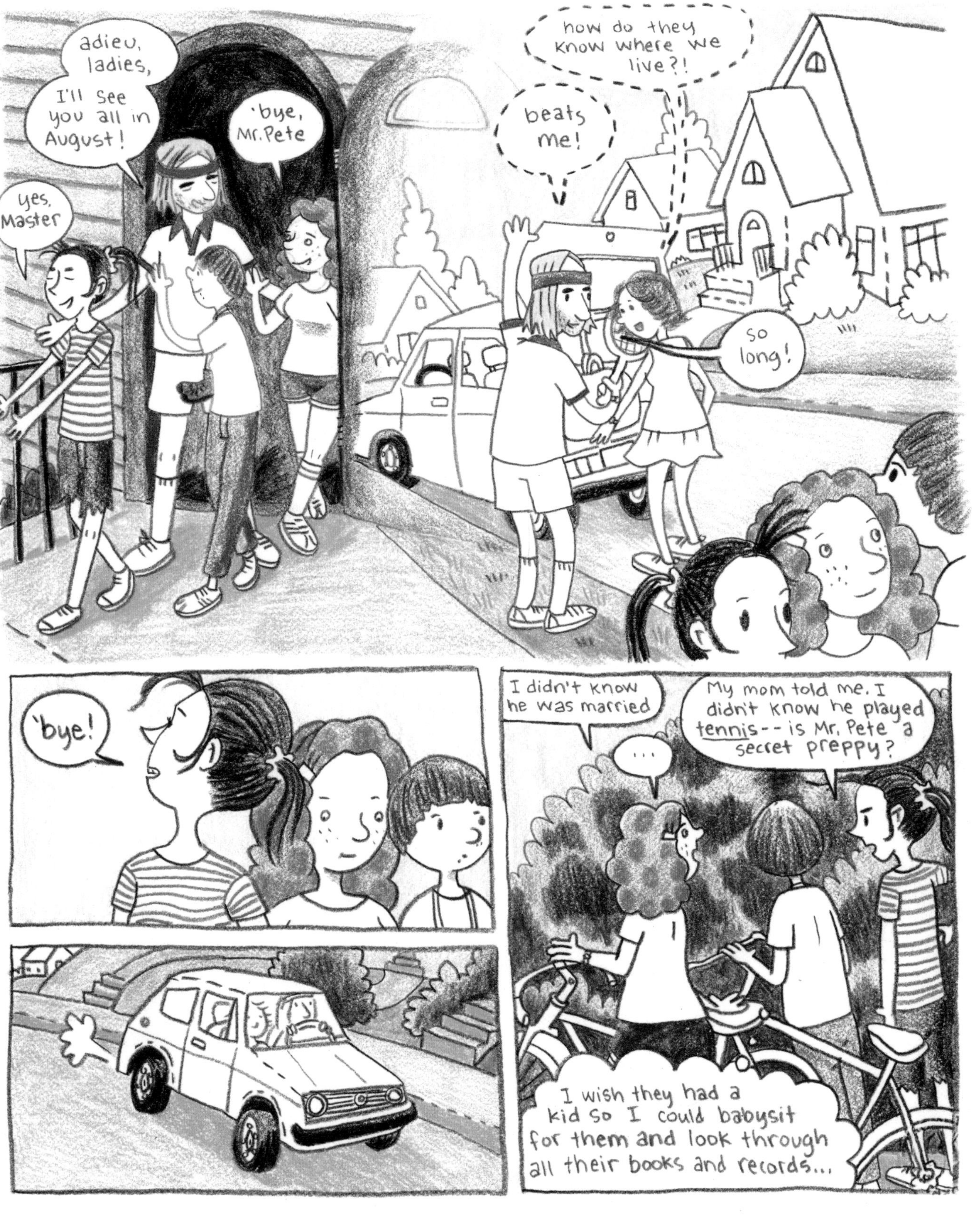
adieu, ladies,
I'll see you all in August!
'bye, Mr. Pete
yes, Master
how do they know where we live?!
beats me!
so long!
'bye!
I didn't know he was married
...
My mom told me. I didn't know he played tennis-- is Mr. Pete a secret preppy?
I wish they had a kid so I could babysit for them and look through all their books and records...

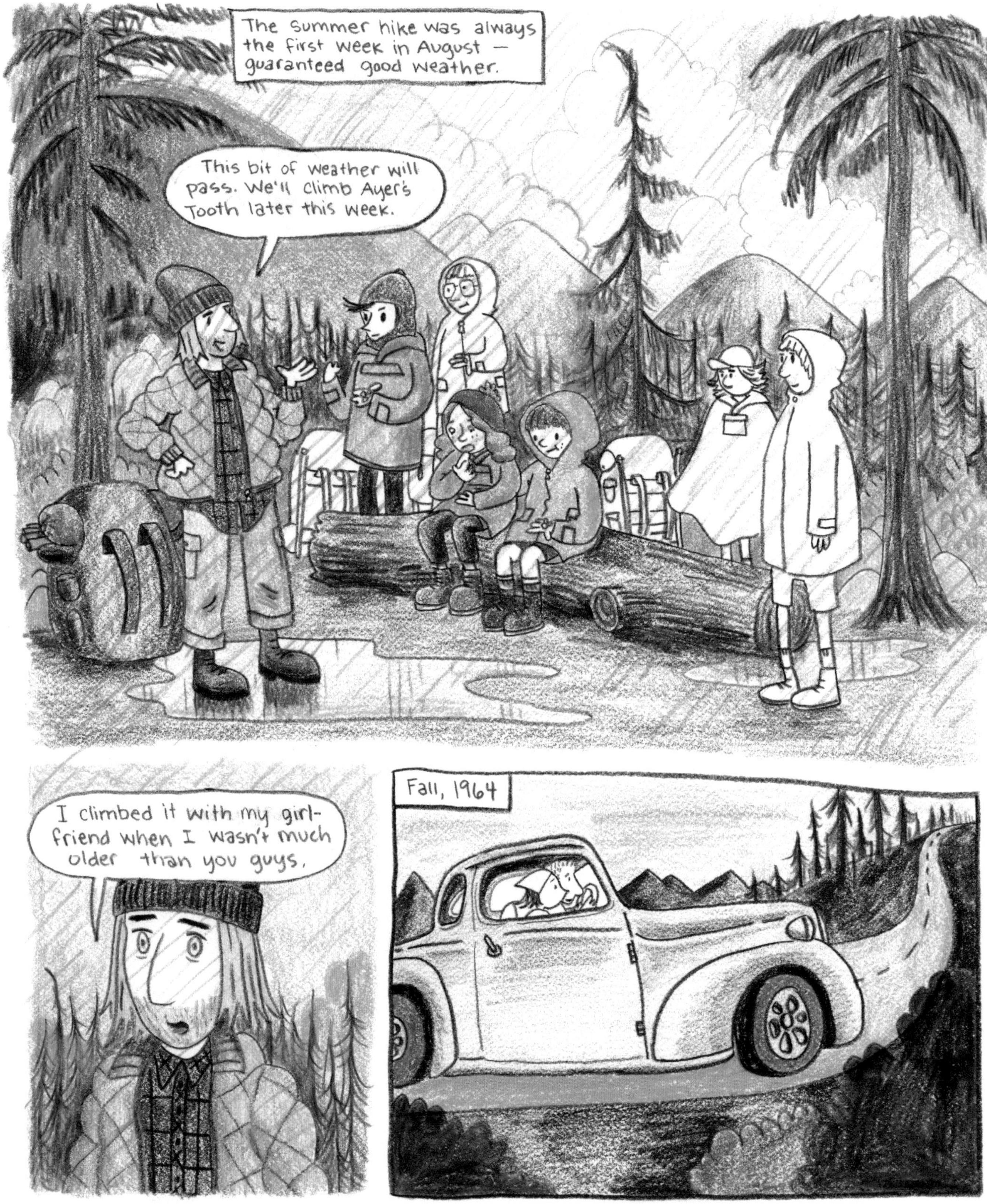
The summer hike was always the first week in August — guaranteed good weather.
This bit of weather will pass. We'll climb Ayer's Tooth later this week.
I climbed it with my girl-friend when I wasn't much older than you guys.
Fall, 1964

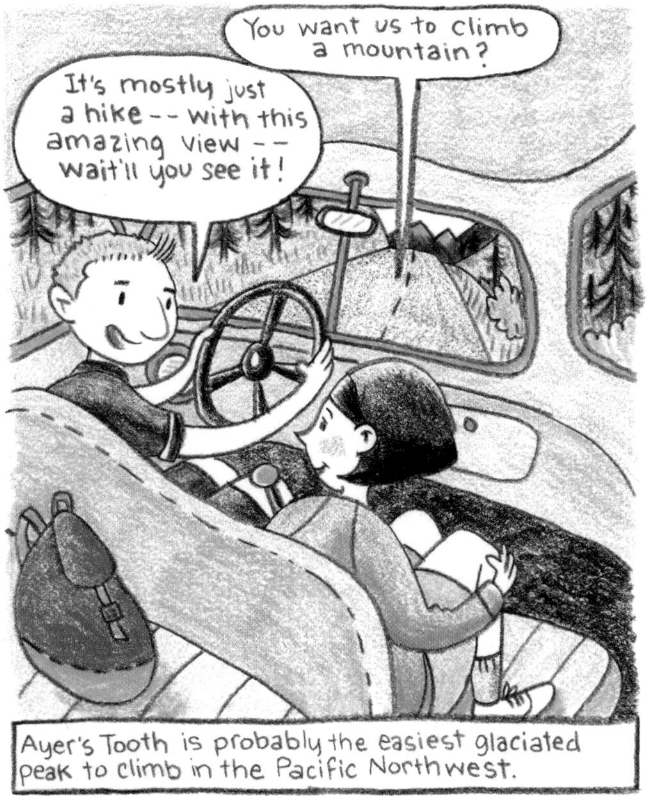
You want us to climb a mountain?
It's mostly just a hike -- with this amazing view -- wait'll you see it!
Ayer's Tooth is probably the easiest glaciated peak to climb in the Pacific Northwest.

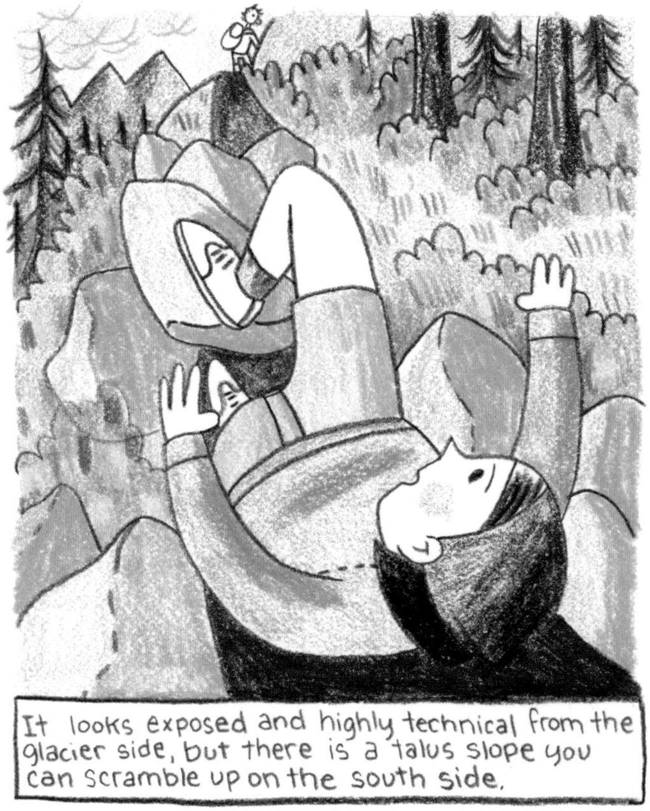
It looks exposed and highly technical from the glacier side, but there is a talus slope you can scramble up on the south side.

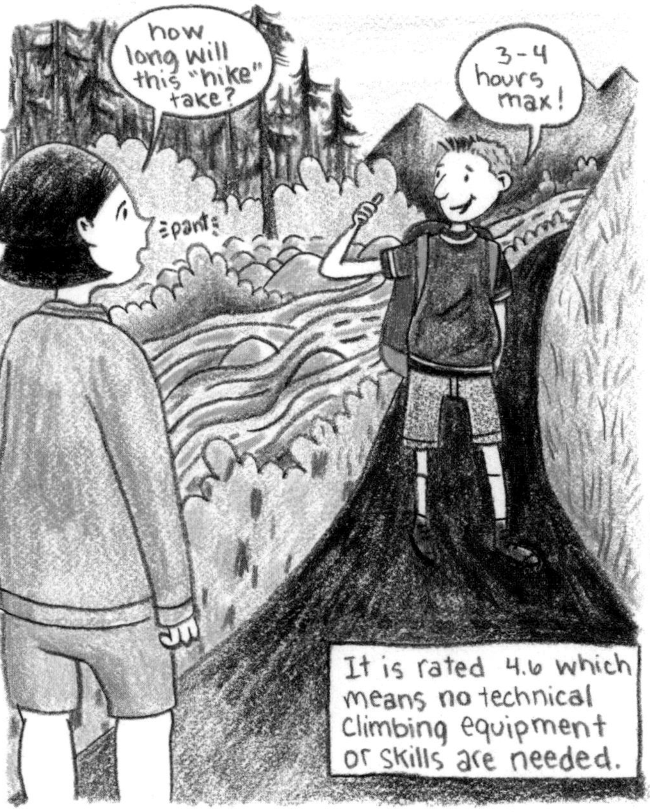
how long will this "hike" take?
3-4 hours max!
pant
It is rated 4.6 which means no technical climbing equipment or skills are needed.

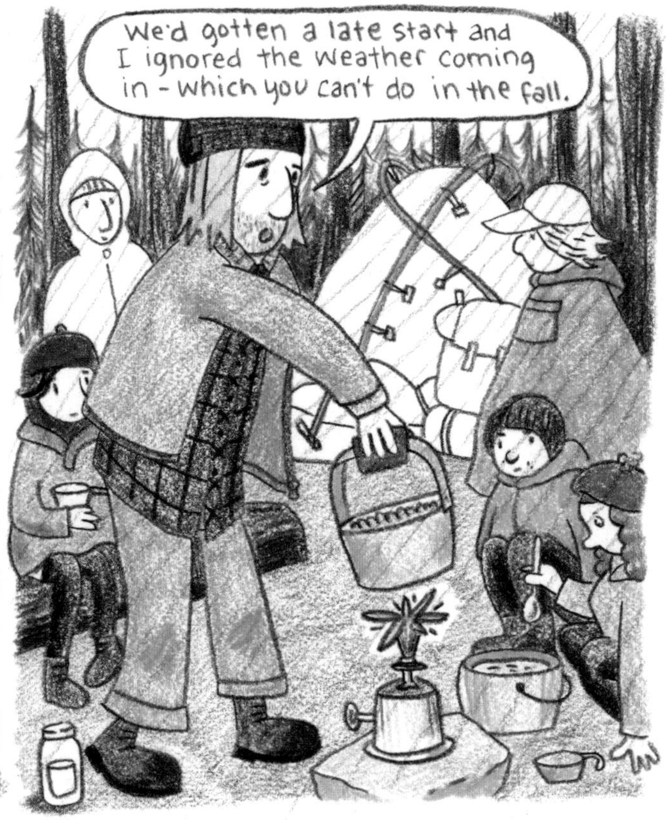
We'd gotten a late start and I ignored the weather coming in - which you can't do in the fall.

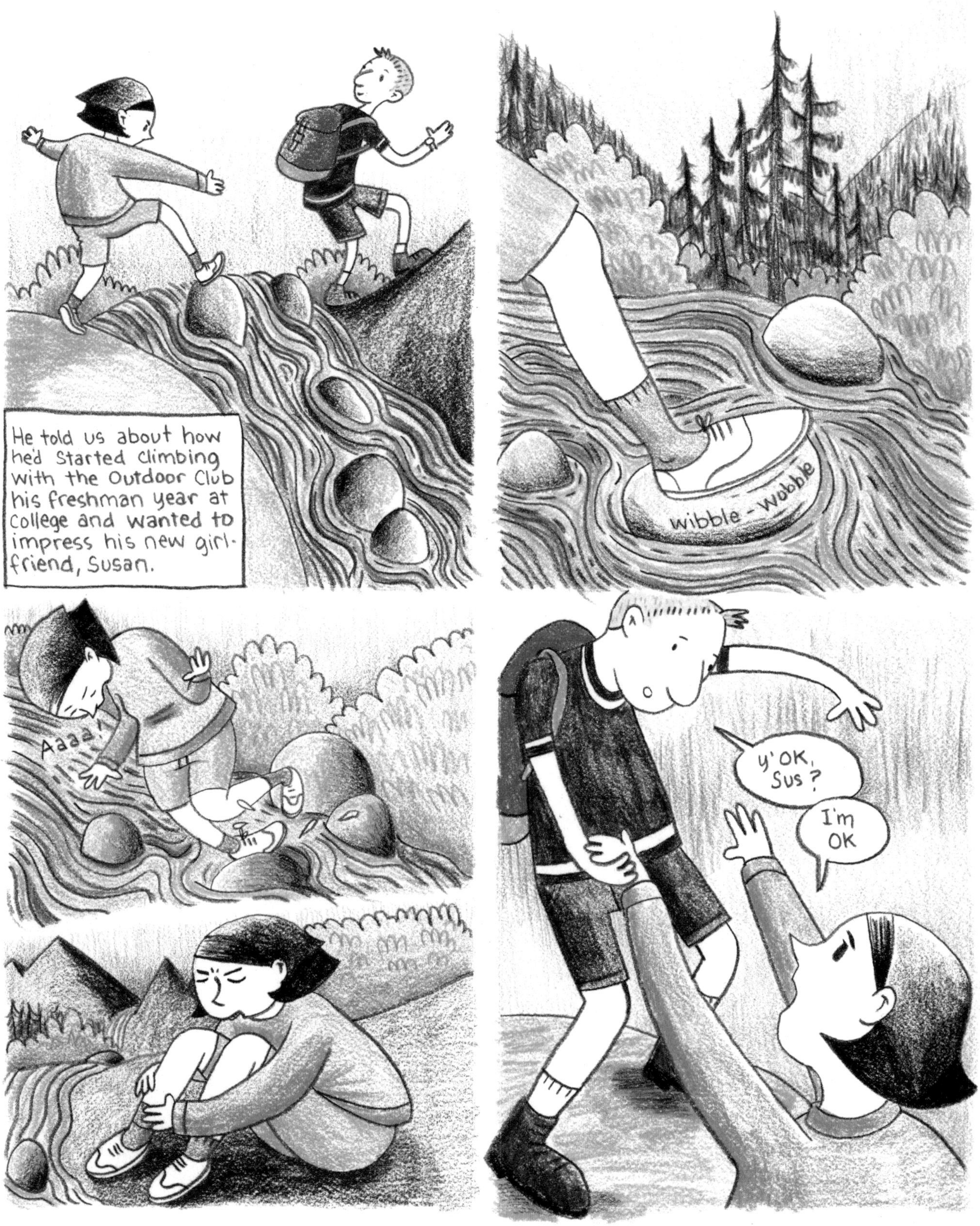
He told us about how he'd started climbing with the Outdoor Club his freshman year at college and wanted to impress his new girl-friend, Susan.
wibble-wobble
Aaaa!
y'OK, Sus?
I'm OK

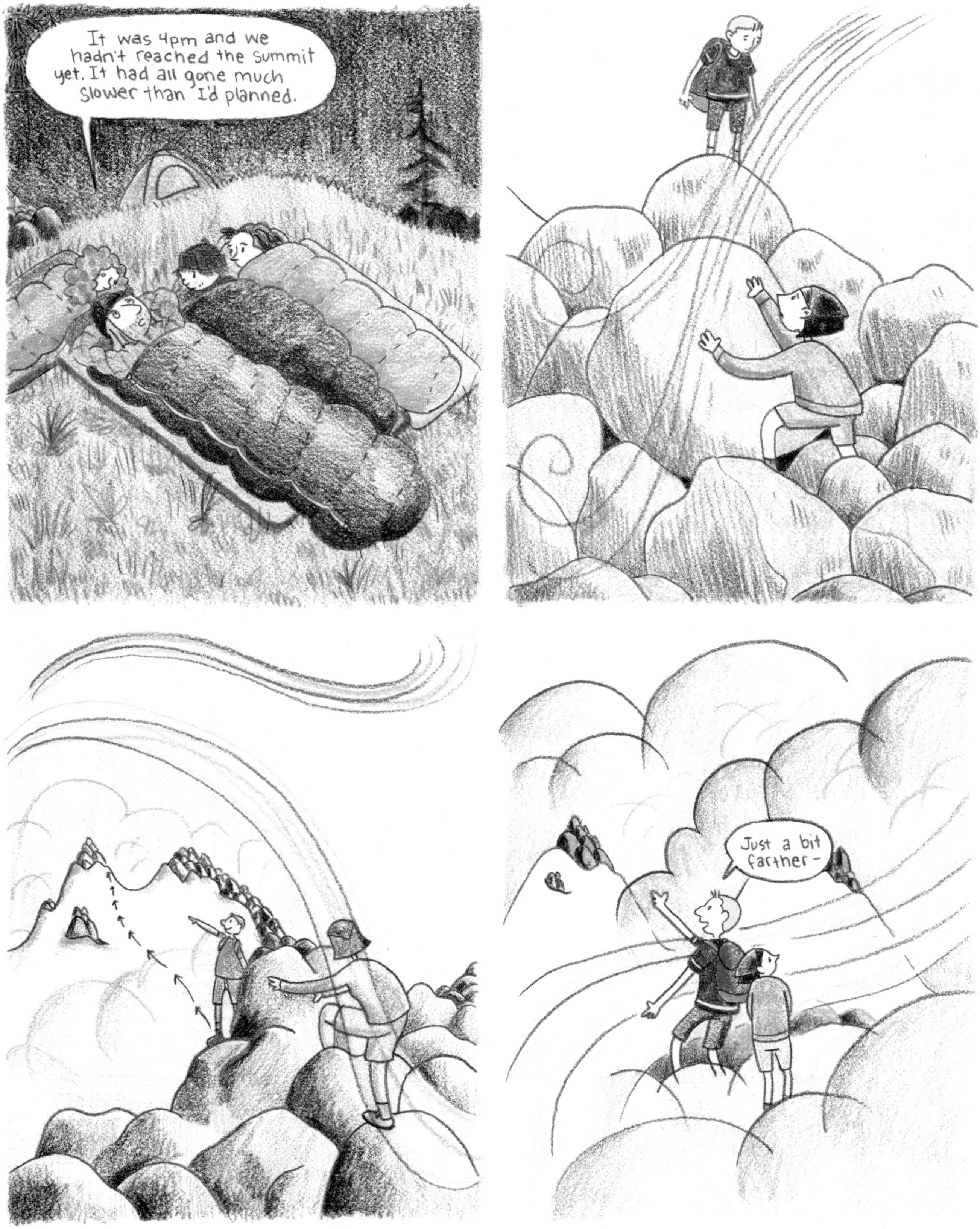
It was 4pm and we hadn't reached the summit yet. It had all gone much slower than I'd planned.
Just a bit farther-

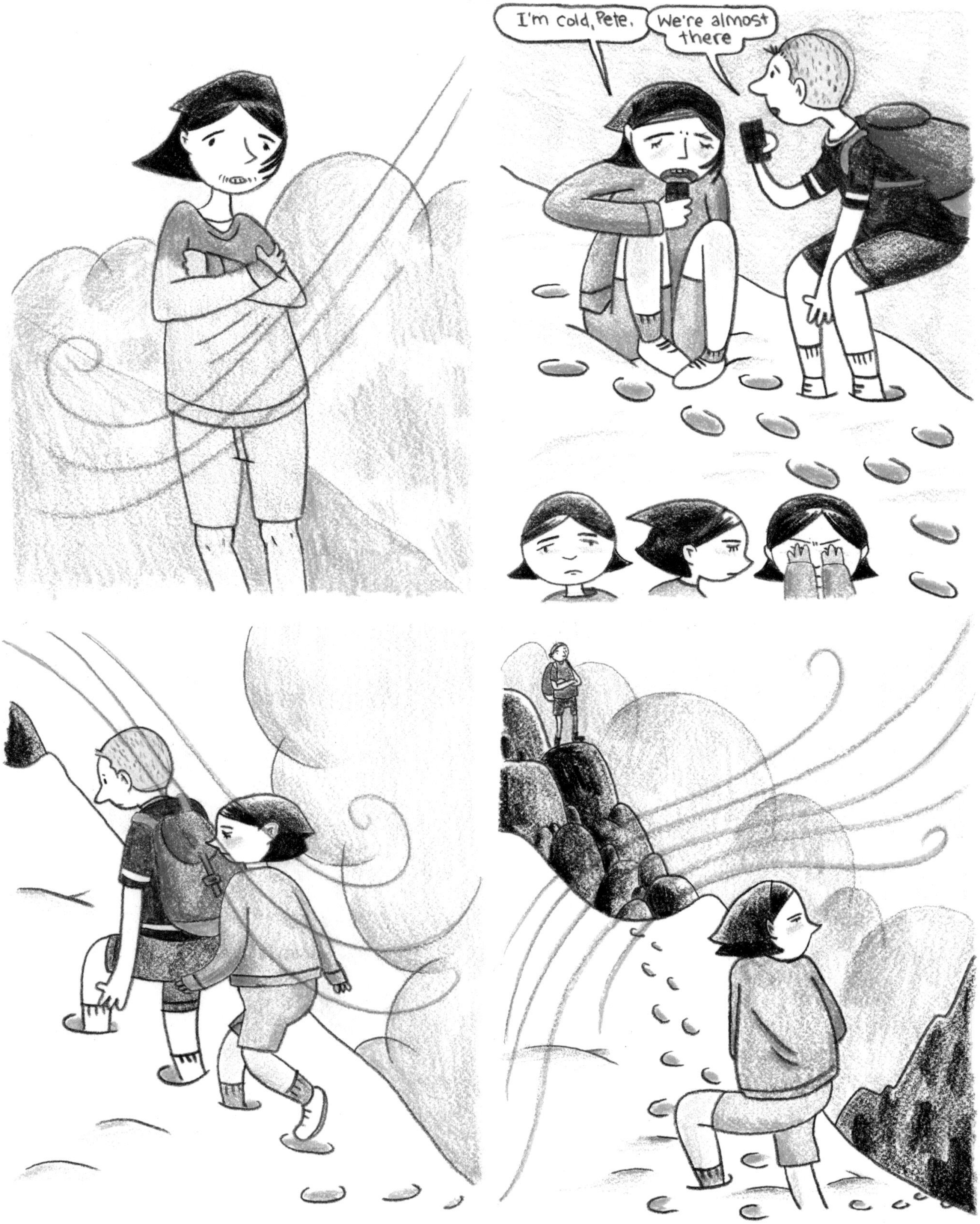
I'm cold, Pete.
We're almost there

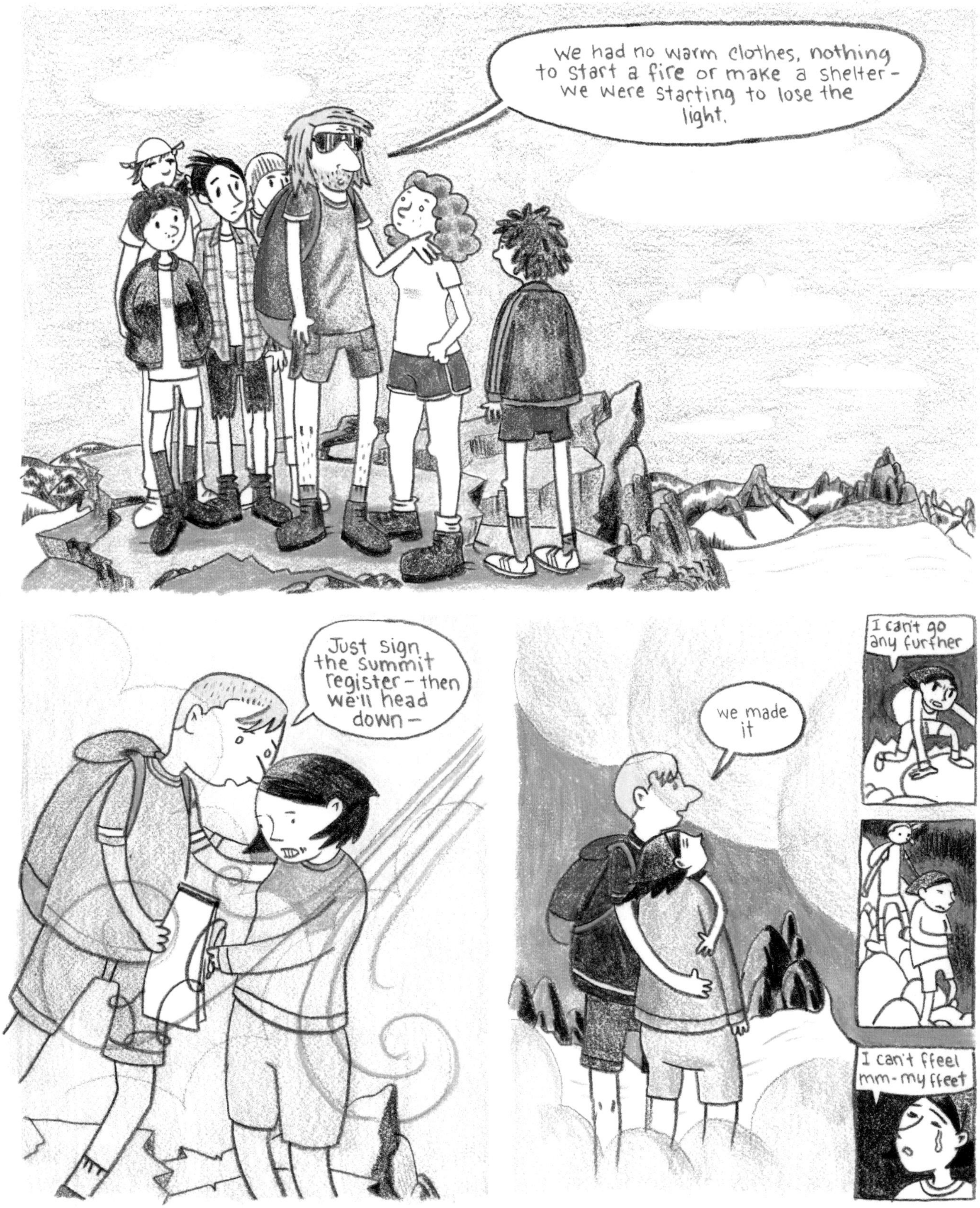

We had no warm clothes, nothing to start a fire or make a shelter - we were starting to lose the light.
Just sign the summit register - then we'll head down -
we made it
I can't go any further
I can't ffeel mm-my ffeet

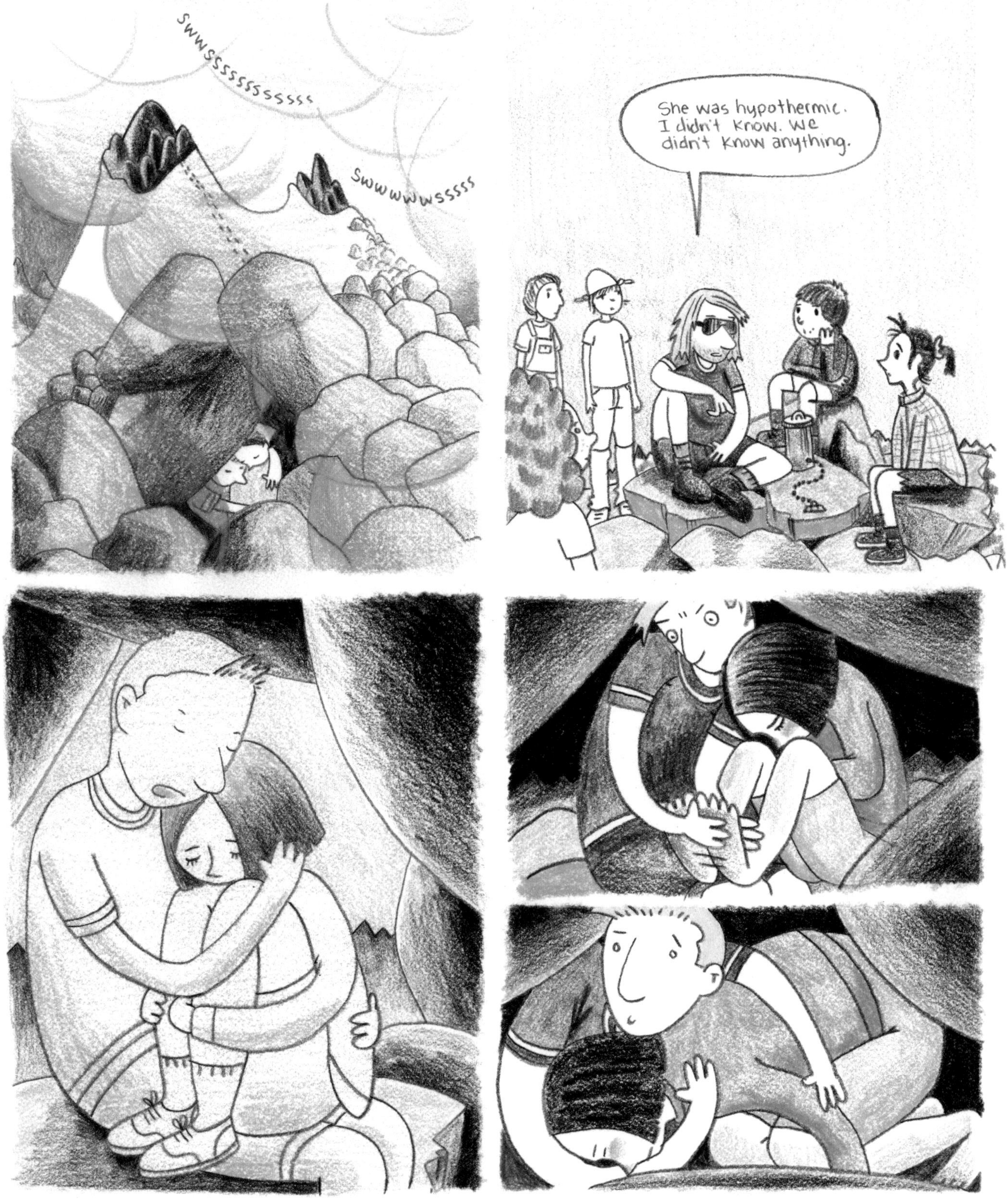
Swwssssssssssss
Swwwwwwsssss
She was hypothermic. I didn't know. We didn't know anything.

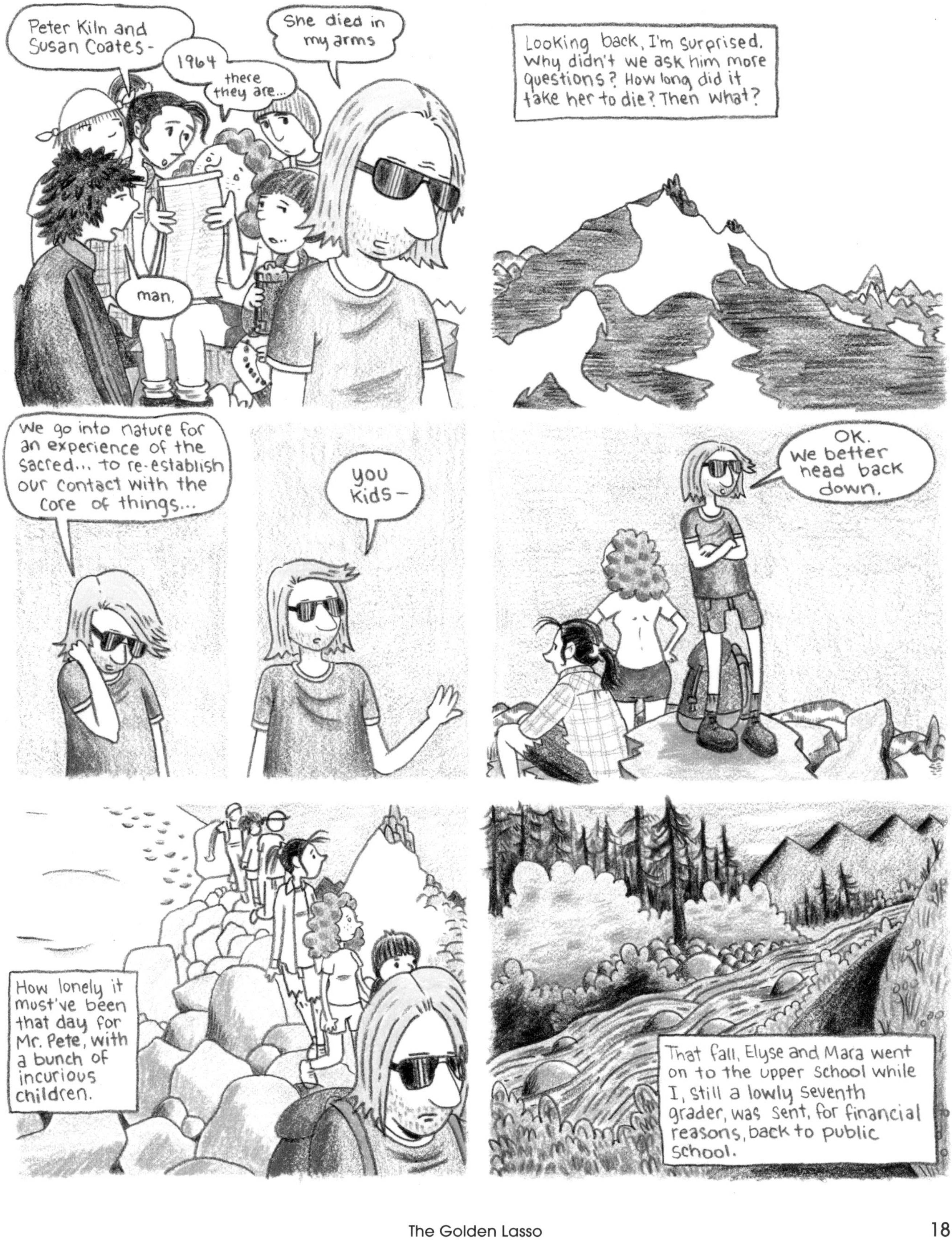
Peter Kiln and Susan Coates -
1964
there they are...
She died in my arms
man.
Looking back, I'm surprised. Why didn't we ask him more questions? How long did it take her to die? Then what?
We go into nature for an experience of the sacred... to re-establish our contact with the core of things...
you kids -
OK. We better head back down.
How lonely it must've been that day for Mr. Pete, with a bunch of incurious children.
That fall, Elyse and Mara went on to the upper school while I, still a lowly seventh grader, was sent, for financial reasons, back to public school.

Finger Jam • Fall, 1980

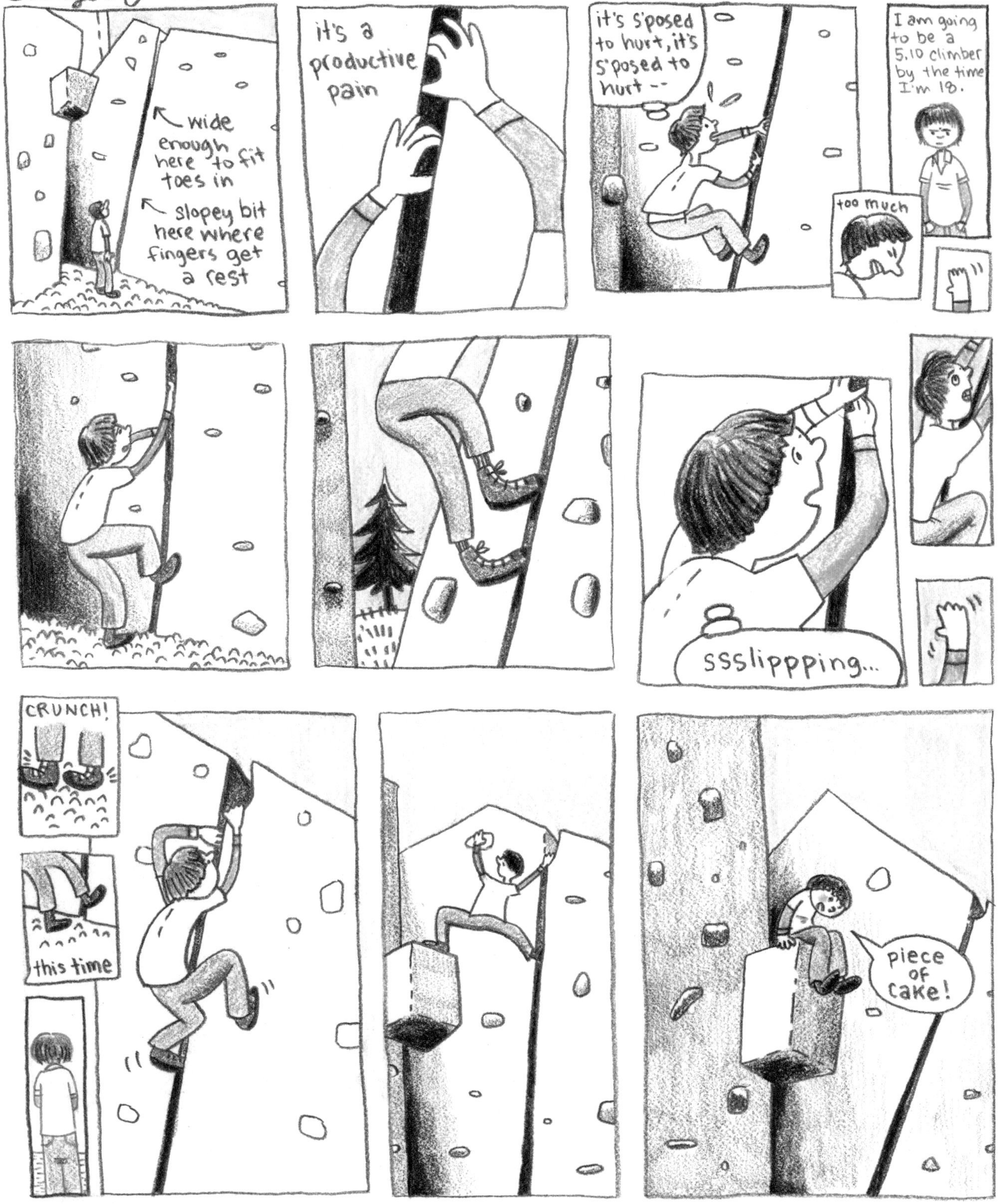

wide enough here to fit toes in
slopey bit here where fingers get a rest
it's a productive pain
it's s'posed to hurt, it's s'posed to hurt --
I am going to be a 5.10 climber by the time I'm 18.
too much
ssslippping...
CRUNCH!
this time
piece of cake!

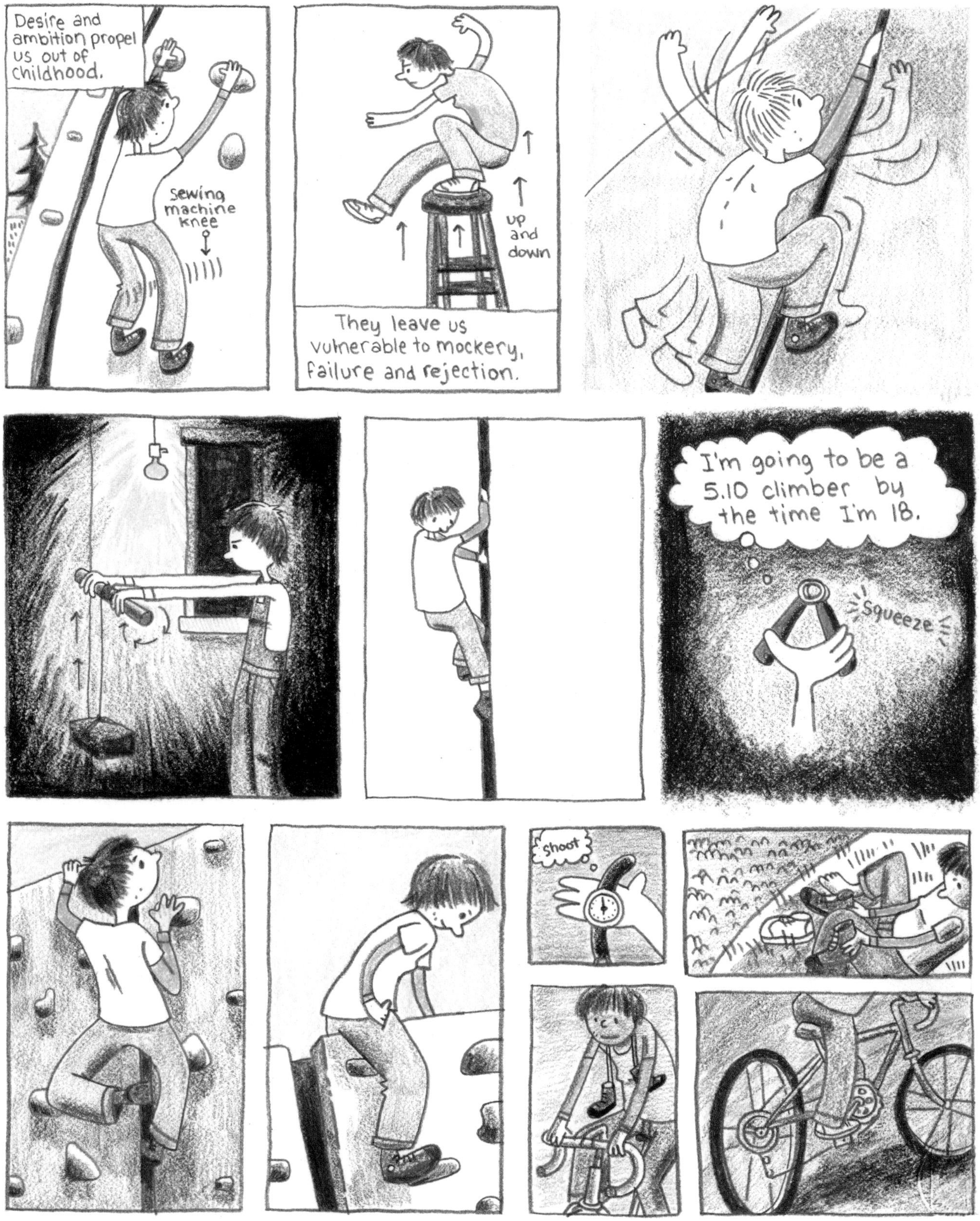
Desire and ambition propel us out of childhood.
sewing machine knee
up and down
They leave us vulnerable to mockery, failure and rejection.
I'm going to be a 5.10 climber by the time I'm 18.
Squeeze
shoot

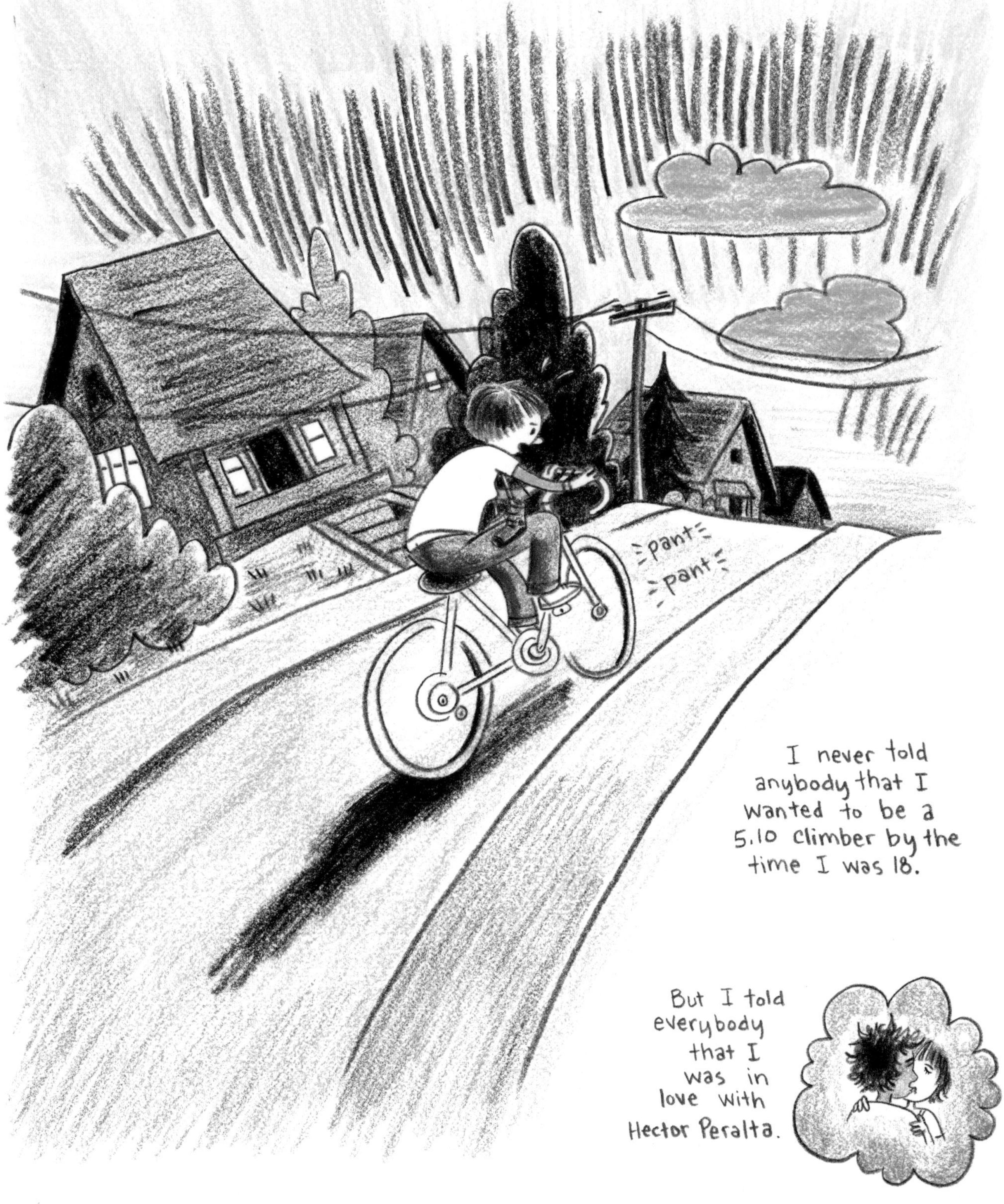
pant
pant
I never told anybody that I wanted to be a 5.10 climber by the time I was 18.
But I told everybody that I was in love with Hector Peralta.

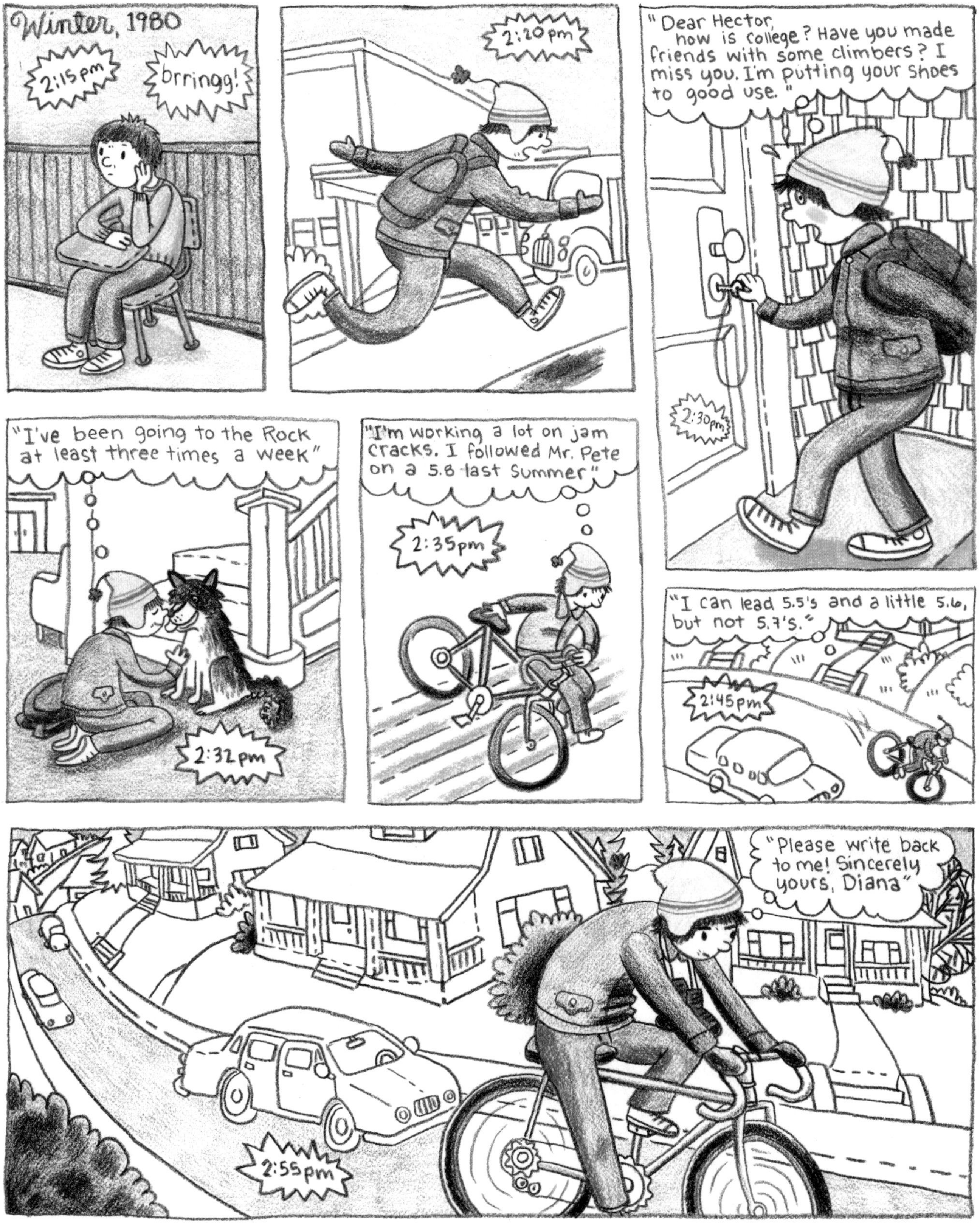

Winter, 1980
2:15pm
brringg!
2:20pm
"Dear Hector, how is college? Have you made friends with some climbers? I miss you. I'm putting your shoes to good use."
2:30pm
"I've been going to the Rock at least three times a week"
2:32pm
"I'm working a lot on jam cracks. I followed Mr. Pete on a 5.8 last Summer"
2:35pm
"I can lead 5.5's and a little 5.6, but not 5.7's."
2:45pm
"Please write back to me! Sincerely yours, Diana"
2:55pm

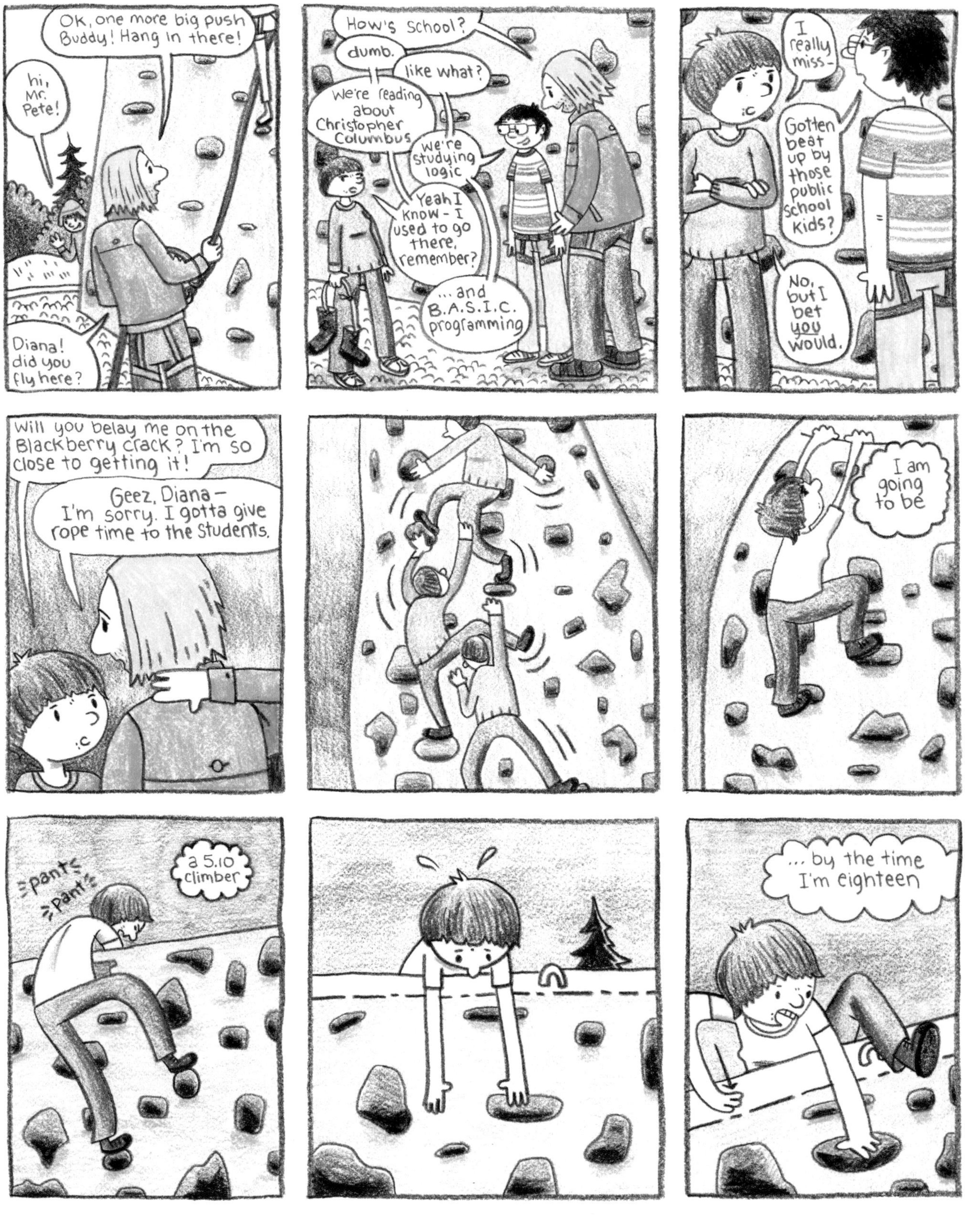

Ok, one more big push Buddy! Hang in there!
hi, Mr. Pete!
Diana! did you fly here?
How's school?
dumb.
like what?
We're reading about Christopher Columbus
we're studying logic
Yeah I know - I used to go there, remember?
... and B.A.S.I.C. programming
I really miss-
Gotten beat up by those public school kids?
No, but I bet you would.
Will you belay me on the Blackberry crack? I'm so close to getting it!
Geez, Diana - I'm sorry. I gotta give rope time to the students.
I am going to be
pant pant
a 5.10 climber
... by the time I'm eighteen

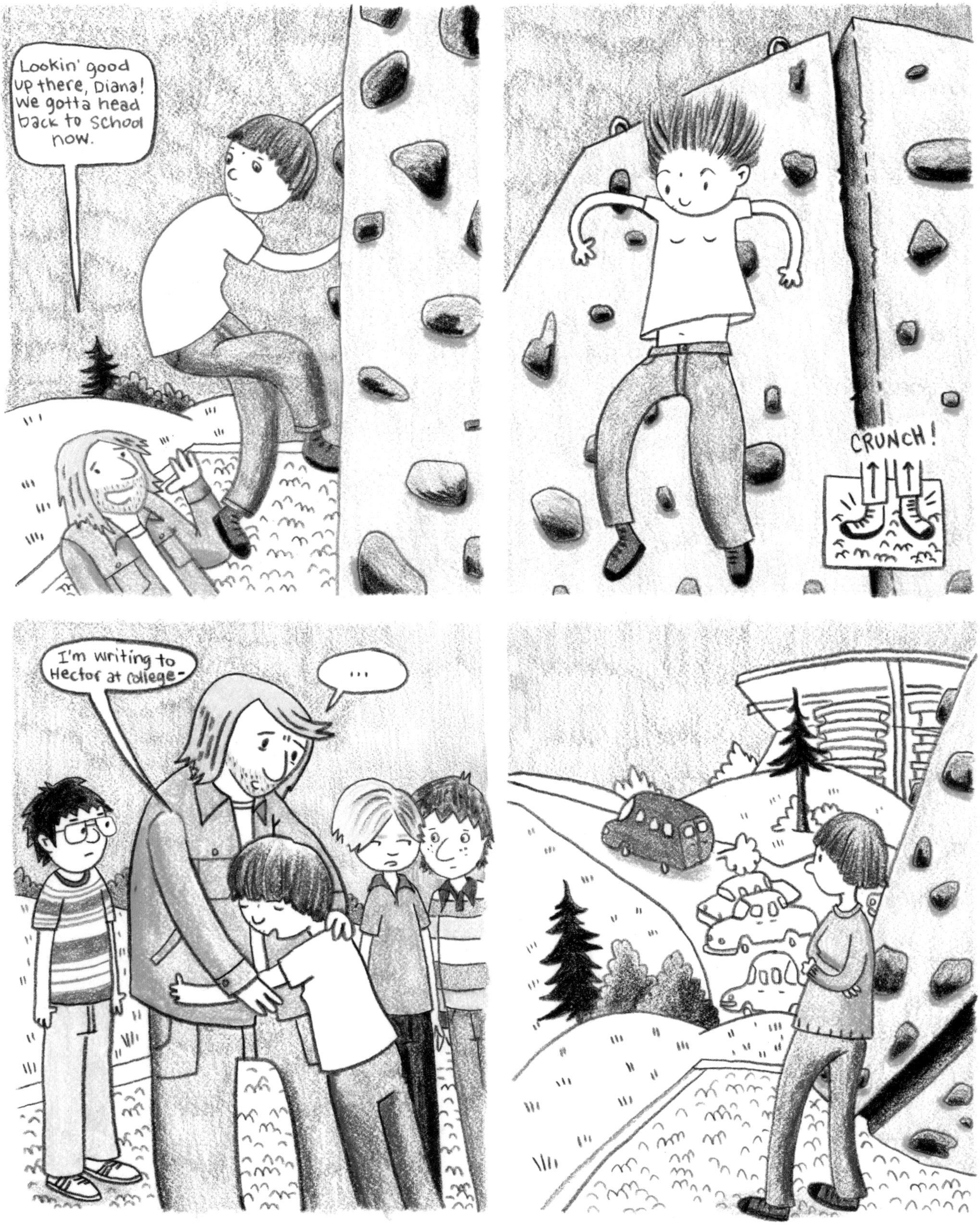
Lookin' good up there, Diana! We gotta head back to school now.
CRUNCH!
I'm writing to Hector at college-
...

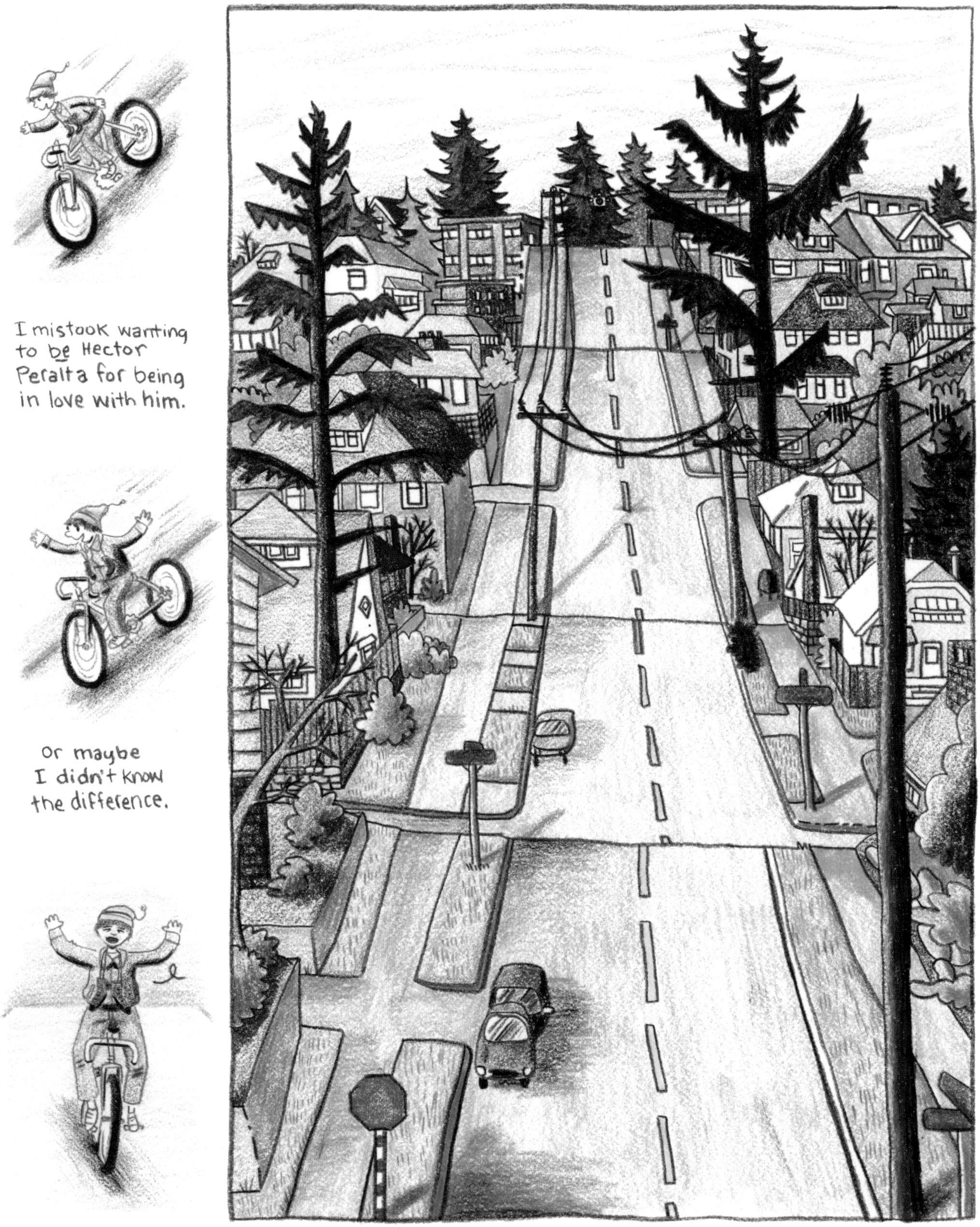
I mistook wanting to be Hector Peralta for being in love with him.
Or maybe I didn't know the difference.

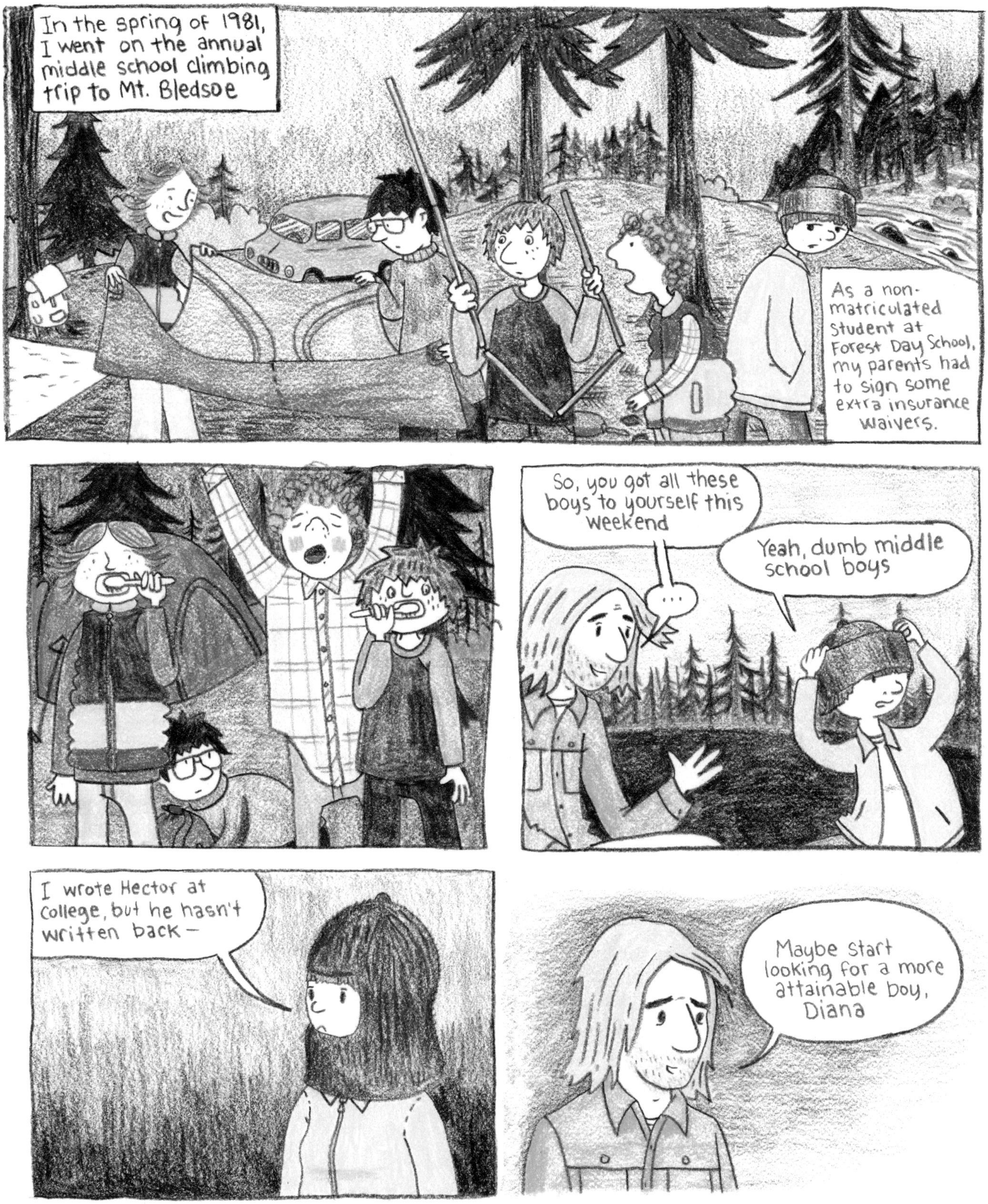

In the spring of 1981, I went on the annual middle school climbing trip to Mt. Bledsoe
As a non-matriculated student at Forest Day School, my parents had to sign some extra insurance waivers.
So, you got all these boys to yourself this weekend
...
Yeah, dumb middle school boys
I wrote Hector at College, but he hasn't written back—
Maybe start looking for a more attainable boy, Diana

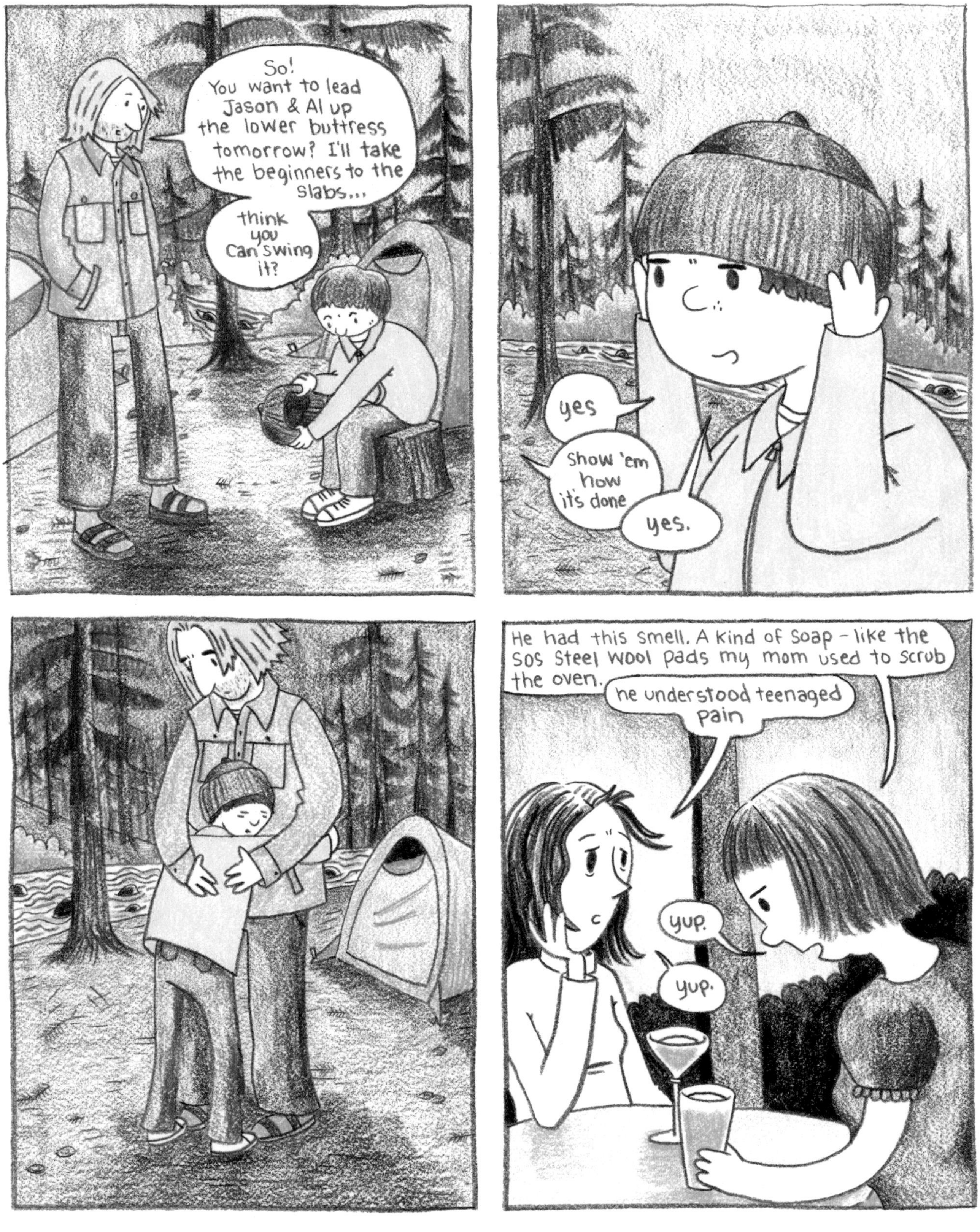
So! You want to lead Jason & Al up the lower buttress tomorrow? I'll take the beginners to the slabs...
think you can swing it?
yes
show 'em how it's done
yes.
He had this smell. A kind of soap - like the SOS steel wool pads my mom used to scrub the oven.
he understood teenaged pain
yup.
yup.

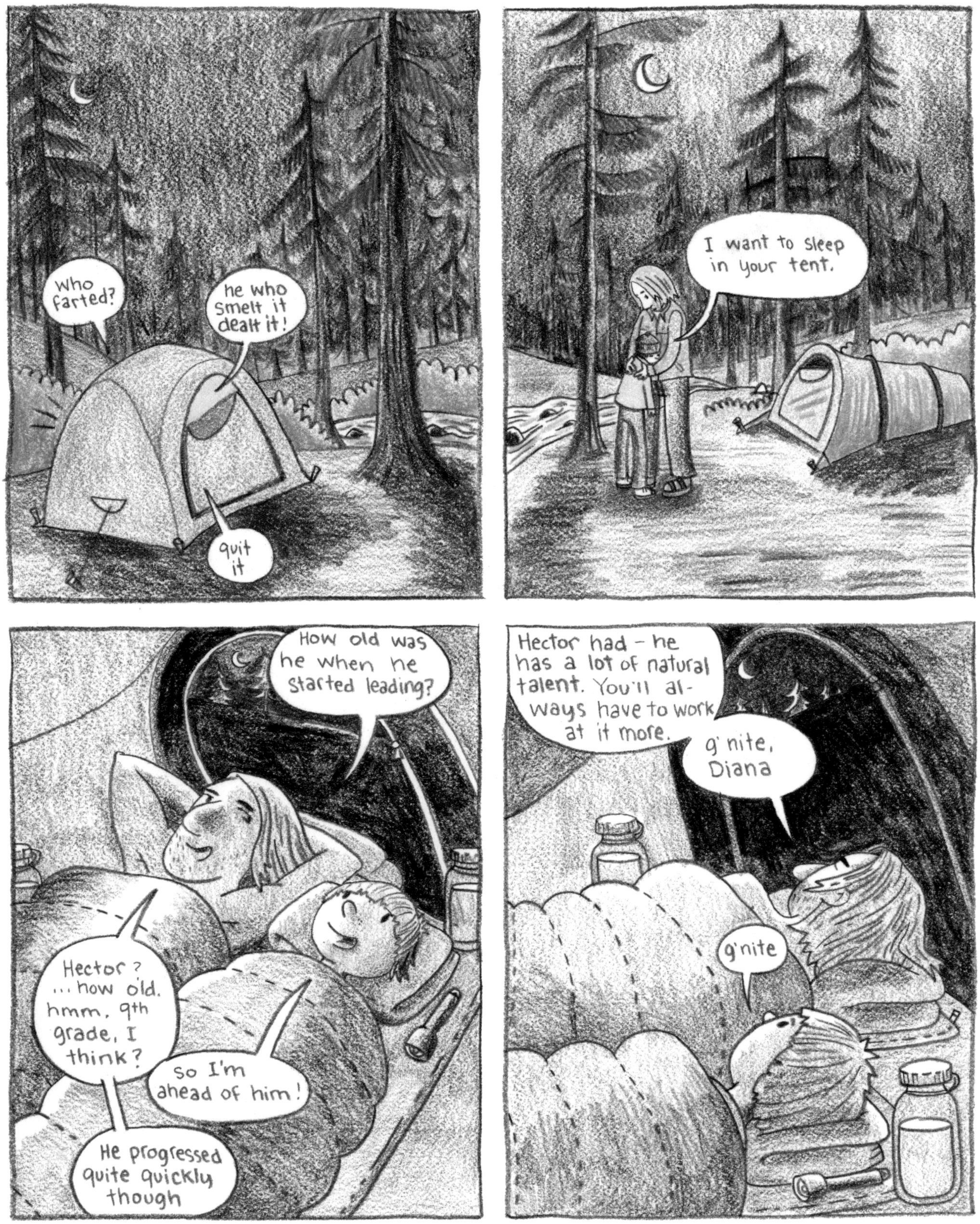
Who farted?
he who smelt it dealt it!
quit it
I want to sleep in your tent.
How old was he when he started leading?
Hector? ...how old. hmm, 9th grade, I think?
So I'm ahead of him!
He progressed quite quickly though
Hector had - he has a lot of natural talent. You'll always have to work at it more.
g'nite, Diana
g'nite

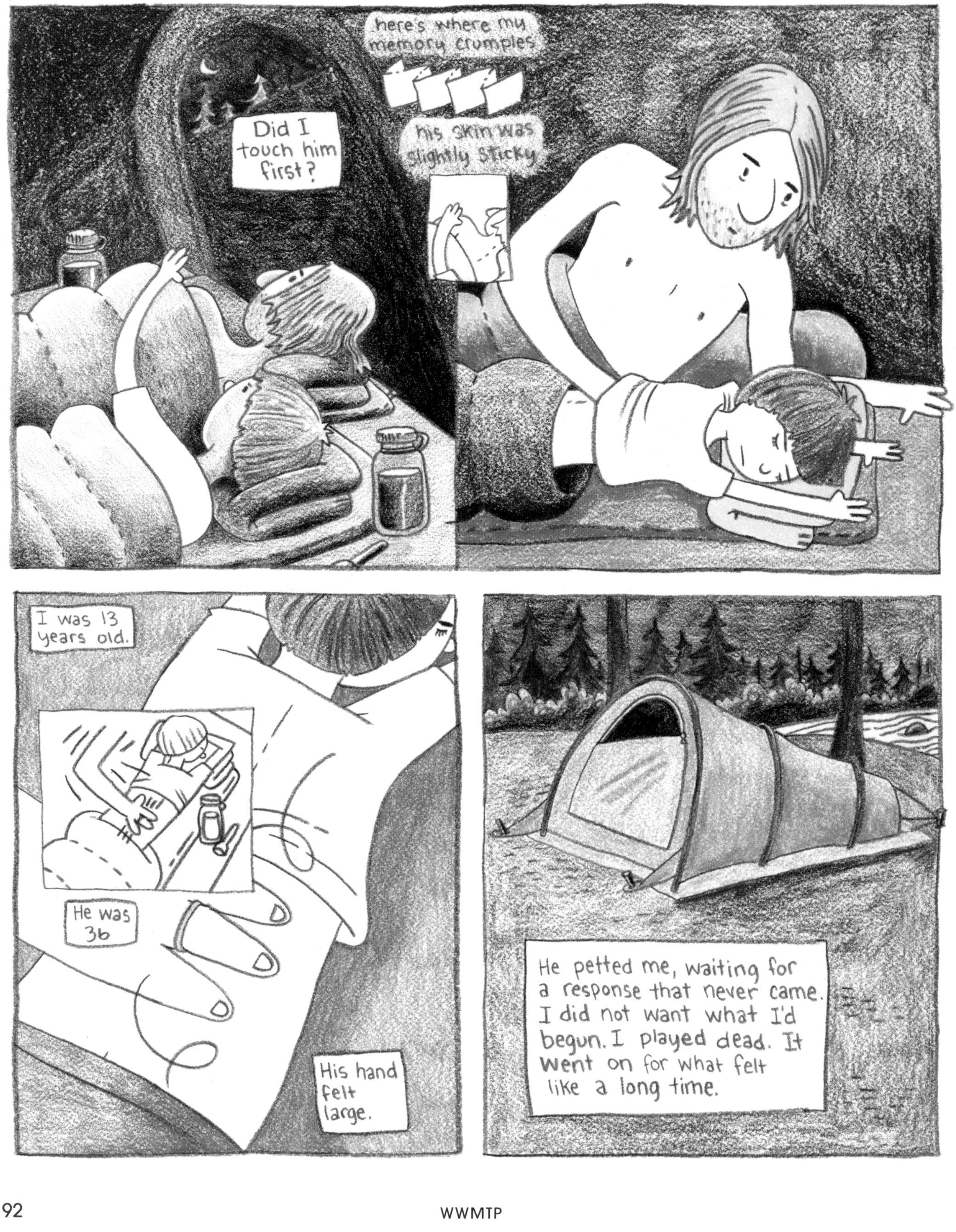
Did I touch him first?
here's where my memory crumples
his skin was slightly sticky
I was 13 years old.
He was 36
His hand felt large.
He petted me, waiting for a response that never came. I did not want what I'd begun. I played dead. It went on for what felt like a long time.

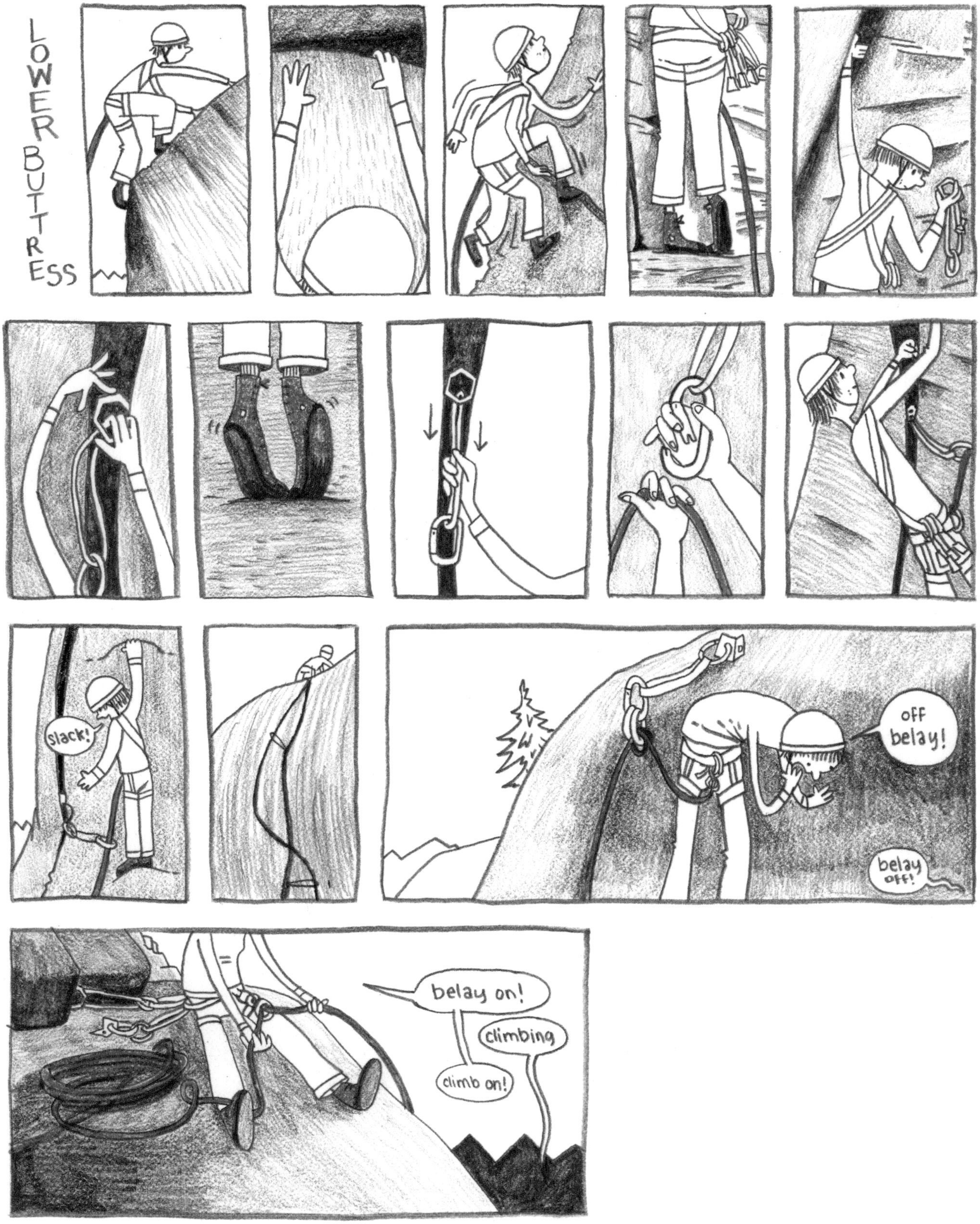
LOWER BUTTRESS
slack!
off belay!
belay off!
belay on!
climbing
climb on!

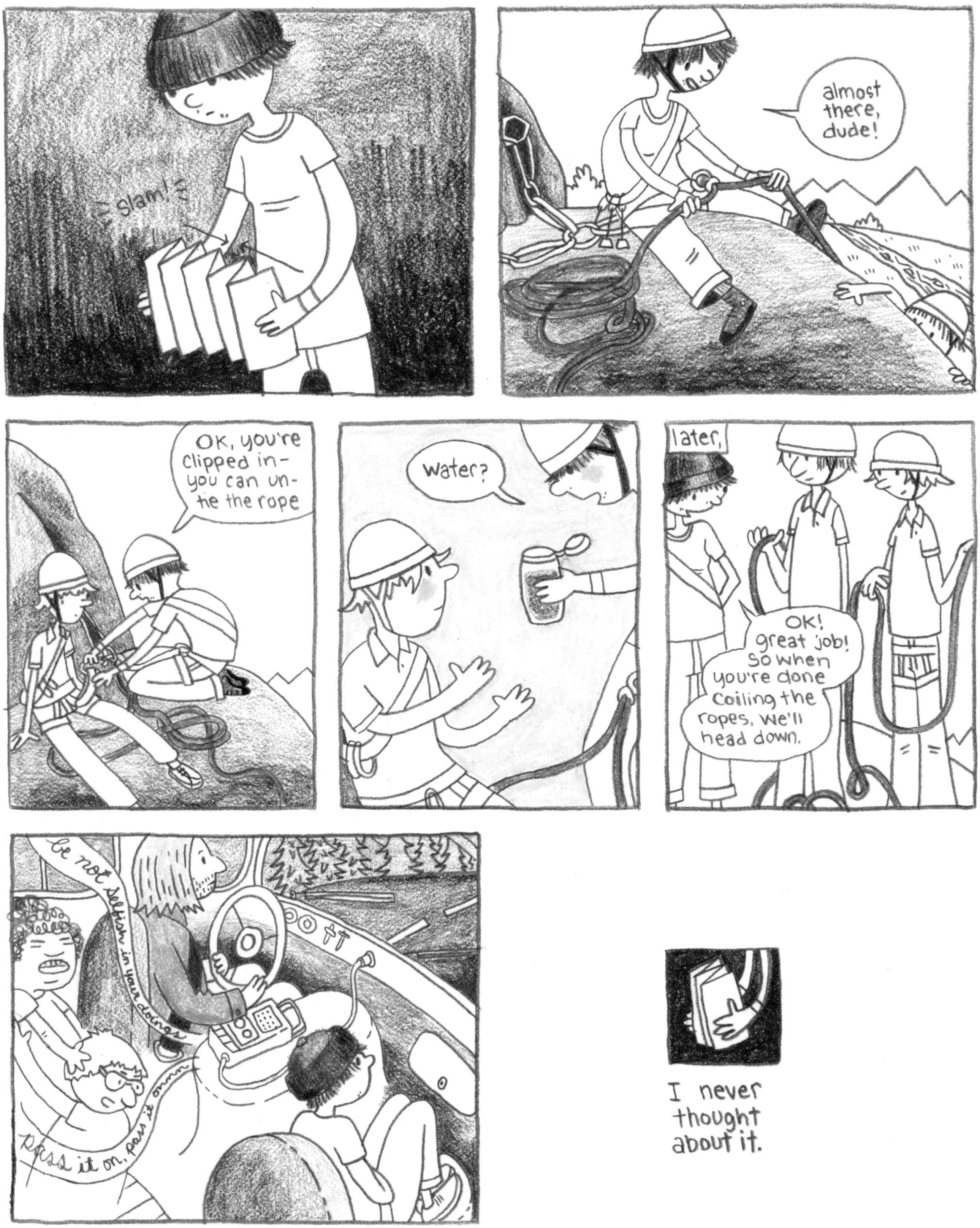
slam!
almost there, dude!
OK, you're clipped in- you can un-tie the rope
water?
later,
OK! great job! So when you're done coiling the ropes, we'll head down.
be not selfish in your doings
pass it on, pass it onnn
I never thought about it.

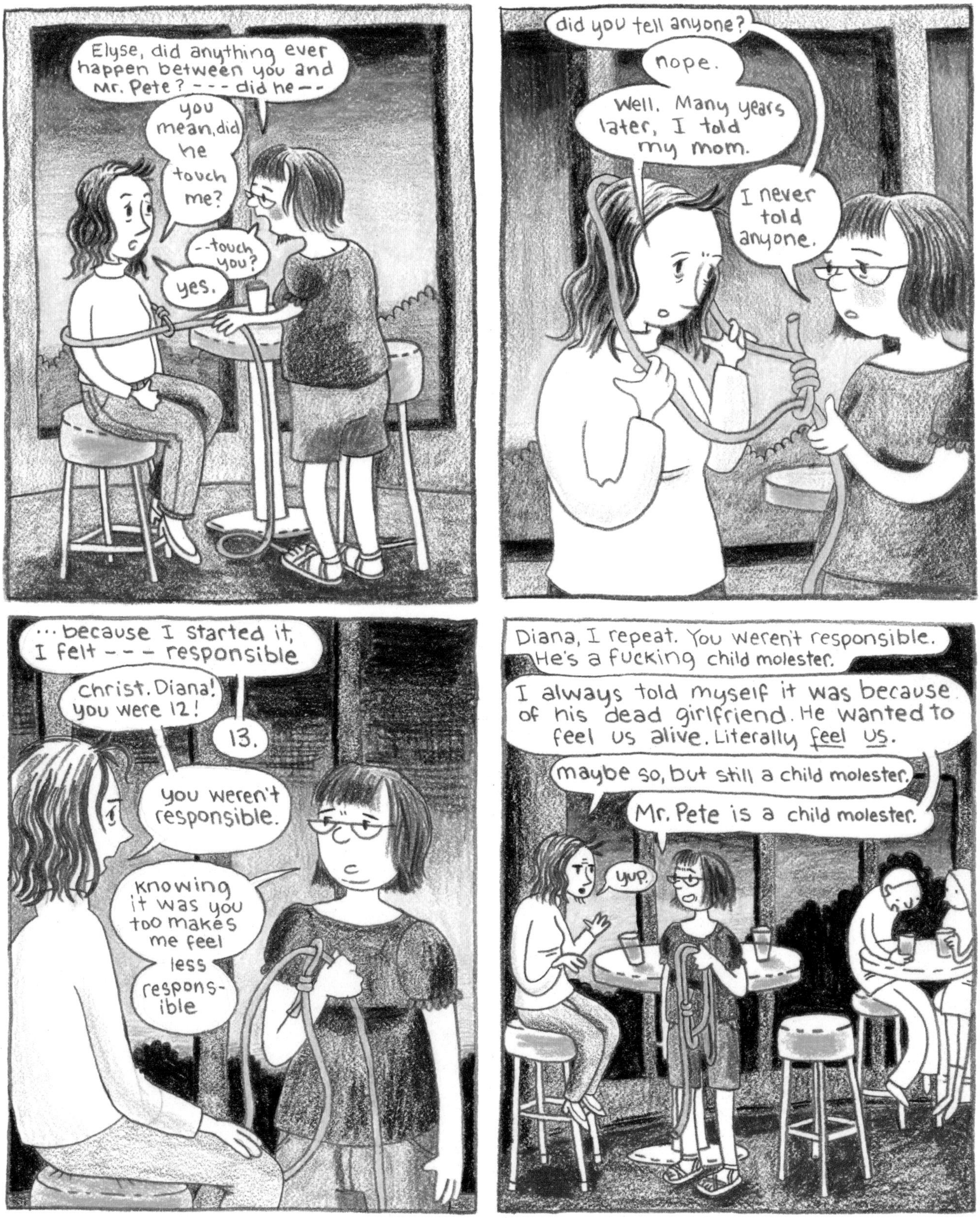
Elyse, did anything ever happen between you and Mr. Pete? --- did he --
you mean, did he touch me?
--touch you?
yes.
did you tell anyone?
nope.
Well. Many years later, I told my mom.
I never told anyone.
... because I started it, I felt --- responsible
Christ. Diana! you were 12!
13.
you weren't responsible.
Knowing it was you too makes me feel less respons-ible
Diana, I repeat. You weren't responsible. He's a fucking child molester.
I always told myself it was because of his dead girlfriend. He wanted to feel us alive. Literally feel us.
maybe so, but still a child molester.
Mr. Pete is a child molester.
yup.

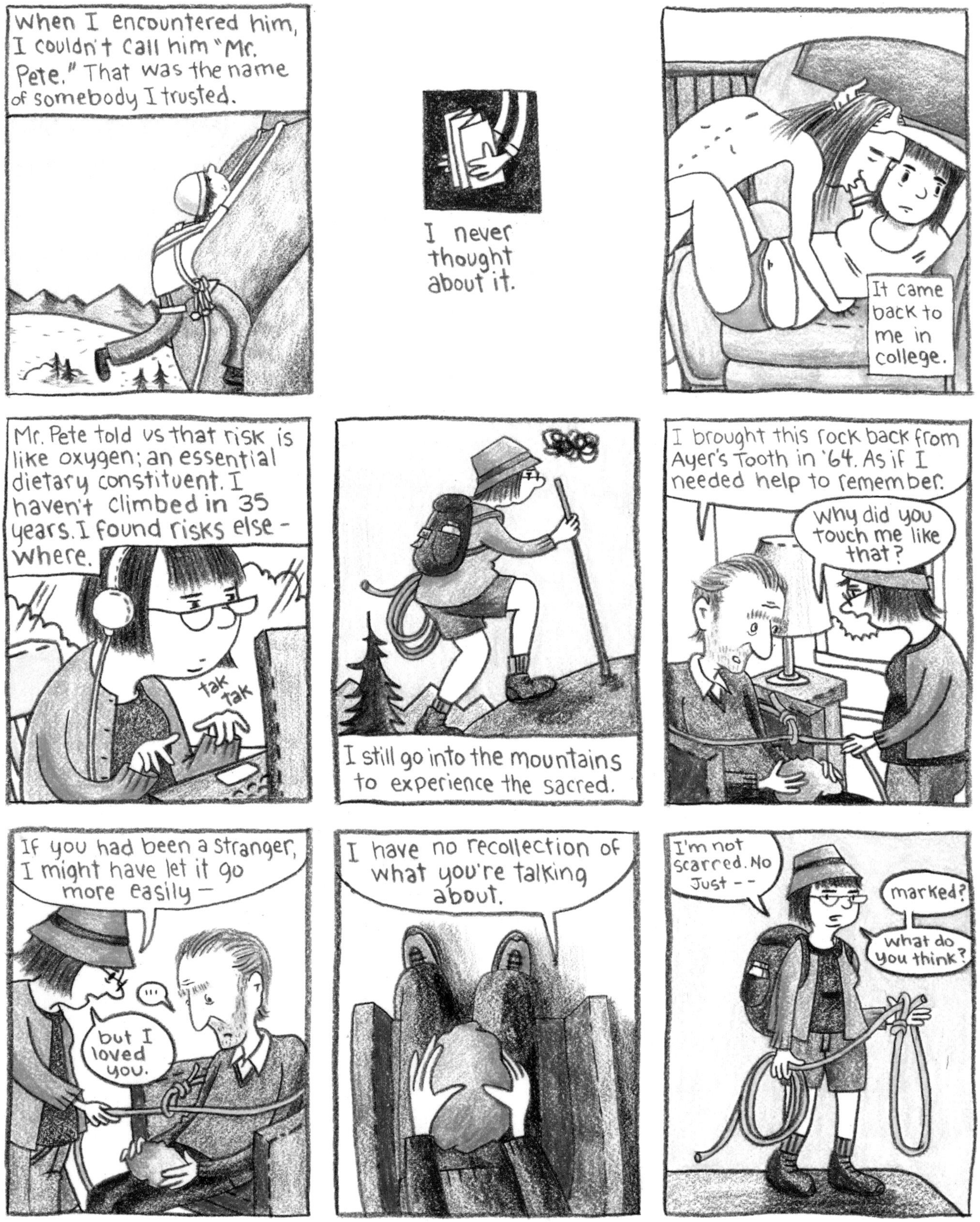

When I encountered him, I couldn't call him "Mr. Pete." That was the name of somebody I trusted.
I never thought about it.
It came back to me in college.
Mr. Pete told us that risk is like oxygen; an essential dietary constituent. I haven't climbed in 35 years. I found risks else-where.
tak tak
I still go into the mountains to experience the sacred.
I brought this rock back from Ayer's Tooth in '64. As if I needed help to remember.
Why did you touch me like that?
If you had been a stranger, I might have let it go more easily—
...
but I loved you.
I have no recollection of what you're talking about.
I'm not scarred. No Just --
marked?
what do you think?

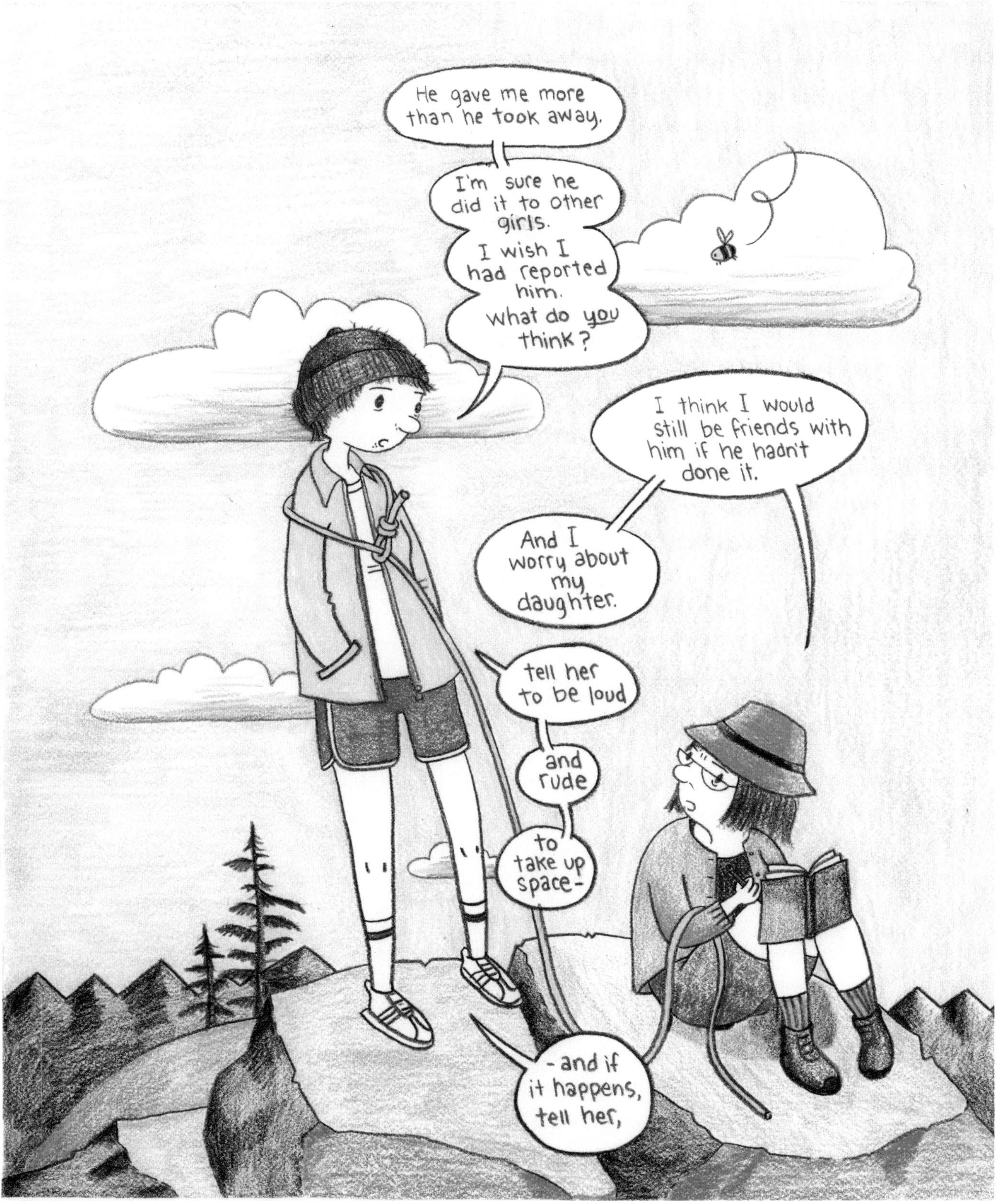
He gave me more than he took away.
I'm sure he did it to other girls.
I wish I had reported him.
What do you think?
I think I would still be friends with him if he hadn't done it.
And I worry about my daughter.
tell her to be loud
and rude
to take up space-
-and if it happens, tell her,

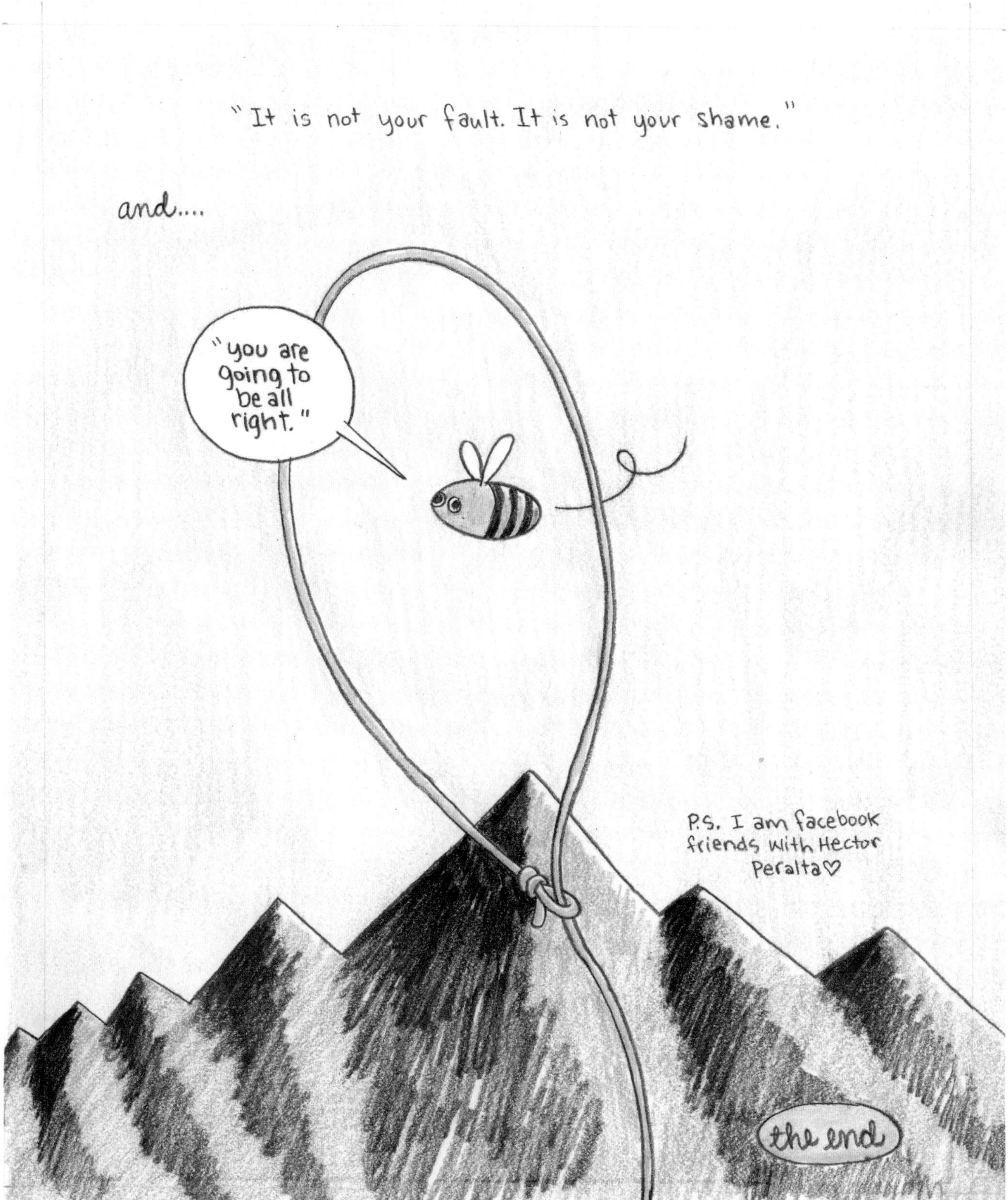
"It is not your fault. It is not your shame."
and....
"you are going to be all right."
P.S. I am facebook friends with Hector Peralta♡
the end

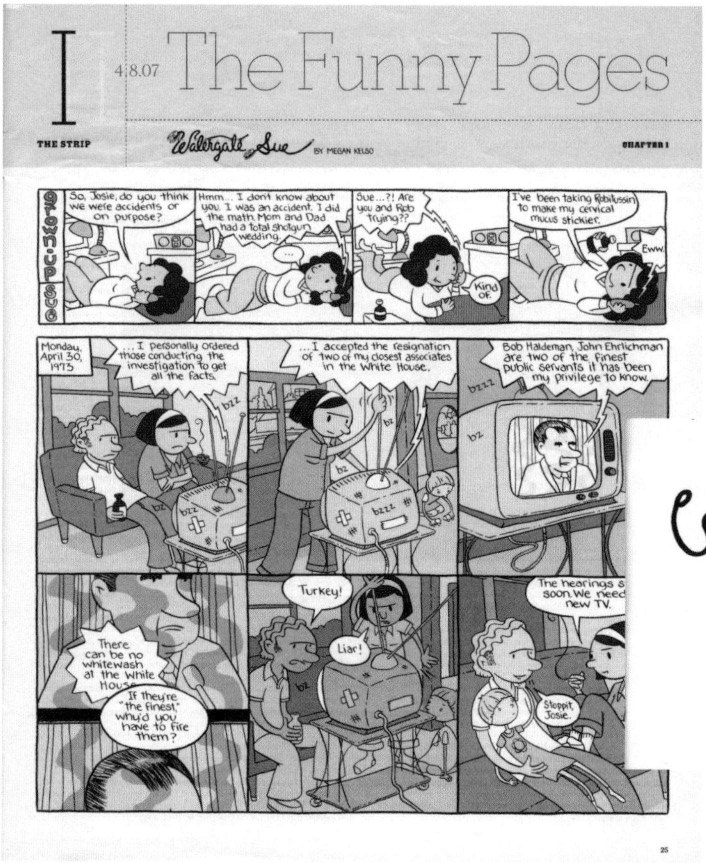
I
4.8.07 The Funny Pages
THE STRIP
Watergate Sue BY MEGAN KELSO
CHAPTER 1
So, Josie, do you think we were accidents or on purpose?
Hmm... I don't know about you. I was an accident. I did the math. Mom and Dad had a total shotgun wedding.
...
Sue...?! Are you and Rob trying??
Kind of.
I've been taking Robitussin to make my cervical mucus stickier.
Eww.
Monday, April 30, 1973
...I personally ordered those conducting the investigation to get all the facts.
bzz
...I accepted the resignation of two of my closest associates in the White House.
Bob Haldeman, John Ehrlichman are two of the finest public servants it has been my privilege to know.
bzzz
There can be no whitewash at the White House.
If they're "the finest," why'd you have to fire them?
Turkey!
Liar!
Stoppit, Josie.
25

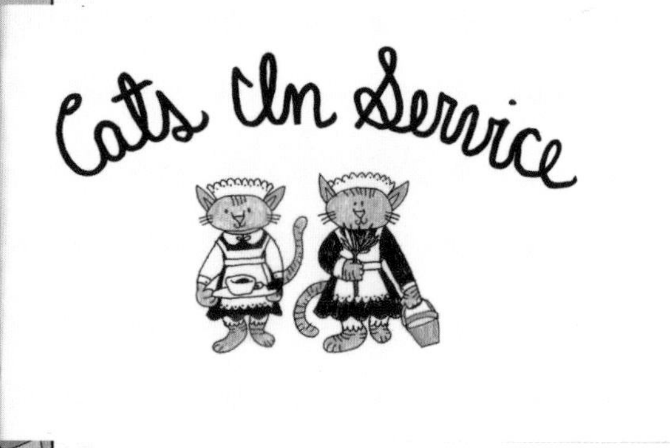
Cats In Service

Notes

WATERGATE SUE originally ran one page per week in the "Funny Pages" section of *The New York Times Magazine* between April and September 2007. The "Funny Pages" feature ran between 2005 – 2009 and presented work from eight different cartoonists.

I started **CATS IN SERVICE** after a fallow period that coincided with my daughter's early years. It was the height of *Downton Abbey* mania and I had a dream that I hired a full staff of domestic servants — but still lived in my 1,000 square foot house. The servants being cats was not part of the original dream. I published it as a minicomic for the 2014 Short Run Comix Festival.

THE EGG ROOM is another story whose original kernel came from a dream. I made notes for it in 2008 during the aforementioned fallow period. I began drawing it at the 2012 Atlantic Center for the Arts comics residency in New Smyrna Beach, Florida. I decided to use watercolor for the final art because it seemed the surest way to capture how the eggs looked to me in the original dream.

The first incarnation of **KORIN VOSS** was called "The Good Witch," and was a one-page comic on the back cover of Ellen Lindner's 2011 *Strumpet* anthology. In 2014, I expanded the idea as a 9-page story in

the good witch
by Megan Kelso 2011
She was a different species:
She had thick, ridged fingernails, droopy earlobes, a smelly apartment.
nicotine stained walls
If grownups are unchanging,
old people are timeless, like a fairy tale.
can we?
She was a good witch with a magic trunk.
I loved her stories but I didn't believe them.
She had never really been a child,
and we would never be old.

FREE
RUNNER
RUNNER
mature readers Please

GUYS-
aw shit-
GUYS!
hang on buddy-

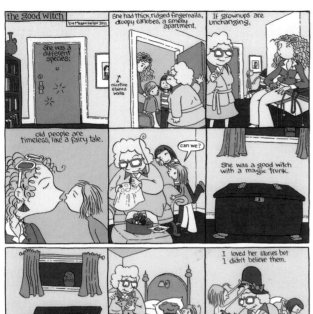

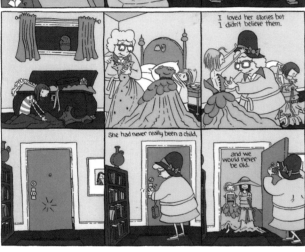

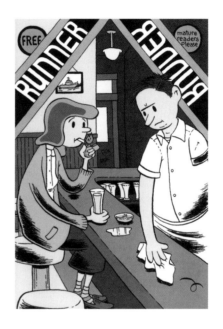

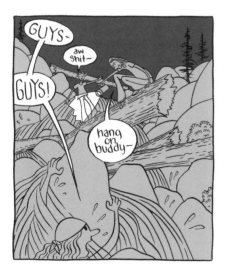

Greg Means' Free Comic Book Day anthology, *Runner Runner*. It was then selected for the 2014 Best American Comics (edited by Bill Kartalopoulous and Jonathan Lethem). By this time, I was at work expanding it further and the witch title was no longer germane, so I renamed it for this collection.

The original version of **THE GOLDEN LASSO** was commissioned for a 2010 performance event in Seattle called Bilocal, an artistic exchange of ideas between Seattle and New Orleans artists, curated by Bob Redmond. It was 14 pages and I presented it as a black and white slideshow and later published it in a minicomic called "Acorns and Pebbles." The story nagged at me; it felt dishonest and incomplete, so I reworked it into its current form over the next 10 years. I chose to do it in colored pencil to show the surface quality of granite.

Acknowledgements

MY SINCERE THANKS to Myla Goldberg, Timothy Kreider, Virginia Carhart, Gabby Gamboa, and Corvie Thykkuttathil for reading the stories at various stages; to Short Run, Atlantic Center for the Arts, the Trailer Blaze alumnae, and the Her Moans alumnae for institutional support and warm collegiality; to Kris Chick, Robin Weatherill, Holly Brown, and Jennifer Smith for friendships that formed me; to Sheila Glaser, Austin English, Greg Means, Bill Kartalopoulos, Ellen Lindner, Bob Redmond, Nick Conroy, and Kelly Froh for opportunities that reminded me I was a cartoonist; to Kari Somerton, Katie McDermott, Joanne McWilson, and Cindy Wu for the special friendship of fellow parents, and finally to my family, the Kelsos, Buckleys, and Smiths, who are the center of my life.

About the Author

Megan Kelso was born in Seattle, WA in 1968. She began making comics in the 1990s when she was a student at the Evergreen State College in Olympia, WA. Inspired by the explosion of creativity that evolved into the Grunge and Riot grrl movements, her first comic book was called *Girlhero*, an edition of 50 copies she made on a photocopier, in the manner of punk zines. She taught herself to be a cartoonist by looking at underground comics, and later found mentors among her contemporaries. In 1992, she was the first woman to be awarded a Xeric grant for self-publishing comics. Kelso has since published three books: *Queen of the Black Black* (1998), *The Squirrel Mother* (2006), and *Artichoke Tales* (2010). In 2002, she was awarded two Ignatz Awards, for Outstanding Artist and Best Minicomic. In 2004, she conceived of and edited the all-women comics anthology, *Scheherazade: Stories of Love, Treachery, Mothers, and Monsters*. In 2007, with "Watergate Sue," Kelso became the first woman to create a weekly comic strip for *The New York Times Magazine*. In 2020, she created the artwork "Crow Commute," an 85-foot-long etched stainless steel comics mural, which is installed at Climate Pledge Arena in Seattle. She lives in Seattle, WA with her husband and daughter.

FANTAGRAPHICS
7563 Lake City Way NE
Seattle, Washington, 98115
www.fantagraphics.com

DESIGNER: Jacob Covey
PRODUCTION: Paul Baresh
PROMOTION: Jacquelene Cohen
VP / ASSOCIATE PUBLISHER / EDITOR: Eric Reynolds
PRESIDENT / PUBLISHER: Gary Groth

ISBN 978-1-68396-670-8
LIBRARY OF CONGRESS CONTROL NUMBER 2022935198
FIRST PRINTING: November 2022
PRINTED IN CHINA

"Korin Voss" includes a passage from Laura Ingalls Wilder's *The Long Winter* (Harper & Brothers, 1940), the sixth of nine books in her Little House on the Prairie series.